Alexander Glass
December, 1943

£10

The

MINISTER'S
ANNUAL

The
MINISTER'S
ANNUAL
1974

by
T. T. Crabtree
AUTHOR-COMPILER

OLIPHANTS
116 BAKER STREET
LONDON W1M 2BB

ISBN 0 551 00448 7

THE ZONDERVAN PASTOR'S ANNUAL FOR 1974
Copyright © 1973 by
The Zondervan Corporation
Library of Congress Catalog Card Number 71-9126
Printed in the United States of America

CONTENTS

Preaching Program

Sermons for Special Days

FOREWORD

As one pastor to another, let me express my deepest gratitude to God for the privilege of being able to send forth this ninth volume of the *Annual*. It is sent forth with a sincere hope and prayer that it might be used of the Holy Spirit to assist other pastors to be good ministers of the Lord Jesus Christ. Letters of appreciation and evaluation have come from pastors and seminary professors from five continents of the world.

In every instance when the burden of preparing the material for the *Annual* became almost unbearable, a letter would come from some pastor in a far-off place expressing deep appreciation for the contribution which this publication had made to his ministry. For this opportunity to serve our Lord and the brethren in the ministry, I am indeed grateful.

With deepest gratitude let me express appreciation to the outstanding pastors who have assisted me as contributing authors by providing selected series of sermons for various sections in the planned preaching program. These sermons represent the earnest, prayerful efforts of pastors who are seeking to obey the Great Commission, and at the same time, to feed the flock of God with whom they have the privilege of worshiping and working.

Let me suggest that if the pastor would use this *Annual* to the greatest possible profit intensive study should be made of the section entitled "A Planned Preaching Program," which serves as a table of contents. This section will make it possible for one to secure a bird's-eye view of a suggested planned preaching program. The Holy Spirit can be just as real and perhaps much more effective if we will permit Him to lead us in planning our preaching program rather than following an "unplanned" preaching program.

There are three books which I would like to suggest to the man who is genuinely interested in developing a planned preaching program. These books were written by professors of preaching and provide excellent suggestions. They are: *Planning a Year's Pulpit Work* by Dr. Andrew W. Blackwood (New York: Abingdon-Cokesbury Press, 1952), *Planning Your Preaching* by Dr. J. Winston Pearce (Nashville, Tennessee: Broadman Press, 1967), and *A Manual for Biblical Preaching* by Lloyd Merle Perry (Grand Rapids, Michigan: Baker Book House, 1965).

I am deeply indebted to my wife and children who have encouraged me and cooperated with me in order that I might respond to the burden of the opportunity which this publication presents. I am also very grateful to my excellent secretary, Mrs. Dale Wiser, for her valuable assistance in making this production possible. There is no way by which I can adequately express my appreciation to the staff and to the congregation of the First Baptist Church of Springfield, Missouri, for their prayers, their encouragement, and for the stimulation which they provide me to do my very best for my Lord as well as for them Sunday by Sunday.

We would send forth this *Annual* with the prayer that our Lord might bless it and that it might be used for His glory.

T. T. Crabtree, Pastor
First Baptist Church
Springfield, Missouri 65806

A PLANNED PREACHING PROGRAM

A Planned Preaching Program

A Planned Preaching Program

JUNE 1974
Morning Theme: *Faith for Frightening Times*
Evening Theme: *The Teenager: His Problems and His Potential*
Wednesday Evening Theme: *The Bible Speaks to Our Condition*

SUNDAY, JUNE 2
A.M. "The Authority for
Faith: the Bible"
2 Tim. 3:15-17   161
P.M. "The Teenager and
Fleshly Lust"   2 Tim. 2:22   164
Wednesday Evening, June 5
"The Bible Speaks to Our
Condition"   2 Cor. 7   166

SUNDAY, JUNE 9
A.M. "The Basis for Faith:
God"   Isa. 45:21, 22   168
P.M. "The Teenager and
Marriage"   Matt. 19:6b   171
Wednesday Evening, June 12
"The Bible Speaks to Our
Condition"   Gal. 1   174

SUNDAY, JUNE 16
A.M. "The Object of Faith:
Jesus Christ"   Phil. 2:5-11   175
P.M. "The Teenager and
Jesus"   Luke 2:52   178
Wednesday Evening, June 19
"The Bible Speaks to Our
Condition"   Eph. 2   181

SUNDAY, JUNE 23
A.M. "An Example of
Faith"   John 4:46-53   182
P.M. "The Teenager and the
Will of God"   Acts 22:10a   185
Wednesday Evening, June 26
"The Bible Speaks to Our
Condition"   Phil. 3   188

SUNDAY, JUNE 30
A.M. "The Outreach of
Faith: the Christian Life"
Phil. 3:3   189
P.M. "The Teenager and
Prayer"   Matt. 6:6   192

JULY 1974
Morning Theme: *The Sins Which Damage and Destroy*
Evening Theme: *The Great Christian Virtues*
Wednesday Evening Theme: *The Bible Speaks to Our Condition*
Wednesday Evening, July 3
"The Bible Speaks to Our
Condition"   1 Thess. 2   194

SUNDAY, JULY 7
A.M. "Man's Plight As
Sinner"   1 John 1:8   195
P.M. "Salvation and Its
Fruits"   Gal. 5:22, 23   197
Wednesday Evening, July 10
"The Bible Speaks to Our
Condition"   1 Tim. 1   200

SUNDAY, JULY 14
A.M. "The Sin of Pride"
Prov. 11:2   201
P.M. "Love: Complete
Living"   Col. 3:14   203
Wednesday Evening, July 17
"The Bible Speaks to Our
Condition"   2 Tim. 2   206

SUNDAY, JULY 21
A.M. "The Sin of Greed"
Prov. 15:27   207
P.M. "Joy: Radiant Living"
John 15:11   209
Wednesday Evening, July 24
"The Bible Speaks to Our
Condition"   Heb. 1   211

SUNDAY, JULY 28
A.M. "The Sin of
Sensuality"   Rom. 8:6   213
P.M. "Peace: Superlative
Living"   Phil. 4:7   215
Wednesday Evening, July 31
"The Bible Speaks to Our
Condition"   Heb. 8   217

AUGUST 1974
Morning Theme: *The Sins Which Damage and Destroy*
Evening Theme: *The Great Christian Virtues*
Wednesday Evening Theme: *The Bible Speaks to Our Condition*

SUNDAY, AUGUST 4
A.M. "The Sin of Envy"
Job 5:2   219
P.M. "Patience: Reconciled
Living"   Eccl. 7:8   221
Wednesday Evening, August 7
"The Bible Speaks to Our
Condition"   James 2   224

SUNDAY, AUGUST 11
A.M. "The Sin of Appetite"
Phil. 3:18, 19   225
P.M. "Kindness: Sensitive
Living"   Col. 3:12   227
Wednesday Evening, August 14
"The Bible Speaks to Our
Condition"   1 Pet. 4   230

9

A Planned Preaching Program

NOVEMBER 1974
Morning Theme: *Taking the Stew Out of Stewardship*
Evening Theme: *The Walk and Work of Faith*
Wednesday Evening Theme: *The Bible Speaks to Our Condition*

SUNDAY, NOVEMBER 3
A.M. "Can a Man Rob God?"
    Mal. 3:10   300
P.M. "Principles for Spiritual
    Victory"   Josh. 8:1, 2   302
Wednesday Evening, November 6
"The Bible Speaks to Our
    Condition"   Luke 15   304

SUNNDAY, NOVEMBER 10
A.M. "Did Jesus Teach
    Tithing?"   Matt. 23:23   305
P.M. "Growing on in Christ"
    Josh. 11:23; 13:1   307
Wednesday Evening, November 13
"The Bible Speaks to Our
    Condition"   Luke 18   309

SUNDAY, NOVEMBER 17
A.M. "Investing in Heaven"
    Matt. 6:19-21   311
P.M. "The Faithfulness of
    God"   Josh. 23:14   313
Wednesday Evening, November 20
"The Bible Speaks to Our
    Condition"   John 1   315

SUNDAY, NOVEMBER 24
A.M. "Giving More Than
    Thanks"   Rom. 14:10b   316
P.M. "Victorious Christian
    Commitment"   Josh. 24:15   319
Wednesday Evening, November 27
"The Bible Speaks to Our
    Condition"   John 10   321

DECEMBER 1974
Morning Theme: *The True Spirit of Christmas*
Evening Theme: *The Missionary Message of Christmas*
Wednesday Evening Theme: *The Bible Speaks to Our Condition*

SUNDAY, DECEMBER 1
A.M. "They Shall Call His
    Name Immanuel"
    Matt. 1:23   322
P.M. "The Contemporary
    Missionary"   1 Cor. 3:9   324
Wednesday Evening, December 4
"The Bible Speaks to Our
    Condition"   John 14   327

SUNDAY, DECEMBER 8
A.M. "Why the Christ
    Child?"   Isa. 7:14   329
P.M. "Do We Look for
    Another?"   Matt. 11:2, 3   331
Wednesday Evening, December 11
"The Bible Speaks to Our
    Condition"   John 21   333

SUNDAY, DECEMBER 15
A.M. "The Christ of
    Christmas"   Gal. 4:4   334
P.M. "God Is Ready When
    You Are!"   Gal. 4:4, 5   336
Wednesday Evening, December 18
"The Bible Speaks to Our
    Condition"   Rev. 1   339

SUNDAY, DECEMBER 22
A.M. "God With Us"
    Matt. 1:23   341
P.M. "And Jesus Begat . . ."
    John 1:11, 12   343
Wednesday Evening, December 25
"The Bible Speaks to Our
    Condition"   Rev. 22   346

SUNDAY, DECEMBER 29
A.M. "Retrospective and
    Perspective"   Matt. 28:20   347
P.M. "You Can Take It From
    Here"   Matt. 28:19, 20   349

ACKNOWLEDGMENTS TO CONTRIBUTING AUTHORS

Fred M. Wood . . . . A.M.: Jan 6, 13, 20, 27
Feb. 3, 10, 17, 24
March 3, 10, 17, 24, 31
April 7, 14, 21, 28

David R. Grant . . . . P.M.: Jan. 6, 13, 20, 27
Feb. 3, 10, 17, 24
A.M.: Dec. 1, 8, 15, 22, 29
Funeral Messages

Morris Ashcraft . . . . P.M.: March 3, 10, 17, 24, 31

James G. Harris . . . . P.M.: April 7, 14, 21, 28

Lowell Milburn . . . . P.M.: May 5, 12, 19, 26
June 2, 9, 16, 23, 30

James E. Carter . . . . A.M.: June 2, 9, 16, 23, 30

Chester L. Smith . . . . A.M.: July 7, 14, 21, 28
Aug. 4, 11, 18, 25
P.M.: July 7, 14, 21, 28
Aug. 4, 11, 18, 25

James F. Heaton . . . . A.M.: Sept. 1, 8, 15, 22, 29

Howard S. Kolb . . . . P.M.: Sept. 1, 8, 15, 22, 29

T. Hollis Epton . . . . A.M.: Oct. 6, 13, 20, 27

Tom S. Brandon . . . . P.M.: Oct. 6, 13, 20, 27
Nov. 3, 10, 17, 24

Tal D. Bonham . . . . A.M.: Nov. 3, 10, 17, 24

E. Warren Rust . . . . P.M.: Dec. 1, 8, 15, 22, 29

B. W. Woods . . . . Lord's Supper Meditations
Messages for Children and Young People

T. T. Crabtree . . . . . All Messages Except Those Indicated Above

SUGGESTED PREACHING PROGRAM
FOR THE MONTH OF JANUARY

With faith in the power of the Good News to be used as the instrument of God for the salvation of a lost world, let us confront our task as pastors and preachers with renewed confidence and devotion. Let us determine to preach the Word at our every opportunity and lift up Jesus Christ as the Truth, the Way, and the Life.

Sunday Mornings

The suggested theme for the morning messages is, "The Life and Works of the Lord Jesus." With the Greeks, let us say, "We would see Jesus." Let us seek to introduce our people anew to the Person, the power, the purpose, and the presence of the Christ who lived, who died, but who lives again victoriously.

Sunday Evenings

The suggested theme is "Great Texts from 1 John." With love and wisdom the apostle of love dealt with the problems that plagued the followers of our Lord during the first century of the Christian era.

His message is relevant for the disciples of our Lord in this century.

Wednesday Evenings

"The Bible Speaks to Our Condition" will be the suggested theme for all of the Wednesday evening services during the year. It is suggested that the pastor lead his people in a daily devotional reading of one chapter every day. This suggested theme grows out of the conviction that Bible Study can be the listening side of the experience of prayer. It is more important that we hear what God has to say than it is that He hear what we have to say.

If this program is followed, every seventh chapter in sequence will serve as the scriptural basis for the time of prayer, meditation, spiritual renewal and rededication on Wednesday evening.

The theme passage for January is, "All scripture is given by inspiration of God, and is profitable for doctrine, for reproof, for correction, for instruction in righteousness: That the man of God may be perfect, throughly furnished unto all good works" (2 Tim. 3:16, 17).

WEDNESDAY EVENING, JANUARY 2

TITLE. "The Bible Speaks to Our Condition"

SCRIPTURE READING: Matthew 2.

Introduction. The Apostle Paul declared "All scripture is given by inspiration of God, and is profitable for doctrine, for reproof, for correction, for instruction in righteousness" (2 Tim. 3:16). If we would grow as the children of God, it is

absolutely essential that we give both time and attention to the reading of God's holy Word. God will speak to our condition if we will but give attention to the reading of His Word in a prayerful, responsive attitude.

It has been said, "An apple a day will keep the doctor away and a chapter a day will keep the devil away." This proverb is probably an over-simplification of both our

13

health and spiritual needs. However, there is a fundamental truth in this proverb that commands serious thought.

A prayerful reading of God's Word has been compared to the listening side of the experience of prayer. God will speak through His Word to those who have an inclination to listen. A thoughtful, careful, prayerful reading of a chapter a day, each day through the new year, will bring untold blessings into the life of each reader.

Let us let God speak to us through Matthew 2.

I. *Wise Men Sought the Savior* (Matt. 2:1-10). Wise men from the East who were students of the stars, men of faith and religion, came seeking the Savior. From whence did these wise men come? How far had they traveled? How had these men seen the star in the East? How much did they know about the Messiah's star? It is impossible for us to answer these and many other questions. The significant truth is that they came seeking the Savior.

We use the highest wisdom that man can exercise when we seek a deeper knowledge and a more intimate acquaintance with the Savior who came to die for our sins. He alone can deliver us from the tyranny of evil. He alone can lead us into the life abundant. He alone can give us victory over death. He alone can lead us into the eternal home of God.

Let each of us seek Him with the same diligence that the wise men sought Him.

II. *The Wise Men Worshiped the Savior* (Matt. 2:11, 12). When the wise men found the Christ child,

they fell on their knees before Him giving to Him the worship of their minds and hearts. They opened their treasures and presented unto Him gifts of gold, frankincense and myrrh.

A. Gold is an appropriate gift for a king. Jesus was born to be a king. He wants to rule, not by force, but through love. He rules the hearts of those who love Him from His cross. We need to crown Him king of our hearts.

B. Frankincense is the gift for a priest. It was in the Temple worship and at the time of sacrifices that the sweet perfume of frankincense was used. Jesus was to be our great High Priest. It is He who has given us access into the very presence of the holy God.

C. Myrrh is a gift for one who is to die. It was used to embalm the bodies of the dead. Christ came into the world to die for our sins.

As the wise men gave of their best, we would be wise to give of our very best into the service of the Christ.

III. *Piety Does Not Guarantee Immunity From Trouble* (Matt. 2:13-18). It has always been a mystery as to why the innocent suffer and why the righteous experience trouble. We will never have an adequate and satisfactory answer to this question as long as we walk the ways of men.

There can be no question concerning the innocence or the righteousness of Joseph and Mary. They were within the will of God. By virtue of their being in the will of God, they found themselves to be the objects of the hostility of an evil king who sought to bring about their destruction.

Much of the evil and suffering

that the innocent and the righteous experience is due to no fault or sin on their part. The devil is responsible for much of our suffering. The wickedness and carelessness of others brings about suffering.

Should we find ourselves as the innocent victims of tragedy as did the parents of the children in Bethlehem, we must look to God for grace and strength to bear the agony of our misfortune.

Piety does not provide us with an immunity from suffering. We must not permit ourselves to lose our faith in the goodness of God if tragedy should befall us or someone very dear and precious to us.

IV. *The Purpose of Our God* (Matt. 2:19-23). Behind everything that is recorded in Matthew 2 we need to see the plan and purpose of God. Repeatedly, the inspired writer refers to the fulfillment of prophecy.

God had been at work through the centuries to accomplish His redemptive purpose. In the fullness of time He sent forth His Son to be our Savior, Lord, teacher, and friend.

God continues to be at work in the world in the present. He is at work in the various congregations around the world seeking to communicate the good news of His love for men, even while they are in the midst of sin and rebellion.

God is at work to accomplish His purpose in our homes. He wants to help us with the responsibilities involved in marriage and the raising of our families.

God is at work in individual hearts seeking to deliver from the tyranny of evil and lead into a life of devoted service.

Conclusion. Are you listening? Did you let God speak to your heart through the verses of Matthew 2? He wants to speak with you. He will speak to your condition if you will listen.

SUNDAY MORNING, JANUARY 6

TITLE: "Jesus Grew"

TEXT: "And Jesus increased in wisdom and stature, and in favour with God and man" (Luke 2:52).
SCRIPTURE READING: Luke 2: 40-52.

HYMNS: "Higher Ground," Oatman. "I Am Thine, O Lord," Crosby. "I Am Resolved," Hartsough.

OFFERTORY PRAYER:

Our Father, this is the first Sunday of the new year. We stand on the threshold of new opportunities but we also feel the responsibility of new obligations. Thou hast led us in the past and we face the future with full assurance of Thy guidance in the days ahead. We thank Thee for open doors and we pray for faith to enter them in Thy strength. Today we bring fresh resolves concerning the stewardship of our lives. Help us to recognize that a part of that stewardship is the bringing of our tithes and offerings. We ask Thy blessings upon each gift, each giver and each cause that we support through our giving. Accept our gifts and use them to spread the Gospel of Thy grace. We pray in Jesus' name. Amen.

Introduction. There is very little material in the New Testament concerning Jesus from the time of His birth until the beginning of His ministry. A few scattered passages tell of the early days just after His birth. Matthew records His flight into Egypt and His return. Luke tells of His presentation in the Temple and the response of Simeon and Anna.

Two silent periods confront us concerning His life. The first is from the time His parents "came and dwelt in a city called Nazareth" (Matt. 2:23) after they returned from Egypt until the time Jesus visited the Temple at the age of twelve. The other silent period is from the return to Nazareth where Luke says, "he went down with them . . . and was subject unto them" (Luke 2:51) until He presented Himself to John for baptism at the age of thirty.

What kind of life did Jesus live during these days? Many apocryphal stories and fantastic legends have come down to us concerning these periods, especially when He was between the ages of twelve to thirty. Most of them have been rejected as untrustworthy. The truth is that we just do not know. Reliable records are not available. Two statements of Luke give us the best clue. Immediately after he records the return of Jesus from Jerusalem following the presentation in the Temple he says, "And the child grew, and waxed strong in spirit, filled with wisdom: and the grace of God was upon him" (Luke 2:40). Luke then tells of the visit of Jesus and His parents to Jerusalem and concludes this ac-

count by saying, "And Jesus increased in wisdom and stature, and in favour with God and man" (Luke 2:52).

When we speak of the growth of Jesus we do not imply either imperfection or immaturity. We are speaking only of the finiteness of His human nature. He was divine, to be sure, but He was human also and had a normal human growth. His human nature had the inexperience of childhood and, therefore, passed in a normal way to wider knowledge and clearer self-consciousness. As His capacity increased, His ability to grow and comprehend increased. There were no pauses nor sinful elements mingled in His growth. His powers were neither deformed nor unduly developed. His growth means merely that He had no failings in His childhood but was taught by life as well as by Scripture and communion with the Father. The silence of the Scripture is as eloquent as if it were vocal with reference to the early years of Jesus. The innocence of Jesus grew into holiness and did so naturally without attracting attention to itself. For this reason, the world did not hate Him as a child for He did not yet, except perhaps by His unconscious example, testify against it concerning its evil deeds. On this first Lord's Day of the new year we consider the growth of Jesus as an example for our growth in every area of our personality.

I. *Jesus Grew Physically.* It is important for us to have good bodies if we are to give our best in God's service. This does not overlook the fact that there have been outstanding examples of people with handicaps who have concentrated upon their work and had amazing success in spite of limited physical abilities. These, however, are glorious exceptions to the rule. Our bodies are the temple or the dwelling place of God's Spirit. We need to obey all the laws of health. There is every indication in the New Testament that Jesus had a vigorous physical constitution. His work schedule was amazing. He became tired, of course, but there is no indication anywhere that He had limited physical capacities. On the contrary, quite often He performed tasks that showed He was a man of great physical strength. The early years of our lives set the pattern for physical strength or the lack of it in the mature years. Boys and girls who are called upon to work hard in the growing years of life may grumble at the time, but later they realize what a privilege they enjoyed. Jesus worked in the carpenter shop. He took care of His body and in the years to come He was able to use it in His work to God's glory.

II. *Jesus Grew Mentally.* Although God warns us many times concerning the folly of trusting human wisdom, this does not mean He is opposed to our intellectual growth. Nowhere does the Bible place a premium upon ignorance. God gave us a mind and He expects us to develop it through study. All other things being equal, the best-trained Christians will be the most effective ones. The boy Jesus must have spent many hours reading the Old Testament scrolls and the writings of the learned men. It is not possible for us to know when He first became aware of what scholars call His "Messianic consciousness" but we are sure that early in His life His human nature found perfect fellowship with His divine nature and He understood His true mission. During the early days His consciousness of divine sonship was real but, as yet, undeveloped. He was not merely a "childlike" God in whom growth was impossible. He was truly human in mind and lived under all the limitations common to man in the mental realm. He, therefore, was required to study in order to grow. In this way He is our example for intellectual achievement. If the Son of God grew mentally, those of us who seek to follow in His steps should take seriously academic development and utilize it to the glory of God.

III. *Jesus Grew Socially.* There is, of course, a danger in striving for popularity. We must not become a "chameleon" and adjust to whatever moral color prevails with the crowd. A Christian must always stand for his conviction and be firm in his decisions for right conduct. On the other hand, however, we must hold our standards with a sweet spirit. This means we must learn to get along with people. A Christian should not make others feel miserable in his presence. He should make them feel relaxed and happy. If we will cultivate the art of making people enjoy our company, we can grow in the "graces" of social life and, at the same time, lead people to respect our Christian principles. People enjoyed having Jesus in their midst. He was invited to their social gatherings. He was "at home" among them without compromising His convictions concerning God and His redemptive purposes.

IV. *Jesus Grew Spiritually.* It was His personal fellowship with the Father that enabled Him to face life victoriously. It is true that He possessed a unique relationship with God but He also maintained an unbroken fellowship with Him. Our relationship with God is established through the new birth. Our fellowship comes through growth in things of the spirit. The public life of Jesus had its roots in His private and personal walk with the Father. His bright faith, optimistic outlook and confidence in God's power to transform others came because He maintained spiritual growth through personal communion in prayer, Scripture study, and constant striving to know God's will and do it. We can be born physically only once but we can grow physically. We can be born spiritually only once (John 3:16), but we can grow day by day in things of the spirit as we feed on God's word and seek to follow His purposes for our life.

Conclusion. The growth of Jesus and our growth may be different in some ways but in many ways it is exactly the same. Jesus possessed two complete natures—the divine and the human. His two natures did not mingle into one with the divine predominating. His two natures remained separate. His human nature could, therefore, grow. The born-again Christian also has two natures. The old nature is still with us but the new nature imparted in the conversion experience is also a reality. We *must* grow. That which fails to progress retrogrades. It is necessary for us to grow if life is to be happy and victorious. The whole personality of man must grow. We are not divided into separate compartments but are one personality. As we grow in each area, life will become meaningful to self, helpful to others and pleasing to God.

SUNDAY EVENING, JANUARY 6

TITLE: "Life in Him"

TEXTS "For the life was manifested, and we have seen it, and bear witness, and shew unto you that eternal life, which was with the Father, and was manifested unto us" (1 John 1:2).

SCRIPTURE READING. 1 John 1: 1-10.

Introduction. It is generally believed that John was an old man and had returned from exile on Patmos when he wrote 1 John. He is revered as the last of the apostles and this is what emphasizes the note of authority. These are the words of an inspired writer who was the most intimate companion of our Lord in the days of His earthly ministry.

First John is a book for Christians in general and "Life in Him" is the theme of the book. Eternal life is not only endless existence, but the life of God revealed in Jesus Christ, and shared by all who put their trust in Him. Believers possess a new moral life, which source is God, its channel is faith, and its issues are goodness and love.

I. *The Relationship to That Life,* (1 John 1:1-4).

A. Life in Jesus is through the Word. In John 1:1 Jesus is called the Word. He is the living Word who possesses this life in eternal fellowship with God. The phrase in

1:1, "from the beginning," shows the infinity of Jesus and goes back behind the Incarnation to the eternal purpose of God.

Three of the human senses are used and their tenses show the reality of Christ's humanity and the qualifications of John to write. "We have heard" is a present active and portrays continuous action. "We have seen" is the same tense and portrays the same continuous action. "We have touched" is an aorist tense and portrays repetition. He was touched time and again.

B. Life in Jesus is properly manifested. John said we have experienced that life and now testify it to you. This testimony is valid because of our experience (1:2a). John goes further and says that you (meaning all) can have eternal life too. This divine life is fellowship. The fellowship is with other believers and with God. The basic idea in fellowship is to have things in common. The specific idea in this passage is Christian fellowship. This is sharing the common life in Christ through the Holy Spirit.

C. There is real joy in this fellowship and in proclaiming it. True joy comes from fellowship with God and the joy is overflowing when it is shared with others.

II. *This Life Is Manifested in Our Conduct* (1 John 1:5-10).
There are three things we do:
A. We proclaim the message (1 John 1:5). The word "declare" in the King James Version means to give a report. The believer tells what has happened to him and can happen to others.

B. We walk in the light (1 John 1:6, 7).

C. We tell the truth about sin.

III. *A Fuller Discussion of These Thoughts Is Seen in An Emphasis of the Negative and Positive.*

A. There is the allegation that one has fellowship with God while he walks in darkness (1:6). The idea of walking refers to conduct or character. God is light. Light is a symbol of splendor and purity. It is that which illuminates our lives. Since God is light, it is not possible to have fellowship with Him while walking in darkness.

1. Walking in darkness means to pursue the daily tasks without reference to the will of God. It means living according to worldly standards and seeking selfish goals. It means excluding the light that is God.

2. Walking in the light is doing righteousness. Righteousness is doing the will of God. This can be done only when we are in fellowship with God and one another.

B. There is the claim that one has no sin and John opposes this (1:8).
The words "no sin" is in reference to no guilt or no principle of sin.

1. A person is shown that all are guilty of sin and responsible for it. One is not to deny it or seek to explain it away.

2. The sinner is shown what to do with his sin. He is to confess it. To confess means to agree with

God. The sinner says to God, "I agree with You. I am a sinner."

C. There is the claim that one has no sin and this makes God a liar (1 John 1:10).

Many verses in the Bible specifically point out that all have sinned. Romans 3:23 is an example. The message of the Bible is that man is sinful and God has provided salvation for him in Jesus Christ.

Conclusion. True life—living—is fellowship with God which is possible through faith in Jesus Christ.

Fellowship at its highest among men is that which comes by accepting the Christian verities. The deepest source of joy is found in Christian service and the highest form of service consists in bringing others into fellowship with the Father through Jesus Christ.

My appeal to you who do not have this life, is to accept Jesus as your personal Savior now and enter into eternal life with Him. My appeal to you who are Christians is to surrender your life to Him in Christian service.

WEDNESDAY EVENING, JANUARY 9

TITLE: "The Bible Speaks to Our Condition"

SCRIPTURE READING: Matthew 9

Introduction. Through the inspired Word of God we can hear the voice of God speaking to the deepest needs of those who look to Him for guidance and help. Only as we listen to His Word can we become equipped to do the good work of God.

Matthew 9 contains material that could command our attention for a week rather than for a single day. It gives to us a picture of the movement and the ministry of our Lord as He met the needs of those about Him. As we study this chapter we can see that He was a very busy man among men. His ministry was needed. His heart was compassionate and He gave himself completely to ministering to the various needs of man.

Matthew reveals in this chapter that our Lord was involved almost constantly in controversy with those who disagreed with His ministry and with His method of doing things. The Pharisees, representing the religious establishment of that day, were His most severe critics. It is interesting to note that our Lord did not let this controversy and disagreement cause Him to swerve from His purpose. Neither did He let their vicious attacks embitter Him and cause Him to retaliate. We see our Lord giving Himself unreservedly to His task and refusing to yield before the opposition of His critics.

"Jesus Christ the same yesterday, and today, and for ever" (Heb. 13:8). If the Christ was concerned during His earthly life by the suffering of those about Him, we can be certain that He is moved with compassion as our eternal Lord. With sympathy and with power, He would minister to us.

I. *The Lordship of Christ.* In Matthew 9 we have an outstanding display of the Lordship of our Lord.

A. We see Him as the Lord over disease (9:1-7).

B. We see Him as the Lord over life (9:9). He issued a call that was to claim the life of Matthew for His service. Matthew gave up a profitable position using His pen to keep tax accounts in order that his pen might be used to write the first gospel.

C. We see Him as Lord over the realm of death (9:18-26).

D. We see Him as Lord over blindness (9:27-31).

E. We see Him as Lord over the demonic (9:32).

Christ is the Lord over the greatest foes that we face. He wants to give us victory over the enemies that would defeat or destroy us. He is worthy to be the Lord of our life and of all that we are and have.

II. *The Importance of Faith.* Matthew 9 speaks dramatically of the importance of faith as the human response which opens the door for God's power to do its work.

A. The faith of the paralytic and his friends brought both forgiveness and the restoration of health (9:1-7).

B. The faith of the grief-stricken ruler made possible our Lord's restoration of his daughter to life (9:18-25).

C. The faith of the woman who suffered from a hemorrhage for twelve long years (9:20-22).

D. The faith of the two blind men who were seeking their sight (9:27-30).

The refusal to believe in Jesus Christ places limitations upon His power to change lives and circumstances that would defeat us.

The Christ of the gospel of Matthew is the Christ whom we should be worshiping today as Lord. We need to trust Him as we face the painful problems of life in order that He might work miraculous changes in us and through us.

III. *The Purpose of Prayer.* Matthew 9 provides us with many samples or examples that disclose the nature and purpose of prayer.

In this chapter we discover that prayer is a dialogue between a needy believer and an all-sufficient Lord. It is a dialogue in which there is communication between ordinary human beings and the unique Son of God.

The chapter opens with a paralytic and his friends petitioning the Savior for the return of health. He responded by granting forgiveness of sin along with the restoration of health.

Then there is a divine side to the experience that we call prayer for we hear our Lord making a request to one who sat in a tax collector's booth. Matthew answered the prayer of our Lord and became one of His devoted followers.

Also, the ruler came petitioning the attention, time and power of our Lord on behalf of his daughter. Our Lord responded by graciously granting his request.

The poor woman, without a word, but with an outstretched hand, requested help. And our Lord responded to her prayer even in the midst of a multitude.

The chapter closes with a word from the Lord to the effect that we are to enter into dialogue with the Father God concerning where and when we are to labor in the fields that are white unto harvest. Our Lord is not suggesting that we rebuke God or overcome His reluctance to send laborers into those fields. Instead, he is suggesting that each of us should report for duty and listen to the divine instructions in order that we might know what part of the harvest field God would have us to labor in.

Conclusion. Let us spend some time listening to what God would say to us through this tremendous chapter from Matthew's gospel.

SUNDAY MORNING, JANUARY 13

TITLE: "Jesus Was Baptized"

TEXT: "This is my beloved Son, in whom I am well pleased" (Matt. 3:17).

SCRIPTURE READING: Matthew 3:1-17.

HYMNS: "My Faith Looks Up to Thee," Palmer. "Down to the Sacred Wave," Smith. "O Happy Day," Doddridge.

OFFERTORY PRAYER:

Our Father, the Father of our Lord and Savior, Jesus Christ, we have come this morning to worship. We see about us the glories of Thy handiwork in nature, and we see the beauty of Thy holiness in many lives who have been transformed by Thy grace. We thank Thee for the privilege of telling others the story of God's redeeming love in Jesus Christ. We bring our offerings that Thy work might be carried on both in the near places and those far away. Our gifts are a symbol of our love for Thee but they are more. They are concrete expressions of our dedication. Our gifts are practical ways in which we demonstrate our love and concern. Through our money our own program can be maintained here, and we can share our witness to many people in faraway places. Accept our gifts and use them in a way that is pleasing to Thee. Bless us in order that we may be a blessing. We pray in Jesus' name. Amen.

Introduction. The subject of baptism has divided Christendom across the centuries. It would be popular perhaps to ignore this event in the life of Jesus when sketching the main events from His birth to His crucifixion and resurrection. Such a course of action, however, would cause us to omit one of the most significant happenings in the life of our Savior. Regardless of the disagreements, we would be spiritually poorer if we ignored a fair and honest look at the baptism of Jesus. We shall seek to profit from the lessons it brings to us.

I. *John's Call to Baptism.* There is no more colorful picture in all the Bible than that of John the Baptizer calling his fellow countrymen to repentance. There was no compromise in his message. He was not interested in statistics. When the Pharisees and Sadducees flocked to him, he said unkind things to them indicating his lack of faith in their sincerity. He was interested in the kind of living which produced fairness and compassion in daily man to man relationships.

The Jews were already familiar with one kind of baptism—that of initiating a proselyte to their religious faith. John's baptism introduced a new element. His was a baptism of repentance. There was no institutional church at that time into which members were received on profession of faith. The kingdom of God was about to be introduced to the world in a new and unique way by the Messiah, the Son of God Himself. John was sent to call the people to repentance and prepare them for the coming of the Lamb of God who through His atonement would take away the sin of the world.

John recognized his role. He never tried to go beyond it or to usurp the dignity and prestige which belonged to the Savior. Later, when his devotees began to leave him to follow Jesus of Nazareth, his only reply was, "He must increase, but I must decrease" (John 3:30).

Another example of John's loyalty to Christ was his insistence that his baptism would be replaced by a greater one. He was not minimizing his own ministry nor was he in any way de-emphasizing water baptism when he insisted that the one following him would baptize "with the Holy Ghost, and with fire." The point was that where John had his limitations, the Messiah would possess perfect insights and be able to evaluate properly and judge fairly with reference to moral and spiritual conduct.

II. *The Baptizing of Jesus.* There is something sweet and tender in the relationship between John and Jesus. At first, John was reluctant to baptize the stranger from Galilee. We cannot be sure that he understood everything about Jesus at that moment. Perhaps it was later, after the baptism and after Jesus returned victoriously from the temptations with a glow of triumph on His face, that John realized the full truth. But as he looked into the face of the One making request for baptism, he immediately recognized the spiritual superiority of this man standing before him. John's reasoning was that if either of the two was to baptize the other with a repentance baptism, he should be baptized by Jesus. The quiet insistence of the Galilean, however, won John over completely and he baptized Jesus.

The theological questions which arose because of later events in the history of the developing Christian faith were not present at the Jordan River that day. Later, Paul, in writing to the Romans, saw much more in baptism than might have been seen by the most observant follower of John on the banks of the Jordan when Jesus came "up straightway out of the water." Paul saw baptism as a symbol of the believer's death to the old life, burial to that life and resurrection to a new one (Rom. 6:4). He saw it further as a picture of the bodily resurrection at the Second Coming of Christ. We must remember, however, that Paul lived on the other side of the historical event at Calvary. The disciples of Jesus refused to believe, until the very end, that Jesus was going to die. They thought in terms of an earthly kingdom in spite of Jesus' insistence to the contrary. The people standing with John and Jesus at

Jordan were completely incapable at that time of understanding all of the teachings which were implicit in this beautiful symbolic act.

Why was Jesus baptized? It was certainly not because He was a sinner and must repent. He was identifying Himself with the repentance baptism of John, not personally repenting of sin. The Bible teaches consistently that Jesus was entirely without sin. Jesus was putting His stamp of approval upon a good act. He was dedicating Himself to the ministry of John and to the message of John because this preaching represented the highest and best in the Judaism of that day. Jesus was about to enter into the public arena of proclamation and service for God. He would take the people where they were spiritually and seek to lead them to where He wanted them to arrive in understanding the true nature of God's kingdom. For Jesus, baptism was a dedication as He began His work. He spoke of it as an act "to fulfil all righteousness."

III. *God's Approval of the Act.* The opening of heaven was a supernatural act. It was for the benefit of Jesus but we learn from John 1:32 that John the Baptist saw it also. We cannot tell from the record whether anyone else other than these two saw and heard. In John 12:28 the people heard a sound from heaven which they thought was thunder, but they were not able to distinguish the words. At the conversion of Saul on the Damascus Road the people with him saw the light and heard a sound but were not able to distinguish the words. The expression "descending like a dove" is not clear as to whether it is speaking of a dove's form or with a dove's manner of descending. Most

scholars, however, believe that some bodily form was present, although certainly the gentleness of the dove is emphasized. The point here is that God was pleased with His Son. This act of dedication by identification with the work of John the Baptist was commended by the heavenly Father.

Baptism is important. If it were not, Jesus would never have insisted that John baptize Him. The water does not "wash the sin away" but the act contains a great message. It may be true that some groups in history have perverted this doctrine by an overemphasis of it or a misinterpretation of it. This, however, is no excuse for one to avoid participation in a beautiful and meaningful experience that was accepted by Jesus and later included in His great commission to His disciples as He sent them out to evangelize the world (Matt. 28:19, 20). Baptism is a part of God's redemptive plan. It speaks a definite message to the new convert. It further enables him to speak a clear-cut message of confession to the world. God said concerning Jesus' baptism, "I am well pleased."

Conclusion. It must be recognized that there are many varying viewpoints among the various groups within Christendom concerning baptism. This is unfortunate and has led, at times, to sharp words between people who should love one another in Christ. The difficulty began early in the history of Christianity. A saving value was attached to baptism that is unwarranted by the Scriptures. The form was changed to accommodate those who were unable to go down into the water and come up out of the water because of illness or other reasons.

Within a few centuries the majority of the Christian world had eliminated the part of baptism which speaks of the burial and resurrection. This is most unfortunate.

It is doubtful that the Christian world will ever be reunited in form on this meaningful observance. We can, however, be reunited in spirit. Baptism is for believers. It is for those who have had a personal experience of salvation in Jesus Christ and wish to confess to the world their identification with Christ in personal faith. Some feel more deeply about the form of baptism than others and some of these are very militant in their views. Whatever our persuasion concerning the form of baptism, we are not justi-fied in being un-Christian in attitude toward those who disagree with us.

The important thing concerning baptism is that it speaks of repent-ance, death to the old life and identification with the new. Unless one has had an experience of regen-eration, he can go down into the baptismal waters a dry lost man and merely come up a wet lost man. It is our experience with Christ as Savior that makes baptism meaning-ful and valid in God's sight.

Jesus was baptized. He did not feel Himself above this experience. He believed it contained a vital part of God's message to the world. The early Christians likewise practiced it and incorporated it into the require-ments for the fellowship of believers.

SUNDAY EVENING, JANUARY 13

TITLE: "Fellowship in Him"

TEXT: "He that saith he is in the light, and hateth his brother, is in darkness even until now. He that loveth his brother abideth in the light, and there is none occa-sion of stumbling in him" (1 John 2:9, 10).

SCRIPTURE READING: 1 John 2:1-11.

Introduction. The Expositor's Greek Testament gives a title of the intro-ductory portion of this scripture as "The Remedy for the Sins of Believers" (volume V, page 172, Eerdmans Publishing Company, Grand Rapids, Michigan). Part of this passage does deal with the rem-edy, but the total passage deals with Christian fellowship—fellowship with God and fellowship with man. The remedy of sin makes this possible.

John uses the term "little chil-dren" advisedly. It is a tender tone. He is an old man and regards his readers as "little children." This was a phrase of Jesus as is seen in the gospel of John (13:33). This tone is assumed because John is about to address a warning to them, and he desires to take the sting out and to disarm the opposition.

I. *Fellowship in Him As It Relates to Sin* (2:1, 2).

A. The believer is exhorted to try to live above sin (2:1). It seems that John had no patience with pro-fessional perfectionists (1:8-10), but he has even less patience with loose lives.

In dealing with these concepts, two dangers are pointed out. One is, since it is impossible to live without

25

sin, why strive after holiness. The argument is that such effort is useless; sin is an abiding necessity. The other danger is to say, why dread falling into sin since it is so easy to escape. We may sin with light hearts, since we have the blood of Jesus Christ to cleanse us.

John writes that he is not trying to discourage his readers in their pursuit of holiness or to embolden them in sinning, but on the contrary, in order that they would not sin. In order for sin to be avoided, two measures must be taken—walk in the light and confess past sins.

B. The believer has a twofold provision for his sin (2:1b, 2). The words, "we have" in verse 1 is a present active indicative which indicates continuous reality. The first provision is found in an advocate as verse 1 mentions. The word "advocate" means to call by the side of, to render assistance. An advocate champions the cause. He pleads the case. He does not plead one's innocence nor does He adduce extenuating circumstances. He acknowledges one's guilt and presents His victorious works as grounds for acquittal.

The second provision is found in the word "propitiation" in verse 2. This word means to appease and render favorable. It means to gain or regain favor. It means to make complete satisfaction for a wrong.

II. *Fellowship in Him Is Determined by the Knowledge of a Believer* (2:3-6). The tense of the verb "know" (2:3), is continuous. One keeps on knowing.

A. One knows Him if he keeps His commandments (2:3, 4). *The*

Expositor's Greek Testament translates this verse, "and herein we get to know that we know Him—if we observe His commandments" (page 174). This knowledge is proof of our propitiation and advocacy.

There are two ways to look at this: first, one gets to know by keeping and second, when one knows, one keeps. Knowledge of God, or fellowship with Him, is tested by obedience to the divine commands. For one to profess to know Jesus and not obey Him, is a contradiction according to verse 4.

B. One knows Him when love is perfected (2:5). The redeeming love of God has attained its end in the man who observes His Word. This is to love one's enemies and such that they might be brethren. By cultivating such love as this, one gets to know that he knows Him. This is also to love sinners as God loved them. This is a forgiving love.

C. One knows Him if he abides in Him (2:6). Evidence of abiding in Him is walking with Him. This is another verb that displays continuous action. Walking in Him is a conformation of one's life to His. The believer gets like Him by imitating Him, and likeness to Him is irrefutable evidence that one is like Him.

III. *Fellowship in Him Is Seen in the Light of a Christian* (2:7-11).

A. The nature of light is love. Love is an inevitable test of fellowship with God. Light keeps one from stumbling. Love destroys the desire to hurt and seeks good. If a person hates, he lives in darkness. Hate shuts out light and thus hinders knowledge of where one goes and destroys fellowship.

Nothing is so blind as hatred. It conceals the person from his own faults and the virtues of others. It keeps one in ignorance of moral peril and indifferent to the consequences of deeds. No one who lives under the power of hatred, or who fails to obey the impulse of love can claim fellowship with God, for God is love.

B. The commandment to love is made new in Jesus. It is new in time, standard, and motive.

One who is walking in light revealed in Christ will not only do what is right in refraining from sin; he will also keep the great commandment of love which Christ gave and Himself fulfilled.

Conclusion. The greatest life one can have is that of fellowship with God. All believers are to resist sin and walk close to God. But when sin is committed, it is adequately covered in Jesus Christ. Turn to Him in faith. Resist evil and test your fellowship by how and whom you love.

WEDNESDAY EVENING, JANUARY 16

TITLE: "The Bible Speaks to Our Condition"

SCRIPTURE READING: Matthew 16.

Introduction. The events and conversations recorded in Matthew 16 focus upon a pivotal point in the life and ministry of our Lord. His opposition was becoming more aggressive. Pointed personal questions provoked a recognition and confession of His Messiahship. He speaks concerning the establishment of His Church and gives voice concerning its undying nature. For the first time He speaks plainly concerning His death and resurrection which is a fulfillment of Old Testament prophecy. The chapter closes with a declaration concerning His ultimate glory.

A proper and prayerful study of this chapter will speak to our present condition.

I. *Our Motive Is Highly Important*

(Matt. 16:1-8). Those who came to our Lord with selfish and malicious motives were not always kindly received. They did not always receive an open and direct reply to their questions or a favorable answer to their prayers.

If we would enter into dialogue with the eternal God, we need to do so with an open mind and a heart that is willing to do His good will.

II. *Daily Bread in Abundance* (Matt. 16:9, 10). As Jesus warned His disciples concerning the erroneous teachings of the Pharisees and the Sadducees, He reminded them of the manner in which God provides for our material needs. He reminded them of how provisions had been made for the multitudes in a time of need and asked the question, "How many baskets did you fill?" God provides in excess of our needs. He provides for us adequately and gives to us a surplus. Our God provides for us in a liberal and generous manner rather than in a stingy manner (James 1:5).

III. *Divine Truth Is Revealed Truth* (Matt. 16:13-17). The real truth about God and life cannot be discovered by the unaided human intellect. The real truth about God is revealed to those who earnestly seek to know Him and to be responsive to His will (1 Cor. 2:14). Peter was earnestly seeking to come to a deeper understanding of the nature and purpose of our Lord. God, according to His own purpose of grace, opened the mind and the heart of Peter and let him grasp the truth that Jesus of Nazareth was indeed the Messiah, the Son of God in human flesh.

It's wonderful to sit at the feet of great teachers and to read the books of outstanding writers. The greatest privilege that we have is that of letting God reveal to us His truth as it speaks to our condition.

IV. *The Peril of False Thinking* (Matt. 16:22, 23). How can one be so open to the truth in one moment and so far from the truth in the next? Peter could speak a word of warning to each of us at this point. In one moment, he was open to a fresh revelation from God. He was granted insight to understand who Jesus really was. From this pinnacle of spiritual insight, we find him descending to the valley of being totally wrong in his understanding concerning the purpose of God in Jesus Christ.

If the thoughts of men and the purpose of Satan could take command of the mind of the Apostle Peter, you and I should be alerted and on our guard. We must not make the fatal assumption that because we have been right about one thing that this guarantees that we will be right always about other things.

If Satan could infiltrate the mind of Peter, he can infiltrate our mind and cause us to think thoughts and accept ideas that are erroneous and hurtful. We need to be on guard against believing "the doctrine of the Pharisees and the Sadducees" and accepting the false teachings of Satan.

V. *Profits That Do Not Evaporate* (Matt. 16:24-28). Our Lord was a life investment counselor. He extended an invitation for His disciples to follow Him in a life of faith and faithfulness. He warned them against living a life of self-centered selfishness that produces the profits that are perishable.

He would encourage us to find the life abundant by losing our life in service to God and to others. He would encourage us to take the long look and to live with the ultimate values of an eternal kingdom uppermost in our mind and movements.

Conclusion. Let us search our heart and look at our motives. Let's trust Him to provide adequately for us through the day. Let's open our mind and will to receive divine truth and to avoid the false way that leads to disappointment. What can we do for His glory today?

TITLE: "Jesus Overcame Temptation"

TEXT: "For we have not an high priest which cannot be touched with the feeling of our infirmities; but was in all points tempted like as we are, yet without sin" (Heb. 4:15).

SCRIPTURE READING: Luke 4: 1-13.

HYMNS: "Stand Up, Stand Up for Jesus," Duffield. "Yield Not to Temptation," Palmer. "May God Depend on You?" Martin.

OFFERTORY PRAYER:

Our Father, we approach Thee as redeemed children of God by faith in Jesus Christ. Part of the Christian life is the bringing of our offering and we do it gladly. We count it not merely a duty but a privilege to bring the tithe into the storehouse that God's work may be carried on both here in our own church and through our mission outreach to the uttermost part of the earth. We know that we can give without loving but we know also that we cannot love without giving. Help us to give and help us also to find joy in giving. Accept our gifts and use them in a way that will glorify Thy name and take the message of Thy Son to many who need Him. In our Savior's name we pray. Amen.

Introduction. It is after moments of spiritual ecstasy that we are most prone to temptation. This is because there is a tendency to relax our discipline and feel we have reached spiritual maturity. Jesus did what we should do when we feel a crisis arising. He went into a place of solitude for prayer and meditation. It was time for Him to begin His life's work and He must listen to the voice of God and set His goals in perfect harmony with the purposes of His Father for Him.

There is no need for a meticulous discussion as to whether the temptations were literal or whether Jesus fought the battle purely within His soul. God is not limited in His means nor in His methods. The Bible teaches clearly the existence of a personal devil—an adversary. In the crisis moments of God's redemptive program, He intervened in extraordinary and unusual ways to accomplish His goal. Unless one is absolutely prejudiced against the supernatural, he can accept without any problem the personal appearance of the Evil One.

The matter of whether Jesus could have sinned or not is also one which should not concern us greatly. Of course, He could have sinned. If He could not, the whole experience is a sham and the recording of it is useless. Jesus had two natures—human and divine. He could have forfeited His right to be the Savior if He had not disciplined Himself to obedience. The experience of Jesus in the wilderness was more, however, than a departure for "devotions." It was a necessary confrontation with Satan at the beginning of Jesus' ministry in order that certain basic issues would be settled. God's Spirit led Jesus into the wilderness. The verb has the significance of "drive" and thus indicates a strong compulsion. He was literally thrust into personal encounter with the one who was head of the dark kingdom of evil.

What kind of Messiah will Jesus

of Nazareth be? The crowds would endeavor to force Him into their mold and place an earthly crown on His head. Jesus must, therefore, come face to face with the options offered by the non-godly forces of the universe and make His choice. He must meet temptation in every area of His personality and decide that the "short cut" through favor with men will never bring long-range approval from either God or man. Every temptation that is possible for man to experience may be categorized in one of the three offered by Satan.

I. *The Temptation to Appetite.* The seclusion of Jesus and the consequent communion with God produced an ecstasy that helped to master the flesh. There are recorded cases in history which verify the ability of high emotion to hold physical wants in abeyance. Everyone, however, must "come to earth" again and feel the reality of physical hunger. Jesus was no exception. There is nothing either right or wrong with hunger. It is independent of all moral considerations. It is, however, how man satisfies the physical craving that determines whether or not he has sinned against God. The suggestion of Satan seemed innocent enough. Jesus, however, saw the bait wound skillfully over the barbed hook. He tore it away and disclosed the sharp point. He refused to claim special privileges because of His unique relationship to God. He had come to be the Savior and this meant identifying Himself with His fellow men. They were not able to command stones to be made bread. If He claimed special privilege or preferential treatment, He would not be playing the game fairly and that

would be sin. The Redeemer must be spotless. This meant He must refuse to claim a way of escape from personal problems and needs which was not open to every man. He was to be a burden bearer. He could not do this by separating Himself from His own burdens. If He was to share the lot of His brethren, He must be content to live as they lived.

All of us meet this temptation. We meet it every day. It may not have to do with stones and bread but it has to do with the hot passions that incite us to satisfy the cravings of our flesh by illegitimate means. The cry of the flesh is normal, but it must not be satisfied in abnormal ways. There must be disciplines in life. We live in a structured society. God has put certain guidelines in our personal relationships and we ignore these at our peril. In the Garden of Eden the woman saw that the tree was "good for food." This means it appealed to the lust of her flesh. How many homes are broken today because one marriage partner has sought to satisfy the cravings of the flesh in a way that violated faithfulness to his/her companion! Or perhaps the passion was satisfied in the pre-marital years but the blot of remorse lingers and clouds the marriage relationship! How many bodies have been impaired for life because the lust of the flesh was satisfied with that which at the last "biteth like a serpent, and stingeth like an adder" (Prov. 23:32)! Every physical drive that is allowed to run uncontrolled threatens future happiness.

The physical is not only subservient to the spiritual but it is dependent upon it. Fleshly needs must be satisfied in ways that are in harmony with spiritual principles. Man needs bread. He cannot live without it, but it must be supplied through processes approved by God and which recognize that nourishment has a divine reference as well as a human one.

II. *The Temptation to Avarice.* Matthew and Luke reverse the order of the second and third temptation. It seems more logical that Luke's account renders the events as they occurred for two reasons. First, Luke made it clear in his introduction that he was writing an "orderly account" (1:3). Second, this temptation to materialism is still related somewhat to the physical for it involved the "lust of the eye" while the third temptation was much more subtle involving the "pride of life." Thus the first two temptations were direct while the third was more indirect (yet perhaps far more appealing than even the first two).

Does Satan have the power to offer the kingdoms of his world? The Faust theme has been predominant in literature. Man *can* sell out to the devil and enjoy temporary success.

III. *The Temptation to Ambition.* In the Garden of Eden the woman saw that the tree was "to be desired to make one wise" (Gen. 3:6) while John speaks of this aspect of temptation as "the pride of life" (1 John 2:16).

It is this desire for sophistication that is perhaps the most subtle temptation of all today. It is not enough to have well-fed bodies and a comfortable bank account. Man wants to be "looked up to" and worshiped as though he were God himself. Some of the things people do today in order to seem presti-

gious would be amusing if they were not so tragic.

If Jesus had jumped from off the pinnacle of the Temple, people would have considered Him outstanding. They would have fed His ego and surely looked up to Him as a god of some kind. But Jesus was not in the business of having His vanity satisfied. He had a message to be delivered and He wanted the people to follow Him in deeds of kindness and service.

This third temptation was the hardest of all for Satan even offered Scripture which seemed to prove His position. It is so easy to find Scripture which seems to justify our position when we want something badly enough. Those who classified the seven deadly sins arranged them in correct order—at least when they put "pride" at the top of the list!

Conclusion. How did Jesus overcome temptation? It is not being tempted that is the sin. It is how we react to the temptation. The example of Jesus is exactly the pattern for us. He met Satan's attack with the written Word of God. Facing each of the temptations He quoted from the marvelous career-climaxing messages of Moses as recorded in the Book of Deuteronomy. It is impossible to overemphasize the importance of being familiar with Scripture. There is a school of thought today which minimizes memorizing lest we let it become a mechanical thing and lose the meaning. This is, of course, always a danger in the amassing of facts, but we should not "throw out the baby with the bath water." The solution is not to quit memorizing Scripture but rather to be sure we understand the meaning as we commit the words to our mind and heart. A college professor years ago insisted in Bible classes that large portions of Scripture be memorized by the students. A young lady years later testified that the Scriptures she memorized in that Bible class had been perhaps the most valuable learning during her entire four years of college. She said she found herself, in times of crisis, referring again and again to verses that she committed to memory.

The way to be victorious in temptation is not merely to clench one's fist, grit one's teeth and stomp one's foot in defiance against the tempter. It is rather to be so saturated with the Word of God that one lives in a living fellowship with Him. This way of life makes one rise above the temptation. The attractions that Satan offers simply have no appeal.

Jesus was here on His Father's business. So are we and we too must be about the things of our Father. Perhaps then we can understand the words of Thomas A. Edison who is reputed to have said, "I am not bothered with temptation. I stay too busy."

SUNDAY EVENING, JANUARY 20

TITLE: "Childhood in Him"

TEXT: "I write unto you, little children, because your sins are forgiven you for his name's sake" (1 John 2:12).

SCRIPTURE READING: 1 John 2:12-29.

Introduction. "The Apostle has been setting forth searching truths and is about to make an exacting claim; and here he pauses and with much tenderness reassures his readers: 'I am not addressing you as unbelievers or casting doubt upon the sincerity of your faith. On the contrary, it is because I am assured thereof that I am writing this letter to you and wrote the Gospel which accompanies it'" (*The Expositor's Greek Testament*, volume V, page 177).

I. *The Writer Sets Forth the Conditions of Childhood* (1 John 2:12-14).

A. Before John establishes the condition of becoming children of God, he explains why he is writing. This is fourfold: to encourage further achievements, to caution against temptation from which his readers cannot be free, and to urge the believer to do righteousness and manifest love. This is not to be done to become a Christian, but because the believer has already enjoyed fellowship with God and is seeking a larger relation of all the privileges that this fellowship allows. The last reason for writing is to warn against perilous allurements of the world.

B. Now John sets forth the conditions of childhood. These conditions are forgiveness, knowledge, faith, and abiding in the Word of God. A discussion of these conditions is found in the way John addresses his readers.

1. The term "little children" refers to believers in general. Here the term "forgiveness" is found. Forgiveness is the initial and funda-

mental experience of a Christian. It is the supreme need of every soul and is the absolute condition of fellowship with God.

2. The term "fathers" is used to portray maturity. The evidence of maturity is seen in the knowledge of the Father. It dates back to the beginning.

Knowledge is made possible through Jesus Christ and is the very essence of eternal truth. It increases in its depth and fullness by the experiences of life, by the pressures of problems, by the stress of sorrows, and by the changes and mysteries of the passing years.

3. The term "young men" is used to describe the strong. They are strong in faith. They have overcome the evil one. They are strong because the Word of God abides in them.

4. Since all people become Christians the same way, it can be conceived that the terms "children," "father," and "young men" are terms used in stylistic writing. Thus, each term is all-inclusive and each statement applies to all others.

II. *The Writer Sets Forth the Manifestations of Childhood* (2:15-17).

A. A negative idea is presented to emphasize the positive, namely, a love for the world.

A love for the world is not in keeping with believers in Christ. The world is the unbelieving men and women. It is the society of the unspiritual and godless. A Christian is not to covet the world. Three terms are used to describe the

world: lust of the flesh, lust of the eyes, and pride of life.

If anyone keeps on loving these things—the world—the love of the Father is not in him. Besides that, these things are temporary—they pass away.

B. The real manifestation of true childhood is seen in a love for the Father. He does the will of the Father.

III. *The Writer Sets Forth a Contrast Between True Children and Those Who Claim to Be* (2:18).

A. A negative is presented to emphasize the positive. There will be crises that arise and adversaries of Christ who will be deceptive. They are the exponents and representatives of the anti-Christ. They are a nuisance party. True children will not be deceived.

Neither will true children fall away (2:19). By falling away or a withdrawal, one proves he never shared the real life and fellowship of the community.

This is one of the most important doctrines of the Church. It is clear that these people had been members of the visible church; they had fulfilled the outward requirements for church membership, but although it was from the fellowship they went out, they were not of them. This reminds one that more than outward membership in the visible Church is required if one is to be a member of the body of Christ, and also one must not expect that the visible Church will always be composed entirely of true believers.

True children will not deny the Father and the Son (2:22). One cannot be a believer in Christ as

Savior and then deny the Incarnation and the filial relation of man to God. The term "Christ" in verse 22 is the Son of God, the Eternal Word, of whom John writes.

B. The positive is now brought in contrast to the negative.

1. True believers have been anointed by the Holy Spirit (2:20, 21), This is the unction of the Holy One.

2. True believers confess the Father (2:24). It is only as one receives Christ that he becomes a child of God (John 1:12); thus, if Christ is resisted—not confessed— it is evident he is not a child. He does not recognize God as Father. Belief is thus shown to be a touchstone of character; it is a test of life. It is more than an intellectual assent to truth. It has its moral elements as well and it consists in submission to a Being who is holy and divine. It is a spiritual experience made abiding by the indwelling Spirit of God.

3. True believers abide in Christ (2:24, 28). That which is heard as is mentioned in verse 24, is the Gospel message of Jesus Christ. As one abides in Christ, he then becomes confident. This abiding results in obedience and this is the greatest manifestation of childhood.

Conclusion. The greatest experience one can have is to become a child of God by being born again. If you have never received Christ as Savior and been forgiven of your sins, this is the time to do it. This is also a good time to examine your life and see how you manifest your relation to God.

WEDNESDAY EVENING, JANUARY 23

TITLE: "The Bible Speaks to Our Condition"

SCRIPTURE READING: Matthew 23.

Introduction. How can this chapter which begins with a warning against the example of the Scribes and Pharisees (23:1-12) and continues with an announcement of seven woes upon these civic and religious leaders of the nation of Israel (23:13-36) be profitable for the people of God in this decade of the seventies? The Holy Spirit did not lead Matthew to write this chapter merely in order to preserve a historical record of the controversy which our Lord had with those who were plotting to bring about His death by crucifixion. This chapter contains something more than ancient history.

The Bible needs to be studied in its historical context. An awareness of the circumstances described in the chapter can help us to make the proper application to our own lives and circumstances in the present.

Our Lord is unchanging in His nature, in His desires, and in His denunciations. We can discover the will of our Lord by examining that which He approved in contrast to that which He denounced. We can be certain that if an attitude of mind or an ambition of life brought displeasure to Him then, that it would do so today.

There are two major pictures of our Lord that have real significance for the present in Matthew 23.

I. *Christ the Critic.* Our Lord was no kill-joy (John 3:17). Our Lord was critical only of that which was hurtful, destructive, negative. His denunciation of evil was but the backside of His love. He could not condone that which was destructive and at the same time be genuinely concerned about the welfare of people.

This passage reveals Christ as a radical critic who was dealing drastically with the malignancy that was destroying the nation and hindering it from fulfilling God's purpose. Let us examine our own lives in the mirror of His criticism of the example of the Scribes and Pharisees.

A. Christ criticizes profession without practice (23:3).

B. Christ criticizes unwillingness to share the burdens of others (23:4).

C. Christ criticizes wrong motivation for religious service (23:5a). The applause of our contemporaries is not an adequate and proper motivation for religious services. While it is important that we stand high in the opinion of others, we must not be guilty of taking a poll of public opinion before we take a stand on moral issues.

D. Christ criticizes an attitude of judging success in terms of a position of prominence rather than in terms of service rendered to the needy (23:6-11).

E. Christ criticizes hypocrisy (23:13-15). Repeatedly, our Lord denounces pretense, sham and phoniness. He uses terms such as "hypocrites," "blind guides," "fools" and a "generation of serpents."

A hypocrite is one who deliberately pretends to be something that he isn't. There is a difference between failing to be fully Christian and pretending to be something on the outside which does not represent the inward reality.

F. Christ criticizes the hindering of others from entering the kingdom of God (23:13).

G. Christ criticizes basic dishonesty in relationship with God and others (23:16-22).

As one listens to our Lord criticize attitudes, actions and ambitions of these religious leaders, it makes one tremble as he examines his own mind and motives in the presence of God.

II. *Christ the Compassionate One* (23:37-39). Christ was at the end of His earthly ministry. The events in this chapter describe His final encounter with the civic, religious and political leaders who were plotting to bring about His death. They had rejected Him as their Messiah and Lord. Our Lord responds with tears of compassionate grief as He beholds the city and addresses it with a broken heart. Luke's gospel records that when our Lord beheld the city and spoke these words that He wept over the city.

A. Our Lord was weeping because of what His people were missing and would continue to miss.

B. Our Lord was weeping because of the foolishness and the hard-heartedness of these people

35

who had turned away from their only hope of salvation.

C. Our Lord was weeping because of the calamity that was going to befall His nation and His capital city.

Conclusion. The words recorded in Matthew 23:37 are some of the saddest to be found in all of the Bible. They reveal the heartbreak of our Savior. He addresses His nation with these sad, pathetic words, "ye would not." Let it not be said concerning us, "ye would not" do the good will of God.

SUNDAY MORNING, JANUARY 27

TITLE: "Jesus Called Men"

TEXT: "Come and see" (John 1:39) "Follow me, and I will make you fishers of men" (Matt. 4:19).

SCRIPTURE READING: John 1: 35-51; Matthew 4:18-22.

HYMNS: "Jesus Calls Us," Alexander. "O Master, Let Me Walk With Thee," Gladden. "Footsteps of Jesus," Slade.

OFFERTORY PRAYER:

Eternal God, our heavenly Father, we are grateful that we are not our own but have been bought with a price. We are thankful that this price was not corruptible things such as silver and gold but was the Lamb slain from the foundation of the world. We rejoice in the blessings that are ours because we are members of God's redeemed family. We stand amazed in Thy presence because of Thy great love for us. We know that we are not all we should be but we are grateful for the privilege of seeking to grow in grace and in further knowledge of Thee.

The offerings we bring this morning are testimonies of our love for Thee. We desire, through our gifts of money, to have a part in Thy work at home and around the world. We thank Thee for every cause that is supported by the gifts that we bring. We ask Thy blessings upon all who are serving in Thy name and trumpeting the message of Christ in any way on this Lord's day.

Receive our gifts as expressions of our dedication. Use our gifts in constructive ways to tell the message of God's redeeming love in Jesus to those who do not know Him. Help us to bring not only our gifts but may this service also be a means of renewing our lives in dedication to Thee. May we make fresh resolves this morning concerning the living of our lives and may we go forth from God's house today to put these resolves into practice. May we do all of this to Thy glory. We pray in Jesus' name. Amen.

Introduction. It is not easy to harmonize the four gospels with reference to the early ministry of Jesus. Most scholars, however, agree that Jesus had a short ministry in Judea before He went into Galilee for an extended preaching tour. In all probability, Jesus went back to

Galilee briefly after His baptism and immediately returned to Jerusalem for the Passover. It was while He was in Galilee that He performed the first miracle as recorded in the second chapter of John. The third chapter of John, including the visit of Nicodemus to Christ, records events which occurred after He returned to Jerusalem. He then, after a brief ministry in this area, returned to Galilee through Samaria where He met and led to saving faith the woman at the well of Sychar. He then began His major ministry in Galilee as recorded by Matthew, Mark and Luke.

Thus we have the record of Jesus, immediately after His baptism, calling several disciples to Himself including Andrew, Peter, Phillip and Nathaniel. Later, we find that in Galilee He called Peter and Andrew once more. The first call, as recorded in John's gospel, was for them to accept Him as a person. It is not incorrect to say this was a "call to salvation." The call which came to them in Galilee was a call to leave their work and be a "full time" follower of Him. Both of these calls were important. There is a twofold sense in which He calls us today.

I. *Christ's Call to Us to Receive Him Personally.* John's gospel is preeminently the gospel concerning the personhood of Jesus Christ. It was written to set forth with clarity and certainty that Jesus was the divine Son of God. This is the emphasis of the gospel from the first chapter until the last. John's gospel records that after Jesus was baptized He began to attract some of John's followers to Himself. John seems to have had only one purpose—that of calling people to repentance. Jesus had a deeper

goal—He sought to lead men to follow Him for further instruction in doing the will of God. Jesus possessed an attractiveness that won people to Him immediately. John declared Him to be the "Lamb of God, which taketh away the sin of the world" (John 1:29). After this declaration of John, some of his followers began to leave him and follow Jesus.

It was Andrew, one of the disciples who spoke least, who recognized Jesus immediately as the Messiah. He went and told his brother, Simon, and brought him to Jesus. The next day Jesus found Philip and called Him unto Himself. Phillip found Nathaniel. An interesting conversation developed between Nathaniel and Jesus. Nathaniel made a great confession concerning Jesus. He called Him, "the Son of God . . . King of Israel" (John 1:49).

What was happening? One by one these men were being brought to Jesus. They would later form the nucleus of His twelve disciples. First of all, however, they must believe in Him as a person.

It is the same with us today if we would serve God. We must accept the personhood of Jesus Christ. We cannot do His work effectively unless we accept Him as Savior. As one surveys the contemporary scene, he becomes aware that too many people are trying to do the works of Jesus without believing in Him. It is necessary for us to decide once and for all what we believe concerning the deity of Christ and His complete equality with God as we begin our service for Him.

II. *Christ's Call to Us for Dedication and Service.* The scene changes! Jesus is no longer in Judea. He is now in Galilee. He is beginning His active ministry.

One thing we should note about His relationship with John the Baptist. Jesus gives us a beautiful example in ministerial ethics! He did not begin an extensive ministry until John the Baptist was off the scene. One of the most significant verses to be found in the Bible is that which says, "Now after that John was put in prison, Jesus came into Galilee, preaching the gospel" (Mark 1:14). Jesus did not want to overshadow John and hence would not begin His active, public ministry until John had gone into forced retirement.

The first thing a good leader does is to try to find good followers. This is in order that he may train them to carry on his work in the event he must step aside. As Jesus began His active ministry, He sought for leaders. Where would He find them? The best answer was some of those whom He had met and won to Himself in Judea while John was preaching. Some of John's early followers made some of Jesus' best disciples.

The record does not tell us what Peter and Andrew did from the time they met Jesus in Judea until He called them by the Sea of Galilee for full-time service. We presume they carried on their work according to their customary business habits. Perhaps they had spoken often of Jesus since meeting Him. Probably they wondered if they would see Him again. The seed had been sown, however, and when Jesus called them they were ready to respond without question.

How like life this is! Although we should accept Jesus as complete Lord of our life in the initial salvation experience, many times we wait a season before we understand the full implications of complete surrender to His will for us. There are amazing examples of people who are saved and called to preach at the same moment but these are the exception. Most of us go through a period of evaluation and establishment of priorities. Many God-called preachers will confess that their call to the ministry was a far greater emotional "tug" than their conversion experience. Perhaps they were converted as a child and the experience was a quiet and peaceful one—although very meaningful. On the other hand, their call to full-time service was a deep struggle of the soul concerning the commitment of a full life.

The fact that the disciples immediately left their nets and followed Jesus indicates two things. First, Jesus possessed a tremendous personal appeal. Second, the previous experience with Jesus in Judea had left its imprint upon them and they were now ready to follow Him wherever He would lead.

III. *Each Call Is Distinctive.* In every encounter between man and God, the individual personality is respected. No two calls come exactly alike. Some are diametrically opposite from others. In some cases two calls may have some similarities but there are still differences that make each person's call a unique one. With some calls, the emotions may be stirred greatly. There may be great sins that have separated man from God and the call to salvation is the call to forsake those sins. In some experiences of salvation, however, it is the still small voice that whispers winsomely and invites to the Savior. The sin element is, of course, present in every conversion experience but it is not articulated as much as in others.

The call to service likewise differs. Peter and Matthew were poles apart. One was a fisherman and the other a tax collector. Yet each heard the voice of Jesus in his own way and each responded according to his background, temperament and life style. We should never try to force another person into the mold of our own exact experience. Our task is to bear witness concerning the claim of Jesus upon life and let the Holy Spirit minister in His own way and lay upon the heart of the person hearing so that response may be made in the way that is consistent with his own personality.

Conclusion. God's call comes continuously. We can reject the call but we cannot ignore it. Indecision is a form of refusal. Yet, God remains ever pleading for us to come to Him and accept His will for our life.

The greatest discovery we will ever make is to find what God wants us to do. The greatest goal we will ever attain is that of accomplishing the purpose that He has for us in this world. The first call comes to everyone for the same purpose. It is for personal salvation. Each one of us needs to be saved from our sins and become a new creature in Christ. The second call may vary in intent as well as in method. God calls some people into definite full-time work as preacher, missionary or a religious worker in a "full-time" sense. Yet, all of us are called to be of service. Although we may not give ourselves in full time in such a way that we depend upon Christian people for financial support for our livelihood, yet there is still a sense in which we are all in "full-time" service for the Lord. Our business is the Lord's business. We may have a trade, merchandise mart, or profession to pay our expenses but we all are called to be a "full-time Christian."

As long as there are lost people in the world who need to be saved and saved people who need to be trained in further growth, we have a mission from the Lord. The same Christ who called Peter, Andrew, James, John, Matthew and Phillip is calling twentieth-century people to Himself. Let us never turn a deaf ear to the Master's call!

SUNDAY EVENING, JANUARY 27

TITLE: "Dignity and Destiny in Him"

TEXT: "Beloved, now are we the sons of God, and it doth not yet appear what we shall be: but we know that, when he shall appear, we shall be like him; for we shall see him as he is" (1 John 3:2).

SCRIPTURE READING: 1 John 3:1-4.

Introduction. In the first two chapters of 1 John, the Christian life has been presented under the figure of a divine fellowship. In chapter 3, it is presented as a result of a divine birth. In the earlier chapters, salvation is presented as what Jesus wrought—propitiation and advocacy. In this chapter, it is presented as an amazing expression of God's love. Chapter 2, verse 29, introduces the idea and it is elaborated on in the following verses.

I. *The Bible Presents Salvation As Something of Divine Dignity* (3:1, 2a). The dignity of being in Christ is a present possession, as well as one of the future.

A. It is based on being children of God. The word "children" draws attention to community of nature rather than rights and privileges. Verse 2 adds to verse 1 in that Christians are not only *called* "sons of God," but that they *are* the sons of God and this is in the present. It is now. To be born of Him, is to be partakers of divine nature. First Peter 1:4 says it is an inheritance which is imperishable, undefiled, unfading, and is kept in heaven. John, in his gospel (3:5, 6), says that regeneration moves one from the sphere of the flesh into the sphere of the Spirit. Second Corinthians 5:17 says anyone in Christ Jesus is a new creature.

B. It is also a product of God's love. Love follows and vitalizes new life. Love bestows on men something of God's nature and thereby installs believers as members of God's family. Love grants to all who believe a change of moral nature, a new disposition, and a spiritual experience. Love is concerned for the highest good. It is not concerned that believers simply be saved from suffering and loss, but in order that they might be styled children of God. This love is not something inherent in human nature, but is due wholly to the love of God.

The dignity that is the believers is not only based on being children of God and is a product of God's love, but is also a gift of God (Eph. 2:8, 9).

II. *The Dignity That Is the Possession of the Believer Presents a Dilemma* (3:1c). A Christian is not ostensibly different from other men. The world did not recognize Jesus as the Son of God. This dignity forms a distinction between the Christian and the whole mass of unbelieving men and women. This is seen in the fatherhood of God. God is the potential Father of all people by creation, but those who believe in Christ are children of a heavenly birth and are real children of God.

The true fatherhood of God is never fully appreciated until one draws near to him through Christ, and the brotherhood of man will never be realized until men find the Father through Jesus Christ.

Those who reject Christ should never expect to understand or be expected to understand the followers of Christ. Thus, the world has no sympathy with the motives and aims and character of the Church of God who follow His steps or reproduce His life.

The believer does not know all of what he shall be, but he knows his destiny is to conform to the image of God.

III. *The Destiny of a Christian Is to Be Like the Son of God* (3:2c, d). To be like the Son is a blessed hope which concerns the character, disposition, and moral nature which were transformed and made perfect (Matt. 5:8). It also includes the transformation of the body which is to be conformed to the body of His glory (2 Cor. 3:18).

For one to be like Him in the life to come, he must practice that likeness now by imitating Him here on earth. This imitation is in the purity of living and is a result of the new birth. No one is content to live in sin when He knows God.

IV. *The Duty of a Christian Is of Concern Along With His Dignity and Destiny* (3:3). The word translated "hope" in verse 3 literally means "rest" in Him. That is, rest in God as Father. Luke 5:5 is a good example. It means relying on the Word of God and Christ is the Living Word.

The word "purifieth" in verse 3 denotes purity maintained with effort and fearfulness amid defilements and allurements. One who is purified is free from contamination (John 11:55; Acts 21:24, 26; Exod. 19:10). It is a personal inner cleansing of the heart (James 4:8), of the soul (1 Pet. 1:22), of the self (1 John 3:3), and of one's word (Phil. 2:12).

Conclusion. Anyone who is not a child of God is short of the dignity man's Creator intended him to be. Those who are not Christians will never reach the destiny planned for them by God, and neither will they be able to perform the divinely ordained duty. If you do not know Jesus Christ as your Savior now, accept Him and become what He wants you to be.

WEDNESDAY EVENING, JANUARY 30

TITLE: "The Bible Speaks to Our Condition"

SCRIPTURE READING: Mark 2.

Introduction. A daily study of the Word of God will provide us with the instruction that is needed for living a righteous and good life. We need a proper attitude toward our Lord and a proper understanding of life with its opportunities and responsibilities. We need the insight and the encouragement of divine instruction every day. Let us open our mind and our heart and listen as God seeks to speak to our condition through Mark 2.

This chapter reveals our Lord as being a very busy man sharing the good news of God's kingdom and ministering to the needs of those about Him. He was the center of attention. It was impossible for Him to hide from the people. There was a magnetism about the personality and teachings of our Lord that attracted the multitudes to Him.

I. *Christ the Great Healer* (Mark 2:1-12). There are three different features of this account that deserve our attention.

A. The helpless man. The man was a paralytic and unable to move from one place to another. Evidently there was some connection between his disease and his sin.

B. The helpers. There were at least four men who were concerned about bringing the helpless man to the great helper and healer. They did so at great inconvenience and with much persistence.

C. The hinderers. There were some who were very critical of our Lord and they were hinderers. The crowd which thronged about our Lord hindered the four from bringing the helpless man to our Lord in the most direct manner.

In the world today there are many helpless ones who need the service of helpers who can bring them to Christ the great healer. Let us make certain that we are not among those who are the hinderers.

II. *Sharing the Good News* (Mark 2:14-17). Our Lord treated each person as a human being. He did not discriminate on the basis of race, religion, culture or profession. Levi, better known as Matthew, was a despised publican in the service of the Roman occupational forces. Jesus loved him and wanted to redeem him. He extended an invitation to Levi and the tax collector responded affirmatively and became Matthew the apostle and writer of Scripture. In these words we have a picture of the response of a redeemed individual who was eager to share the good news of his experience with Christ with his friends. How natural that Levi should gather all of the publicans together in his house for a banquet with Jesus as the guest of honor. Matthew was eager for these other publicans to learn what he had learned about Jesus and to experience what he had experienced.

Matthew was using a natural and normal method for sharing the good news with his friends. His method was effective and appropriate. He gave proof of the genuineness of his relationship to Jesus Christ by immediately becoming concerned that others might come to know Christ as he did. Each of us could make a similar response and be a tremendous blessing to our friends who do not yet know Jesus as Savior.

III. *The Joy of Our Lord and His Disciples* (Mark 2:18-20). The sculptors and the artists have given to the world a false concept of the Messiah. Instead of His being a sad individual filled with melancholy, our Lord was characterized by a radiant personality that attracted men to Him and caused them to give to Him their undying loyalty.

When the enemies of our Lord inquired concerning why He and His disciples did not fast, He described Himself as a bridegroom, and He described His disciples as being guests at a wedding feast. Bridegrooms and their guests were happy, light-hearted, delightful individuals to be around.

A sad, long face is a poor advertisement for what it is like to be a Christian. Christ came to make joy possible and to give us a faith to sing about (John 15:11).

IV. *The Purpose ∂f the Sabbath* (Mark 2:23-28). Our Lord was in a constant controversy with the religious leaders of His day concerning the proper use of the Sabbath. Their traditions and laws had caused the Sabbath to become a blight rather than a blessing. Our Lord insisted that the Sabbath was made for the good of man. He did not look upon it as a ritualistic requirement that men must observe in order to earn the favor of God.

The Sabbath was intended as a day of rest. Man was not made as a machine of perpetual motion. He must have relief from the grind and the struggle of labor to restore the vital energies of life.

Jesus used the Sabbath to relieve

suffering. He insisted that one should always do what was right on the Sabbath day.

Conclusion. On the Lord's Day, the modern follower of Christ should spend some time in rest, some time in worship and some time in service. To ignore the day set apart by the Lord is to deny our essential nature as being spiritual. We expose our children to the peril of secularism and materialism.

The Sabbath was made for the good of man. We should make certain that it is used in a manner that will produce good in our own lives and in the lives of others.

SUGGESTED PREACHING PROGRAM FOR THE MONTH OF FEBRUARY

Sunday Mornings

Continue the series of morning messages using the theme, "The Life and Works of the Lord Jesus."

Sunday Evenings

Conclude the series based on John's first epistle with the theme, "Great Texts From 1 John."

Wednesday Evenings

"An apple a day keeps the doctor away, and a chapter a day keeps the devil away" is a common proverb. Continue to emphasize the habit of reading one chapter each day in order to let "The Bible Speak to Our Condition."

The theme passage for February is, "Open thou mine eyes, that I may behold wondrous things out of thy law" (Ps. 119:18).

SUNDAY MORNING, FEBRUARY 3

TITLE: "Jesus Taught Regeneration"

TEXT: "Ye must be born again" (John 3:7).

SCRIPTURE READING: John 3:1-18.

HYMNS: "Since Jesus Came Into My Heart," McDaniel. "Ye Must Be Born Again," Sleeper. "Come, Thou Fount of Every Blessing," Robinson.

OFFERTORY PRAYER:

Our God and our Father, help us to recognize the privileges that come to us from Thy gracious hand. Give us the wisdom to use the opportunities of our lifetime during the lifetime of our opportunities. May we never be too busy with the trivial to do those things which are eternal. May the relationship that we have in Christ produce a daily fellowship which enables us to meet problems victoriously. We pray that God's majesty and power may inspire us to give our best in faithful service. As we bring our tithes and offerings, may we do so in the spirit of gratitude. May we see beyond the narrow walls of self to a world that needs the Gospel of Christ. In this spirit, may we give joyfully and generously. We pray in Jesus' name. Amen.

Introduction. It would have been difficult to have found a better moral man in all Judea than Nicodemus. He was an outstanding leader among the Jews. He may have come to Jesus by night because of fear of what others would say, but the reason may have been because both he and Jesus were busy and met by appointment. His opening words were designed to pay respect to Jesus. It may be that he believed flattery would win a favorable acceptance. The reply of Jesus in verse 3 to the introductory statement of Jesus in verse 2 is, if not sharp, certainly straight to the point. There are three stages in the conversation between these two men. First, they spoke face to face. Next, they challenged each other mind to mind. Finally, the discussion became heart to heart. Most scholars believe the words of Jesus in verse 10 extend through verse 21.

I. *The Nature of the New Birth.* The transformation which comes when Christ enters one's life cannot be explained. Neither can it be analyzed completely. It can, however, be visualized. There are three distinct results. First, there is a *divine* change. The new birth is not a product of human ability or effort, nor is it to be explained in terms of reformation. God acts upon the heart of the individual and works a work which causes his attitude to be different. The change is a *complete* one. It af-

fects every part of a man's personality. One cannot hold back any area of life from God. This does not mean he will be a sinless person but it does mean he has surrendered himself completely to God's will for his life. The change is also a *permanent* one. This is the basis for the great doctrine of eternal security. The new birth is not dependent upon one's relationship to a visible church. Neither is it dependent upon the observance of Christian ceremonies. Verse 5 does not teach that baptism is essential for personal salvation. Several other interpretations have been offered. One of the most accepted is that water is a symbol for the Word of God. There are two distinct births in one's life—the physical and the spiritual. We become a member of our earthly family through a physical birth. We become a member of God's family through a spiritual birth.

II. *The Necessity for the New Birth.* It is man's sinful nature which makes it essential that he be born again. He has no righteousness of his own. He must be justified upon the basis of Christ's atonement. When he trusts completely in Jesus as Savior, God accounts it to him for righteousness, but He does more. God's Holy Spirit gives him a new nature. Jeremiah prophesied concerning the change God would work in the hearts of people when he spoke of a New Covenant. He said, "I will put my law in their inward parts, and write it in their hearts; and will be their God, and they shall be my people" (Jer. 31:33). Ezekiel prophesied, "A new heart also will I give you, and a new spirit will I put within you" (Ezek. 36:26). It is necessary for man to have a new heart and a new nature because his natural state is enmity against God. In Romans 3:10-18 Paul presents a mosaic concerning sin. He selects quotations from the Old Testament to show that every part of man's personality has been affected by his transgressions. Everyone stands equally guilty before God because when we are guilty of one sin we are guilty of all (James 2:10).

III. *Negotiator of the New Birth.* Throughout all of the Bible God's Holy Spirit is represented as the agent in salvation. Men are convicted of sin by the Holy Spirit. Jesus said that the Holy Spirit, "will reprove the world of sin . . . because they believe not on me" (John 16:8, 9). Men are regenerated through the work of the Holy Spirit as they are brought through repentance and faith into a right relationship with God through Jesus Christ. It is through the Holy Spirit that we become conscious of our sonship in the divine family. It is the Holy Spirit who becomes the pledge of our final redemption as He forms Christ in us as the hope of glory. It is unfortunate that because some people have perverted the doctrine of the Holy Spirit we often have been guilty of saying too little about the subject. The Holy Spirit is a Person, not merely an influence. It is His work that brings us from a sinful state of alienation from God to a right relationship with God through a redemptive experience.

IV. *The Now of the New Birth.* As Jesus and Nicodemus discussed the matter of being born again, Nicodemus became profoundly interested. He asked, "How can these things be?" Jesus replied with a simple illustration from the life of Moses.

The Israelites, while enroute from Egypt to Canaan, had been the victim of fiery serpents. The situation became acute and Moses prayed to God. He was told to place a brass serpent on a pole and put it up outside the camp. Those who would go and look at the serpent would be healed. Jesus told Nicodemus that the Son of man would be lifted up in the same way and whosoever placed his faith in Him would have eternal life. Jesus used the expression that meant "lifted up on a cross for execution" and referred to His coming crucifixion.

The closing verses of the conversation between Jesus and Nicodemus reflect the urgency of the Master's appeal. There are two good reasons for coming to Jesus in the "now" of life. First, we do not know when we will die. It is a fearful thing to pass from this world unprepared to meet God in eternity. It is the course of wisdom to come to the Savior now for it is the only safe path to pursue. Second, the sooner one comes to Christ, the sooner a life of happiness and joy will begin. Of course, one who is still lost does not know of this happiness and joy, but he should receive the testimony of others who have found happiness in surrendering to Jesus. Today is the day that salvation is available and today is the day that salvation should be appropriated. The new birth is God's way for making a sinful person a new man in Christ Jesus.

Conclusion. One does not cease to be a sinner when he becomes a Christian. The new birth gives us a new nature but the old nature is still present. In Romans 7 Paul describes the eternal conflict between the old nature and the new nature within the saved man. The new birth, however, does give man a new affection and a new desire. The person who has been born again has one great goal in life. He wishes to serve Jesus and please Him in every action of life. The judicial act in salvation is justification. The dynamic act is regeneration or being born again. Both take place when one has a genuine experience of salvation. Justification has to do with man's guilt before God. The new birth relates to the change in attitude and therefore the change in activity of the Christian. One of our pioneer preachers, George Whitefield, used to preach over and over on the subject, "Ye Must Be Born Again." One day a lady asked him, "Why do you preach so much on that subject?" He replied, "Because, lady, ye must be born again."

SUNDAY EVENING, FEBRUARY 3

TITLE: "Obligation in Him"

TEXT: "Whosoever abideth in him sinneth not: whosoever sinneth hath not seen him, neither known him" (1 John 3:6).

SCRIPTURE READING: 1 John 3: 5-10.

Introduction. In the previous verses of 1 John, John has pointed out such things as life in Christ, fellowship in Christ, childhood in Christ, and dignity and destiny in Christ. In the verses under consideration, John points out the obligations that arise out of such relationships. This is simply saying that after a person has been begotten of God—born again—there are some obligations involved.

I. *All Sin Has Its Origin in the Devil* (3:8). The devil has been a sinner from the beginning. This is his career and his normal life, and those who imitate him become his spiritual children.

A. This sin is lawlessness (3:4). The law is the revelation of God's will. It is the Father's require-ment of His children. Sin is the operation of the will against and in defiance of the law of God. It is the refusal to live in accordance with the revealed standards of right and wrong. Lawlessness and sin are con‧vertible and coexistent terms. They are interchangeable. Sinning is the converse of doing right.

B. This sinfulness is a true manifestation of the true self (3:10).

II. *All Sin Has Its Remedy in the Son of God* (3:5). The mission of Christ—His coming into the world—was to perform a remedy of sin. His very work emphasizes sin. He was manifested to take away sin (3:5). In the life of all people, there is an eternal conflict between Jesus and Satan, but victory over Satan is certain. The purpose of the Incarnation was to take away sin—past, present, and future. Jesus is qualified to do this because there is no sin in Him.

The nature of this removal is found in the words "take away." It means to lift up and carry away (John 1:29). It is complete expiation wrought by Christ on Calvary.

The word "destroy" in verse 8 is used metaphorically as loosening an obligation or bond, or relaxing an obligation.

III. *The Obligation in Christ Is to Live Righteously* (3:6, 7, 9). The word "righteousness" simply means right living. It is doing what is right. It means practicing what is right.

Here then is the true obligation in Christ. It is to live rightly according to the standards of God. The tenses of the verbs in verses 6, 7, and 9 are continued action verbs. The one who has the habit of sin and keeps on doing it shows he is not a true child of God. The words, "doth not commit sin" (3:9), means the child of God does not have the habit of sin. He does not keep on sinning. Verse 6 points out that the one who keeps on abiding in Christ does not keep on sinning. The reverse is also true; that is, the one who keeps on sinning—lives a life of sin, not mere occasional acts of sin—has not seen the Father. The habit of sin is the proof that one has not the vision or knowledge of Christ. From all of this, it is understandable that if a man is a Christian, he will do what is right. If he is a child of God, he is expected to resemble Him in righteousness. This is his obligation.

IV. *This Obligation Shows a Major Contrast.* Sin in all its forms is the very antithesis of that which is in Christ. There is incompatibility between sinfulness and Christian profession, and the Christian must never grow complacent in his attitude toward sin. A life of sin is proof that one is a child of the devil and not of God (John 8:33-39). Truth and falsehood, good and evil, right and wrong, God and the devil are irreconcilable opposites. So are sin and holiness, lawlessness and righteousness opposites. Sin is wrong doing, and righteousness is doing right.

Conclusion. The most wonderful thing that can ever happen to a person is to become a child of God. The greatest achievement of a child of God is to become righteous like God. I plead with you to surrender your all to Jesus Christ for cleansing of sin. Resist the devil and he will flee from you. Draw close to God and He will draw close to you. Then assume the obligation that is yours in Him.

WEDNESDAY EVENING, FEBRUARY 6

TITLE: "The Bible Speaks to Our Condition"

SCRIPTURE READING: Mark 9.

Introduction. The psalmist prayed, "Open thou mine eyes, that I may behold wondrous things out of thy law" (Ps. 119:18). Only the Spirit of God can open up your mind to understand the Holy Scriptures. Our Lord opened up the Scriptures so that His disciples could understand the nature and the necessity of His death and resurrection (Luke 24: 45). As we develop and maintain the habit of reading at least one chapter of the Bible each day, we need to do so with the awareness that we must let God speak through His Word if this spiritual exercise would be truly profitable.

Let us try to let God speak to us through Mark 9.

I. *The Purpose of Spiritual Retreats* (Mark 9:2-8). Repeatedly our Lord took His disciples and went aside into private places for prayer, rest and instruction. The experience described in these verses was unique. It occurred some six months before our Lord's death. Luke's gospel tells us that our Lord took Peter, James and John and went up into a mountain to pray (Luke 9:28). As our Lord communed with our Father God, He was transfigured before them. His humanity slips into the background and we see a manifestation of His deity. The Shekinah glory of the eternal God was seen upon His face and countenance. He entered into dialogue with Moses and Elijah, representing the law and the prophets concerning His forthcoming death or exodus. The word which is translated "decease" really means His "exodus." Our Lord was strengthened and encouraged for the ordeal which confronted Him. The voice from heaven identified and confirmed Him as the Son of God and gave specific instructions to the apostles concerning their response to Him.

This experience was not understood by Peter, James and John at the time. It was a part of the training that they were receiving that could be understood only after His death, resurrection and the coming of the Holy Spirit on the Day of Pentecost. In this retreat on a mountaintop with their Lord, the apostles were given some new truth about God and some new instructions for their own life.

Each of us needs to find a place and a time for a retreat into solitude that we might listen and hear what God would say to us.

II. *Suffering in the Valley* (Mark 9:14-29). We must beware lest we envy those who have mountaintop experiences with God. We need to be on guard lest we interpret our own mystical experiences with God in terms of something merely to enjoy and to be grateful for.

At the foot of the Mount of Transfiguration, there was a distressed father who in his agony was seeking help for his unfortunate child who was demon possessed and suffering from epilepsy. On previous occasions the disciples had "cast out demons" (Mark 6:13). In this situation, however, the nine who remained at the foot of the mountain were powerless and unable to help.

The desperate father brought his plea to the Lord. He spoke in terms of the necessity of faith and prayer as being necessary if miracles were to take place. The father spoke for most of us when he pled, "Lord, I believe; help thou mine unbelief" (Mark 9:24).

We need to utilize all of the trust that we have as we face the needs of those who suffer in the world's valleys, highways and byways today.

III. *Only Those Who Serve Are Truly Great* (Mark 9:33-37). The apostles of our Lord were very human at the point that they were motivated by low and selfish motives much of the time like the rest of us. They were seeking for position, power, prestige, comfort.

Our Lord rebuked them for their self-centeredness and declared that if in the kingdom of God they would find greatness, they must do so in terms of the denial of their selfish self and a giving of themselves unreservedly to meet the needs and the problems of others.

Kingdom greatness is not determined by how high our position is or by how many people we have supervision over. Kingdom greatness is to be thought of in how many people we serve and bless and help.

Let each of us make certain that we serve others today instead of seeking to be served by others.

IV. *Tolerance Is Essential* (Mark 9:38-41). For some strange reason, human nature causes us to want all others to conform to our own pattern and our own way of thinking and serving. Our Lord rebuked the attitude of narrow exclusiveness which required that everyone march to exactly the same tune in the verses which we read today.

Our God is not limited to one individual or congregation to accomplish His work. Let us be thankful that God does not wait for us to attain perfection or conformity in every respect to His will before He works miracles through us.

V. *Faithful Discipleship Involves Radical Surgery* (Mark 9:42-50). How are we to interpret this passage of Scripture? Must we interpret every phrase of it in a very literalistic way? How many folk do you know who only have one hand, one foot or one eye? Did our Lord mean that we should literally place our hand upon a chopping block and cut it off? Was He suggesting that we amputate one of our legs?

Was He demanding that we gouge out one of our eyes? He, who restored the withered hand and made the lame to walk and gave sight to the blind, would never literally expect us to lame ourselves in this manner.

Our Lord is recommending in the strongest words that could be used that we deal drastically with those attitudes, affections, appetites, ambitions or actions that would have a tendency to lure us away from the way of the cross. He is suggesting that we must not tolerate evil in our life. He is suggesting that we walk the high road of self-discipline and dedication to the good will of our God.

Conclusion. No one can draw aside and do our praying for us. No one can go down into the valley of human suffering and render the service that we are capable of rendering. If we would find true significance in life, we will find it through the pathway of the cross that involves humility, the repudiation of our selfish self, the toleration of those who do things a bit differently from the way we would, and by a continual program of voluntary self-discipline and dedication.

Read the chapter again and let God speak to your heart.

SUNDAY MORNING, FEBRUARY 10
(Race Relations Sunday)

TITLE: "Jesus Gives New Meaning to Life"

TEXT: "But whosoever drinketh of the water that I shall give him shall never thirst" (John 4:14).

SCRIPTURE READING: John 4: 1-26.

HYMNS: " 'Tis So Sweet to Trust in Jesus," Stead. "I Heard the Voice of Jesus Say," Bonar.

"My Faith Looks Up to Thee," Palmer.

Our Father, we are grateful that You know far more about us than we know about ourselves. We are thankful that You are more concerned about us than even we are concerned about ourselves. We are grateful that because of Thy insight into us Thou art able to provide for our needs. We make mistakes when we try to plan our life without Thee. We can be our best only when we are in the center of Thy will. This morning we come to Thee with our problems and ask for Thy guidance. We come with our weakness and ask for Thy strength. We come with our needs and ask for the fullness of Thyself. We come with our gifts of money and ask that Thou shalt accept these gifts and use them in the furtherance of Thy work. Help us to realize that the gift without the giver is bare and thus to dedicate not only our possessions but our influence, our enthusiasm, our loyalty and all that we are in the work of Thy kingdom. We pray in Jesus' name. Amen.

Introduction. The fourth chapter of John's gospel follows closely in chronology the third chapter. Jesus had spent a brief time in Judea and was now ready to go into Galilee for a lengthy ministry. How would He go? If He had followed the traditional route, He would have gone to Jericho and crossed eastward over Jordan into Perea and gone north until He passed Samaria and then cut back westward across the Jordan into Galilee. In this way He would have escaped the Samaritan country. This half-breed race was despised by the Jews. Because of their prejudice, they would not even pass through the country of the Samaritans, much less associate with them.

The compulsion which caused Jesus to go through Samaria was twofold. First, His disciples must learn a great lesson. They must be made to realize that God loves all people without distinction as to race or ethnic background. Second, Jesus knew there would be a woman at Sychar who needed the Living Water. He wanted His disciples to witness God's grace extended in saving power to a hated Samaritan.

I. *The Approach of Jesus.* Because the woman had some deep personal problems, Jesus felt it was best to deal with her alone. He chose an opportunity while His disciples were gone away into the city to buy food. He made it His business to be at a place where the woman would come. He waited by the well.

Jesus did not use a direct approach. Some people can be approached in this manner but others must be approached indirectly. Jesus realized the woman would be quick to jump to the defensive. In the first place, she was a Samaritan. She would be suspicious of any Jew who sought conversation with her. Second, she had deep moral problems and, therefore, would be slow to become interested in spiritual things, especially when such interest would involve coming face to face with her sin.

The simple request of Jesus was that she give Him a drink of water. Few, if any, women would be unwilling to do such a small favor for a weary traveler.

II. *The Answer of Jesus to Opposition.* It is not possible for us to know the attitude with which the Samaritan woman spoke the words in verse 9. Some feel she spoke sharply to Jesus, being enraged that He would dare to make a request of her. Others feel that the words represent one weary of life and defeated in spirit, being surprised that a Jew would be willing to socialize with her especially in view of her background which she probably thought everyone knew.

The answer of Jesus in verse 10 was designed to stir curiosity and interest. He probably felt the woman would recognize the spiritual overtones of the statement. The woman's answer reveals she did not yet fully appreciate the significance of Jesus' words. The answer of Jesus in verses 13 and 14 contained further spiritual implications, but it is doubtful as to whether or not she completely understood His message. Her reply in verse 15 still seems a bit shallow, although we cannot be certain at this point.

Jesus recognized the necessity of bringing her face to face with her sin. This is the significance of His statement that she call her husband. It worked! It gave Jesus a springboard from which to bring her face to face with her former life and even her present one. The woman then tried to change the subject by starting a religious argument. Jesus, however, continued to press His point.

III. *The Announcement of His Messiahship.* There had been a controversy for many years between the Jews and Samaritans concerning the proper place of worship. The Samaritans were halfbreeds. The race had been formed after Assyria captured the northern kingdom. They were a mixture of the lower elements of the Assyrian and Israelites. The Samaritans, however, insisted they were the true descendants of Abraham. They had their own version of the Pentateuch. Their worship place was Mt. Gerizim, and they refused to recognize Jerusalem as the true place for religious ceremonies.

Before identifying Himself, Jesus realized the necessity of presenting to the woman the true nature of worship. It is not forms, ceremonies or institutions that bring one to God. One must discover God through a spiritual experience. As Jesus presented this truth to her, she seemingly was not able to grasp the full significance of it. She dismissed it with a casual, "Messias cometh, which is called Christ: when he is come, he will tell us all things." This gave Jesus the perfect opportunity to announce to her exactly who He was. He had paved the way by His unique approach. Now she is face to face with a decision.

IV. *The Attitude of the Woman.* There is no record concerning her reply to him. The scene is interrupted by the coming of the disciples. Obviously, they recognized an important conversation was taking place for no one asked Jesus why He was talking with the woman. They must have sensed that He was discussing spiritual matters. John resumes the narrative concerning the woman in verse 28. The woman was, no doubt, very much impressed with Jesus because she left her waterpot and went into the city to tell the men of her new discovery. These were, in all probability, men who knew her well—perhaps a part of her clientele. A great transformation must have come to remove her inhibitions toward religion. It should be pointed out, however, in fairness to the woman, that throughout the entire story she seems to have a religious background. She knew of Jacob. She was informed concerning the worship habits of the Samaritans and the Israelites. She also knew that the Messiah was coming. What led her into a life of sin, we are not told. We are only given an account of the One who transformed her life.

Conclusion. Although the Samaritan woman was familiar with Scripture, she did not know about divine grace. Her broken life had affected her attitude and perhaps caused her to be cynical of anyone who spoke concerning spiritual matters. It is only grace that can bring forgiveness. One who is presenting the Gospel message of grace should seek the best time to approach the individual and should also be tender and gentle in his appeal. God's grace accommodates itself to the temperament of each individual. One of the most convincing proofs of God's ability to forgive is the change that comes to an individual when he experiences divine grace. To see a life made anew is indeed a miracle. A true conversion comes from a power greater than any human effort or ability.

From this story we should learn that all things are possible through God's divine grace even if the difficulty seems insurmountable. The story of Nicodemus (last Sunday) shows us that there is no man so good but that he needs a new birth. This story teaches us that there is no person so sinful but that he can be changed through a new birth.

The sequel to the story should not be overlooked. Jesus gave an object lesson to His disciples concerning true values. There is a place for physical food. The disciples had gone into the city to secure nourishment for their bodies. Jesus used this encounter with the Samaritan woman to teach them that our lower desires in life must be subordinated to the higher ones. Jesus never neglected the claims of the body. In fact, He worked miracles to supply people with food. He insisted, however, that the highest duty of man is not to attend to the desires of the body but to do the will of God. The hunger of His soul for the spiritual experience of leading the woman to new life was greater than His physical fatigue or appetite. The joy which came with this experience brought Him inspiration. He glowed with inward spiritual energy as He explained to His disciples where they would find their greatest joy.

SUNDAY EVENING, FEBRUARY 10

TITLE: "Assurance in Him"

TEXT: "And hereby we know that we are of the truth, and shall assure our hearts before him" (1 John 3:19).

SCRIPTURE READING: 1 John 3: 11-24.

Introduction. In 1 John 2:7-11, the apostle reiterates the old commandment as not only the paramount duty of believers, but the evidence of their sonship. He said that the evidence lies in doing righteousness. Now he defines righteousness as loving the brethren.

The previous paragraph (1 John 3:1-10) applies to the test of righteousness. Here is applied the test of love. John regards love as an obvious test. He declares that the whole message of the life and character of Christ is a message of love. In these verses (1 John 3:11-24), it is pointed out that the Christian's whole duty is summed up in the obligation to exercise love.

I. *Love Is Manifested Toward One Another* (3:11-18).

A. This love is a natural result of childhood, but it is also a commandment (3:11-13). Hate, envy, or jealousy has no part in one's true Christian nature of love. Cain is used as the example (3:12). If one is animated by hate, then evidently he is still in a state of spiritual death. He has not been born of God; he is not a child of God (3:14).

A lack of love is an indication of one who is still in the death of sin, being, in fact, a murderer, for the essential part of being a murderer, at least from the divine point of view, is the inward attitude of which the outward deed is but the expression.

B. This love is a testimony of one believer's experience of grace—the new birth (3:14-18).

The words "we know" in verse 14 are so located in the original language as to make them emphatic. This is in contrast to the unregenerated world. The words "passed from" in verse 14 mean to pass over from one place to another; to migrate out of death into life. The believer does this while here on earth. Verses 14, 16, and 18 give a positive affirmation of love. Jesus is the example. By dying, He showed a divine love toward men who had sinned against Him and God. The practice of love, therefore, can be broadly described in terms of the imitation of Christ.

The Christian's love is not seen in empty air, not with word and tongue, but in the midst of deed and truth. It is seen in warm words accompanied by warm deeds. It is the willingness to surrender that which has value in one's own life to enrich the life of another (3:14, 18). It is shown in daily living.

Verse 17 points out the negative. If one closes his heart to the needs of others, God's love does not abide in him.

C. This love is identified with the world.

II. *The Assurance of the Christian Is Seen in a Free Conscience* (3:19-24). Verse 19 may be translated, "In the presence of God, we shall have confident assurance because God understands us."

A. The conditions of a free conscience are: to believe in Him (3:23), love one another and abide in Him. Believing in Christ is the summary of all His commandments (Mark 12:28-31). To believe in the name of Christ is to believe in all that He is. The Christian abides in God, and God in him through the Holy Spirit (John 14:10; 17:21, 23). A person remains in Him only as he imitates the example of

Christ. This is seen as the believer is loyal to the Gospel.

B. The conscience is free because the Lord frees it and this is a contrast to the believer's own freedom (3:20, 21). The human being in his own weakness will condemn himself of sin. Condemn means to know something against. He knows his failures and they rise up to condemn him. This challenge may come from within or from without. But the most serious is the doubt in the heart. The wonderful thing, though, is that a man's own heart is not the final judge (1 Cor. 4:4, 5). When sin is confessed, the Lord removes it from the confessor and no longer holds it against him. He is greater than the human heart. He links omniscience with love and sympathy. He is bigger and final, and when He forgives, we have assurance in Him.

This is not a claim to sinlessness, but of a claim to a consciousness of fellowship with God.

C. When the conscience is free, the Christian's prayers are answered and this is another assurance (3:22). There are no limitations to prayer, but there must be a complete surrender of the one who is praying to the will of God (Mark 11:24; Luke 11:9). The answer may not always be in the form expected, but will be better.

To pray in the name of Jesus is to pray in virtue of union with Him. That union is love and obedience in which Christ's love and obedience to the Father is reproduced in the Christian through faith.

Conclusion. There is nothing that produces insecurity like a lack of assurance. A man's uncertainty with God is his greatest frustration. Hear the words of this passage, believe in Him, abide in Him, pray in Him, and love in Him, then you can walk with assurance—assured of being His child, assured of being forgiven, assured of a free conscience.

WEDNESDAY EVENING, FEBRUARY 13

TITLE: "The Bible Speaks to Our Condition"

SCRIPTURE READING: Mark 16.

Introduction. The last chapter of the gospel of Mark contains the account of the events surrounding the Resurrection of our Lord. It makes mention of several appearances of our Lord to various disciples and groups of disciples.

When the risen Christ first appeared to Mary Magdalene, she did not recognize Him (John 20:14). The two travelers between Jeru-

salem and Emmaus were blind to the true nature of the person who joined them for their journey homeward (Luke 24:16, 31). As we read this account of the resurrection of our Lord, we could pray as did the psalmist, "Open thou mine eyes, that I may behold wondrous things out of thy law" (Ps. 119:18).

I. *He Is Risen* (Mark 16:6). The angelic announcement concerning the Resurrection of Jesus Christ was truly the best news that has ever fallen upon the ears of man. Each believer needs to enter into the heritage which is his by virtue of the fact that ours is a living Christ.

A. The Resurrection was a dramatic declaration of the victory of Jesus Christ over sin, death, the grave and all of the forces of evil. We worship and serve a triumphant Christ.

B. By His conquest of death and revelation of the reality of immortality, our Lord gave to His disciples a hope and a faith in victory over death and the grave.

C. By His conquest of death, our Lord was raised to a position of authority. He is granted the authority to both invite and to command His disciples to share the significance of His redemptive achievements with a needy world.

We need to respond to the great truth announced by the messenger who spoke to the women when they visited the tomb of our Lord.

II. *He Goeth Before You* (Mark 16:7). The Resurrection of our Lord was to have continuing significance for His disciples. It provided for them the abiding presence of their living Lord who was to be their companion along the road of life.

A. He goes before us as our teacher. The other gospels relate how that our Lord continued to teach His apostles following His Resurrection. He sought to help them understand the prophecies that had predicted His death and His triumphant Resurrection. Our Lord continues to be heaven's authoritative teacher for us today.

B. He goes before us to provide guidance. The Christ of history wants to be the Christ of our personal experience. He wants to provide us with light for all of the dark mysteries of life in the present (John 8:12). Today, we need to follow Him in faith and obedience.

C. He goes before us to provide for our needs. Out of the abundance of His grace, He will minister to our needs in whatever circumstances we find ourselves. He is the Christ who fed the multitudes to the extent that there was always a surplus. We can trust Him for what we need today.

III. *Our Continuing Commission* (Mark 16:15). The commandment which our Lord gave to His disciples was not intended to cease with them. It was an imperative command with future significance for every follower of the way of the cross.

Each of us is in a process of going about from place to place. In our going about from place to place, we are to announce the good news. The phrase "preach the gospel" is not to be limited to a formal worship service with a minister behind the pulpit. It really means that each of us in our daily walk is to be engaged in communicating the good news of God's love as we have experienced it in Jesus Christ.

We are to continue to share this good news until every creature on the face of the earth has had the privilege of either accepting or rejecting Jesus Christ as Lord.

Conclusion. How have you related to this great commission? Have you professionalized it and let it apply only to the clergy? Have you internationalized it and applied it only to those who are vocational foreign missionaries?

Each of us must put himself in the middle of this continuing commission if Christianity is to be relevant for us and helpful to others.

SUNDAY MORNING, FEBRUARY 17

TITLE: "Jesus Loved People and Believed in Them"

TEXT: "When he saw the multitudes, he was moved with compassion on them" (Matt. 9:36).

SCRIPTURE READING: Matthew 9:35-38.

HYMNS: "Send the Light," Gabriel. "Tell Me the Story of Jesus," Crosby. "Jesus Calls Us," Alexander.

OFFERTORY PRAYER:

Our Father, we need a closer walk with Thee. Help us to know that it will not come to us accidentally nor incidentally. Make us willing to accept the disciplines of life that lead us closer to Thee. Help us to be willing to take the initiative in self-sacrifice as we dedicate ourselves completely to Thy purposes for us. Help us to recognize that we are incomplete until we have laid our all on the altar. Give us both the grace and the knowledge to grow toward Thy likeness. May we find Thy presence more real each day as we give ourselves more completely. Forgive us where we have sinned and strengthen us where we are weak. Let our love to Thee be unreserved. Help us ever to live in the light of the glorious Gospel of our Lord and seek to make Him known to others. Bless us as we bring these tithes and offerings and use them for Thy redemptive purposes in the world. We pray for Jesus' sake. Amen.

Introduction. Matthew's gospel is mainly topical. Much of the material is grouped under certain subjects. The great Galilean ministry lasted at least eighteen months. It would have been virtually impossible to have recorded every event. Chapters 8 and 9 of Matthew's gospel record representative episodes in the life and ministry of Jesus during the early part of the Galilean ministry.

The schedule of Jesus was a busy one. No person living today maintains such a rigid discipline or reaches out to touch the lives of more people. Yet, Jesus was always ready to lend a helping hand to anyone regardless of his need or social status.

In chapters 8 and 9 we see Jesus healing a leper, healing the servant of a centurion, healing the mother-in-law of Simon Peter and casting out demons from those who were possessed with them. While He was at rest in a boat, a mighty storm arose on the Sea of Galilee. Jesus rebuked the wind and the sea and there was a great calm. Jesus went to the other side of the Jordan and cast demons out of two men. He came back west of the Jordan and healed a man sick of the palsy. He called a man named Matthew to follow Him. He healed a woman who had a problem with hemorrhaging for twelve years, and He healed the daughter of one of the rulers of the city. Two blind men followed Him and He healed them. He cast the devils out of a dumb man. Everything He did was to help the life of people physically, mentally and spiritually.

The close of the ninth chapter gives a summary of everything He did. He engaged in a threefold ministry—teaching, preaching and healing. This is still a part of the basic Christian message and ministry. When Jesus took time to view the people it brought a sense of pathos to His soul. The tenderness of His heart caused Him to identify with them and make their suffering become a part of His own. He then uttered a command to His followers to "get into the action" and use their talents to help spread the message of God's kingdom and help heal humanity's spiritual hurt. These verses bring to us a threefold picture of the Master as He viewed the multitudes.

I. *He Saw Confusion.* If any people in the world have ever been confused as to their state of life and ultimate security, it was the Jewish people of Jesus' day. They had been in bondage, with the exception of a few years, to a foreign power since the days of the Assyrian and Babylonian empires. They had been kicked up and down the field of international politics like a football. False messiahs had arisen, and they had gone after them. The Book of Acts (5:36, 37) tells of two leaders who had arisen and deceived the people. They had come to the place that they did not know whom they could trust or to whom they could turn. They were confused.

Their world was not unlike our day. We too live in a day where it is difficult to know what the real issues are in national life. Our political life is definable in simple terms. One party is in and the other wants in now. Militarily, we are confused. Some feel we should seek peace by preparing a strong defense against possible aggression. Others believe we should disarm completely and immediately and thus show others our good faith. Economically, we are in a state of confusion. Most of us, unless we have suffered a recent reverse, have more material possessions than we have ever had in our life. Yet, there is more uncertainty and anxiety concerning our economic situation, as we look to the future, than we have ever had in the history of our nation. In the realm of morals, we are equally perplexed. Convictions that we have held as necessary to life itself have been given up in favor of a permissive approach that justifies anything. The black and white distinctions have faded to a dull gray with nothing being really wrong— that is if we can get away with it! Sin consists in getting caught—not in performing the wicked deed!

II. *Jesus Felt Compassion.* As Jesus viewed the spiritual dumbness of these people, as well as their other needs, he was stirred within the recesses of his soul. All suffering mankind comes within the orbit of Christ's interest. Jesus was aware that many of the people had been disappointed in life and it crushed His heart. To see one without an aim or purpose causes any sensitive person to feel deeply. The word "compassion" means literally "suffering with" and is one of the most meaningful words in our language.

One of our greatest needs today

is for men who are strong enough to be leaders and yet tender enough to feel deeply concerning the deficiencies of others. Jesus was and is such a person. No one ever possessed such a drive and dynamic in His personal life. Yet no one was more sympathetic with people who could not keep up with His pace. Jesus knew of the scattered world which had lost the sense of its oneness and it grieved Him because the Father never intended such a situation to develop in the beautiful world He created.

The godlessness of our day is enough to bring a shock of concern to any person who is spiritually sensitive. If life is to be worth living for the multitudes, there must be courageous men possessed with the love of God in Jesus Christ who will minister to their needs and point them to the One who can make their life anew.

Jesus saw with the eye of God, and He felt with the heart of both God and man. We associate the word "pity" with the idea of divinity, but the word "compassion" actually belongs to divinity incarnate. One of the tragedies of our day is that we can walk the streets of our towns and cities and never feel one touch of emotion when we see people who are torn, weary, without a shepherd and without any hope in this world or in the one to come. It is only the compassionate love of Christ in us that can motivate for effective Christian service. Jesus not only loved people, but He also believed in them. The crowd would have looked at Matthew and not been impressed that he had spiritual potentiality. Jesus saw him and realized immediately that here was a man who could become one of His inner circle and write one book concerning His life.

Jesus spoke to him and let Matthew know that He saw good in him. The good came forth and developed under the teaching of the Savior. It was compassion that led Jesus to think Matthew had possibility for growing.

III. *Jesus Gave a Commission.* One thing we must never forget! If you excite emotions that are intended to lead men to action, the action should follow! If it does not, the emotion without the proper action will make the heart grow much harder than it was in its previous condition. An old truism says, "Impression without expression leads to depression."

Jesus pointed the group to the possibilities for service. He pictured these opportunities as a harvest which is truly plenteous but with only a few laborers. The injunction of Jesus was that we should pray for the Lord to thrust forth laborers into the harvest. Jesus realized that if people will pray sincerely concerning a need, they will eventually offer themselves to meet that need. It is quite significant that the next chapter tells of how Jesus called His twelve and sent them out to witness concerning Him. It is unfortunate there is a break in the chapter division at this point. Actually, the calling of the twelve follows immediately upon the statement of Jesus that we are to pray the Lord to send forth laborers into the harvest.

Conclusion. How much do you really care about people? Does it really matter to you that hearts are broken, lives are torn, hopes have been blighted and many people are living without a sense of direction in life? Jesus cared. He did not set up an office in Capernaum with a shingle outside of it which said "Jesus of Nazareth. Office Hours 9 to 5. May Be Seen By Appointment Only!" He went where the people were. He made it His business to be at the very place Zaccheus was in order that He might win Zaccheus to faith in Himself. The best way in the world to lead a person to higher aims and ideals for their life is to believe in them. If we make people think we do not have faith in them, they will never feel a compulsion to rise above mediocrity. If, on the other hand, we let them know that we feel they have infinite possibilities, they will do their very best to live up to our hopes and dreams for them. With the tremendous pressures that are in the world today, Christian people cannot afford to become complacent. We must think as Jesus thought, feel as He felt and work as He worked to God's glory and the helping of lost and defeated humanity.

SUNDAY EVENING, FEBRUARY 17

TITLE: "Knowledge in Him"

TEXT: "Hereby know we that we dwell in him, and he in us, because he hath given us of his Spirit" (1 John 4:13).

SCRIPTURE READING: 1 John 4:1-21.

Introduction. It is noticeable in 1 John that the work of the Holy Spirit is related almost exclusively to the imparting of faith. Therefore, belief in Jesus Christ is related to the presence and work of the Holy Spirit. Chapter 4 opens with the assurance that one is a child of God based on confession and inspired by the Holy Spirit.

I. *Knowledge Is Imparted by the Holy Spirit* (4:1-6).

A. There are some false spirits that would lead a seeker astray (4:3, 5).
Some victims fall easily to spiritualistic humbuggery. This is the work of false spirits—known as the anti-Christs. These anti-Christs are in the world now and seek to make Jesus and Christ separate (4:3).
In verse 5 these anti-Christs are characterized. They are spoken of as prating. The word is "say" or "speak." The world listens to those who speak in its own language. The false prophets and the world are in perfect union. The false prophets have gone out and left the Church and joined the society of the godless and unbelieving. They claim to be spiritual, that is, to be Christian. They claim to be divinely inspired, but in reality their spirit was that of the devil.

B. The Holy Spirit testifies to the truth (4:2-4, 6). The Holy Spirit testifies about the Incarnation which is the real test that Jesus is the Christ. The crucial test is their attitude toward Him. He also overcomes false testimonies (4:4). The faithful (not false) are God's delegates bearing their Master's commission and continuing His warfare (John 20:21), and they have shared His victory. This comes through the working of the Holy Spirit.
The faithful can claim final vic-

tory over false prophets, and the reason lies in God who abides in them (3:20, 24). God is greater than Satan who is in the world, the prince of the world (John 12:31; 14:30), the god of this age (2 Cor. 4:4).

The Holy Spirit accentuates the Christian testimony (4:6). The "we know" in verse 6 is for emphasis in the sentence. This is in sharp contrast with the false prophets and the world. The Christian knows because he is in tune with the infinite God. The reason sermons are inspiring or dull is because both the preacher and hearer are in continuous contact with God or because they are not. The Christian knows by personal experience, and there is no reason for him to be duped by the spirit of error.

II. *Knowledge Is Manifested by Love* (4:7-12).

A. God is the source of love. Love is the divine nature, and those who love have been made partakers of the divine nature (2 Pet. 1:4). By the practice of love, they get to know God more and more.

It is true that God is love, but love is not God. They are not interchangeable. Not every manifestation of love, kindness, benevolence, or sacrifice is a sign of a new birth or of being a child of God. Godly love is sure to result in confidence toward God and love toward men.

B. Because God is love and so loves, the believer ought to love also (4:9-12).

The Incarnation is the supreme manifestation of the love of God. This love was manifested that man might receive life. This life is eternal. It is present and in harmony with the true order of things. God's children must have something of this love. It is their nature. This love is an indication of God indwelling the child of God.

III. *Knowledge Is Proved by Christian Witnessing* (4:13-21).

A. He has given the Spirit so that the ones who believe in Him may know and witness (4:13, 14).

Believers are the sphere in which the love of God operates. The gift of God is proof of fellowship with Him. The witness is that He is the Savior of the world (4:14). Jesus is in the world unseen and it is the business of the Christian to make Him visible. The Christian is to Him now what He was to the Father in the days of His flesh.

B. Witness is born in confession (4:15). This is a confession born of persuasion. This conviction implies fellowship with God. A confession of the deity of Jesus Christ implies surrender and obedience and not mere lip service (1 Cor. 12:3; Rom. 10:6-12). Confession is proof of fellowship with God. It follows experimental and confident trust.

C. There is a love in the believer that casts out fear and instills confidence (4:17-21).

Love is a heavenly visitant sojourning with the believer. It has been carried to its end when the believers are like Jesus and are His visible representatives. It casts out fear of judgment and establishes the right relations everywhere. Fear does not exist in real love. It harbors no fear and no dread.

Conclusion. The Bible teaches that all believers are indwelt by the

Holy Spirit. The passage here teaches that the Holy Spirit imparts knowledge, which is manifested by love and is proved by Christian witnessing.

Each person needs to examine himself to make sure the Holy Spirit is in control of his life and that this control is seen in the relation to the believer's fellowman.

Right now, will you make a total surrender to Jesus Christ for salvation and to the Holy Spirit for power?

WEDNESDAY EVENING, FEBRUARY 20

TITLE: "The Bible Speaks to Our Condition"

SCRIPTURE READING: Luke 7.

Introduction. As we follow the habit of reading God's Word each day, we need without exception to pray, "Open thou mine eyes, that I may behold wondrous things out of thy law" (Ps. 119:18). Luke 7 is something more than an unrelated collection of incidences in the life of our Lord. Seemingly, the inspired writer is trying to help his readers understand the nature and the scope of the ministry of Jesus. This chapter begins with the healing of a slave of a Gentile military officer and concludes with the forgiveness of the sins of a prostitute. Between these two extremes we can get a small picture of the range and the scope of our Lord's ministry to the needs of men.

I. *Gentiles Are the Objects of Our Lord's Concern* (Luke 7:1-10). Our Lord did not belong exclusively to the Jewish race. His concern was not limited to Jewish needs.

This incident reveals that our Lord included those outside of Israel in the scope of His compassionate concern.

Here we see that our Lord revealed His authority over disease at a distance. He did not have to be present and place His hand upon a sick man in order to heal him.

The Gentile military officer was a man of both faith and humility. He believed in the authority of Jesus and at the same time did not feel worthy to approach Jesus personally.

We would experience more of the power of our Lord if we expressed both faith and humility toward Him.

II. *Concern for a Grieving Widow* (Luke 7:11-17). With compassionate eyes, our Lord looked upon the distressed condition of a grieving widow who was following the body of her son to the place of burial. Our Lord was moved with compassion toward her and utilized His power and His authority over death to restore her son, to comfort her heart and to provide for her future.

If Christ is the same yesterday, today and forever, we can be assured that He suffers with us in our suffering and grieves with us in our grief. Ultimately, the family of faith will be reunited together.

This incident reminded the people of the actions of Elijah (1 Kings 17:17-24) and Elisha (2 Kings 4:21-37). The people believed that Jesus was a prophet sent from God.

III. *A Ministry of Mercy Contrasted With a Ministry of Military Might* (Luke 7:18-23). John the Baptist found himself imprisoned by Herod (Luke 3:20). It was only normal that he should be eager to have an authentic word from Jesus concerning His ministry. Perhaps John the Baptist was eager for our Lord to assert His Messiahship and exercise some of the popular concepts of what the Messiah would do. Perhaps John was hoping that Jesus would raise an army and rescue him from the discomfort and despondency of imprisonment. We can sympathize with John.

Our Lord replied to the inquiry of John's disciples by describing the nature of His ministry in terms of its being a ministry to the blind, the lame, the lepers, the deaf, the dead and to those who were spiritually bankrupt (Luke 7:22). Jesus' performance was in line with His Messianic platform as announced earlier (Luke 4:18, 19).

We need to be certain that our expectations from the Lord are in harmony with the purpose of His ministry lest we be caused to stumble and fall.

IV. *The Response of a Fickle People* (Luke 7:31-35). Jesus contrasts the reactions of the crowd to the ministry of John the Baptist and to His ministry. He reveals how fickle and how changeable they were. Consequently, many of them missed the blessings of God because they responded neither to the ministry of John nor to the ministry of our Lord.

Each of us needs to beware lest we miss what God has to offer us.

V. *The All-Inclusiveness of Our Lord's Love* (Luke 7:36-50).

A. Our Lord's concern for Pharisees. Most of us have categorized the Pharisees as those who were completely beyond the range of our Lord's concern. We remember that they were His foes and His critics. A close study of the gospels will reveal that our Lord was concerned about reaching these people with the message of His love. Repeatedly we find Him eating with them and in conversation with them. They needed a Savior. He offered them God's love.

B. Concern for a prostitute. This passage is a compressed account of the events that took place during an entire dinner in the home of a Pharisee. This sinful woman sensed a concern and an attitude of acceptance in Jesus that caused her to respond to Him in faith. She expressed her gratitude for His forgiveness in a spontaneous and extravagant, and at the same time, very appropriate manner.

Because of her deep awareness of full forgiveness, she loved much.

The proof of our experience of forgiveness will be indicated by the expression of our gratitude to our Lord.

Conclusion. How grateful are we to our Lord? How do we express our affection for Him? Is it possible that we are like the self-righteous Pharisee who felt no need for forgiveness?

The woman trusted Christ. She experienced forgiveness. Forgiveness produced love. Love demanded self-expression. This she did by anointing His feet. This was a most appropriate thing to do in that day.

Genuine love will find an appropriate avenue for expressing itself.

TITLE: "Jesus Taught Us to Pray"

TEXT: "Your Father knoweth what things ye have need of, before ye ask him" (Matt. 6:8).

SCRIPTURE READING: Matthew 6:5-15.

HYMNS: "What a Friend We Have in Jesus," Scriven. "Did You Think to Pray?" Kidder. "Near to the Heart of God," McAfee.

OFFERTORY PRAYER:

Our Father, we are citizens of heaven but we live upon earth. We lie exposed to the rough storms and troubles of temptation. We must live day by day with those who are not in sympathy with Thy purposes in this world. Help us to overcome the struggle with our own cowardice, negligence and indifference. Give us the strength to discipline our wills, cultivate our minds and harness our powers. As the crises of life arise, make us equal to them. Deliver us from the sin of shrinking from our responsibilities. Give us faith in the greatness of life and in the adequacy of Christ as we march into the future. Help us to live by faith but give us always the strength to show our faith by our good deeds. As we bring our tithes and offerings today, make us mindful that this is as much a part of the worship service as the praying, the reading of Thy Word and the preaching from the pulpit. Thou hast blessed us in many ways. We return to Thee a portion of that which Thou hast given us. We invest this in the work of Thy kingdom. We dedicate this money to the proclamation of the Gospel in the many various ways that the talents of people differ. Use this money to Thy glory and make us a witness of Thy grace through our gifts. We pray for Jesus' sake. Amen.

Introduction. The work of Jesus was not all activity and service. He was also a teacher. He recognized the need to instruct the people in order that they could carry on His work and live by His principles after He had gone. This was especially true of His disciples. Before Matthew took two chapters to outline the Galilean ministry in miniature, he told of the great sermon which Jesus preached. It is called the "Sermon on the Mount." The fact that portions of it are repeated elsewhere in the ministry of Jesus in no way reflects on the integrity or the unity of Matthew 5-7. Speakers often repeat themselves on other occasions. This sermon was delivered near the beginning of Jesus' ministry in order to set forth the guidelines of living for those who would follow Him.

The middle chapter of the three is, in many ways, the heart of the sermon. Jesus began this section with a warning against an ostentatious display of one's good deeds. He then immediately applied the same principle to prayer. We are not to pray in order to be seen of men. We are praying to God and should realize this both in our method of praying and in the words that we use in our prayers.

I. *The Command to Pray.* Jesus prefaced one of His parables with the statement that "men ought always to pray, and not to faint"

(Luke 18:1). This is more than a suggestion that spiritual power is available for those who wish to have it. Jesus is making it clear that a supreme obligation of the Christian life is to be constantly in prayer. In the Sermon on the Mount, however, Jesus makes it clear that this does not mean we are to pray on the street corner to be seen of men. Paul's exhortation to "Pray without ceasing" (1 Thess. 5:17) is in harmony with the command of Jesus. Neither does Paul, however, mean that we are to make ostentatious display of our personal communication with the Father. To be constantly in prayer means we are to be always attuned to the will of God and always in such a frame of mind that He can speak to us, and we can in turn be responsive to any word He may have for us on a given occasion. An outstanding preacher of another generation was once asked what it means to be filled with the Holy Spirit. He replied, "It means to be extremely God-conscious in one's life." Some may feel this is an oversimplification, but the full truth is certainly implicit in the words of the great minister. Likewise, to be constantly in prayer means to be always in a frame of mind that puts us in perfect fellowship with the Father. Prayer is an act, of course, but it is also an attitude—a way of life that recognizes God's presence and stands always ready to submit to His leadership. We can do more than pray after we have prayed, and we should, but until we have prayed concerning a matter, it is doubtful we can do anything effective concerning it.

Prayer has been called "the lost word" in the Christian life. This is not an overstatement. Our power-lessness is often, if not always, due to our prayerlessness. The greatest people on the earth today are those who have a proper prayer life. This does not mean those who talk about prayer or those who say they believe in prayer or even those who can explain prayer. The greatest people are those who *take time* and *pray*. It is not easy. The circumstances of life have a way of pressing about us and seeking to claim our priorities. We must put prayer first in our life and that means *taking time* from other things in life's schedule and giving that time to prayer. Those who pray are those who are doing the most for God in winning souls, in solving problems, in leading churches to renewal and in supplying both men and money for the mission field. God reaches lost people in this earth through the willingness of His born-again children to witness. It needs to be emphasized again and again, however, that God can only do with a man's life what a man allows him to do. A large part, if not all, of our personal surrender to God's will is directly proportionate to our personal prayer life.

II. *A Pattern for Prayer.* The passage in Matthew is often called erroneously "The Lord's Prayer" but it is rather a "model" prayer. If we are actually looking for a "Lord's Prayer" we probably should consider the prayer of Jesus in John 17:1-26 as constituting it because these words are literally a prayer of Jesus in the Garden of Gethsemane. The words of Jesus in the Sermon on the Mount are not meant as a prayer for us to repeat word for word and thus substitute as a prayer. This does not mean it is wrong to repeat this prayer in a worship assembly, but it should never be repeated mechanically as a substitute for our own personal prayer. There are values, of course, in repeating it in a worship service, but the greatest value is that it should serve as a model or guideline for the kind of praying in which we should engage.

Jesus addressed His prayer to the Father and began with a reverent honoring of the Father's name. This is important. One's name stands for his character. We cannot be irreverent toward a person's name without minimizing if not actually blaspheming the personal characteristics of the one whom the name represents. It is important that we constantly keep a high regard for the name of our God. The Jews reverenced the name of Jehovah. They were so afraid, at one time in their history, they would use His name lightly and irreverently that they refused to speak the sacred name but rather substituted another word for it. This was probably an overemphasis, but the lesson comes to us forcefully. We must honor the person, as a person, to whom we pray.

The kingdom of God is both present and future. It exists today as a spiritual reality. It will come to full consummation when our Lord comes again. There is nothing inconsistent with praying for His kingdom to come in the hearts of people on earth even though we know that it will never come completely until Jesus returns personally. The kingdom of God now is the rule of God in the hearts of people. As we pray, we need to ask God to help each of us individually to let His will be done in our lives now even as it shall be done in the day when the kingdoms of this world become the kingdom of our Lord. God's will is being done now in heaven. We should pray for it to be done on earth now as we grow in grace and knowledge of His will and as we are more surrendered to His purposes for us.

There is nothing wrong in praying for our temporal needs. The suggestion of this petition, however, is that God should give us day by day the things we need rather than giving us several years' supply in advance. The Israelites, during their wilderness wanderings, were given manna for their sustenance. It is significant, however, that they were only given enough each day for that day's needs. A part of prayer is faith. Faith means living "one day at a time" and being perfectly willing to trust God for future needs as we try to do His will in the "todays" of our life.

Verse 12 is quite significant. Jesus made it clear that there is a relationship between our willingness to forgive others and our personal forgiveness by the Father. This is not inconsistent with the doctrine of the atonement or justification by faith. It rather suggests that the truly "born again" person will be one with a forgiving spirit. Earlier in the Sermon on the Mount Jesus said, "Blessed are the merciful: for they shall obtain mercy" (5:7). One who is unwilling to forgive those who have sinned against him should reexamine the genuineness of his own personal experience with the Lord in salvation.

The words concerning temptation do not mean that we are led into temptation by the Father and here we are asking Him to reconsider His normal course and refrain from leading us into temptation. James (1:13, 14) makes it very clear that we are not tempted by God. God cannot be tempted with evil. He does not tempt any man. James says, "But every man is tempted, when he is drawn away of his own lust and enticed." The petition in the "model" prayer is paraphrased by Phillips, "Keep us clear of temptation, and save us from evil."

The "model" prayer ends on the same note that it begins. The Father is great. His sovereignty must be recognized and His character respected. He is the one who rules now, will rule always and because of His moral purity *must* rule. To Him, all praise and all honor is due now and forever.

Conclusion. One who prays constantly and according to the guidelines set forth by Jesus will be a person with a spiritual dynamic. As we think magnificently of God and adore Him, His characteristics will unconsciously be reproduced in our own life. A man becomes what he loves. When he finds delight in fellowship with the divine he becomes more like the divine. When one wrestles with God in prayer he will find himself becoming equipped to wrestle with the problems of the world. True prayer is hard work. A man does not necessarily need immense and commanding powers of thought in order to pray but he does need to bring that which he has to God in an immense and powerful way if he would learn the secret of spiritual strength. The greatest and grandest subject in the universe is the infinite God. When we have been in fellowship with Him we shall go out prepared for the problems of life. George Truett once said, "The closet with the closed door is the trysting place for power. Men and women who come from it come with faces that shine, with visions that inspire and with power that shakes the world."

SUNDAY EVENING, FEBRUARY 24

TITLE: "Faith in Him"

TEXT: "Whosoever believeth that Jesus is the Christ is born of God: and every one that loveth him that begat loveth him also that is begotten of him" (1 John 5:1).

SCRIPTURE READING: 1 John 5:1-12.

Introduction. In the verses of the Scripture passage listed, one finds the molding thoughts of the epistle. The life God imparts to His children is tested by righteousness, love, and belief. The passage also points out the close relation between the three elements of the Christian life; love is shown by righteousness, and righteousness is secured by faith, thus, the title "Faith in Him."

I. *Faith Is the Condition of Salvation* (5:1a). Faith has three components—knowledge, belief, and trust. It is not merely intellectual conviction, but full surrender to Jesus Christ as Lord and Savior.

The object of faith is Jesus Christ. The term "Christ" refers not only to the redeeming work of Jesus, or to His "anointing" by the Spirit of God for that work, but more specifically to His divine nature as is seen in verse 5—"the Son of God."

The person who so believes is a child of God, but one who does not believe has no right to the name Christian, for to deny this truth is to manifest the spirit of anti-Christ. John presents "belief" as the absolute proof that one is a child of God.

II. *Faith Results in Love and Obedience* (5:1a-3). There are two commandments of God.

A. The first commandment is love—love God and love the brotherhood.

Love is the natural expression of the new life imparted by God. It is defined as keeping the commandments of God.

B. The second commandment is obedience. Obedience is a proof of love. The commandments of God are not grievous (5:3), that is, they are not irksome. The standards of obedience are of the highest, but the believer is given the Holy Spirit so that He may keep them. The commandments are not hard to obey for God gives the grace one needs for fulfillment, even though effort is required.

III. *Faith Overcomes the World* (5: 4). The world is in opposition to God. The world's maxims, principles, ideals, and spirit are all contrary to the will of God. It is the sum of all the forces that are antagonistic to the spiritual life.

God gives the believer victory through his faith. The word "overcome" is found twice in verse 4. The first time it is a continuous action, thus, a continuous victory because it is a continuous struggle. One keeps on overcoming the world. The second is a punctiliar

action. It is a single experience. It is the victory over one temptation at a time.

Jesus won the victory over the world (John 16:33) and God in the believer (1 John 4:4) gives him the victory. The faith is not in human merit but in God and in what Jesus Christ has done. This power is only operative in believers.

For the Christian, there is conflict, but victory is assured. The energy imparted by God is mightier than that of the world. The believer's weapon is faith.

IV. *Faith Has Some Witnesses* (5:7-10).

A. The strongest witness of faith is the Holy Spirit (5:7). The Holy Spirit testified to Jesus at His baptism (Matt. 3:16, 17; Mark 1:9-11; Luke 3:21, 22). Jesus was baptized with the Holy Spirit (Matt. 3:1; Mark 1:8; Luke 3:16). Acts tells that the Holy Spirit was poured out upon the apostles (Acts 2:33).

B. Another witness is seen in the water and blood (5:8). It is commonly believed that the water is referring to the baptism of Jesus and the blood to His death. In these two, Jesus is manifested as the Savior of the world.

C. The third witness is the human witness (5:9). The conditions of a legal, valid witness are found in Deuteronomy (19:15), Matthew (18:16), John (8:17; 10:25), 2 Corinthians (13:1). The human witness is a valid one.

D. The fourth witness is human experience (5:10). He that believes on the Son of God has the witness in himself. The one who believes on Christ comes to possess a deepening consciousness that He is the divine Savior. He is cleansed and pardoned. He has peace and power. He has victory.

V. *Faith Results in the Possession of Eternal Life* (5:11, 12). Belief in Jesus Christ is a sign that one has experienced the new birth and is a child of God.

Eternal life is quality as well as duration. It is life like God's or the life of God. It is a present posses-sion and is eternal in duration. Dur-ation is less prominent than the moral character. Eternal life is the very life of God, manifested in Christ—thus, a life like that of Christ.

Conclusion. The one greatest thing a human being can do is to exercise faith in Jesus Christ and receive eternal life. If you have never done that then you are urged to do so right now. Bow your head, confess your sin, receive Jesus as your Savior and receive God's life.

WEDNESDAY EVENING, FEBRUARY 27

TITLE: "The Bible Speaks to Our Condition"

SCRIPTURE READING: Luke 14.

Introduction. The habit of open-ing up God's Word and studying a chapter a day gives us an opportu-nity to have eyes that are open to see wonderful things out of God's holy Word. The chapter which is suggested for this date closes with the phrase "He that hath ears to hear, let him hear" (v. 35). This is an imperative. We are not only to hear, but we are to heed that which God communicates to us through His precious Word.

I. *The Priority of the Law of Love* (Luke 14:1-6). In the days of our Lord, the ritual and traditions asso-ciated with the law of Moses took precedence over all other consider-ations. In this incident in which our Lord healed a man on the Sabbath day, He declared by His actions that the law of love takes precedence over all other customs, traditions, or accepted interpretations of the law of God. The Pharisees believed that the Sabbath should be observed neg-atively in terms of doing no labor and positively in terms of resting and feasting. The Sabbath was made for man and was intended to be a continual reminder that God was his creator, redeemer and sus-tainer. By healing the sick man on the Sabbath day, our Lord was saying that the expression of genu-ine good will must never be restrict-ed to a particular time or to a particular place. It must be free to minister.

II. *Humility Leads to Honor* (Luke 14:7-14). Our Lord spoke to those who had been invited to the feast concerning the fact that selfishness and disregard for others disqualifies one for the place of honor at God's banquet table. He points out that in the practice of hospitality we should not restrict ourselves to an exclusive circle of self-serving friends, but that we should become concerned about the unfortunate, the needy, the helpless. He speaks concerning the fact that service to those who cannot return the favor will be remembered by the Father God on the day of Resurrection.

III. *Beware of Making Excuses* (Luke 14:15-24). Our Lord warned those who considered themselves to be inside the circle of God's favor against the peril of making excuses for themselves which would lead to exclusion from the favor of God. Something in the nature of man causes him to have an inflated concept of his own piety and acceptability in the sight of a Holy God.

It is always possible to find excuses for neglecting to respond to the invitations which come from God to His people. We need to beware lest we rationalize and exclude ourself from some experience with God when His invitations come to us. These invitations usually come in the form of a command. Every command contains within it a promise. To make foolish excuses for not obeying God's invitations or God's commands is to deny ourselves the privilege of experiencing the fulfillment of His promises.

IV. *The Demands of Discipleship* (Luke 7:25-33). Our Lord never offered any easy, cheap, inexpensive, convenient way to achieve success. While salvation may be the free gift of God's grace, there is no easy way

to be faithful to the claims of discipleship.

Our Lord never held out a promise of peace, prosperity and plenty without struggle if we would but confess Him to be Lord and Master.

The passage under discussion is not teaching that we must hate instead of love. Rather we have here an example of the use of hyperbole which is very normal among Orientals as they seek to speak in the strongest words possible to convey an important truth. Our Lord is declaring that if one would be His disciple, then the claims of this discipleship must have priority over all personal relationships, interests and ambitions. There must be absolutely no competing loyalties if one would be a true follower of Jesus Christ.

Our Lord is suggesting that potential disciples count the cost of discipleship before they begin the journey. He is suggesting that those of us who claim to be disciples examine the quality of our followship.

Conclusion. As you read Luke 14, do you have ears that hear? Do you have a heart that is open and receptive? Are you willing to begin to do as our Lord taught that we should? Not to do so is to bring discredit upon the cause of Christ, and it is to place ourselves in the category of salt which has lost its saltiness.

Sunday Mornings

Continue the series based on "The Life and Works of the Lord Jesus."

Sunday Evenings

The theme for the Sunday evenings is "The Biblical Doctrine of the Forgiveness of Sins." These five messages were provided by Dr. Morris Ashcraft who has authored a splendid book entitled *The Forgiveness of Sins* (Broadman Press: Nashville, Tennessee, 1972). This book would provide excellent supplementary material for a series of messages on the forgiveness of sin.

Wednesday Evenings

Continue the program of encouraging the reading of at least one chapter each day in the belief that "The Bible Speaks to Our Condition."

The theme verse for the month is "But his delight is in the law of the LORD; and in his law doth he meditate day and night" (Ps. 1:2).

SUNDAY MORNING, MARCH 3

TITLE: "Jesus Founded His Church"

TEXT: "Upon this rock I will build my church; and the gates of hell shall not prevail against it" (Matt. 16:18).

SCRIPTURE READING: Matthew 16:13-18.

HYMNS: "The Church's One Foundation," Stone. "Faith of Our Fathers," Faber. "I Love Thy Kingdom, Lord," Dwight.

OFFERTORY PRAYER:

Our Father, Thou hast taught us that our hearts will be where our treasures are. Give us, therefore, the divine grace and the personal wisdom to lay up our treasures in heaven in order that our interests on earth may be in spiritual things. By Thy generosity we have received all that we have. Help us to use the things which have been entrusted to our care in a way that may make us more truly Thy servants. May we ever hold before our minds the truth that as Thou hast blessed us so we should seek to be a blessing to others. May our gifts be used here in our own church and to the uttermost part of the world for the building up of Thy kingdom in the hearts of people. We pray in Jesus' name. Amen.

Introduction. During the Galilean ministry, Jesus took His disciples on several retreats away from the thronging crowds. The retreats were twofold. First, the disciples needed physical rest. Second, He desired to instruct them more thoroughly in order that they could carry on His work after He left.

One of those retreats was as far away as Caesarea Philippi, quite a number of miles north of the Sea of Galilee and not far from Mount Hermon, the probable site of the Transfiguration which occurred a few days later. Jesus had been with the disciples for some time now and

He wished to know how much they understood concerning His nature. His first question was a general one. He probably was not as much interested in knowing what the multitudes thought of Him as He was in knowing how the disciples felt and how they interpreted the ideas of the masses. The first question paved the way for the second one which was more intimate.

Simon Peter had a way of speaking first whether he knew the correct answer or not. This time, however, he was exactly right. Jesus assured him that his answer had not come upon the basis of human knowledge. It was revealed to him by the Father—and for a particular purpose. Jesus used it as the basis upon which to instruct His disciples more clearly and give them a basis for evangelization.

I. *The Foundation of the Church.* Peter said that Jesus was the "Christ, the Son of the living God." The word "Christ" means "Messiah" and this means Simon Peter was recognizing Jesus as the One whom God had promised to send to His people. But Peter said more. He identified the Messiah as the Son of God. There was not complete agreement among all Jews concerning the coming Messiah. There was not even a unanimous understanding among the people that the Messiah would necessarily be equal with the Father. As there are various ideas and understandings of the Scripture today concerning the Second Coming of Jesus, there were various ideas concerning the First Coming of Jesus. These were based on interpretations of Old Testament passages. Simon Peter's statement, however, rang the bell loud and clear. Jesus of Nazareth was the Son of God. Implicit in his

statement are all the later teachings we have concerning the complete equality of the Son with the Father and the complete deity of the Savior. It was indeed a marvelous confession!

Jesus said He would build His church on this fact—that He is the Son of God. There have been various understandings as to the exact meaning of Jesus' words. Some have felt Jesus made a "play on words" in His statement. The word "Peter" means "rock" in the Greek language. Some have suggested that the difference in the two Greek words used for rock in the text means that Jesus was saying to Peter that he is a "movable" type of rock, but He (Jesus) is the solid rock that cannot be moved. There may be a basis in the text for such an interpretation. Others have felt that Jesus meant He would build His Church on Peter's confession or even upon Peter's faith and, therefore, upon the faith of others who would come along with and after Peter in accepting this truth. Whatever shade of interpretation we give to the confession, one thing is certain. The Church of Jesus Christ is built upon the fact of His complete deity and His equality with God the Father. Jesus was born of a virgin, possessed a unique nature and, although He identified Himself with man, He was, nevertheless, God in the flesh.

The Church is built upon this truth and when any local congregation minimizes it, the truth of Scripture is compromised. Unless a church believes in the deity of Christ, it will seek to win the lost in vain. When a church falters on this truth, it is not long before the church is compromising in other areas. It is important that every minister and every teacher of any kind maintain the first fundamental truth about Jesus—He is the Son of God.

II. *The Nature of the Church.* The word translated "church" comes from a Greek word which means literally "called out" and this is the true nature of Christ's Church. It is composed of those who have been called out from sin and the world and made new people in Jesus Christ. This same word is translated "assembly" in Acts 19:41.

The church consists of born-again believers. When Jesus spoke of His Church in this passage before us He was speaking, of course, in terms of a concept. There were no buildings or church organizations as we know them today. It was later that people gathered themselves together in local congregations and constituted assemblies known as churches. In the New Testament we read of the "church at Corinth" or the "church at Ephesus" or "the churches at Galatia." These churches were visible bodies and consisted of born-again people. The ideal for our churches today is that every member of each local assembly be a born-again Christian person. No one should be admitted to membership in a local body unless he has had a genuine experience of regeneration. There have been times in the history of Christianity when a person was required to give his personal experience with Christ in salvation before he was admitted to membership in the local church. Unfortunately, some congregations have been more lax and have failed many times to require or even to emphasize the new birth experience as a prerequisite to membership in the local group. When this is done we lose our influence with non-believers.

There are a few places in the New Testament where the Church is spoken of in a general institutional sense rather than speaking of the local body. This is similar to the way in which we speak of "the Christian home" in America. Each Christian home in America is a separate entity even though we speak of "the Christian home" in our nation. Likewise, our churches today are local, visible bodies even though we sometimes speak of the Church in a general sense.

There are those who speak of "the church universal," meaning all saved people regardless of their affiliation, or lack of it, with a local congregation. This is sometimes spoken of as the "universal" church or the "catholic" church. Protestants today speak of the "holy catholic church" while the Roman Catholic church speaks of their church as the "Roman" catholic church. The expression "kingdom of God" may also be used to refer to the universal body of saved believers. Many people believe this is a better expression to describe the invisible body of believers.

Whatever terminology we use in describing the Church, we should remember that the Church is composed of people who have had a personal experience with Jesus. The word "called out" signifies that those who comprise Christ's Church should be different from the world. They should have had a personal experience in the forgiveness of sin through Christ and their life should reflect this change.

III. *The Promise to the Church.* Jesus gave a great assurance to His Church. He said, "The gates of hell shall not prevail against it." Many have seen this passage as teaching that Jesus is promising the Church will never go out of existence. It will remain until His Second Coming. This may be what Jesus meant in this passage, but there is another possible interpretation. When the Church goes on the offensive the forces of hell will not be able to withstand the onslaught of Christian people banded together in militant action. In other words, the Church is not on the defense. The Church is marching under the orders of Christ. The combined forces of evil will not be able to resist this onward march. This interpretation magnifies the conquering power of the Church under the leadership of the Holy Spirit in today's world.

Conclusion. Are you a member of Christ's Church? Have you had an experience with Him that has caused a transformation in your life? You should belong to a local congregation and invest your talents in the work of Christ through that church. No church is perfect. This is because churches are made of people and no people are without fault. Your life will be better, however, if you will find a place of service in a local congregation with fellow believers.

Joining a local church does not bring personal salvation. This comes only through an experience with the Savior. There is great value, however, in being associated with other Christians in a local body. If you are not a church member, will you give serious consideration to belonging to a church? This is, of course, on the condition that you have been saved. If you have not been saved, your first step is to receive Jesus as personal Savior.

Those who are church members should give loyalty to the church where they belong. To "flit" from one church to another Sunday after Sunday does not deepen one's life nearly as much as finding a place of service in one church and being loyal to that church. This does not mean that there are not legitimate times when we can visit other churches. On the whole, however, our loyalty should be to the congregation where we hold our membership.

SUNDAY EVENING, MARCH 3

TITLE: "The Keys of the Kingdom"

TEXT: "And I say also unto thee, That thou art Peter, and upon this rock I will build my church; and the gates of hell shall not prevail against it.

And I will give unto thee the keys of the kingdom of heaven: and whatsoever thou shalt bind on earth shall be bound in heaven: and whatsoever thou shalt loose on earth shall be loosed in heaven.

Then charged he his disciples that they should tell no man that he was Jesus the Christ" (Matt. 16:18-20).

SCRIPTURE READING: Matthew 16:13-20.

Introduction. Jesus used many bold figures in teaching the disciples. They remembered these striking expressions, parables, and figures, and repeated them many times in their own witnessing. Some of these expressions have come to us in the

New Testament in such a way as to be difficult to interpret. One such expression is that which relates to the "keys of the kingdom."

It is common knowledge that one famous interpretation of this passage suggests that Simon Peter and his successors were endowed with the authority from Jesus Christ to open or close the doors of heaven by their control of the Church and its sacraments. It is my belief that this passage has to do with the Church and with the forgiveness of sins, but not in this authoritative sense. It is also my conviction that this expression conveys a very significant message regarding the Church and the forgiveness of sins.

I. *The Rock.* The "rock" on which the Church is built is the confession of faith in Christ and Christ's acceptance of the confessor. In the passages before us we have the great confession at Caesarea Philippi. In response to Jesus' question, Peter, whose name means rock, confessed to Jesus, "Thou art the Christ, the Son of the living God." Thereupon Jesus responded, "Blessed art thou Simon Bar-jona: for flesh and blood hath not revealed it unto thee, but my Father which is in heaven. And I say also unto thee that thou art Peter, and upon this rock I will build my church. . . ." The rock is not the man Simon Peter nor is the Church built upon a man. When Peter confessed his faith that Jesus was the Christ, and Christ accepted Simon Peter on the basis of that confession, the foundation was laid for the Church. In short, Jesus said, "I can build my congregation of the faithful on this foundation."

II. *The Church.* For "the Church" is not primarily an institution; the Church is the community of the "people of God" gathered into a fellowship by this experience of faith in Jesus Christ. In the New Testament there are several ways in which the word "church" is used. The two most significant ones designate the Church in its universal sense, and the church as a local body. In the first sense, "the Church" includes all of the Christians of all of the ages. This idea is prevalent in Ephesians and Colossians. It is the "people of God," the "body of Christ," and the "fellowship of the Holy Spirit." By far the most frequent use of the word "church" has to do with local congregations.

III. *The Churches.* Wherever the early Christian missionaries went preaching the word, communities of the faithful originated. These are the "churches." Each of these churches is a genuine manifestation of "the Church." In Matthew 18:15-35, Jesus establishes the connection between forgiving sins, the Church, and the "binding and loosing." In that passage, the spirit of the Church is seen in Jesus' statement "for where two or three are gathered together in my name, there am I in the midst of them."

IV. *Binding and Loosing.* "Binding and loosing" refer to the Church and to the forgiveness of sins. We have noted in Matthew 16:19 that Jesus promised "the keys of the kingdom" and then said "whatsoever thou shalt bind on earth shall be bound in heaven; and whatsoever thou shalt loose on earth shall be loosed in heaven." In Matthew 18:18 Jesus repeats the identical statement after He has instructed Christians in the settlement of disputes among themselves. Then in verse 20 he speaks of the Church as the place where "two or three are gathered together in my name." Then, Peter asked the question (v. 21) "Lord, how oft shall my brother sin against me, and I forgive him?" This seems to leave no doubt as to the meaning of the keys of the kingdom and the binding and loosing. If any doubt remained it would have been removed by Jesus' statement after His resurrection, "And when he had said this, he breathed on them and said to them, 'Receive the Holy Spirit. If you forgive the sins of any, they are forgiven; if you retain the sins of any, they are retained' " (John 20:22, RSV).

V. *The Forgiveness of Sins.* In the passages cited, the contexts and specific statements require us to understand that Jesus intended the "keys of the kingdom" to be understood in terms of the Church and the forgiveness of sins. The binding and the loosing have to do with the forgiveness of sins.

Does this mean that the Church forgives sins? Not in the sense that the Church authoritatively or arbitrarily forgives or retains sins. However, it does mean that the Church knows about God's forgiveness and proclaims the message of the forgiveness of sins. Since the Church proclaims the promise of forgiveness, it does "open the door" for people to enter into the kingdom of heaven. On the other hand, if it fails to proclaim the Christian message of forgiveness, people remain outside the kingdom. When Jesus said that the actions of His people are binding in heaven, He meant that the decisions made in these congrega-

tions in response to the message of forgiveness are eternally binding. In short, when we preach the Gospel and offer the forgiveness of Jesus Christ, people make decisions which determine eternal destiny.

This interpretation of the keys of the kingdom as the forgiveness of sins is consistent with other New Testament teachings; the interpretation of sheer authority is not consistent with the New Testament. For instance, in the immediate context of this statement (Matt. 18:1-4), when the disciples asked, "Who is the greatest in the kingdom of heaven?" Jesus replied by calling a small child to Him and by indicating that the greatest is the humblest. On another occasion, when an ambitious mother specifically requested that her two sons be given priority in Jesus' organization, He expressly refused the request and prohibited such "exercise" of "authority" as was later claimed for Simon Peter. Jesus said, "You know that the rulers of the Gentiles lord it over them, and their great men exercise authority over them. It shall not be so among you; but whoever would be great among you must be your servant, and whoever would be first among you must be your slave; even as the Son of man came not to be served but to serve, and to give his life as a ransom for many" (Matt. 20:25-28, RSV). It is unthinkable that Jesus intended to imply that the keys of the kingdom and the binding and the loosing should be tied to any view of the authority or the primacy of Peter, his successors, or an institution which would claim to admit or exclude people from heaven. But it is a fact that the passages involved do relate the Church to the forgiveness of sins through its faithful proclamation of the message of Jesus Christ.

Conclusion. And Jesus said to us in the Church, "I give you the keys." Will you faithfully proclaim the Gospel of forgiveness so that people may enter the kingdom?

WEDNESDAY EVENING, MARCH 6

TITLE: "The Bible Speaks to Our Condition"

SCRIPTURE READING: Luke 21.

Introduction. With eyes open for truth and with ears attuned to listen to God, let us approach this great and perplexing chapter from Luke's gospel.

The events described and the teachings recorded in Luke 21 come from the last week of our Lord's life. The events described follow His triumphal entry into Jerusalem and precede His arrest, trials and crucifixion by a matter of hours.

I. *Commendation for a Spirit of Sacrifice* (Luke 21:1-4). Our Lord was watchful as the people made their contributions to the treasury of the Temple. He beheld the manner and the motive behind their gifts. Without criticizing the rich who came giving generously, He highly commended the widow who gave sacrificially. He was particularly impressed with the fact that she gave to the extent that there was nothing remaining for her.

What attitude does our Lord have toward our spirit of giving? How much sacrifice is involved in our giving? Do we even know how to spell the word "sacrifice"?

II. *The Danger of Being Deceived* (Luke 21:5-9). In all ages man has been subject to deception. We can be deceived by others, by the devil and by ourselves. Our Lord warned His disciples against the peril of listening to false claimants to being the Messiah.

III. *On a Collision Course With Catastrophe* (Luke 21:10-24). This particular passage is very difficult for the casual reader to understand. Our Lord uses apocalyptic language to communicate truths to His disciples that were easier for them to understand than for the modern reader. Apocalyptic language was used by Hebrew sages and prophets to express their hopes and dreams for a divine, dramatic manifestation of God's work, particularly in a time of national stress. Often Jewish prophets and writers used apocalyptic terminology to describe the ultimate consummation of the ages.

The verses under consideration deal both with the catastrophe that Jerusalem faces, and, at the same time, the final windup of human history. Because our Lord is speaking concerning both of these events, the casual reader can be confused as he reads this passage.

There are several thoughts and impressions that come through clearly as we read this passage.

A. Disciples of our Lord are always exposed to the peril of trouble. These were facing the possibility of imprisonment and persecution from both the Jewish authorities and from pagan kings and governors (Luke 21:12).

B. A time for testimony (Luke 21:13-15). Whatever life brings, the follower of Christ should look for an opportunity to give a verbal testimony concerning his experience with Jesus Christ. God will bless his effort. We should trust the Holy Spirit for leadership when the opportunity occurs.

C. Enduring faithfulness leads to ultimate victory (Luke 21:19). There will be trouble along the way. Persecution may be our lot. We may experience physical injury. Our ultimate security is with God. The faithful will be rewarded even if martyrdom comes.

D. Jerusalem is to be destroyed (Luke 21:20-24). Israel had rejected her Messiah. Israel had rejected the plan of God for their life. Instead of being a missionary force among the nations of the world, Israel had retreated into a narrow, nationalistic exclusiveness. Israel refused to be a channel through which the grace of God and the message of God could reach the world. By her rejection of God's plan, she chose a pathway that was leading to oblivion.

IV. *Victory Belongs to the Lord* (Luke 21:25-28). In apocalyptic language our Lord speaks of the consummation of history. In a time when the nation was being threatened by the power of Rome, the followers of Christ are to recognize that above and behind it all, the Lord will rule sovereign and supreme.

V. *Be Alert and Ready* (Luke 21:29-36). The overwhelming impression that comes through this passage is that each disciple of the Lord Jesus should live each day in readiness for the final victorious return of Jesus Christ. We should not be overly concerned about the day by day events that precede His coming. We should concentrate on being faithful and obedient and let God take care of the ultimate outcome.

VI. *In the Presence of God and Among the People* (Luke 21:37, 38). At night our Lord drew aside that He might go into the presence of the Father God. In the early morning our Lord went among the crowds to be their teacher, comforter, healer and guide.

Conclusion. If we would face the trials and trouble and fears of the present, we need to spend time in the presence of our Father God. Each day we should find a place of retreat and solitude in order that we might let God speak to our condition.

TITLE: "Jesus Was Dedicated to Duty"

TEXT: "And it came to pass, when the time was come that he should be received up, he steadfastly set his face to go to Jerusalem" (Luke 9:51).

SCRIPTURE READING: Luke 9: 43-56.

HYMNS: "Jesus Calls Us," Alexander. "O Jesus, I Have Promised," Bode. "Our Best," Kirk.

OFFERTORY PRAYER:

Our Father, Thou art a merciful God. Grant that we may ever seek the constant aid of the Holy Spirit in order that we may follow each day of our lives after those things which build us up in Jesus Christ. We praise Thee and bless Thee because of Thy great power and because of Thy great goodness. Thou hast given us the ability to work and to earn money. We come now to bring our tithes and offerings to Thee. Our gifts represent our life. May we recognize that the giving of money is not only symbolic but is actually the giving of our life for it has taken hours of our life to earn the money. We give these offerings to Thee because we love Thee and we wish to have a part in Thy work around the world. Use these gifts to advance the work of Thy kingdom in the hearts of people. Most of all, use us individually and collectively as instruments of Thy grace and Thy peace to touch the lives of people and bring them to a knowledge of Thee. We pray these things in Jesus' name. Amen.

Introduction. The major part of Jesus' ministry was in Galilee. Matthew and Mark major on this great Galilean ministry which lasted at least eighteen months. It may have been interrupted by brief visits to Jerusalem, but the eighteen-month period is considered as one unit comprising this ministry in Galilee. It may have been even longer than eighteen months.

On the other hand, Luke's gospel majors on the last period of Jesus' ministry of approximately six months consisting of a "later Judean ministry" and followed by a "Perean ministry" before the last days in Jerusalem immediately preceding His death.

In Luke 9:51 we find the "watershed" of Jesus' ministry. This verse identifies the time that Jesus left Galilee as a sphere of operations and headed His face southward—a decision that set Him squarely on His journey to the cross. In all probability, the material in Luke 9:51-18:14 is parallel with John 7:2-11:54. Also, three passages in John (7:2ff.; 11:17f.; 12:1) correspond to the three times that Luke speaks of Jesus' going to Jerusalem (9:51; 13:22; 17:11). As said before, Jesus may have come back for a brief period in Galilee and joined the pilgrims coming to Jerusalem, but Luke 9:51 represents the great decision to leave Galilee as the major field of ministry and when He set His face toward Jerusalem and toward His death.

I. *Jesus Had One Great Mission in Life.* Although our Savior was a great teacher, this was not His primary mission. He indeed taught the crowds and He spoke as no other man has ever spoken. His wisdom was far greater than anyone who had ever come to the world or has ever come since His day. He used some material that existed, but He gave His individual touch to it. He spoke with authority—not as one merely reciting the opinion of others. Likewise, Jesus worked miracles. He did supernatural things in order to help those who were weak and needy and also in order to show His power. Every part of the Savior's life was a blessing to others and an example of how men should live.

Yet, the mission of Jesus, from the beginning, was to die. He did not come so much to preach the Gospel as He came in order that there might be a Gospel to be preached. Everything in His ministry pointed toward His passion. It was necessary for Him to live a perfect life in order that He might be the Lamb of God without spot and blemish. The life itself, however, was not the sin offering. It is true the Scriptures speak of our "being saved by his life," but this does not refer to the initial experience in salvation by which we become justified in God's sight through the death of the Savior. It refers to the process of growth whereby we are saved daily from the "power" of sin rather than to the original experience in which we are saved from the "penalty" of sin. It is the death of Jesus that makes atonement for sin and makes it possible for us to find redemption through His blood. This was the over-arching purpose of Jesus' life, and His mind was on the cross from the beginning of His ministry.

II. *The Time for Decision.* One of the most important things we face in life is our decision as to *when* we shall do a thing. Jesus felt it was necessary to have an extended ministry in Galilee before His final "clash" with the religious authorities at Jerusalem. If Jesus had stayed in Galilee, He would never have been crucified. His problem in Galilee was that He was too popular. The people wanted to make Him a king. They wanted to force Him to become a political Messiah and lead them in rebellion against the Roman government. Jesus sought during His entire Galilean ministry to instruct the people in this section of Palestine concerning the spiritual nature of God's kingdom. At certain periods, He withdrew with His disciples for special "in depth seminars." The time came when He felt He had instructed them sufficiently and must leave them on their own. He wisely stayed away from a lengthy sojourn in Judah where Jerusalem was located during this period of instruction to the common people in Galilee. The visits there to the religious feasts were brief. His premature death would have interfered with the plan the Father had for Him. Timing is very important in one's life and Jesus had the exact time planned when He would leave Galilee and concentrate on the provinces of Judah, Perea and later the city of Jerusalem itself.

III. *Dedication Means Complete Surrender to a Cause.* Once Jesus set His face toward Jerusalem, He never looked back. Although He realized it meant His death, we see in His decision the "completed surrender of a spotless soul." Everything that happened subsequent to Luke 9:51 was under the influence of the cross. Throughout the rest of the gospel we are constantly reminded that the destiny of Jesus is Jerusalem. We know that He will confront the religious leaders in the capital. We know also He will be rejected and put on the cross. Jesus accepted the divine imperative under which God had placed His life. He did it voluntarily. God was in charge of His life and He was completely surrendered to the Father's purpose for Him. Jesus was not a helpless victim of circumstances. He made the choice deliberately. He was fully aware of all that was involved but He also knew that by giving His life He would in reality realize it most completely. This is the true meaning of dedication. In the Old Testament the word "dedicate" or "consecrate" comes from a root which means "to cut off" and has the further meaning of "to separate for a special purpose." This is the true nature of dedication. When we are dedicated to God we are cut off from the rest of the world and separated completely unto Him for holy living and for unselfish service.

There have been many illustrations of true consecration. One of the best illustrations is that of the words of General Pershing, commander of the American troops, to General Foch, commander of the Allied Forces in World War I. Pershing brought his forces to Foch and said, "Our men, our equipment, our supplies are yours to use as you wish." What a change we would see in the world if every Christian would surrender to God completely and say, "My time, my talents, my money, my enthusiasm, all that I have is Yours to be used completely in Your service."

Conclusion. How dedicated are you? Robert E. Lee insisted that the word "duty" is the sublimest in our language. He once said, "You can never do more than your duty. You should never wish to do less." We must always realize, of course, that the highest motive in service is love. We should seek to serve Christ because it is a privilege not because it is our "ironclad" duty. We should, nevertheless, find a joy in doing our duty. We should come to love to do those things which we should do. In this way love and duty are blended into one beautiful action. The doing of our duty is similar to learning how to obey the rules. The obeying of rules is, likewise, not the highest form of Christian living. We should seek to live on such an exalted level of Christlikeness that we act superior to the law and have no need for laws or rules. There is, however, a great value in learning to obey the rules and also to do our duty. These approaches to life deepen character. When we fail to do our duty or obey the rules we find ourselves deteriorating in our personal growth. On the other hand, the doing of duty and the obeying of rules contributes to the developing of a great personality. We should always let love be the supreme motivation, but we should find joy in the simple doing of our duty.

TITLE: "The Church As the Community of Forgiveness"

TEXT: "Put on therefore, as the elect of God, holy and beloved, bowels of mercies, kindness, humbleness of mind, meekness, longsuffering:

Forbearing one another, and forgiving one another, if any man have a quarrel against any: even as Christ forgave you, so also do ye" (Col. 3:12, 13).

SCRIPTURE READING: Colossians 3.

Introduction. The Church is a community of the "forgiven." One may join human institutions in various ways. Entrance requirements to some churches range all the way from very strict to almost none at all. But, a man may join a "church" only if he comes through the door of the forgiveness of sins. In Biblical faith all men have sinned against God and have thereby suffered estrangement from Him. God's call to repentance is a call for man to come back to God; man does this only by accepting the gracious forgiveness of God. A true church is composed of the forgiven. It goes without saying that we Christians should have real joy in the acknowledgment that we were sinners and that Christ forgave us. This witness constitutes one of our strongest appeals to those who have not yet been forgiven.

I. *A Church Is a Community of "Forgiving" People.* In the Sermon on the Mount Jesus stated, "For if you forgive men their trespasses, your heavenly Father will also forgive you; but if you do not forgive men their trespasses, neither will

your Father forgive your trespasses" (Matt. 6:14, 15, RSV). On another occasion, Jesus was asked how many times a Christian should forgive an offending person. There was an old adage that a righteous man might forgive someone as much as seven times in a day. Jesus required His followers to forgive not "seven times in a day" but "seventy times seven times" (Matt. 18:21; Luke 17:3).

It is also quite important to recognize the role of forgiving in the Christian life. It is universally acknowledged that Christians, regrettably, sin after conversion (1 John 1:9). But when they do, Christ forgives them, and they mutually sustain each other by forgiving one another when they sin (Eph. 4:32; Col. 3:13). When Christians worship, they confess their sins and accept forgiveness. If Christians are genuinely true to their nature, it may be said of them, "Behold how they forgive one another!"

II. *The Church Is Committed to a Ministry of Forgiveness.* In the writings of Paul, forgiveness is the same as reconciliation and he refers to the Church as having the "ministry of reconciliation" (2 Cor. 5:18). The Church exercises this ministry by proclaiming "the message of reconciliation" (2 Cor. 5:19). As the Church proclaims this message, and as its members live the example of forgiving, they show estranged sinners the gracious forgiveness of God.

III. *As Christ's Body on Earth, the Church Is Concerned for Persons.* The Church heals its own members by forgiving them, and it restores persons to healthy human relations by forgiveness. When the Church forgets its ministry of healing by forgiveness, and clamors over principles instead of witnessing to persons, it abandons its task. All around us there are persons burdened down to the point of collapse by the guilt for their own sins. Families are divided within; individuals are crushed; institutions are rent with controversy. The only cure for these situations is for the persons to forgive one another. The Church knows how to forgive and proclaims the message of forgiveness.

Conclusion. Men and women without faith in Jesus Christ live their lives in lostness. The churches whose members know God's forgiveness and the message of forgiveness stand as their only hope. When the Church is faithful in its ministry of proclaiming forgiveness, it opens the door of heaven.

WEDNESDAY EVENING, MARCH 13

TITLE: "The Bible Speaks to Our Condition"

SCRIPTURE READING: John 4.

Introduction. The chapter for today is one of the great chapters of John's gospel of love. The events in this chapter were to have a profound effect upon the life and ministry of the apostles.

By these words and these events, our Lord was speaking to His apostles and to His future followers. John, the writer of this gospel, under the inspiration of the Holy Spirit selected these events that help prove that Jesus was indeed the Christ and that men could find eternal life through faith in Him.

I. *The Scope of Our Lord's Loving Concern.* There are very few chapters in the New Testament that reveal the scope or the range of our Lord's concern for all men as does this chapter.

A. Loving concern for the Samaritans (John 4:4-42). The revolutionary nature of our Lord's love is revealed in this experience with a Samaritan woman who had a very low moral standard, even among the Samaritans. Our Lord entered into dialogue with this woman who was ostracized by Jews because of her sex, her race, and her religion. Our Lord was eager to make available to her the fountains of living waters from which she could quench the thirst of her soul.

It was not because of a desire to make a hasty trip from Judea to Galilee that our Lord decided to go through Samaria (4:4). Our Lord deliberately went through this area that was avoided by orthodox Jews in order that He might register the divine concern for a disenfranchised people.

B. Loving concern for Jewish people (John 4:43-45). Christ was returning from Jerusalem to Galilee. He was genuinely concerned about His nation and the people whom God had chosen to be the instruments of His redemptive love.

C. Loving concern for Gentiles (John 4:46-54). The text does not declare that the officer was a Gentile, but it implies such. Perhaps he was very sympathetic toward the Jewish faith and the Jewish people. He had heard about Jesus. He felt a desperate need for the help of the Christ and came searching and pleading for His assistance.

Our Lord revealed His concern and performed a miracle of healing in response to the Gentile official's plea for mercy and assistance.

Our Lord's love crossed all natural and artificial barriers that normally separate men. If we would be His true followers today, we must have a universal concern for the needs of all men.

II. *The Spirituality of Worship* (John 4:21-24). We should not assume that places dedicated to prayer and worship were considered to be unimportant by our Lord. However, in His conversation with the Samaritan · woman, He emphasized that worship is the response of the heart to God rather than merely going to a place and observing certain rituals or ceremonies.

Our Lord declared that God is Spirit, and that they who would worship Him must worship Him in spirit and in truth.

Genuine worship is a spiritual response to a spiritual God. As the instrument of the Spirit, the body with all of its faculties is to be put at the disposal of God.

We can rejoice in the fact that God is accessible to us in any place, at all times, and under every possible circumstance. God is not limited to a specific place and to a particular time. He is always present and always available to those who will worship Him in spirit and in truth.

III. *The Joy of the Harvest* (John 4:35-42). Our Lord used terminology that was appropriate to His listeners. Here He speaks in terms of people in need of the grace of God as being compared to a harvest field that was ready to be harvested. He emphasizes the perennial nature of the spiritual harvest.

He saw the Samaritan people as people who were hungry for and eager to respond to the good news of God's universal love.

Some serve as sowers and others serve as reapers. In the end, God will reward each according to his labors. The spiritual harvest will have eternal significance for those who labor in the fields for the Lord.

IV. *The Avenue of Faith* (John 4:46-54). In this miracle of healing, our Lord emphasized the necessity of faith in the person, the presence, and the power of God. Our Lord responded to the deep sense of need and to the faith which the official focused upon Him.

The Lord revealed His power to heal at a distance without being present to actually touch the body of the one who was sick.

As a result of the man's faith, Christ was provided an avenue through which He could work, not only upon the man's son, but also within his household.

When Jesus returned to Nazareth, He was unable to do many mighty works because of the unbelief of the people. This is perhaps the explanation for the failure of so many of us today. We either refuse to believe or we neglect to believe in the promises and in the power of our Lord.

Conclusion. A survey of the Bible and a consideration of Christian history will reveal that the spiritual giants that have walked across the stage have been men and women who out-believed their contemporaries. Through this great chapter, God would encourage us to have a greater faith.

SUNDAY MORNING, MARCH 17

TITLE: "Jesus Changed People's Lives"

TEXT: "And Zacchaeus stood, and said unto the Lord; Behold, Lord, the half of my goods I give to the poor; and if I have taken anything from any man by false accusation, I restore him fourfold" (Luke 19:8).

SCRIPTURE READING: Luke 19: 1-10.

HYMNS: "Stand Up, Stand Up for Jesus," Duffield. "Since I Have Been Redeemed," Excell. "Standing on the Promises," Carter.

OFFERTORY PRAYER:

Our Father, we are grateful that we know Thou art with us in every circumstance of life. We pray that Thou shalt help us recognize our dependence upon Thee, Thy saving help, Thy guidance and our constant need of forgiveness. Help us now as we bring our tithes and offerings to Thee to rejoice in the privilege of giving. Our gifts shall support many causes and we ask Thy blessings upon all of them. Bless Thy servants who are laboring in places that are difficult and places that are even dangerous. Use our gifts in the proclamation of Thy Gospel and use us as personal witnesses for Christ in the place where we live. We pray these things in Jesus' name. Amen.

Introduction. The last six months of Jesus' ministry were busy days for Him. As was pointed out last week, Luke's gospel majors on this period. Luke 9:51 through 18:14 contains the record of events that occurred during this time. The parallel section John 7:2-11:54 records the happenings in this same period. Although it cannot be irrefutably established, in all probability the material beginning with Matthew 19:1 and Mark 10:1 occurred in this latter part of Jesus' ministry after He left Galilee as a sphere of operations. Luke records much more of this latter period of Jesus' activities than Matthew or Mark because they major on the Galilean ministry. The fact that some words of Jesus seem to be repetitions of things He said during His Galilean ministry does not reflect on their integrity. It is inconceivable that Jesus would not have repeated Himself on numbers of occasions as He taught. He met with similar problems and people with similar questions. Naturally, He gave similar answers. Jesus touched the lives of many people during this last six months of His ministry. Perhaps the most significant of all, however, was His visit to Jericho. Luke's gospel tells of a blind man who cried for mercy and how Jesus gave to him his sight. Immediately following this account we have the record of the

84

life-changing experience of Zacchaeus.

I. *The Money-mad Man.* Zacchaeus was a tax collector. These men were perhaps the greediest of all the Jews. The Roman government had a system of farming out tax-collecting privileges. They would select a Jew and give him the authority to collect taxes in a district. Anything he collected over the stipulated fee to the Roman government would belong to him. Naturally, this encouraged greed on his part and, therefore, the temptation was to be overbearing with his fellow countrymen. Zacchaeus, as a publican or tax collector, was, no doubt, one of the most unpopular men in Jericho. He must have been a lonely man as the people had surely ostracized him from their social life. One writer suggests with creative imagination that perhaps Zacchaeus lived in the last house of a dead-end street and that he had a large fence or hedge around his home. It was strictly private for no one ever came to see him.

II. *The Man With Lonesome Longings.* Surely, Zacchaeus wanted a better life. No one could have remained happy under such conditions. In the early stages of money-making one may believe he is securing happiness. Later, however, he realizes the true values of life are not material successes. Zacchaeus had, no doubt, heard about Jesus. People had told him that those who came in contact with Jesus went away changed. Perhaps Zacchaeus thought to himself that he, too, would find a new life if he saw Jesus. There was probably some curiosity in his climbing the tree to see Jesus, but it was also based on a higher motivation. Perhaps someone had told him about the woman who merely touched his garment and was healed. Zacchaeus may have reasoned that if Jesus could do this, something similar might happen if he climbed the sycamore tree and saw Jesus as He passed. When one is in desperate circumstances he will "grab at any straw" which he thinks can help him. Life was crowding in on Zacchaeus and he followed the only course he knew to guarantee a personal glimpse of Jesus and perhaps a glance or even hopefully a word from the One who had changed the lives of so many people.

III. *The Savior's Sudden Statement.* How surprised Zacchaeus must have been when Jesus spoke his name! But how much more surprised he was at the words which followed! Jesus was going to Zacchaeus' house for a visit! Luke does not tell us many of the details which we would love to know. The short man hurrying down the tree must have made some of the people laugh unless they were among those who were filled with jealousy at the personal attention Jesus was showing to Zacchaeus. Although the text does not state the fact definitely, we rather gain the impression that Jesus had a meal with Zacchaeus. This seems to be the normal interpretation of "gone to be guest with a man."

When did the change of Zacchaeus come? Was it the minute he saw Jesus in the tree and obeyed His voice? Was it as they walked along the way toward Zacchaeus' home? Was it as they broke bread together and Jesus led the family in prayer? Was it as they sat together in the home of Zacchaeus and talked about spiritual things and the possibility of a new start for this "rich little runt" who had messed up his life so badly? We do not know when the change came but we do know it came!

IV. *The Meaning of Conversion.* Salvation is more than an external transaction regarding God and man whereby the latter has a new standing with the Lord. When one is truly converted there is a change in every area of his life. He becomes a "new man in Christ Jesus." The things he once loved he begins to hate. The things he once despised he begins to love. He has a new sense of values. His priorities are different. His very reason for living has changed. Zacchaeus revealed by his testimony that a transformation had taken place. He began with an act of benevolence—half of his possessions would be given to the poor. To the Jewish people, there was nothing which indicated godliness more than one's willingness to help those who were underprivileged. His second evidence of conversion was his willingness to make restitution where he had wronged his fellow man. The Mosaic law only required that a man restore twofold, but Zacchaeus went far beyond the command. We have no way of knowing what a "dent" this put in Zacchaeus' personal fortune. It could have taken most of his material net worth. There is no evidence that Jesus required him to make such a strong statement of his intention. It could be that Jesus, however, pointed out to him the necessity for stripping himself of that which had come to be his God—personal wealth. Jesus made an even greater demand on the rich young ruler. God does not require everyone to make such a radical distribution of his earthly possessions. There are many whose besetting sin is in another realm. Before anyone can experience true conversion, however, he must look at himself honestly and turn over to Jesus his entire life. This involves a surrender of anything and everything that stands between him and complete commitment to Christ.

V. *A Reaffirmation of Christ's Mission.* Verse 10 contains, no doubt, the words of Jesus, not the comment of Luke. This occasion gave our Savior a marvelous opportunity to give a comprehensive statement concerning His ministry. There is probably no finer summary of Jesus' purpose in coming to the world than these words. Jesus came to save, but He did more. He came to seek those whom He would save. Our Master is always taking the first step toward the sinner. He took the first step when He went to the cross of Calvary. He takes other steps toward us long before we move toward Him. Through the Holy Spirit, He leads friends to witness to the lost. He leads people to write tracts, build church buildings, make personal visits and many other avenues of approach to the lost man. This is Jesus "seeking" the lost today. How marvelous to know that the Savior is still at work! No one is too sinful for Him. He loves us all. We should remember, however, that although He does love us, we must be willing to make radical changes in our life and attitudes before our sorrow for sin is genuine repentance which is productive of salvation. We must not be merely sorry we are "caught up with" in our sinning. We must be sorry enough for sin that, as best we can, we will forsake it.

We shall never live perfect lives for this is impossible. Even after we become a Christian, we are still human beings. The Master came, however, to put within us a new heart and a new spirit. Zacchaeus, after this experience, could have testified in the words of the song writer, "No One Ever Cared for Me Like Jesus." This is why Jesus came to earth. He came because He loved. He was sent because His Father loved. God continues to love us today and His greatest desire is that lost people shall repent of their sins and turn in saving faith to Jesus Christ.

Conclusion. Can a human life be changed? There are those who say that once the pattern of life is set nothing can be done about it. The message of Jesus Christ says human life is the one thing that can be changed. The stars are fixed in their courses. The laws of nature are immutable. Personality, however, has been and can be changed. Man's free will guarantees his ability to make choices that alter his outlook, attitude and way of life.

SUNDAY EVENING, MARCH 17

TITLE: "The Keys of the Kingdom: a Blessing and a Burden."

TEXT: "And I will give unto thee the keys of the kingdom of heaven: and whatsoever thou shalt bind on earth shall be bound in heaven: and whatsoever thou shalt loose on earth shall be loosed in heaven" (Matt. 16:19).

"Verily I say unto you, Whatsoever ye shall bind on earth shall be bound in heaven: and whatsoever ye shall loose on earth shall be loosed in heaven" (Matt. 18:18).

"Whose soever sins ye remit, they are remitted unto them; and whose soever sins ye retain, they are retained" (John 20:23).

SCRIPTURE READING: Matthew 16:13-20.

Introduction. Each one of us who has faith in Jesus Christ knows the joy of being forgiven. We recall the burden of sin and the guilt which hung on our consciences. Then someone witnessed to us about the promise of Jesus Christ and we came to know the forgiveness of our sins. Liberation from bondage resulted in a joy unspeakable. To be forgiven is to live a life of blessing.

I. *The Blessing of the Keys.*

A. Sharing forgiveness. It would be difficult to exaggerate the blessing of being able to share this message and promise of God to others who are burdened by sin. Along the route of our pilgrimage we meet so many people who are burdened down by their sin, but who come to know the joy which we know merely by our witnessing to them. Can you imagine a greater blessing than to be in a position such as this so as to be able to share the unsearchable riches of Christ with one so freely? This is what it means to have the "keys of the kingdom."

To be able to forgive another is a tremendous blessing. There are people who live their lives under the severe burden of a grudge. There are those who fool themselves into saying, "I forgive him but I cannot forget." To remember the sins of another is to refuse to forgive him. The person who does not or cannot forgive an offender must live with the shackles upon himself. To be able to forgive another is to get rid of those shackles and to be freed. To be able to forgive is to know a great blessing.

B. Forgiveness cures sin. Along the journey we meet people whose lives are distorted by sin. Sometimes the individual life which is distorted has also distorted that of a family and other human relationships. When we faithfully witness for Jesus Christ to this person sometimes we see the complete transformation of his life and the resultant transformation of his family life. The Christian must sense a joy comparable to that of a physician who by using his skills, restores a sick person to health. In our case however the transaction is eternal. It is a blessing beyond description to be able to witness to such a person; this is the legitimate use of the keys.

II. *The Burden of the Keys.* But it also follows that the possession of the keys imposes a tremendous burden. Those of us who know the forgiveness of God are under the burden of sharing that good news with others by our teaching, witnessing, and actual forgiving. To know the forgiveness of God and to refuse to share it with others is an unspeakable crime.

Since we do know the message of forgiveness and have the assurance that God will forgive sinners, we are under the burden of having to

be faithful to that witness, available to those who need forgiveness, and sensitive to those persons around us. In short, this means that we are "not our own" but that we belong to Him. Therefore we must give ourselves as He gave Himself.

It may be possible that possession of the keys would tempt some persons into being presumptuous. If this is so, a word of warning should be sufficient.

When we meet in our churches to pray, to sing, to worship, to speak and hear the word of God we need to be reminded that we are holding the keys of the kingdom of heaven. The decisions are binding in heaven. These decisions are made in response to the church as it witnesses about God's forgiveness. When the church is faithful in its witness, it actually opens the doors for people to enter into the presence of God.

When a person who is mentally or emotionally ill goes to the psychiatrist, he receives the best treatment that the psychiatrist can give. However, he must often be sent back into the situation which produced his illness in the first place. In the church, however, we surround the new Christian by brothers and sisters who love and know how to forgive. In that context he can recover from his sin and can grow into a strong person. There is no setting in the world like that of Christian fellowship in which people can be made whole.

Conclusion. And Jesus said to those of us in the church, "I give you the keys of the kingdom of heaven. If you are faithful in your ministry, the door is open and they will enter. What will you do?"

TITLE: "The Bible Speaks to Our Condition"

SCRIPTURE READING: John 11.

Introduction. When John wrote his gospel, he was inspired by the Holy Spirit to select certain great events in the life of our Lord that served as signs or as pointing fingers that would indicate something about the unique nature and purpose of the Lord Jesus Christ (John 20:30). Each of the great miracles was something more than a miraculous event. These miracles had a teaching purpose. They were designed to reveal something to the hearts of men concerning Jesus Christ and God's great purpose in and through His life and ministry.

If we exclude the sign of our Lord's death and resurrection, we come to perhaps the most significant sign concerning our Lord in the raising of Lazarus from the dead.

I. *A Disclosure of the Power of the Son of God* (John 11:4, 25, 26, 40-44). In this great chapter we are confronted with mystery and miracle. That which happened was mysterious and miraculous. There is no way to explain this event except on a supernatural level.

Our Lord revealed His lordship over physical death and His power to restore one to physical life. He did this in order to reveal and to declare that He also had the power to bestow and to impart the gift of eternal life.

II. *The Creation of Faith* (John 11:15, 45). Our Lord used the death of His friend, Lazarus, as an occasion to deepen the faith of His disciples and to create faith in the hearts of those who did not yet have faith.

Without faith, it is impossible to please God. Without faith, we face life with human resources alone. Without faith, we will hesitate to attempt to do anything above and beyond what common sense would dictate.

Our Lord recognized that we needed faith in the greatness and in the goodness of our God. Through this miracle of raising Lazarus, He would strengthen our faith in both the goodness and in the power of our Lord.

III. *The Devotion of a Disciple* (John 11:16). In the midst of this great chapter there is a verse that reveals the devotion of a disciple that could be easily overlooked by the casual reader. Thomas, who is often criticized because of his doubts, here reveals the depth of his devotion and the extent of his loyalty. He recognized the danger which our Lord would be facing if He returned to Bethany. He knew that great risk was involved. He was willing to face that risk with the Lord, even if it meant a tragic death. He encouraged the other disciples to join with him as he journeyed with the Lord into dangerous territory.

Are we willing to risk our life out of devotion and loyalty to our Lord?

IV. *The Sorrow of the Savior* (John 11:35). One of the most beautiful pictures of our Lord to be found in all of the Holy Word is found in these two words that make up the shortest verse in the Bible. Our Lord wept in the midst of their sorrow and in the presence of their agony. We are not going too far when we assume that He weeps

89

with us when We weep. He suffers with us when we suffer. He is a compassionate Savior.

V. *The Victory of Life Over Death* (John 11:43). Jesus would lead us to believe that instead of living to die, by divine grace we die to begin really living. Lazarus' restoration to physical life is but a prophecy of our resurrection to an eternal life that will never end. The body will perish, but the spirit will continue to live in a new body that will not be subject to disease or to death (John 11:25, 26; 1 Cor. 15:49-57).

Conclusion. Through this miraculous event, our Lord would speak to us today and help us overcome our fear of death. He would seek to relieve our anxiety about those who have entered death ahead of us. He would assure us that life, rather than death, is permanent.

SUNDAY MORNING, MARCH 24

TITLE: "Jesus Went a Little Farther"

TEXT: "And he went a little farther" (Matt. 26:39).

SCRIPTURE READING: Matthew 26:36-46.

HYMNS: "Trust and Obey," Sammis. "Did You Think to Pray?" Kidder. "Close to Thee," Crosby.

OFFERTORY PRAYER:

Our Father, we bring to Thee our grateful praise that in every circumstance of life Thou art present with us. It is Thou who hast made us. It is Thy Son who has redeemed us. It is Thy Holy Spirit who is our Comforter and Energizer. As we bring our money to Thee, we are expressing our gratitude for blessings that have been sent to us. Thy mercies are so great they cannot be numbered. We are showing our interest in the work of Thy kingdom. We are seeking to invest ourselves in the bringing of others to a saving knowledge of Thee. We pray that these gifts may help others to proclaim boldly the message of Christ—the joy of receiving Him as Savior and the folly of refusing His call. May these gifts be used to convert unbelievers, give strength to the weak, health to the sick, rest to the weary and to make the world a better place in which to live because the message of Christ has been proclaimed. We pray these things in Jesus' name. Amen.

Introduction. The life of Jesus was filled with interesting and meaningful incidents. The gospel of John says "there are also many other things which Jesus did, the which, if they should be written every one, I suppose that even the world itself could not contain the books that should be written" (John 21:25). In a series of messages on the life of Jesus, therefore, it is necessary to be selective in the material.

The last week of Jesus' life was spent in and around the city of Jerusalem. He made His headquarters in Bethany at the home of Mary, Martha and Lazarus. He made arrangements to eat the Passover in the upper room of a home. After the meal was finished, He went with His discipes to the Garden of Gethsemane for prayer.

This was a time of deep emotion for our Savior. He warned the disciples that they would be embarrassed that night because of Him. Simon Peter insisted he would never be offended because of Jesus but Jesus warned him he would deny his Master three times before the cock crew. Some of the greatest spiritual truth in the Bible is found in the Gethsemane experiences of our Lord.

I. *Jesus Had an Inner Circle.* All great leaders have a few men who are close to them. In a sense the entire twelve was Jesus' "select group" but in an even greater sense it was Peter, James and John who understood their Master best. It was these three who went with Him into the house when He raised Jairus' daughter from the dead. It was this same three who accompanied Him on the Mount of Transfiguration where they viewed Moses and Elijah and Jesus in their glorified bodies.

Often in a church it is necessary for the pastor to have "key members" who help him in a most significant way. This does not mean the pastor is playing favorites, although he may sometimes be accused of it, but it means rather that there are always certain people who are more receptive to suggestions and seem to possess keener insight into God's work. Peter, James and John were being trained for greater service. Two of them became outstanding evangelists after the Ascension of Jesus.

II. *Jesus Identified With the Sins of the World.* The Bible says that Jesus spoke of His soul as being "exceeding sorrowful, even unto death" and asked these three to stay at a certain spot and watch with Him. He had already left eight of them at a spot near the entrance to the garden. It is difficult for us to realize the burden that was on the heart of Christ. He knew the significance of the night. He knew that He would be arrested shortly and the next day He would be crucified. Nevertheless, He was more concerned about His followers than He was about Himself. He had already said to them earlier, "Let not your heart be troubled" (John 14:1). There is a great lesson for us. When we think constantly of our own distresses, they become greater. The best way to forget our own problems is to help others in the sharing of their burdens. The cold man warms himself in seeking to minister to another who is freezing. Likewise, our burdens disappear when we help others. Paul tells us to "Bear ye one another's burdens, and so fulfil the law of Christ" (Gal. 6:2).

III. *The Secret of It All—Go a Little Farther.* Of course, these words in Matthew's gospel refer to geographical distance. Jesus left a group of eight in one place, a group of three in another place and went deeper into the garden. Yet, we are doing no violence to the Scripture when we lift this phrase out and give it an even deeper meaning. Every part of Jesus' ministry was a "going farther" than anyone else.

A. Jesus went farther in His interpretation of the law. Many scholars have pointed out that very little in the teachings of Jesus was entirely new. Almost all of His sayings find parallels or near-parallels in the Old Testament. It was not the newness of the material but the freshness oi interpretation that made Jesus stand out as a teacher with authority. He did not merely recite the interpretations of the rabbis. He gave His own meaningful exposition of the law. He breathed a spirit into it that far surpassed anyone who had gone before him. We are not to obey in the letter of the law, according to Jesus, but in the sweetness and reasonableness of spirit. Murder is more than an act. It is an attitude. The same is true of adultery and all of the other commandments concerning man's relationship with man. It is out of the heart that the mouth speaks and from the heart come the issues of life.

B. Jesus went a little farther in His refusal to retaliate. This is true throughout all of His ministry. He recognized that God's kingdom could be extended in the hearts of people only by unselfish love. During His earthly ministry He refused to take issue with the Roman government who ruled the people at this time. He would not fulfill the popular Jewish notion of a politically-oriented Messiah by leading a revolt against the Roman establishment. He insisted we are to love our enemies, bless those that curse us and pray for the ones who despitefully use us. A few moments later, here in the Garden of Gethsemane, He demonstrated this spirit. Judas, who had already left the Twelve, came with a great multitude to take Him away for trial and later for crucifixion. Peter drew his sword and struck a servant of the high priest, but Jesus rebuked him with the warning, "they that take the sword shall perish with the sword" (Matt. 26:52).

C. Jesus went a little farther in His concern for a lost world. This was the fundamental point of Jesus' ministry! He came to be our Savior by going to the cross. From the beginning of His ministry He saw the act on Calvary by which He would redeem mankind. Every part of His earthly activity pointed to this solemn and serious hour. Jesus has left us an example of concern for the lost that should inspire full commitment to this cause. The dedication of our Lord calls forth for our own dedication to live lives that are devoted in discipline in order that we may lead others to the Savior.

The winning of lost people is not an elective in the Christian's curriculum. It is a required course. The Lord's one purpose in His ministry was to find people and win them to Himself. No sacrifice was too great for Him and nothing should stand in our way of making soul-winning the first priority in daily living. We should take advantage of every contact and indeed, should seek to make contacts that will give us opportunity to give testimony to the lost. It is only as Christians are willing to follow the Master's example of going "a little farther" in this area that our rapidly deteriorating world can find redemption and salvation from the ills that threaten our extinction.

Conclusion. How far do you go? It is those who go farther in every category of life that make the great contributions to humanity. Those laboring in the scientific laboratory go far beyond the point of duty. The business executive who arrives at his office early to chart the work for the day long before the "paid staff" come in is the one who builds a great organization. The teacher who spends extra time with the child who is backward in order to bring him up to a normal level or spends extra time with the exceptionally talented child in order to make him a leader is the one who is truly great in his field. The joys of life are present for the person who gives himself beyond measure. The one who lives merely by the "what do I *have* to do" rule never finds real fulfillment. When Phillips Brooks, the great New England clergyman, was being buried someone said to his brother, "If Dr. Brooks had just held himself back and not pushed himself so hard, he might have lived longer." His brother replied, "Yes, but if he had done that, he wouldn't have been Phillips Brooks." This does not mean that we ought to "burn out" prematurely, but it does mean that those who make great contributions in life are those who are willing to go far beyond the normal call of what "ought to be done" and see rather what "should be done" if the godly causes in this world come to fruition.

SUNDAY EVENING, MARCH 24

TITLE: "The Forgiving Father"

TEXT: "It was meet that we should make merry, and be glad; for this thy brother was dead, and is alive again; and was lost, and is found" (Luke 15:32).

SCRIPTURE READING: Luke 15.

Introduction. Luke records four parables of Jesus in the fifteenth chapter of Luke. These parables tell about a lost animal, lost money, and two lost sons; but, they are primarily speaking about the seeker who turns out to be God. For instance, the parable is not about a prodigal son but about the forgiving Father.

I. *The Four Parables Speak of God the Father.*

A. The lost sheep. Jesus' parable about the lost sheep is very unusual. It seems somewhat dangerous that the shepherd would leave ninety-nine sheep in the wilderness while going after one sheep which had strayed away. However, this is the nature of shepherds who feel responsible for the sheep. Upon finding the sheep there is a period of rejoicing by the shepherd and his neighbors. The parable teaches that there is joy in heaven when a sinner repents and is brought back to the fold of God.

The lost sheep, with no sense of direction, is completely helpless while he is lost. Nevertheless, in spite of his innocence in straying and his helplessness in being lost, he is in great danger until someone finds him. This parable speaks of the nature of God who goes seeking after His lost creatures and rejoices upon restoring them to the fold. It also implies something of our missionary task in the Church, that of seeking the lost for God.

B. The lost coin. The coin was lost by the carelessness of someone else. However, it is just as lost as if it bore responsibility for its own condition. It can do nothing until someone looks for it. It may be that many people are lost because of the carelessness of someone else; it is definite that many people can be saved only when someone else begins searching for them.

This little story portrays the nature of God as One who goes searching for the lost until He finds him and then rejoices over one sinner who repents.

C. The lost son. The prodigal son was lost by his own choice. He demonstrates disobedience, disrespect, and willful turning from God. He exhibits the waste of his talents and resources, the dissipation of his family name and respect, the shame of sinful existence, and the desperation of being lost. He also comes to know the betrayal of his sinful friends, but he remembers the nature of his father and is thereby motivated to return.

The father is the main character of the story. He is portrayed both in strength and love. He waits, understands, receives the son, forgets the wrong, restores and rejoices over the return of a wayward son.

D. The older brother. The older brother was lost, too. But he didn't know it. Actually, he was farther from his father than the prodigal son who journeyed to a distant land. Nevertheless, he deluded himself with external evidence in his futile attempt to prove his faithfulness to the father. Adjacency is not the same as companionship. The older brother was unwilling to forgive his younger brother. He showed his lack of filial loyalty in that he would not rejoice with the father at having another opportunity to make a man out of the younger son.

The older brother represented the critics of Jesus on this occasion who considered themselves the elect of God, but who were very unforgiving toward the sinners about them. It is also possible that this parable may indicate to us that the forgiveness of God does not mean that the personal relationships fractured by our sins are automatically and immediately mended.

These parables teach clearly the nature of God as heavenly forgiving Father. They portray that men may be lost in various ways, but they are saved only when someone searches for them or motivates their return to God. The parables teach that God cares for His own and searches for them. They teach that God freely forgives and restores sinful men when they do return. They portray the great joy in heaven when sinners repent.

II. *The Father Forgives Our Sins.*

A. Forgiveness is personal. In Biblical faith sin is a personal act against God and sins are personal acts against other human beings. The result is estrangement from the person against whom the sin is committed. Forgiveness is the personal act of removing that sin and restoring the broken relationship.

Consequently, forgiveness must never be thought of as a legal transaction. It is not a bargain, a truce, or a settlement. It is rather a personal act which involves the will and the feelings of a person toward another. The judge on the bench may exercise leniency within the guidelines spelled out by the law, but he does not forgive the criminal. The criminal has not sinned against the judge. There is no personal relationship broken or to be mended between the criminal and the judge. The judge represents the law and the court. This is an entirely different situation from that which we know in forgiveness.

B. Forgiveness removes the barrier of sin. It is not easy to say how forgiveness does this. The sin becomes a reality and is like a barrier between the persons involved. With time the barrier appears to get larger. In most instances, one cannot return to undo the damage done by sin. Time moves on. Consequently the only way to destroy this barrier is to will it out of existence. In short, a person can decide that it will no longer remain as a barrier between him and another. He wipes it out; he destroys it; he forgets it. This is precisely what God does with reference to our sins.

C. Forgiveness is reconciliation. Sin separated men from God and men from men. Forgiveness brings them back together. Forgiveness reestablishes the harmony that was broken. It is always an extremely personal and human act. It is reconciliation. This is one of the most beautiful New Testament words for salvation. It portrays salvation not as something one gets; rather, it portrays salvation as a relationship with God into which one enters by faith in Jesus Christ. Forgiveness in the New Testament always includes the reconciliation of the parties involved. It can never be reduced to a decision to tolerate or endure.

D. Forgiveness is restoration. When the prodigal son returned home, the father restored him to his original place as a son and as a member of the family. Sin had disrupted all of that. In sin man falls from God and is cast out of Eden.

In forgiveness man is restored to God and is restored to the relationship he lost.

Men are tempted to see forgiveness in terms of less than full restoration. We should guard against this compromise. Forgiveness is not probation; it is restoration.

III. *The Father's Forgiveness Is Free But Costly.*

A. God forgives us freely. The New Testament abounds with reminders that our salvation is a gift of God. It is the result of His grace freely given. Sinners stand before God with empty hands; they have nothing to bring to Him with which to secure the forgiveness of their sins.

In most instances there is nothing we can do to undo the damage caused by our sins. Our evil deeds have happened; they are irrevocable. They go on having their influence long after we have ceased to remember them. It is unthinkable that we could repay the damage or that we could undo the wrong which we have done. Forgiveness is the gracious act of God in which He freely erases the records of our sins and gives us a new start in life without a mortgage.

B. But forgiveness involves the cost of the cross. Salvation was not free to God; it cost the life of Jesus Christ His Son. Somehow in the mystery of God only in the cross do we see our sin in all of its evil and God's grace in all its majesty. At the foot of the cross we meet God. In our rejoicing at the greatness of His redemption let us not be ungrateful for the tremendous price that Jesus Christ paid for our reconciliation.

C. Forgiveness may not remove all the costs of our sin. The prodigal son squandered a fortune; he disgraced the family name; he violated his own conscience; the cost of his acts may not be recovered. Sin always comes at a very high price and continues to collect compound interest from those who engage in it. The prodigal son may well rejoice in the freeness of God's forgiveness; however, he may not be able to reclaim the years which the locusts have eaten.

D. His forgiveness may not recover the cost of personal injury to others. Many people who know God's forgiveness of their sins cannot understand why other people will not so readily forgive them. Admittedly, we should forgive others when they repent, but actually many people will not do so. The sinner, although he enjoys the forgiveness of God, must often live with the lack of forgiveness from those against whom he has sinned.

The older brother is a glaring example of the cost of the younger brother's sin. The older brother will not accept him back as freely as did the father. Now, he must live with the ill-will from the brother against whom he sinned. In time perhaps the older brother may forgive him as genuinely as the father did; in the meantime, the younger brother will be painfully aware of the cost of his sin.

Conclusion. The Christian faith proclaims a message of forgiveness to the entire world. On the basis of Jesus Christ's life, death, and resurrection, we extend to you this day the promise of forgiveness. He has authorized us to offer you free forgiveness for your sins. There is no need for you to carry your sins any longer or any further; God will forgive you; He will remove the burden from your back. God is anxious to forgive your sin just as the father is anxious to forgive his son and have him back at home. God will not charge you for forgiveness; but remember that your sin goes on exacting a dreadful price for each day you exist within it.

WEDNESDAY EVENING, MARCH 27

TITLE: "The Bible Speaks to Our Condition"

SCRIPTURE READING: John 18.

Introduction. When we try to let God speak to us through John 18, we need to be aware that this chapter describes the events which took place on the night before our Lord's crucifixion. It is an awesome experience to solemnly read of our Master's march toward His cross. With humility, with sorrow, with joy, with gratitude, we should contemplate the spirit of sacrifice that possessed our Savior as He came to these moments in His life.

This is a chapter characterized by an unusual number of great questions.

I. *The Questions of Jesus.*

A. A question repeated to the soldiers (18:4, 7).

B. A question directed to Peter (18:11).

C. A question to the high priest (18:19-21).

D. A question directed to the servant of the high priest (18:23).

E. A question directed to Pilate (18:34).

II. *The Questions Directed Toward Peter.*

A. The question of a maid at the door (18:17).

B. The question of one standing by the fire (18:25).

C. The question of the servant of the high priest (18:26).

III. *The Questions of Pilate.*

A. A question to the Jewish officials (18:29).

B. A question concerning Jesus' kingship (18:33).

C. A sarcastic question (18:35a).

D. A pointed question to Jesus (18:35b).

E. A searching question directed to Jesus (18:37).

F. A very important question (18:38).

G. A question to the angry mob that was seeking to crucify Jesus (18:39).

Conclusion. One cannot read this chapter without being impressed with the calm, compassionate courage of our Lord Jesus as He approached the hour when He was to suffer for our sins. It would appear that instead of our Lord being on trial, Annas, Caiaphas and Pilate, the Jewish and Roman officials, were the ones really on trial. Our Lord was determined to register the degree of God's great love for sinners and succeeded beyond power of words to describe.

This chapter contains the record of Peter's threefold denial of a knowledge of the Lord. Perhaps he was frightened. Perhaps he was hoping to rescue his Lord. Our Lord knew of Peter's peril and had predicted Peter's disgraceful denials (John 13:36-38). Our Lord was to give Peter a threefold opportunity to reaffirm his love following His resurrection (John 21:15-17).

We face the peril of following in the train of Peter's denial. If we live an unworthy life and claim to be a disciple of our Lord, we are denying the power of His presence in our life. We deny Him when we are unfaithful to the highest and to the best to which the divine Spirit calls us. We deny a transforming experience with Him when we remain silent in the midst of men's need for the Good News. We deny Him when we do not give ourselves in positive obedience to the Great Commission.

As the Lord forgave Peter and utilized Him, so the Lord wants to forgive us and utilize us as a blessing to others.

TITLE: "Jesus Did God's Will"

TEXT: "Thy will be done" (Matt. 26:42).

SCRIPTURE READING: Matthew 26:36-46.

HYMNS: "I Am Resolved," Hartsough. "Make Me a Channel of Blessing," Smyth. "Wherever He Leads I'll Go," McKinney.

OFFERTORY PRAYER:

Our Father, we know there is much to be done in this world for Thee. We know that we can never do it all, and yet we are grateful we can do some of these things. We would like to be able to do more. There are many places we cannot go individually. We are grateful that through our gifts of money we can go other places to tell Thy message. Help us to see beyond the four walls of our own church building. May we see the world and all of its need. Help us to be always conscious of Thy all-inclusive love for all men everywhere. Help us to remember the words of our Lord who said, "It is more blessed to give than to receive." Forgive us when we are more concerned with the fact of getting than the act of giving. Help us to lay up treasures in heaven where moth and rust cannot corrupt. Take these gifts that we bring to Thee. We offer them with love and gratitude. We pray these things in Jesus' name and for His sake. Amen.

Introduction. The life of Jesus is now in the shadow of the cross. The purpose for which He came is now squarely before Him. A decision must be made. Thus far, Jesus has met every test and emerged victoriously. The Tempter has endeavored in vain to dissuade Him from His task. Yet, the biggest test of all is immediately before Him.

It is impossible for us, as human beings, to understand the great soul agony of Jesus that night in Gethsemane. He had no sin in Him but, as He prayed in the garden He felt the pressure of all the world's sin upon Him. Because of His divine nature, He could foresee all of the things that awaited Him on the cross. Yet, because of His human nature, He sought an escape. Was there an escape? Was there any other way for God to redeem the world? If so, what was it? Jesus prayed, "If this cup may not pass from me, except I drink it, thy will be done." The divine plan for redeeming the world was formulated before the world was created. Peter speaks of our redemption and then refers to our Redeemer, "Who verily was foreordained before the foundation of the world" (1 Pet. 1:20). The implied answer to the Gethsemane prayer was that Jesus must fulfill God's plan by going to the cross. There was no alternative.

I. *God Had a Will for Jesus—and He Has a Will for Every Life.* As the babe lay in Bethlehem, God had already mapped out His life. Jesus kept before Himself constantly the Father's will. When His parents rebuked Him, at the age of twelve, for staying behind and talking with the religious leaders in the Temple, His reply to them revealed His dedication to God's purpose for Him. He said, "wist ye not that I must be about my Father's business?" (Luke 2:49).

Likewise, God has a plan for each individual life. If not a single sparrow is forgotten before God, much more does He know each of us by name and has a plan for every life. John Wesley once said, "To find God's will is man's greatest discovery and to do God's will is man's greatest achievement." God even uses those outside His divine family to accomplish His redemptive purposes. When the Jewish nation was in Babylonian exile God turned to a pagan ruler and laid upon his heart His purposes for His chosen people. As a result, Cyrus issued a decree that the Jews could return to their homeland. God thus used one who knew Him not to accomplish His purpose. One of our great preachers preached a great sermon on "Every Life a Plan of God" based on the words of the Old Testament prophet, "I will gird *and* arm you though you have not known Me" (Isaiah 45:5 *Amplified Bible*).

II. *Man Can Pervert the Purposes of God.* Although God is sovereign, man has a free will. It is possible, therefore, for man, finite though he is, to shake his fist in the face of Almighty God and say, "I will not do that which is Your plan for me." History is filled with nations who have ignored the moral laws of God and plunged over the precipice into catastrophe. Men with great potential for making major contributions to civilization have chosen to rebel against the purposes of God and have ended up on the rocky shores of frustration and misery. Could Jesus have rebelled against God at the last moment and refused to go to the cross? Another question is parallel to it. Could Jesus have yielded to the tempter at the begin-

ning of His ministry? The answer to both questions must be "yes" for Jesus had a completely human nature as well as a completely divine one.

What about our temptations to pervert God's purposes for us? Are there safeguards we can set up to help us avoid the pitfalls of disobedience? One of the best ways to guarantee that we shall fulfill God's purposes for us is to remain close to Him in daily fellowship and thus find infinite resources available for the doing of His will. It is not easy! There are many things to pull us away from dedicated devotion. The pressures of this world, as well as our personal ambitions, seek to alienate us from a spiritual approach to life. When we allow these things to overcome us we find the beautiful possibilities of life can become twisted and defeat will be imminent.

III. *How Can We Know God's Will?* Although the first requirement for doing God's will is to want to do it, there is a great need for guidelines to help the sincere Christian evaluate in day to day living the impressions he receives concerning God's will for his life. There is an *intentional* will of God. He desires that all men be happy. Yet, we are thrown into life situations which are influenced by the presence of sin in the world. These circumstances force us many times to make adjustments. We need to distinguish between God's *intentional purpose* and God's *circumstantial will* because of human conditions which are brought about by the sins of society. We cannot tell a woman whose son has been hit by a drunken driver that this was the "will of God" that her son die and she must accept it.

Drunken driving has nothing to do with the will of God. This young man was caught in a circumstance which was beyond his control and he suffered for it. We are guilty many times of glibly saying this is "God's will" when we should examine the situation further. We receive many good things in life because good men before us have been dedicated in some field of research. Likewise, we will receive many evil things in life because evil men have lived and set into motion the law of sin and retribution for society. We are bound together in a bundle of life and we cannot ignore the implications of living in tight knit circumstances.

Are there not, however, aids for our own individual choices concerning God's will? To be sure, there are. Much has been written on the subject. Some have pointed out that conscience helps us. It does indeed but it is never an infallible guide. We should listen to our conscience but be careful not to be deceived by an untrained conscience in the hands of a rationalizing sinner. Others have suggested a lowly signpost that we call "common sense." Others have suggested we counsel with friends and heed closely their advice. We can use the mind and wisdom of others as we read it in great literature. We can listen to the voice of the Church and its feelings about matters. The Quakers have spoken of the inner light which is probably another way of saying "be led by the Holy Spirit." One of the most meaningful illustrations, however, that has ever come is the one of the man who was bringing the ship into harbor. A passenger asked him how he was able to be certain he would bring it into port correctly. He pointed to three guiding lights and said to the passenger, "When I line this ship up according to these three lights I know she's in perfect shape."

Conclusion. In seeking for a practical application, we should recognize that God's will should be considered in a twofold manner. First, we should ask ourselves the question, what should be the plan of my life with reference to God's will concerning long-range goals. Every life should have ideals and plans for the future. The person who has projected himself as to what he wants to be and do with his entire life is one who will be happy and much less liable to waste time in either immoral living or superficial living. On the other hand, we need to be asking ourself each day concerning God's will for us each moment. Of course, the cumulative total of our actions day by day will result in our accomplishing or failing to realize God's will for our entire life.

It is not easy to know God's will because God's will is not a static thing. It is progressive and often flexible. We should meet each day with the determination that we will approach every event in the light of what we feel Jesus would have us do. We must not be conformed to the will of worldly people, but we should rather be transformed as our lives are hid with God in Christ. In this way we can both find and do His good and perfect will.

TITLE: Forgiveness: the Goal of Church Discipline"

TEXT: "Moreover if thy brother shall trespass . . ." (Matt. 18: 15).

SCRIPTURE READING: Matthew 18:7-22.

Introduction. Modern churches do not usually exercise church discipline as churches in the past have done. At least this is true in the formal sense of the term "church discipline." However, it is probable that modern Christians do exercise more informal discipline over one another than most of us realize; and probably, this is the best kind of church discipline after all. Informal discipline may limit knowledge of the offense to the smallest number of persons possible thereby minimizing the damage and the needless talk about the event. However, there may still be occasions in which church congregations must exercise discipline over their members.

I. *A Definition of Forgiveness.* In Biblical teaching there are two emphases in the term forgiveness: (1) the removal of the barrier of sin; and (2) the restoration of fellowship. The offense committed forms a barrier between man and God and between two men thereby alienating the two. Forgiveness is the gracious act which removes that barrier and restores the fellowship of the persons involved.

In the Old Testament, sin is against God. Consequently, only God can forgive sin. Sin may be a transgression against God, disobedience to God's law, unbelief, rebellion, etc. Sin becomes a kind of reality standing between man and God. To forgive it means (1) to send it away, (2) to lift it up as one would lift a burden, (3) to cover sin, or (4) to blot it out.

In all of these instances sin becomes a barrier which stands in the way of fellowship and, like a stain, demands cleansing or removing. Forgiveness is the act of God which removes it or blots it out.

In the New Testament there are some distinctively new ideas about forgiveness. Jesus forgave sins "in his own name" thereby incurring the charge of blasphemy since only God forgives sin. Jesus taught that men can not know the forgiveness of God unless they are willing to forgive other men. Evidently, one who is not sensitive enough to understand the suffering in the conscience of the sinner is not able to accept God's forgiveness. Jesus taught that repentance precedes forgiveness as in the case of the Pharisee and the Publican. When asked how often a man must forgive, Jesus responded that a man must forgive seventy times seven times. One of the clearest insights in the New Testament regarding forgiveness is that it is a personal act, never a legal act.

II. *Three New Testament Passages Dealing With Church Discipline and Forgiveness.*

A. When the church is called on to settle personal disputes (Matt. 18:15-22).

When Jesus instructed His disciples about settling disputes between brothers, He first advised the offended party to take the initiative and go to the offender in a personal attempt to solve the problem. Jesus said, "If he listens to you, you have gained your brother." It should be noted that this method limits the knowledge, and, consequently, the damage of the offense to the smallest number of persons. If the two men are reconciled at this point, there is no reason for anyone else to know about the problem.

If the first step fails, Jesus advised the Christian to take two or more brothers with him and try again to talk to the offending brother. This method accomplishes three things: it provides witnesses who will know exactly what was said and be able to overcome the subjective prejudice of the two members; it will therefore offer a better opportunity for settling the original problem; it still limits the knowledge of the problem to a small circle of people.

When both attempts have failed, Jesus counseled His followers to tell it to the church. There are several implications in this action. The action assumes that both men are members of the church and that their membership means something to them. It also implies that the church, like a family, is involved when two of its members are at outs with each other. It seems to imply that the congregation will care enough to want to settle the problem thereby redeeming both persons involved and the fellowship of the congregation. It should be noted, however, that reporting personal difficulties to the church is a last resort; this is done after all other attempts have failed.

When reconciliation is not achieved even in the context of a church hearing, Jesus advised that the church should regard the offender as an "outsider." This implies that in the teaching of Jesus, there is no notion that the church would do any kind of punishing. The most severe action is to regard the offender as outside the fellowship.

It is highly significant that Jesus, after stressing the importance of men's action on earth and in the church, which has the power of binding or loosing in heaven, went on immediately to answer Peter's question about forgiveness. Peter asked, "Lord how oft shall my brother sin against me, and I forgive him? till seven times?" Jesus responded, "I say not unto thee, until seven times: but until seventy times seven" (Matt. 18:21, 22).

This brief paragraph establishes at least two major Christian emphases: (1) the whole point of personal and congregational efforts to deal with those guilty of offending is that they be forgiven; (2) and, the church must never set a limit on how many times a person will be forgiven. He will be forgiven as often as he asks to be forgiven even to the point of "seventy times seven" times.

B. Church discipline in the case of immorality (1 Cor. 5:1-5). In this passage Paul wrote to the Corinthian church about the case of serious immorality among them. He did not give details regarding the efforts which had been made in the past to correct the wrong of this man who was guilty of incest. The implication is that these efforts had been made and had failed. Paul recommended that this person be removed from the church.

Paul suggested that the church in assembly should take official action which would exclude the man from formal membership in the body. He used language which is strange to us when he said, "You are to deliver this man to Satan." This should not be understood to imply that Satan is some kind of agent for God, or that

Christians in a sense use him as a sort of prosecuting attorney or prison warden. Instead, Paul alludes to the Christian conviction that within the fellowship of the Church, one enjoys the protection of God, the fellowship of the Holy Spirit, and the prayer and the encouragement of fellow Christians. In this context, one can be secure from the destructive power of sin. However, if the Christian is separated from this setting, he will be overcome by sin. In other words, out in the realm of Satan he has no protection and no defense. But the purpose of this action, according to Paul, is that the man, "may be saved in the day of the Lord Jesus."

It is highly important that in this instance of the worst kind of immorality, exclusion is the most serious act of the Church, and the purpose of that act is that the offending man will eventually be brought to the awareness of his sin so that he can be saved or forgiven.

C. Forgiveness must follow punishment (2 Cor. 2:5-11). Paul writes here about some brother in the church in Corinth who has committed a serious act which is both against Paul and the church. While no details are given, we would assume that he has done something which has undermined or attacked Paul and has in the process disrupted or divided the congregation. It would be unwise to speculate as to what this is or to give illustrations from modern times. However, in this instance, the church has taken some kind of formal or official action against this person. Paul referred to it as "punishment by the majority."

The most significant theme in this passage is that Paul advises that their punishment or censure is "enough." Then he said, "You should rather turn to forgive and comfort him, or he may be overwhelmed by excessive sorrow. So I beg you to reaffirm your love for him" (2 Cor. 2:6-8, RSV).

This entire passage deals almost exclusively with the Christian theme that the person guilty of offending the church should be forgiven and that the sole purpose for any action against him is that he be brought to forgiveness. Paul wisely enjoins the congregation to forgive him quickly lest he be driven into depression as a result of the action against him.

A great deal of injury is done to persons when they are left in their guilt and in punishment for a long period of time. When parents use discipline on their children, they are wise if they limit the punishment to a very short period of time and then fully restore the children to the family fellowship. Exclusion or rejection of a person from the family is a very severe punishment which is usually attended by the deterioration of the person. The church family may be required to take action against its members on occasion, but it is "Christian action" only if its eventual purpose is to bring about the reconciliation of the person involved.

Conclusion. Just as Jesus Christ came to reconcile sinful men to God, so He left His Church as a reconciling agent in the world. He has entrusted to us "the message of reconciliation" (2 Cor. 5:19).

The Church is made up of those who have been forgiven by God. They have learned the meaning of forgiveness and they forgive one another. The Church as such is in the business of forgiving. All around the Church there are individuals and families estranged from each other desperately needing help in the achievement of forgiveness. The Church knows best how to do this and should be diligent in the practice.

The passages which we have studied clearly lay out a number of lessons for Christians to follow.

To care for other persons and deal with their offenses is not necessarily meddling. It takes a great deal of courage and concern for a Christian to go to another person who has offended him and attempt to settle that problem before it becomes serious. The passages indicate that if an individual or small group will go to the offending person at an early stage, they may save him and prevent him from going deeper into the wrong thereby hurting himself and others. These passages suggest that knowledge of personal difficulties should be restricted to the smallest number of persons possible. Confession of sin is the honest acknowledgement of it to the person or persons against whom the act is done. Disclosure of such information beyond this circle is not confession but publicity.

These passages do indicate that the Christian has responsibility for his brother and on occasion must do the very difficult task of going to one who is an offender and seeking to solve a serious problem. It may seem unfair that the offended person must take the initiative, but in reality, he is more able to take up the problem because of his sensitivity to the wrong. Also, it is just possible that the offender is not aware that he has offended. The most important single emphasis of these passages is that the Church may have to exercise discipline over its members, but when it does, it must do so with the goal of reconciling the person or persons involved.

". . . and be kind to one another, tenderhearted, forgiving one another, as God in Christ forgave you" (Eph. 4:32, RSV).

SUGGESTED PREACHING PROGRAM FOR THE MONTH OF APRIL

Sunday Mornings

Conclude the series on "The Life and Works of the Lord Jesus." The month of April provides an excellent opportunity for preaching the Gospel in all of its grace and glory.

Sunday Evenings

There is always a need to improve the quality of our worship experiences. The pastor is a leader of worship. Our people need to worship in Spirit and in truth. The suggested theme is "Making Our Worship More Meaningful."

Wednesday Evenings

Continue with the series, "The Bible Speaks to Our Condition."

The theme verse for the month is "Thy word is a lamp unto my feet, and a light unto my path" (Ps. 119: 105).

TITLE: "The Bible Speaks to Our Condition"

SCRIPTURE READING: Acts 4.

Introduction. The chapter which serves as a basis for our Bible study today will provide us with light for the road ahead. In the first verses we find the apostles being obedient to the Great Commission in the manner in which our Lord intended that all of us should be obedient. In their going about from place to place, they were sharing their information and their experience of what Jesus Christ meant to them. They had not internationalized or professionalized the Great Commission. They simply went about talking to people about the Lord Jesus.

I. *Filled With the Spirit* (4:8). To be filled with the Spirit means to be aware of His indwelling presence and to be committed fully to His guidance and leadership. It means to consciously be dependent upon Him for wisdom, knowledge, guidance and spiritual vitality which is necessary for the doing of God's work. All of us are commanded to "be filled with the Spirit" (Eph. 5:18). To neglect or to refuse to be filled with the Spirit is to be disobedient to the will of God for our lives.

II. *The Only Way of Salvation* (4:12). In dramatic words which would bear memorization, the apostles declared that Jesus Christ is the only way to salvation. This salvation is more than a ticket to heaven. It provides forgiveness from the penalty of sin which is death. It offers power for the living of a victorious life in the present. It promises deliverance from the very presence of evil in the future. This salvation can be experienced only through our Lord Jesus.

This declaration from the lips of Peter should challenge each of us to recognize the world's desperate need for Jesus Christ. By virtue of the fact that we know Christ, we are under obligation to share Him with all of those in our individual personal world.

III. *The Command to Be Silent* (4:18-23). In these words we have a clear command from the religious and political authorities of that day to the apostles that they be silent rather than talkative concerning Jesus Christ. Our Lord had commanded them to be His witnesses, testifiers, testators.

Most of us are guilty of the terrible crime of being silent concerning the Lord even though we have received no commandment to be silent. Our command is that we be talkative about Him and that we communicate with others concerning what Christ means to us.

How would we react if the political authorities commanded us to say absolutely nothing about our Lord? Would we be intimidated, and would we be obedient to them? Or would we react as did the apostles and continue to speak boldly in the name of our Lord?

These early Christians had an inner compulsion to give their Christian testimony which they refused to repress. May God grant to each of us such an inner compulsion to oral confession of our experiences with Jesus Christ.

IV. *The Open Door of Prayer* (4:24-31). In times of difficulty and need the early Christians entered the throne room of the Father

105

God that they might obtain mercy and find grace for help in every time of need. It is interesting to note that in this experience of prayer they quoted to their own hearts the great promises of God's Word and claimed the promises of God as they presented their needs before the throne of grace of their heavenly Father.

Instead of praying for release from the command to be witnesses, they prayed that God would grant to them greater boldness with which to speak in the name of the Lord. Their prayer was heard and God answered by granting their requests.

V. *Great Fellowship* (4:32-37). The fellowship one with another and the fellowship that they experienced with God was unparalleled and is indescribable in human terminology. The Holy Spirit filled them with His presence and power. They were united in heart and soul. They were overwhelmed with a spirit of generosity that caused them to share with and to meet the needs of others. They were unusually effective in communicating the message of God's grace as they had experienced it in Jesus Christ.

Conclusion. Let us pray that God will overwhelm us with the wonders of our great salvation. Let us pray for a new awareness of the presence of the Holy Spirit within our heart, and may we be more responsive to Him. Let us pray for an inner compulsion to share the good news of God's love with those about us. As we do so, others will come to know our Savior as we know Him, and our joy will be like the joy of these early followers of our Lord.

SUNDAY MORNING, APRIL 7 (Palm Sunday)

TITLE: "Jesus Died for Our Sins"

TEXT: "God commendeth his love toward us, in that, while we were yet sinners, Christ died for us" (Rom. 5:8).

SCRIPTURE READING: Matthew 27:33-50.

HYMNS: "Glory to His Name," Hoffman. "Beneath the Cross of Jesus," Clephane. "Near the Cross," Crosby.

OFFERTORY PRAYER:

Our Father, we recognize Thee as the Eternal One. Thou hast been our dwelling place in all generations. As we bring our offerings this morning, we pray for all who shall be supported by these gifts. Bless the work of this local church. Bless the causes we support in ,the larger ministries of God's kingdom. We thank Thee for Thy blessings which are so numerous they cannot be numbered. We bring these gifts with joy and thank Thee for the privilege of sharing in the witness of the Gospel. We pray these things in Jesus' name and for His sake. Amen.

Introduction. When we come to deal with the crucifixion we are at the heart of the Gospel. The Old Testament symbolized the death of Christ in many ways. All of the predictions and types converged and found fulfillment on that day when Jesus hung for six hours on the cross. The events leading up to Christ's death are all filled with emotion, but it is when the Lamb of God becomes the substitute for man that we stand speechless before the infinite grace of God.

It is the general verdict of scholarship that Jesus was crucified on Passover Day. He had eaten the supper with His disciples the preceding night. They had prayed in the garden. Jesus was arrested, and before 9 A.M. the next morning He had been tried six times—three times before a Jewish group and three times before a Roman court. He refused to speak in His behalf. False witnesses were hired against Him. He was treated shamefully. There were many illegal acts performed in connection with His trials. They placed on Him a crown of thorns and spat upon Him. At His crucifixion they parted His garments and gambled for them. They put Him on a cross and crucified Him between two thieves. All of these events show the mockery and ridicule as well as the downright insults that accompanied His crucifixion.

Yet God was at work! That which the Satanic forces of wickedness did in an attempt to eliminate Jesus of Nazareth was the one act that God used to bring redemption to the world. No one has ever completely understood the cross and its meaning. No one illustration can gather up within it all of the truths contained in the redemptive message of Christ that was made reality through the Atonement. If the cross were not too broad for human comprehension, it would be too narrow to meet human need. God is above man and, therefore, His thoughts are above man. Yet, when we come to the cross in faith saying, "I am a sinner but I fling myself upon the mercy of God as revealed in the death of His Son," then a miracle happens within our life. Paul called it "being saved" and Jesus spoke of it as being "born again" while many other metaphors and similes are used throughout the New Testament to describe the wonderful thing that happens when a sinful man comes face to face with himself and his God in the saving work of Jesus Christ. Although we cannot explain the cross completely, we can analyze it prayerfully.

I. *The Man of the Cross.* Jesus was a man. He was more than man but He was a man. He was the best man who ever lived. He was the only man who was born of a virgin and conceived by the Holy Spirit. Those who knew Him in the flesh testified concerning His true nature. At Caesarea Philippi, Simon Peter called Him, "the Christ, the Son of the living God" (Matt. 16:16). John the Baptist testified, "Behold the Lamb of God, which taketh away the sin of the world" (John 1:29). After the resurrection, Thomas exclaimed, "My Lord and my God" (John 20:28). History is filled with the testimony of men who, though they lived after Him, have felt the full impact of His mission to the world and have joined those who knew Him in the flesh in proclaiming, not merely His greatness as a man, but His unique deity and His co-equality with the Father.

II. *The Maker of the Cross.* Who was responsible for the death of Jesus? If we were to look at the matter from merely a human standpoint, we might say the Roman soldiers who nailed Him to the cross were actually the doers of the deed. They carried out the execution orders and did a job similar to the one they had done many times before in a routine manner. If we want to go back a little farther, we might say that Pilate was the one who caused the cross for he failed to set Jesus free when the evidence clearly indicated there was no guilt. He took a bowl of water and washed his hands declaring that he was innocent of the blood of "this just person." If we wish to go back still further, we can blame the Jewish people for, in reality, they were the ones who brought about the act. They delivered Him because of envy. Jesus refused to accept their type of religion—a legalistic code of obedience to externals with little or no spirit and far less human compassion. Even further back we might blame Judas. He identified Jesus in the garden in order that the Roman soldiers might arrest Him.

Yet, all of these are superficial ways of placing the blame. The death of Jesus was more than another death of another man. This was an event that had been in the mind of God from the creation of the world. All of God's dealings with man had pointed toward it. This was the Lord's doing! It was necessary that Christ die in order that God's redemptive program be consummated.

What made redemption a necessity? It was the sinfulness of man. There are many Scriptures which "prove" that man is a sinner. Man, however, is not convinced of his sinfulness through logic or proof. It is when the Holy Spirit convicts him through the use of the written Word

that man realizes his sinfulness before a holy God. Man is a sinner, both by nature and by practice, and he can never be good enough to save himself. It was man's sin that drove Jesus to the cross. The poet says:

'Twas I that shed the sacred blood
I nailed Him to the tree
I crucified the Christ of God
I joined the mockery.

Of all that shouting multitude
I feel that I am one
And in that din of voices rude
I recognize my own.

III. *The Mercy of the Cross.* It is on Calvary at the death of Jesus that we see the heart of God as no other place in the Bible. Christ poured out His soul as an offering for our sin when He gave His life. His life was not taken away from Him. He gave it. He made it very clear while in the days of His flesh that He laid down His life of His own free will. In the Garden of Gethsemane He said to Peter that He could pray to the Father and more than twelve legions of angels would come to His rescue. The reason He offered no resistance to His arrest and crucifixion was because of His great love for sinful humanity.

A lost man does not need justice. He needs mercy. If God dealt with us on the basis of justice, all men would be lost. Our salvation is all of grace because God loves the undeserving. Grace has been defined as the free and undeserved mercy of God.

IV. *The Message of the Cross.* There is a twofold call that comes from Calvary. To the one who has never repented of his sin and trusted in Jesus for salvation, the message is to receive Christ as personal Savior. When Jesus died on the cross God put the sin of every individual on the back of Jesus. He suffered all that the sinner deserves to suffer throughout eternity. Because He was God in the flesh, He had infinite ability to suffer everything that man deserves to suffer. The cross of Jesus calls for repentance of sin and complete trust in Jesus as personal Savior. One begins his life as a Christian when he has the birth from above that comes when he accepts the justification that awaits him at Calvary. In justification, man receives a new standing before God. Man is justified upon the basis of the One who has died in his place. Accompanying justification is regeneration. This is the change that takes place in the heart of man when the death of Christ on the cross moves upon his heart and the Holy Spirit makes him a new person in Jesus Christ.

For the one who has already been saved, the cross has a continuing message. We are to live constantly beneath its shadow and never forget that we are redeemed through the blood. The same blood that washed us from our sins signed us up to a life-long commitment to the Lordship of Christ. It is not enough to be saved from sin. We are saved for godly living and unselfish service. Every time we think of Calvary we should remember afresh that it is through His mercy, not through works of our own, that we are children of God.

Conclusion. Do you know the peace that comes by surrendering your will completely to God? It comes, first of all, through the initial experience of becoming a Christian. This involves denying our own merit and accepting the merit that comes through the shed blood of the One who died on the cross and rose again. Happiness comes by being a Christian. Being a Christian comes by a visit to "the old rugged cross" and finding there full pardon and complete forgiveness.

SUNDAY EVENING, APRIL 7

TITLE: "Why People Do Not Go to Church"

TEXT: "Not forsaking the assembling of ourselves together, as the manner of some is" (Heb. 10:25).

SCRIPTURE READING: Hebrews 10:23-27.

Introduction. The twentieth century has been a time marked by the resurgence of religious interest. In 1900, less than 35% of the population of the United States claimed membership in any kind of church. Today, over 63% of our citizens are members of churches. Before we get too comfortable, let me remind you that this leaves 70,000,-000 unchurched people to be won.

Despite this impressive percentage of church members, we are told that two-thirds of the members of Protestant churches are absent on any given Sunday. There has come an erosion of loyalty and faithfulness that is distressing. Church attendance is partly a habit, and church people are out of the habit.

Never did the church have such facilities for worship. Rarely does a church build with a capacity equivalent to the resident church membership. If every member decided to come one Sunday, it would create a hopeless crisis in any church. A church sanctuary is rarely filled on Sunday mornings. It is usually more than half empty on Sunday nights. More and more churches are dark and forsaken on Sunday evenings. Defeat has been acknowledged.

Religious freedom means not only the freedom to worship, but also the freedom not to worship. In early American life, the church was the center of the social life as well as the religious life in the community. The Lord's Day was observed as a holy day instead of a holiday. In Colonial times, you either went to church or you had no place to go.

Today, there are many other appeals competing for our loyalty. Sunday is a workday. In many stores, it is the busiest day of the week. Proprietors work to make money. Some employees cannot come to church services because the public demands their services on Sunday. The boat, the lakeside cabin, the professional game, the television set, the interstate highway—these all beckon to the family. The church is more and more the loser to spectacular and exciting substitutes.

A young preacher was having a hard time with his sermon. He had experienced many interruptions during the week and he was not well prepared. He perspired as he tried to rise to the occasion. The scattered congregation was half asleep. It was with relief that he came to the close of the sermon and dis-missed the people. Rushing to the door, he took his place to greet the worshipers as they left. A stranger started out. The minister gripped his hand and uttered the cliche, "Come back again." The stranger looked him in the eye, and responded with the shattering question, "Why?" Are people staying away from church because they are not helped when they come? Empty pews are a liability any way you look at them. Empty pews are a warning. They say something to us.

The absence of some people may be a compliment. When someone says, "I quit the church because they welcome people of all races," this is a tribute to the church being the church. If people stay away because the preacher is a prophet and they only desire to hear pleasing platitudes and gushing flattery about their so-called goodness, the church is not to be condemned. If the presence and power of the Holy Spirit is so intense that people stay away because they are running from God and the claims of Christ, we are not responsible.

But some people stay away who desperately need to come. There are people absent whose needs could be supplied if they regularly attended worship services in the church.

I. *Our Own Unworthy Lives.* People are watching us. If our lives reflect that our faith means little to us, these observers conclude that it will mean little to them. Some tell the truth when they say, "I'm better than some of those down at the church." I know that "being good" isn't all of it, but not being good turns off many people who need the Lord.

In his early adult life, Mahatma Gandhi found himself in South Africa on a Sunday. Although he was not a Christian, he greatly admired Jesus, and he decided to go to church. He was turned away at the church door by a white-faced, black-hearted usher who mistook him for a Negro. He vowed never to enter a Christian church again. And Gandhi had a way of keeping his vows.

II. *They Do Not Know We Care.* How can they know if we do not let them know? Some do not come because they have not been invited. If we do not care enough to invite them, we do not care very much.

Some come but do not return because we do not let them know we missed them. How far we have drifted from the Great Shepherd who missed the one sheep and who left the ninety-nine to bring him back.

III. *The Church Service Fell Short in Their Need.* Perhaps they were not made to feel welcome and wanted. We are too concerned with our own little circle of friends to widen the circle and include a stranger. Maybe the service was cold and formal. Or maybe the service was ill-prepared and disorganized. Could it be that they looked up to be fed and went away hungry? What a responsibility and privilege when people in need come to worship!

Conclusion. In the latter years of the last century, a man made a large fortune in mining operations in Montana. He decided to spend some of his money building the "ideal community." He dedicated 1,000 acres and laid out the town site. He paved the streets and laid the sewers and water lines. He developed parks and built school houses. There was a theater, a dance hall, and several saloons. Businesses were established, and homes built in neat lines.

The pet aversion of this man was the church. He had a reversionary clause written into every deed that if property were sold for religious purposes, it would revert to the original owner. Then he invited people to come. Soon 4,000 or 5,000 arrived. But there were no women school teachers. The other kind of women were plentiful. Highminded parents would not come for they did not want their children to grow up where there was no church. Within five years the bottom dropped out, and bankruptcy proceeded. The owner issued the following Manifesto:

"God knows that there is no such person as God, and my motto has always been, 'To hell with religion.' But for some fool reason which no man can fathom, I have found from experience that we cannot do business in this country on any other basis than that silly bit of sentiment which we stamp upon our coins, 'In God We Trust,' and 'we are going to build a church.'" Thus ended his ignoble experiment.

WEDNESDAY EVENING, APRIL 10

TITLE: "The Bible Speaks to Our Condition"

SCRIPTURE READING: Acts 11.

Introduction. The chapter from which we seek light for the road of life today marks a dramatic new beginning in the life and activity of the early disciples. This chapter reveals the result of what God was trying to communicate to Peter and through Peter to the church through Peter's experience with Cornelius the Gentile. The one great truth that comes through in Acts 11 is the all-inclusive nature of the love of God. Up to this point, the church has been a Jewish institution primarily. From henceforth it includes Gentiles as well as Jews.

I. *The Dissolving of Racial and Religious Prejudice* (11:1-18). To this point in the history of the Christian movement, it has been primarily a Jewish movement. Even the apostles were the children of the age in which they lived. The Jewish people had been very narrow and nationalistic and exclusive. They refrained from any contact with anyone other than the other Jewish people. They did not believe that Gentiles were included in the loving purpose of God. It took repeated efforts on the part of God to convince Peter that Gentiles were also included in God's love (Acts 10:10-16). In addition to this threefold vision, Peter heard the voice of the Spirit of God commanding Him to follow through and to go with the men who were at the gate inviting him to the house of Cornelius (Acts 10:19). It was not accidental that Peter took six witnesses with him on this trip (11:12). Jewish law required that there be at least two witnesses. Peter took three pairs of witnesses with him so that these events could be firmly established in the minds of everyone when he came back to report to the church in Jerusalem.

The gift of the Holy Spirit to the house of Cornelius convinced Peter and the witnesses with him, as well as the church in Jerusalem, that God had also granted to the Gentiles the gift of repentance and faith that brought life and immortality to the Gentiles.

II. *The Purpose of God Includes the Gentiles* (11:19-24). Following this experience in the household of Cornelius, some of the disciples went to Antioch and preached the good news to non-Jews, and they believed and were converted. This concerned the church at Jerusalem to the extent that they sent Barnabas to investigate. Barnabas was a great and good man under the control of the Spirit of God. He evaluated what God was doing and did all he could to encourage these Gentiles to trust in and to obey the Lord.

What happened in Antioch was a new departure in the redemptive program of God as far as the Jewish believers were concerned. This was to produce controversy and conflict that would lead to the great church conference later (Acts 15).

III. *Christian Conduct Results From Christian Teaching* (11:25, 26). It is interesting to note that at the end of the year of teaching activity, the disciples of our Lord were called Christians. Today we identify a new believer as a Christian instantaneously with his profession of faith. It is questionable whether we should do this. To be Christian is to be Christlike. Conversion does not instantaneously produce Christian character and Christian conduct. We probably would be more correct if we identified the new convert as a believer, as a disciple, as a child of God. The term "Christian" should be a title bestowed upon the believer when others can see the beauty of Christ in him.

IV. *The Practice of Generosity* (11: 27-30). The early Christians possessed an attitude of compassionate concern toward others who were in need. Evidently they believed as our Lord taught that more happiness was to be experienced as a result of giving than could be experienced by getting. Not because of a command, but because of compassion, they shared with those in need.

Conclusion. In the light of this chapter, let us examine our hearts to see if racial or religious prejudice is hindering our religious testimony. Are we fully aware that everyone is included in the loving purpose of God? Do we possess in our own attitudes, actions and ambitions the spirit that would cause others to call us Christian? Are we generous and gracious in ministering to the needs of others? May God the Father grant that we respond fully to the from His Word.

great truths revealed in this chapter

SUNDAY MORNING, APRIL 14 (Easter)

TITLE: "Jesus Arose With Power"

TEXT: "That I may know him, and the power of his resurrection" (Phil. 3:10).

SCRIPTURE READING: Matthew 28:1-10.

HYMNS: "Crown Him With Many Crowns," Bridges. "Christ Arose," Lowry. "He Lives," Ackley.

OFFERTORY PRAYER:

Our Father, we come on this Easter Sunday morning recognizing Thee as Lord of life. Thou art the author and finisher of our faith and we are grateful because we know that Thy first desire and purpose is to make life more abundant for all men everywhere. We are grateful that even as the discouraged, disappointed and seemingly defeated disciples were transformed by the risen Christ so we today can participate in

His triumph and find radiant hope as we walk with Him in faith. We now bring our gifts to Thee. We are grateful that Thou hast given us the ability to earn money. We count it a joy to invest in the work of Thy kingdom through the bringing of tithes and offerings. May we find deep satisfaction in obedience to Thy command of bringing all of the tithe into the storehouse. Give us eager hands and willing hearts to do more than the mere bringing of money. May we dedicate ourselves in personal service and never grow weary in well doing. We pray in Jesus' name and for His sake. Amen.

Introduction. Christianity is a supernatural religion but it has its basis firmly rooted in history. The greatest miracle of all is the Resurrection of Jesus Christ from the grave. All of our faith depends upon it. The issue is clearly drawn—either Jesus Christ arose from the dead or He did not. The Bible says He arose. The history of Christianity proves He arose. Eleven men were depressed and nearly defeated. Something completely transformed them and set them on fire with a zeal that could not be quenched. The personal experience of every born-again believer agrees with the Biblical record. Jesus Christ is alive.

I. *The Fact of His Death.* There have been attempts by skeptics to explain away the Resurrection of Jesus by contending that He never actually died. The famous "swoon theory" has, however, been repudiated even by some of the skeptics. It is rather ludicrous to think one could come from the grave weak and ill in need of medical treatment and tender care but at the same time inspire His followers so dynamically that He changed their sorrow into enthusiasm and elevated their reverence into worship. The Biblical record makes it clear that Jesus died. The soldiers broke the legs of the two thieves who were crucified with Jesus, but when they came to Jesus they found He was dead already. They, therefore, did not break His legs. There is no external evidence of any kind to indicate the scriptural account is erroneous in any way. Joseph of Arimathea begged for the body of Jesus. He took it down from the cross, wrapped it in linen and laid it in a sepulcher. Matthew tells how the Pharisees came to Pilate and asked him to be certain the sepulcher would "be made sure" to prevent His disciples from coming and stealing Him away. According to Matthew's account, this was done and thus every bit of evidence points to the fact that Jesus died.

II. *The Events on the Resurrection Morning.* One of the strongest proofs that Jesus actually arose is the fact that His followers were so slow to accept His Resurrection as a fact. The four gospel writers tell the story —each from his own viewpoint. Although each gives his own interpretation of the facts, as he was inspired by the Holy Spirit, there are no contradictions and the stories blend into one beautiful account.

The first persons to see Jesus alive after His Resurrection were the women who came to the tomb early that morning. They wondered concerning the great stone in the door of the tomb but found, when they arrived, it had been removed and the tomb was open. Mary Magdalene ran immediately to find Peter and John and tell them someone had taken the body of Jesus away. While she was gone, the other women entered the open tomb and saw the angel who told them Jesus had arisen. They departed quickly to tell the disciples. Meanwhile, Mary Magdalene found Peter and John. She told them what she had seen and then returned to the tomb. It seems Peter and John arrived before her. John ran faster than Peter. He arrived first, but looked in the tomb and did not enter it. When Peter came he at once entered the tomb and then John followed him. They saw the linen cloths lying together and the napkin that had been around the head of Jesus rolled up in a place by itself. John immediately knew no grave robbers had been at the tomb. He was the first of the apostles to believe that Jesus had actually arisen from the dead.

After Peter and John left, Mary Magdalene arrived a second time. It was then she saw Jesus. This was the first post-resurrection appearance of Jesus and is one of the most tenderly touching passages in the New Testament.

From then on events happened quickly. Jesus met the women as they were going to carry the apostles news of the Resurrection. He next appeared to Simon Peter. His fourth appearance was to the two disciples journeying from Jerusalem to Emmaus. He then appeared to the disciples in the Upper Room, minus Thomas, and a week later to the disciples including Thomas. Judas was, of course, absent having killed himself after betraying Jesus.

Long before the modern skeptics with their fine-spun theories, there were those who imagined the whole story to be the wild imaginings of a group of excited and hysterical women. Subsequent events, however, proved undoubtedly that their enthusiastic testimony was true. After the first few fears of the disciples were dispelled, they became men of joy, boldness and dynamic energy. They left those feelings of depression and self-pity which had characterized them during those hours between the burial of Jesus and the time when they were convinced beyond doubt of His Resurrection. The events were proof in themselves. Jesus was alive.

III. *The Power That Came.* There has never been in the history of the world a transformation so immediate, radical and thorough as the Resurrection of Jesus Christ. It turned eleven men who were utterly defeated into a bold, death-defying, completely committed band of witnesses. They became the nucleus of the greatest group of people the earth has ever seen—the true believers in Jesus Christ, His militant army that has marched forward

through the centuries. This power cannot be explained on naturalistic or psychological grounds. These trembling followers were standing helpless before their hopeless inadequacy and suddenly they flamed with assurance and became irresistible with their rock-like spirit. Anyone who thinks he can explain this in terms of auto-suggestion or deal with it on the basis of a non-supernatural theology is simply ignoring the facts.

Is that power available for us today? In many ways our world is living under the same conditions as those discouraged, depressed and defeated disciples were from burial day to resurrection day. It is true we have not been with Jesus historically as they were in the days of His flesh. This does not mean, however, that we are, in any sense, limited. Actually, there is a sense in which even more power is available to us for the greatest victories come through complete faith. Jesus recognized that Thomas believed because he saw, but He said, "blessed are they that have not seen and yet have believed" (John 20:29). We are in that great group. We have seen and believed not with the eyes of flesh but with the eyes of faith.

It is faith that brings power. When we link our lives with a great ideal there is no estimating the dynamic which is available. When that ideal is personified, as in Christianity, with a person who has unlimited compassion and unlimited resources, it is impossible to imagine the potential which may be realized. When Paul wrote to the Philippians (3:10) concerning the great desire of his life, he said, "That I may know him, and the power of his resurrection."

Conclusion. It was in the power of the risen Christ that the early Christians went forth to change the face of the world. Because of their fresh and vital experience with the resurrected Christ, they were able to work miracles in His name. In what sense is that power available to us today? Could it be that we are weak and anemic in our faith because we simply have not surrendered ourselves completely to the risen Christ? A minister in Birmingham, England, tells how one Saturday afternoon when he was making his final preparation for the Easter Sunday morning message that the truth suddenly gripped him that Jesus was alive. He says that although he had believed this before, it gripped him in a new way. A new world opened to him and his ministry underwent a change that was nothing short of miraculous. Do you need this change in your life? Perhaps we need the faith of the little girl in school whose teacher asked the class to list the three greatest living people. The little girl wrote on her paper, "General MacArthur, President Eisenhower and Jesus Christ." Her teacher corrected her by saying, "The first two are fine, but I asked you to list *living* people." The little girl replied, "O, yes, ma'am, I understand. But Jesus Christ *is* living. He's alive. He rose from the dead." When this fact grips our hearts as it should, we can begin to live in the power of the risen Christ.

SUNDAY EVENING, APRIL 14

TITLE: "Why People Do Go to Church"

TEXT: "I was glad when they said unto me, Let us go into the house of the LORD" (Ps. 122:1).

SCRIPTURE READING: Psalm 122.

Introduction. We are told that 40,000,000 Americans attend church on Sunday morning. Why do they come? Not because of coercion. We live in a free country. Attendance is optional. It is not for amusement. The world has the Church beat a mile when it comes to sheer entertainment.

In fact, some who attend church regularly find themselves wondering why some people come to church. Dr. Leslie Wetherhead retired a few years ago from a distinguished ministry with the great City Temple of London. He commented, "Now I am at the listening end of services. Sometimes I come away feeling frustrated and angry that a vital, glorious, joyous thing like the Christian religion should have been made so dull, so boring, so irrelevant, and so meaningless!"

Jesus attended the synagogue regularly. When he returned to Nazareth, where he was brought up, *"as his custom was,"* he went into the synagogue on the sabbath day" (Luke 4:16). He had a habit of going to church. He did not wait to see if it was raining or if He had a headache before He decided whether He would attend. He certainly did not agree with everything the speaker was saying. I am sure that many services were boring. But He found His way to God's house. We are not following the example of our Lord if we do not have the custom of going regularly to God's house.

Some people are in church through unworthy motives. They go for respectability or status. They go to see the latest fashions or to salve their conscience because of their uncommitted lives. They go just out of habit.

But there are proper reasons for going to church.

I. *To Worship God.* In the heart of each of us is a need for God. In the soul is a capacity to worship God. God can be worshiped anywhere, but He can be best worshiped in His house. Someone said, "I can worship God in the out-of-doors, on the lake, or on the golf course." President Theodore Roosevelt's answer to this is a classic, "You can, but you likely won't." Worship involves purpose. Worship involves other people. Where even two or three are gathered in Christ's name, He promises to be in their midst. There is something about singing together and praying together and listening together and responding together that makes for a satisfying worship experience. Worship involves praise, the highest type of worship.

II. *To Experience Forgiveness.* Worship also involves confession. The Church is for sinners. In fact, you cannot be received into the Church membership unless you confess you are a sinner, saved by grace. When we confess our sins, we experience the forgiveness of God. There we find the atmosphere that makes it possible to forgive ourselves and to forgive others.

III. *To Find Christian Fellowship.* It is not the job of the Church to furnish fellowship. It is the mission of the Church to be a fellowship. We are made for each other. There is loneliness in isolation. We bear one another's burdens. We pray for each other. We love one another. A church that is a warm, dynamic fellowship is a going church.

IV. *To Be a Part of God's Great Movement.* Jesus said, "Thou shalt worship the Lord thy God, and him only shalt thou serve" (Matt. 4:10). We enter to worship. We depart to serve. For a long time we equated the work of the Church with what happened inside her walls. Now we realize that the "church" is not "over" when the congregation is dismissed.

In her services of worship, we witness "the Church gathered." Our minds are instructed. Our hearts are inspired. Our souls are fed. Our wills are motivated. Then we go out into the world, still the Church, but now "the Church scattered."

Both roles of the Church are vital. The Church is not a fortress where we gather in isolation to enjoy God and each other. Neither is the Church a scattered activist group without organization or roots or permanency. Such is a movement and not a church.

If this concept is true, then what happens inside the church building is more important there. What happens to us in the Church will determine our effectiveness later when we become the Church in the world.

Conclusion. A family in Ohio claims to have the smallest church in the world. A tiny church building has room for only two pews facing each other, with an altar in the midst. The message and the mission of the church are absent. It is not enough just to meet and talk and sing and listen and have fellowship. The Church must make disciples

117

and grow mature Christians and must change the world. True worship of God by the church is a vital and necessary part of that mission.

WEDNESDAY EVENING, APRIL 17

TITLE: "The Bible Speaks to Our Condition"

SCRIPTURE READING: Acts 18.

Introduction. In seeking light for the road of life today, it is always helpful if we can understand the controlling purpose of the scriptural writer. It has been suggested that Acts 18 reveals one of the major purposes that Luke had as he wrote the book that we know as the Acts of the Apostles. In this chapter we have the dramatic point at which the official Jewish position toward the Christian movement is articulated. They had repudiated Jesus Christ. They continued to reject the apostles' interpretation of His life, His death, His resurrection, and His continuing redemptive purpose. Paul turns to the Gentiles with the Gospel.

It has also been suggested that one of Luke's controlling purposes was to demonstrate that in every contact with Roman judicial authorities, Christianity had been revealed to be a religious movement rather than a subversive organization that threatened the Roman government. Gallio refused to indite Paul. He found nothing for which he should condemn Paul.

I. *A Blessing in Disguise* (18:1-3, 18, 19, 26-28). We can well imagine the inconvenience and trouble to which the decree of the Roman emperor put Aquila and his wife, Priscilla, when they had to leave Rome. They could not know at that time that this decree would lead them into contact with Paul through their common trade. This contact with Paul was to lead to their conversion and to their use by God for the advancement of His redemptive purpose.

That which appeared to them as a calamity turned out eventually to be God's great and good blessing for them. God is at work in all things for good for those who love Him. Have you experienced some failure, some tragedy, some great disappointment? Is it possible that God has something better in store for you? By faith, look for it. Let Him bless you as He did Aquila and Priscilla. Not only did they experience conversion, but they became the companions of Paul, and they proved to be a great blessing to Apollos who was one of the Lord's chosen servants.

II. *The Mission to the Gentiles Begins* (18:4-6). When Ananias received the commission from God to go and minister to Saul, the new convert, he was informed that Saul was a chosen vessel who would give testimony concerning Jesus Christ before the Gentiles (Acts 9:10-15). Many days and many events were to take place before Paul was to actually begin his evangelistic and missionary ministry to the Gentiles. This ministry was to begin when the Jewish rejection of the Gospel was to bring about their self-exclusion and the opening of the door of opportunity to Gentiles.

God is eager to use any and all

who will open their minds and hearts to Him. Let us be cautious lest our unbelief and disobedience cause us to exclude ourselves from God's redemptive purpose.

III. *The Encouragement of God* (18:9, 10). The Apostle Paul ministered in the face of severe criticism and hostility. There was great opposition to him in the city of Corinth as is revealed by his later arrest and presentation before the court of Gallio (18:12, 17). In the time of danger, God came to Paul and gave to him an awareness of the divine presence with him at all times. There was given to him a promise of protection. The promise that was given to Paul is the promise that our Lord gave to His disciples when He gave voice to the command which we know as the Great Commission (Matt. 28:20).

God will come and give to each of us encouragement as that encouragement is needed. We can depend upon the divine presence and divine provisions as we are obedient to His command.

IV. *The Need for Spiritual Strength* (18:22, 23). In the last verses of this chapter we have a very compact account of Paul's journey from Corinth by way of Ephesus to Jerusalem and his return to Antioch and then the beginning of another missionary journey. It is declared that as he went from church to church which had been established on previous missionary journeys, he concentrated on strengthening the disciples.

God's children continue to need the strength that comes through devotional study of His Word. Let us let God speak to our condition through the pages of His Word.

We need the strength that comes through earnest, sincere prayer. Let us be certain that we listen as we pray as well as present our petitions in prayer.

We need the strength that comes through the testimony of others who have obeyed God and found Him faithful to all of the promises that He has made.

We need the strength that comes through an awareness of the abiding presence of the Holy Spirit within our heart. The Holy Spirit can make us sufficient and adequate for any crisis, need, or opportunity that presents itself.

Conclusion. The Bible is not a mere record of what happened in the past. It is a record of what can happen in the present as we walk and talk with our Savior and as we minister in His name.

Let us look for the blessings that come to us in disguise. Let us be open to new ministries that the Lord might have for us. Let us always respond and trust in the encouragement that God sends to us.

SUNDAY MORNING, APRIL 21

TITLE: "Jesus Is Coming Again"

TEXT: "This same Jesus, which is taken up from you into heaven, shall so come in like manner" (Acts 1:11).

SCRIPTURE READING: Acts 1:1-11.

HYMNS: "Praise Him! Praise Him!" Crosby. "He Lives on High," McKinney. "We'll Work Till Jesus Comes," Mills.

OFFERTORY PRAYER:

Our heavenly Father, we bow our heads and our hearts in Thy presence to remind ourselves again that we are dependent upon Thee not only for the necessities of life but for life itself. Thou hast been our dwelling place in all generations. Thou hast been our help in years that are gone. Thou art our hope for days yet to come. We are Thine today and we must give every moment to Thee. This is the part of the service where we bring our tithes and offerings that the work of Christ might be carried on here in our own congregation, among our own people, and through our mission causes to the ends of the earth. Bless those today who are serving Christ in places that are difficult and be in a very special way with those that are serving where it is dangerous. May we feel a kinship this morning through our gifts with everyone who is proclaiming the saving name of Christ to those who do not know Him. We pray these things in Jesus' name Amen.

Introduction. Although Jesus had discouraged His followers from expecting a temporal kingdom, the idea was so deeply ingrained in them they could not forget it. After His Resurrection, Jesus was seen by them forty days. He showed by many infallible proofs that He was alive, and He spoke to them of things pertaining to God's kingdom. The final question recorded as coming from the disciples to Jesus was an inquiry concerning the restoration of the Jewish monarchy. Jesus gave them a mild reprimand. The Father has the future planned and we are not to worry ourselves with that which He has reserved for Himself. The true task of the believer is to be a witness for Christ, beginning where he is and reaching out as far as his influence and resources will carry him. The disciples were promised a visit of enabling power to assist them in the proclamation of the Gospel message.

As He finished speaking, while they were still watching, Jesus was taken up into heaven. The men stood by in wonderment, and two heavenly messengers spoke to them. Their words consisted of a firm declaration that Jesus will return to earth the same way He ascended into heaven. Nothing is clearer or plainer. Jesus of Nazareth ascended in the flesh. It is true He had a glorified body, but He was the Jesus whom they knew. This same Jesus is going to return. This message has found itself being proclaimed over and over through the centuries. It is the hope of Christian people for vindication in this world of sin.

I. *The Fact of His Coming.* Christianity was revealed to the world in a historical situation. Likewise, it will be consummated within a historical framework. Spiritual truth has been brought to the world within the context of historical fact. The vehicle by which the message is brought contains accurate information regarding the environment in which the message lived and came to fruition.

The return of Jesus to earth is not something about which men

120

speculated and believed *should* happen. It is that which God, through His divinely inspired Word, has said *will* happen. God's Word makes it abundantly clear. One has only to look at books such as Matthew (24:30; 24:44), Luke (21:25, 27), 1 Thessalonians (1:10; 3:13; 4:16, 17; 5:1, 2, 6), 2 Thessalonians (1:7-10; 3:5), Hebrews (9:27, 28) and 2 Peter (3:10-14) to see that God's Word is clear on the subject.

It is significant that among many scholars there has recently been a renewed emphasis of, and interest in, the return of the Lord. The Second Coming has always been prominent in fundamentalist circles but this revival of interest is present in many modern liberal and neo-orthodox writers as well. The blessed hope of Christ's coming is being seen by more and more people as the only hope for our confused and troubled world. Human ingenuity has failed to solve the problems that are with us, and many thoughtful people are coming to the conclusion that, although we still need to work to solve our problems in everyday living, the only permanent solution will be God's intervention by the sending of Jesus Christ back to the world to consummate history.

II. *The Purpose of His Coming.*
The return of Christ to earth will reveal His infinite glory and majesty. In the days of His flesh He often limited Himself and did not express the fullness of the divine glory that belonged to Him. At His second appearance, however, every eye shall see Him in the fullness of the divine majesty that is His as the second member of the Trinity.

At His coming He will receive His saints. We shall be caught up in the clouds and be forever with Him.

At that moment, the dead in Christ shall receive their new glorified bodies. Those who are living at the time of His coming will be transformed immediately and given their glorious bodies. The redeemed family of God shall be received unto Jesus and shall "ever be with the Lord" (1 Thess. 4:17).

At His coming, He will reject the lost. It will be a time for judgment for those who have refused to receive Him as personal Savior. The Bible says the ones whose names are not written in the Lamb's Book of Life will be cast into a lake of fire. There shall be eternal punishment for all who have refused to submit themselves to Jesus, receiving Him as Savior and crowning Him as Lord of life.

III. *The Nearness of His Coming.*
There are many signs that the coming of Christ will be soon. The Jews have been restored to their homeland and are now once more a nation. Although there are various ideas concerning the program of events at the coming of Jesus, one thing is clear. The Second Coming of Jesus is always associated very closely with the return of the Jews to their homeland. They are now there! The nations of the world seem to be dividing themselves upon the basis of pro-Israel or anti-Israel. All of this seems to be pointing to a great battle in which Israel will be the central figure.

The moral and spiritual conditions have deteriorated as the Bible writers predicted would happen immediately before the coming of Jesus. Of course, the world has always offered enticements to people and in every generation there have been those who turned away from God. In this day, however, it seems we have unparalleled falling away from godly living. This age of permissiveness has come upon us with a force that leaves us baffled as to how we can contend with it. Wickedness in high places threatens our national life. The same is true with other nations.

There is a turning away from sound doctrine even as the Bible predicted would occur. People have little or no interest in spiritual things. They follow clever and cunningly devised fables and leave the Word of God. A return to paganism in the midst of a sophisticated society shocks those who believe in the integrity of God's written Word.

It looks as though the coming of Christ is near. Every sign points toward it.

IV. *Preparation for His Coming.* There is only one way to be saved. The door of mercy is open now. Christ stands as our counselor. He will intercede for us if we will turn ourselves over to Him in complete surrender and trust. The preparation for His coming is to "repent of sin and trust in Christ as personal Savior." This is the only way to be safe in that day when He shall come again. If we receive Him as Savior, we will be one of those who joins Him in the sky at His coming. We will have a transformed body. If we are in the grave as one asleep in Christ, we will be awakened by the trumpet sound and be immediately raised up with a new and glorified body. If we remain until His coming, and are saved, our vile body will be transformed that it might become like His glorious body (Phil. 3:21).

Conclusion. There are many schools of thought with reference to the program that shall occur at the coming of Christ. There is no possible way in one sermon to harmonize all of these various interpretations. The Bible is clear, however, beyond the shadow of a doubt on one thing—Jesus is coming again. He is coming personally, visibly, in the same manner He left and for the purpose of revealing His glory, receiving His saints and rejecting the lost.

The business of the Christian is to wait, witness and work till Jesus comes. The lost man needs to repent before the day of judgment comes. Jesus is Savior now but if He is rejected His presence will be a terror to those who have ignored His plea of grace.

The non-Christian should not be disturbed about the divisions concerning the events that shall occur at His coming. There have always been disagreements among sincere Christians concerning certain facts with reference to Christ's Second Coming. There always will be until He comes again. The wise course is to trust Him as Savior now. In-depth Bible study concerning this and other subjects should be a part of Christian growth, but becoming a Christian by receiving Jesus as Savior is a priority.

TITLE: "The King Is Dead"

TEXT: "In the year that King Uzziah died I saw also the Lord ..." (Isa. 6:1).

SCRIPTURE READING: Isaiah 6:1-13.

Introduction. In the year 1952, the sad word went forth from London, "The king is dead." King George VI had died in his sleep at the age of fifty-six. He was a modest, retiring man, greatly respected and admired. His reign had carried him through the rigors of World War II, the election of a Socialist government, and the dissolution of the world-wide colonial kingdom. His tired heart gave away. Britons flocked to the churches to worship, to pray, and to seek comfort and hope.

In the year 1963, the shocking word encircled a disbelieving world, "The President is dead." John F. Kennedy, young, vibrant and dynamic, was cut down by the assassin's bullet, and a nation was plunged in grief. There had been sorrow when President Franklin D. Roosevelt died, but he was old, his children were grown, and he died in bed. People flocked to the churches in the greatest numbers since the announcement of the close of World War II. Ministers changed their texts and sermons and preached to the people of America a gospel of healing and hope.

About 700 years before Christ was born in Bethlehem, the sad announcement was made, "The king is dead." King Uzziah, the eleventh king of Judah, had died. Crowned at the age of sixteen, he had reigned fifty-two years. Despite his failings, he was the greatest king since David.

The heart of young Isaiah was broken. Uzziah was not only his king, but he also was his friend. In his heartbreak, he made his way to the Temple to worship and to seek comfort and renewed faith. The house of God is a good place to go when sorrow comes. Some Christians stay away from church for months after a loved one dies. Then they find that the first Sunday they return is a hard one. We should pray for strength and courage to be good stewards of our sorrow. Seeing us promptly back in God's house will impress others that we have inner resources that are adequate even in such a time of grief.

Isaiah learned that the king was dead, but God was not dead. He had lost his king, but he discovered the King of Kings. He had an experience of worship that radically changed his life.

I. *He Saw the Lord.* He saw God in His proper nature and character. He saw Him high and lifted up. He saw Him as Lord upon His throne. He saw Him the object of praise, surrounded by heavenly courtiers. He saw Him in all His glory. He saw Him in perfect holiness.

It is interesting to note that in that service, only Isaiah saw the vision. Even those seated beside him and around him had no such experience. There is a sense in which corporate worship is still a very individual matter. One person is moved to tears. Another on the same pew is unmoved. One repents and another trusts in his own self-righteousness. One responds to the claims of Christ and another vigorously resists the persuasion of the Holy Spirit.

123

II. *He Saw Himself.* He did not see himself as a good person, deserving the commendation of God and the plaudits of man. He didn't say to himself, "I must be a good person. I must be the best person here, for God has honored me alone with a vision of Himself." Instead he cried, "Woe is me! for I am undone; because I am a man of unclean lips. . . ."

The closer we get to God, the more clearly we see our sins. The contrast between His holiness and our unholiness gives us a vivid awareness of our sinfulness. The times we feel we are good Christians is when we neglect to pray and worship and feel the presence of the Holy Spirit. When Peter was closest to Jesus, he said, "Depart from me; for I am a sinful man." When the vision of Christ the King was revealed to John on Patmos, he wrote, "I fell at his feet as dead." A lost sense of God brings a lost sense of sin.

III. *He Saw God's Cleansing Power.* When Isaiah confessed his sin, God was faithful and just to forgive his sin, and He cleansed him of all his unrighteousness. The burning coal of purification and cleansing was applied to the member of his body that betrayed openly his inner sinfulness. This was his unclean lips. God's messenger applied the touch to his tongue. And he experienced the sweet, clean feeling of forgiveness and peace. This is the blessing of confession in worship.

IV. *He Saw His Work.* He heard the voice of the Lord saying, "Whom shall I send, and who will go for us?" I can hear Isaiah saying, "Would God call a sinful man?" There are no other kind. Sometimes God calls the most sinful man to preach His Word. The chief of sinners was not too sinful. Yes, He calls sinners to go for Him. He doesn't call sinless angels. He calls sinful men.

But He sends men out only after they have been cleansed of their sins by His grace. The message of God must be spoken through clean lips. The work of God must be poured from clean vessels.

Conclusion. Isaiah did not say, "Where do You want me to go?" "What is in it for me?" "What are the calculated hazards involved?" "What is the salary?" "What are the retirement benefits?" Isaiah signed a blank check. He drove no bargain with God. He negotiated no compromise. God called. He answered. God commanded. He obeyed. Such an unconditional response comes only through the inspiration of the vision through worship.

The same thing can happen to us in this worship service today. It can happen in this hour. The King is alive! He was dead, for He died for our sins on the cross. But He arose from the grave and lives today, and is alive forevermore. Jesus is Lord. He requires unconditional surrender. He commissions us to look upon the fields so white with harvest and to go into all the world as His witnesses. God help us to say, "Here am I; send me!"

TITLE: "The Bible Speaks to Our Condition"

SCRIPTURE READING: Acts 25.

Introduction. This chapter portrays the perplexity of the Roman officials as they sought to articulate an accurate and worthy charge to be brought against the Apostle Paul when he stood before Caesar's judgment seat. Paul was no criminal. He had committed no crime against the nation of Israel or against the Roman empire.

Dr. Frank Stagg takes the position that one of Luke's controlling purposes as he writes the Book of Acts is to reveal that Christianity was not a subversive movement that threatened the Roman empire. In every instance where there was a legal or judicial confrontation between the early Christians and the Roman officials, the decision of the court revealed that Christians were innocent of the charges brought against them. Christianity was not a threat to the Roman empire as such, consequently, the Roman empire should not seek to eradicate Christianity from its borders (Frank Stagg, *The Book of Acts,* Broadman Press, 1955).

I. *Undeserved Sufferings.* This chapter opens with Paul still in prison in Caesarea. He had remained in prison for the last two years. He was guilty of no crime except that of preaching the Gospel of God's grace to Gentiles as well as Jews.

He was the object of the hatred and the hostility of those who opposed his viewpoint and who would have brought Christianity to an end. Seemingly, Paul responded to the situation in which he found himself positively and triumphantly.

A. Not all suffering is the result of sin committed by the sufferer. We must repudiate the idea that all suffering is due to some failure or due to some error in the life of the one suffering.

B. There are many causes for undeserved suffering.

1. We suffer because of the carelessness of others.

2. We suffer because of the selfishness of others.

3. We suffer because of the suffering of others.

4. We suffer because of the activity of the devil.

5. We suffer sometimes because of our own carelessness.

6. Sometimes there is absolutely no explanation for the suffering that we have to endure.

C. We could find some comfort in the truth that no suffering comes to us outside of the permissive will of our loving God.

II. *Opportunity for Unique Witnessing.* As we search for some light from this chapter for the road of life today, we can be reminded of the fact that every situation provides some opportunity for a Christian witness. Paul had given his Christian testimony time and time again to Felix and Drusilla, his wife (Acts 24). In Acts ·25 Paul had the privilege of giving his Christian testimony to Festus, the Roman procurator, and to King Agrippa and Bernice, and to the other Jewish and Roman officials who must have been present on this occasion.

This experience provides Paul with the opportunity to fulfill the intent which the Lord had for him at the time of his conversion and call to a missionary ministry (Acts 9:15). Paul was experiencing what our Lord had foretold would happen to His faithful disciples (Matt. 10:18).

Conclusion. Today, like yesterday and tomorrow, will provide us with some unique opportunities to share with others the Good News of God's love and grace as we have experienced it in Jesus Christ. May we seize our opportunities and use them for His glory as did the Apostle Paul.

SUNDAY MORNING, APRIL 28

TITLE: "What Will You Do With Jesus?"

TEXT: "What shall I do then with Jesus which is called Christ?" (Matt. 27:22).

SCRIPTURE READING: Matthew 27:15-26.

HYMNS: "O Jesus, Thou Art Standing," How. "How Sweet the Name of Jesus," Newton. "Tell It to Jesus," Rankin.

OFFERTORY PRAYER:

Our Father, we recognize this is a day when, as never before, we are utterly dependent upon Thee. The problems that face us in this world are too great to be solved by human ingenuity. As we approach Thee this morning we recognize our inadequacy but we also have confidence because of Thy resourcefulness. We are glad because we know that Thou dost love us and that Thou dost desire for us the best in life. Help us to realize, however, that we must respond with dedication if we are to realize the fruits of Thy love.

As we come to make our offering this morning, may we realize that this is a needy world. Wilt Thou make us aware anew that only the Gospel of Jesus Christ can bring permanent peace to troubled and rebellious heart. Use these offerings to Thy glory and to the proclamation of the message that Jesus Christ died for our sins, was resurrected for our justification and is coming again to receive the saved unto Himself. We pray these things in Jesus' name. Amen.

Introduction. For a number of weeks we have looked at the life of Jesus. We have endeavored to see His ministry in miniature. The major events that are representative of His work have been emphasized. Underlying all of these truths has been the fact that He came into the world on a redemptive mission—to seek and to save that which was lost. A study of the life of Jesus in history lays the foundation for a great question. This morning we consider the all-important matter of our own individual relationship to Him. What have we done with Him personally? Have we received Him into our hearts as both Savior and Lord? Is He a part of our daily experiences in life?

Pilate faced the question of a decision for Jesus. He wanted to remain neutral but he could not push aside a decision. So it is with us. To refuse to decide for Jesus is to reject Him. The question which Pilate asked is a comprehensive one. Some other questions arise from it.

I. *Who Is Jesus?* If the Bible is so bold as to proclaim the necessity of our making a decision concerning Jesus, surely we have the right to ask concerning Him and His nature. Was He just another teacher, preacher or religious reformer? Or is He more? The verdict of history is that Jesus was far more than just an ordinary human being. When Ralph Waldo Emerson finished his work entitled *Representative Men* someone asked him why he did not include Jesus Christ. He replied that it would require too much strength of constitution to put Jesus Christ in the same category with ordinary human beings. All of us who know Jesus in personal forgiveness of sin recognize that though Jesus was a great teacher and preacher, He was far more. We should remember, of course, that Jesus can truly be understood only from within the context of a personal experience with Him. It was when Thomas finally understood Jesus in the fullest that he shouted, "My Lord and my God" (John 20:28).

The man who dares to come and demand a decision from us is not merely a peasant from a small town in a captive province. He is the One who has proved to the world both in the days of His flesh and in subsequent history that He is worthy of complete allegiance and is alone the Lord of both death and life.

II. *What Can You Do With Jesus?* There are only two possibilities open concerning Jesus. He may be accepted. You may receive Him into your heart as Savior. You may recognize your own sinfulness and inadequacy to cope with the problems of life, death and eternity. You may see that in Him the Father's love is demonstrated. In Jesus our guilt may be removed. We may be justified by His grace. We may accept the Atonement as the substitute for the penalty of our sins and become a redeemed creature and a member of God's family. This is what every wise person does when he hears the Gospel preached in its fullness.

There is another alternative, Mortal man may reject the divine Christ. Regardless of our beliefs about predestination or God's foreknowledge, the fact remains that man has a free will. Man *can* refuse God. Even though Christ died for all, all will not be saved. Only those who receive Christ as Savior will enter into the fullness of joy that God has provided for His redeemed people. You can receive Jesus, but you also *can reject Him.*

There is no third alternative. Actually, there is no essential difference between rejecting Jesus outright and postponing the decision. Both are dangerous and both can be fatal to one's spiritual destiny. The Gospel of Jesus Christ is actually a very dangerous thing. When it is preached to an individual, it has one of two effects. Either that person receives Christ as Savior or else his refusal to accept Christ drives him farther away from the salvation God offers.

III. *What Does It Really Matter?* Is there any real great issue at stake?

After all, Jesus lived so many hundreds of years ago. Does it really matter whether I make a decision concerning Him or not?

The verdict of history proves it does matter—it matters much. First, it matters in this life. Those who are followers of Christ are the truly happy people. They are the ones who are making this world a better place in which to live. If there were no such thing as a life beyond, it would still be a wise course of action to be a Christian because of the joy that comes in this life to those who are surrendered to the Lord's will.

Second, it matters in death what we do with Jesus. Daniel Webster was once asked what was the greatest thought that had ever entered his mind. He answered with great emotion, "My personal responsibility to God." Death comes to all of us. It comes to the aged person as he walks falteringly. Often its trumpet sound is heard by one who is barely halfway in the journey of life. Many times its icy grip hushes the laughter of little children. Salvation through Jesus is *more* than merely "death insurance" but it is this—if one wishes to call it by that name. On his deathbed, a great scientist was asked, "What are your speculations now?" He replied, "Speculations? I have none. I know whom I have believed." To be able to face death calmly and with assurance that all is well, is a worthy goal. For one to have Jesus as personal Savior and the witness of the Spirit within, produces a peace that the world cannot give and cannot take away.

There is a third reason why our decision concerning Jesus matters greatly. We will spend eternity somewhere. The Bible does not hold out three possibilities—only two. There is a heaven prepared for those who love Jesus, and there is a hell for the devil and his servants. Eternity is forever. Throughout its endless ages we shall reap the result of our decision concerning the Savior. It matters greatly what we do with Jesus!

IV. *Who Will Decide the Question?* In the light of normal intelligence, to ask this question is but to answer it. There is nothing in the Bible nor in the processes of rational logic to give us any hope that someone else can answer the question for us. There have been wives who would answer this question for their husband if they could. There have been parents who would answer the question for children and sometimes children for parents and husbands for wives. Friends have often pleaded with friends to receive Jesus but this was as far as they could go. The question is an intensely personal one. Joshua spoke to an audience of perhaps two million Jews. He recited the history of God's providential dealings with the nation and then he pleaded, "Choose you this day whom ye would serve" (Josh. 24:15). It is significant that he used the second person singular pronoun which indicated that although he was addressing a multitude of people the choice was a personal one. Each must decide for himself.

V. *When Should the Question Be Decided?* An ancient minister was pleading with his people to turn to God. One asked him when he should do it. He replied, "On the last day before you die." "But I do not know the day I will die." The minister then answered, "Then come to God today." The matter of life's uncertainty is, of course, a strong reason for coming to Jesus today. There are, however, other motivations. The longer we put off our decision for Christ, the harder it becomes. Just as Pharaoh's heart was hardened each time he rejected God's will in the days of Moses, so we jeopardize our ability to make a decision in the future when we turn down God in an earlier encounter.

The highest reason for coming to Christ *now* is that the sooner we become a Christian the sooner we begin to enjoy the fruits of the Christian life. This is the motivation that a lost man can seldom understand. It is usually the crisis concerning our lostness and the punishment that awaits which leads us to Jesus as Savior, but it does not need to be this reason. Jesus offers an abundant life. We are not only saved from hell but we are saved to a spiritual fellowship with our Lord that begins in this life and continues throughout eternity.

Whatever motivation moves one, he should act from it and decide today. It is the safe course to pursue and the one which will begin spiritual dividends that shall last throughout eternity.

Conclusion. This series of messages has sought to bring us face to face with the living Lord. God revealed Himself through Jesus in history, but His revelation is above history. Jesus is timeless because He is truly the "Man for all seasons." The same Jesus who nestled in His mother's arms as a babe, walked the dusty streets of Galilee and the rocky plateaus of Judah, who was nailed to the cross and arose from the tomb is the Jesus who confronts us today and demands our allegiance. His voice is tender and winsome, but it is also stern and challenging. What have you done with Him? What will you do with Him? Life's momentous issues will be decided by the answer we give in our heart to His call.

SUNDAY EVENING, APRIL 28

TITLE: "The King in His Glory"

TEXT: "And as he was praying, the fashion of his countenance altered, and his raiment became white and dazzling" (Luke 9:29, ASV).

SCRIPTURE READING: Luke 9: 28-37.

Introduction. Many of the greatest scenes in the Bible took place on mountains. Most of them were viewed by very few witnesses. They proved to be mountaintop spiritual experiences. It was on Mount Moriah that Abraham offered up his son, Isaac. It was on Mount Sinai amidst the lightning and thunder that Moses received the Ten Commandments. It was on Mount Carmel that Elijah called down the fire of God and devastated the religion and priests of Baal. The wilderness temptations included one from the mountaintop as this world. It was on Mount Calvary that He died. It was on the Mount of Ascension from which a cloud received Him out of their sight.

129

It was probably on Mount Herman where Jesus received His transfiguration experience. Jesus went apart for some very obvious reasons.

First, to seek the guidance of the heavenly Father. He was on the way to the cross. He felt the need to pray. He never took a step without listening to the voice of God. When He had a problem, He did not proceed on human advice. He sought out the lonely place where He could have fellowship with God.

Second, to seek strength. He was under tremendous pressure. Those who sought His life were closing in. He was misunderstood, even by His friends. He was lonely, for even His most devoted disciples rebuked Him when He sought to inform them of His impending death. His human nature recoiled against the prospect of death. He sought the fellowship of God. He received the fellowship of heavenly visitors who understood His mission.

Moses represented the law. He was the lawgiver and could see the fulfillment of the law in Jesus. Elijah represented the prophets. He was the greatest of the prophets. Some even mistook Jesus as Elijah arisen from the dead. The two conversed with Jesus about His "decease" (Luke 9:31). The word "decease" in the New Testament comes from the word "exodus" in the Old Testament. "Exodus" means "going out." The second book of the Bible is titled, "The Book of Exodus," meaning the children of Israel going out of the bondage of Egypt into the Promised Land, flowing with milk and honey. What a description of the death of the believer! Death to the Christian is the going out of the bondage of this life into the freedom of that glorious land our Savior is preparing for us.

As Jesus prayed, He was transfigured. A radiance shone from within. A cloud descended and the voice of God spoke His pleasure in His Son. It was a high and holy hour.

The three disciples who accompanied Jesus were deeply impressed and moved. The spiritual ecstasy Peter experienced surpassed any other event in his life. The wonder and adoration of the moment were overwhelming. We can hear him saying, "Lord, it is good to be here. Let's stay here. This is as near heaven as I care to be. This is as near heaven as I can stand. Let us build three tents, one for You, one for Moses, and one for Elijah. As far as John and James and I are concerned, we'll be happy to sleep on the ground."

Jesus rebuked him and led them down into the valley where a crisis awaited them. The nine remaining disciples had sought to heal a tragically ill boy. Nothing had happened. The enemies of Jesus were exultant. It was a crisis for the kingdom as well as a crisis for a father and his sick son. Our impotence is an embarrassment to Jesus. Our lack of faith reflects upon Him. With a word He healed the boy and gave His disciples a lesson on faith.

There are two vital lessons we learn from this experience of worship on the Mount:

I. *Communion With God Transfigures.* Worship changes the worshiper. The disciples could see the difference in the countenance and bearing of Jesus. The face of Moses shone as he came down from Mount Sinai after a time with God. The face of the martyr, Stephen, shone as he looked up and saw

Jesus standing at the right hand of God. Neither one of these men was aware that his face shone. If it is a genuine radiance, we are the last to notice it.

Dr. George W. Truett, pastor of the First Baptist Church, Dallas, for most of the first half of the twentieth century, was a man of deep spirituality. His prayer life was deeply devout. A columnist for the *Dallas News* wrote an article about the great pastor just a few years before he died. Dr. Truett went one day from his study to an urgent appointment in downtown Dallas. As he walked down the busy street, his eyes straight ahead, his mind intent upon his mission, a man coming from the opposite direction got one glimpse of his face. That man's feet were bent upon a mission of evil. He did not know the pastor. He had never seen him before. But there was something about his face, his eyes, his bearing, that prompted that man to turn aside from his sinful errand. And Dr. Truett never knew of it until he read it in the *Dallas News*.

II. *Prayer Equips for the Valley.* Peter wanted to prolong the great moment on the Mount. He wanted to just live up there. But there was a need down in the valley, and Jesus and the disciples could supply that need.

We cannot live all our life on the mountain. Neither must we live all our life in the valley. We must climb the mountain and experience the worship of God. Then we must take the mountaintop back into the valley to those who had not been up the mountain. We must witness the glory of God on the mountaintop so we may minister to the misery of man in the valley. We cannot live Sunday all seven days of the week. We must worship God and renew our bodies and minds and spirits. Then God gives us six week days back in the valley to take the spirit and inspiration and witness of the Lord's Day to the people. We must meet God in the secret place and the church meeting place so we may meet sinful and needy men in the marketplace. We take our needs to God so we may be strengthened to meet the needs of other men.

Jesus said, "Thou shalt worship the Lord thy God, and him only shalt thou serve." We have not really worshiped unless it equips and motivates us to serve.

Conclusion. As a college student, I was privileged to attend a weekend retreat with students from all over the state. Friday night was a helpful service. Saturday the spirit rose higher and higher. On Saturday night we were on the mountaintop. In a testimony service, students shared their dread of having to go back to their cold, secular campuses the next day.

Finally a new Christian began to speak, "You think you've had a great experience! Think about me. A few weeks ago, I didn't know anything like this existed in this life or in a life to come. It is great! It is wonderful! And I can hardly wait for it to terminate tomorrow so I can get back on our campus and share it with everybody I see."

He had caught the vision. How we need the fire of God within us. How we long for the transfiguring experience of exalted worship that we may be equipped to minister to the multitudes who hurt in the valley.

SUGGESTED PREACHING PROGRAM
FOR THE MONTH OF MAY

Sunday Mornings

The suggested theme for the month is "The Needs of the Family." Messages designated to strengthen home life are suggested for the month following Mother's Day.

Sunday Evenings

The suggested theme for the evening messages is "The Teenager: His Problems and His Potential."

The young people in our congregation need specific guidelines and encouragement as well as warnings from the pulpit.

Wednesday Evenings

Continue the series of Bible studies with the theme, "The Bible Speaks to Our Condition."

The theme verse for the month is "These were more noble than those in Thessalonica, in that they received the word with all readiness of mind, and searched the scriptures daily, whether those things were so" (Acts 17:11).

WEDNESDAY EVENING, MAY 1

TITLE: "The Bible Speaks to Our Condition"

SCRIPTURE READING: Romans 4.

Introduction. In the chapter for today, Paul is seeking to clarify the way of salvation as being by grace through faith rather than by obedience to the law. He has contended that the believer finds a condition of acceptance before God on the basis of faith rather than by the works of the law (Rom. 3:24, 28). Abraham, the father of the faithful, illustrates this thrilling truth.

I. *Abraham Received Justification on the Basis of His Faith* (4:1-8). The word "justification" is a legal term and refers to the activity of God. It is that act of God in which He declares one acceptable in His sight. God justified Abraham on the basis of Abraham's faith.

II. *Abraham Received Justification Before He Received Circumcision* (4:9-12). Circumcision was a sign or seal of the covenant relationship. Paul affirms that the covenant relationship was established prior to circumcision. Circumcision followed justification rather than justification following circumcision.

III. *Abraham Received the Divine Promise Before the Giving of the Law* (4:13-15). Abraham preceded Moses by 400 years. There was no way by which he could have kept the law of Moses and as a result receive the divine promise.

Israel had made the fatal mistake of substituting the law of Moses for the faith of Abraham as a way of finding favor in the presence of God. They substituted law for faith. We need to beware of the same peril.

IV. *Abraham Would Encourage Us to Claim the Promises of God* (4:16-25). We receive justification from God through faith that it might be based upon God's grace rather than upon man's achievement.

132

Abraham believed God. He was a great believer. He put confidence in the promises of God. He was not weak in faith. He did not stagger back in unbelief when God came to him with some great promises. Abraham was persuaded that God was faithful, dependable and trustworthy, and that you could depend upon God to keep His promise.

At this point, Abraham would speak to us in the present. He would encourage us to discover God's promises, claim God's promises, and march forward depending upon God to keep His promises.

We have this record recorded in Scripture not in order that we might merely know about Abraham, but that we might be encouraged to trust God as did Abraham. "Lord, increase our faith."

SUNDAY MORNING, MAY 5

TITLE: "Maintaining Communication Lines Within the Home"

TEXT: "A soft answer turneth away wrath: but grievous words stir up anger. The tongue of the wise useth knowledge aright: but the mouth of fools poureth out foolishness" (Prov. 15:1, 2).

SCRIPTURE READING: 1 Peter 3: 1-12.

HYMNS: "Love Divine," Wesley. "The Christian Home," Spitta. "Lead Me Gently Home, Father," Thompson.

OFFERTORY PRAYER:

Our heavenly Father, we thank Thee for Thy blessings upon us through the home. May our tithes and offerings be used to bring about the conversion of boys and girls, men and women, who will be able to serve Thee better in their homes. Bless this act of worship as each of us brings of our gratitude and to indicate our material substance to express concern for the advancement of Thy kingdom through Jesus Christ our Lord. Amen.

Introduction. We live in a fantastic age of instant world-wide communication. We watch and listen as men converse with each other on the other side of the earth. We watch and listen by means of television as men converse while they walk upon the surface of the moon. We are able to do this because of the excellent communication facilities that modern technology has made available to man.

It is no accident that the American Telephone and Telegraph Company is one of the largest corporations in America. They advertise the fact that they are in the communication business. All of us are involved in the communication business in one way or another.

Man is a communicator. This is a part of his uniqueness as the crown of God's creation made in the image of the Creator.

The Bible teaches us that God is a communicator (Heb. 1:1, 2a). The Bible is the record of God's self-revelation and His effort to communicate His goodwill to man. God continues to seek to communicate with man through the pages of the Bible and through the experiences that His children have through faith and obedience.

133

The experience that we call prayer is actually an experience of communication with the Father God. The believer not only approaches the throne of grace in prayer to present his confessions, praises and petitions, but if prayer would be meaningful, he must listen. God is a communicator and man has a built-in receiving set.

Our Lord, following His victorious Resurrection from the dead, charged His disciples to become communicators. The Great Commission is concerned with communication. There is no way by which we can think of continued existence except in terms of both giving and receiving communications from others. In no area of life is good communications more important than within the family circle.

I. *A Marriage Is a Result of a Communication Process.* It is often said that people get married because they fall in love with each other. The experience of falling in love is the end result of a process of communication.

It is possible for us to communicate by means of the written page. We can utilize the telephone to talk with people at a distance. The radio and television make it possible for one to communicate with millions of people beyond the range of his personal contact. By these modern means of communication we can see and hear those who wish to communicate with us even from the opposite side of the world.

Before a home is established by a marriage, there is a communication process between a man and a woman. In their own unique way they communicate with each other that one is male and the other is female. By the process of courtship, they sell each other on the idea that their greatest future happiness is to be found in a union of their two lives in marriage.

The process of communication which leads to marriage may take many different forms. The man and woman may communicate by means of the dialogue of many different conversations about many different subjects. They may communicate with each other by means of letters through the mail. They may utilize the telephone to converse with each other when they are separated by great distances. They may communicate with each other by means of gifts that are exchanged. This communication may take the form of a smile or a frown. Holding hands is a form of communication. A kiss is a form of communication.

Because the man communicates something which is very desirable to the woman, and because the woman communicates something that is very desirable to the man, they decide to enter marriage that they might live in communication with each other on a continuing and permanent basis.

Marriage is the result of love, but it is also the result of a process of favorable communication between a man and a woman.

II. *The Peril of Poor Communications in the Home.* There are many dangers that imperil the lines of communication in the world. There can be a power failure. There can be an accident that grounds the lines of communication. There are many hindrances to good communication. The same is true concerning good communications within the home.

A successful marriage requires effective and benevolent communications between husband and wife and between parents and children. Communication is a primary problem in all types of family difficulties.

A. Some marriages fail because the couple ceases to communicate with each other. The wise man said, "Death and life are in the power of the tongue" (Prov. 18:21a). Are you using types of communication within the home that will destroy the desire of others to be in communication with you?

B. Some marriages fail because of destructive and inappropriate types of communication. Examine the types of communication that you use within the home.

1. Beware of the cutting criticism that creates hostility. The courtship process consisted of a man and a woman bestowing one compliment after another upon each other. If marriage is to continue to be happy and satisfying, there must be a continuation of the expression of compliments and approvals. If criticism is ever offered within the home, it should be combined with compliments.

An appropriate time and mood should be selected for the expression of any criticism.

2. Beware of the emotional outbursts. Regretfully, much of the destructive communication within the home takes place on the level of an emotional outburst.

We need to beware of the dated emotion. An unpleasant experience in our early life can so injure us as to cause us to react in an unfavorable manner at any time when similar circumstances remind us of the pain that we experienced at that time.

We need to beware of the displaced emotion in which we express anger toward one person when, in reality, we are upset about something else.

3. We need to beware of the dogmatic attitude which does not consider the opinions of others. One man said with sarcasm, "My wife has never made a mistake in the fifteen years of our marriage." She was a dogmatic soul who could never admit being wrong.

4. Beware of insulting each other. An insult will always provoke an angry retaliation. Husbands and wives often insult each other. Parents have been guilty of insulting their children, and then they wonder why their children are angry.

5. Examine the tone of your communications within the home. You may communicate more by the manner in which you speak than with the words with which you speak. The wise man said, "A soft answer turneth away wrath." He also said, "A word fitly spoken is like apples of gold in pictures of silver" (Prov. 25:11).

III. *Building Good Communication Lines Within the Home.* When a husband and wife have broken the lines of communication between themselves, there are times when a third party is necessary if they would reconstruct these lines. A couple went to their pastor with the apology saying, "Pastor, you may think that we are crazy, but we need help. We do not want to get a divorce, but somehow our marriage has ceased to be beautiful and meaningful like it once was. Can you assist us?" The pastor congratulated the couple on their wisdom and sought to listen to their problems, and then suggested some guidelines for re-building the lines of communication that had been so meaningful to them in the past. His suggestions may prove helpful to you.

A. Ask the Lord for help. Establish a time each day in which together, even if you pray silently, that you lift your home with its problems and potential up before God's throne of grace.

B. Accept the fact of human frailty and imperfection. Do not expect perfection on the part of the members of your family and be certain to recognize your own imperfection and incompleteness.

C. Develop a concern for the feelings of others. Both a husband and a wife have individual personal feelings that are of supreme importance to them. A child has emotional needs that need to be met. We need to be as concerned about the feelings of others as we possibly can.

D. Apologize for incorrect and hurtful words and actions. Ask the good Lord for help at the point of being able to say "I am sorry" to the members of your own household when you have been guilty of mistreating them. This takes faith and courage and grace.

E. Practice the fine art of forgiveness. Because God has forgiven you, you can afford to forgive. Renounce the right to retaliate and restore a warm feeling.

F. Recognize the importance of listening to others. It takes time to listen. One must concentrate to listen. One needs to listen. Others need to know that we are listening.

G. Determine to become a giver and recognize the good and the positive in others.

1. Give praise to others in the household.

2. Express gratitude to others in the home.

3. Express confidence in others in the home.

4. Create a sense of high esteem in others. Don't chop others down. Don't put them down. Build them up and encourage them.

Conclusion. Good communication is a dialogue rather than a monologue. Listen to those in your home as well as speak to them.

God is seeking to communicate with you His love, His forgiveness, His hope, His help, and the happiness that can be yours.

Decide now to listen to the Lord, hear His words, believe His promises. Confess your need for Him. Invite Him into your heart and into your home. Welcome Him now.

TITLE: "The Teenager and Rebellion"

TEXT: "As soon as ye hear the sound of the trumpet, then ye shall say, Absalom reigneth in Hebron" (2 Sam. 15:10b).

SCRIPTURE READING: 2 Samuel 15:1-14.

Introduction. There is a long-haired youth in the Bible who reminds me of some of our teenagers today. His name was Absalom. He had many fine qualities. Of all David's sons, he was the most promising. He was handsome, attractive, intelligent. He had leadership of a rare sort. He had a sense of humor. He had a magnetic personality. He was adventuresome and ambitious, wholehearted and daring. He had an unembarrassed confidence in his own ability. He lived magnificently in the king's palace. People loved him. He was an aristocrat, but was not aloof. He drove a chariot with fifty men running before him. He drove the wildest, fastest horses in the royal stables.

Absalom was a genius with the human touch. Then, one day in the name of youth as against experience, he revolted against his own father. He stole the hearts of the people. It was the new generation challenging the old. With his admirers and loyal friends and leaders about him, Absalom crowned himself king in Hebron. Absalom had revolted.

I. *Age of Rebellion.* What happens when one doubles up his little fist and shakes his little head and stomps his little foot and looks up to heaven and says, "I'm not going to do it! Let me alone, God. I'm going to live my own life." Absalom is what happens. Judas Iscariot is what happens. Adolph Hitler is what happens. Communism is what happens. Las Vegas is what happens. Reno is what happens. Fifty-one per cent of all those arrested for serious crimes in New York City were youth under twenty-one. That is what happens!

The rebel spirit is as old as the Garden of Eden. Adam and Eve were rebels when they chose to eat of the fruit of the tree of knowledge of good and evil. The children of God rebelled against His ways and sought to build the tower to heaven. The prodigal son rebelled against his father, and went away to the far country. It is the nature of youth to rebel. It is written deep in the very nature of everyone who lives on this earth. The question is, how to make this rebellion creative, for it can either be creative or destructive. We can either gather up these tendencies and be carried to the heights or these pent-up emotions can cast us down to the depths. Anyone can break an egg, but who can put Humpty Dumpty together again?

I wonder if our society is not aiding the rebel spirit? Absalom's society, home, his environment, all added fuel to the flame of his rebel spirit. Too much leisure time, a father who lavished every luxury and comfort upon him, giving him expensive gifts, the finest clothing, horses and chariots, encouraged his rebellion. Today it would be automobiles. His father gave him everything materially, but he neglected his moral and spiritual training. There are those of us who give our children everything except the one thing that really counts most, companionship which understands and which the child can understand. A society which distributes obscene literature, portrays filth and immorality in the movies, encourages a bad environment and insecurity and running with the wrong crowd and longing for love—these are all a part of the fuel that adds flames to the fire of a rebel spirit of our generation. What if this revolt is a symbol of a deep hunger and thirst within for God and for a deeper meaning to life?

II. *Avenues of Rebellion.* Absalom revolted against authority and restraint. He was a victim of self-will. "I will do what I want to do. I will do as I please. I will love my own life. No one can stop me. Leave me alone." This is rebellion against any demands, against any discipline, rebellion against the cross. A new resident of the town informed the visiting minister when he called that she and her family were looking for a good, "modern church which won't make any demands on us." This is a part of the spirit of our age.

Another avenue of rebellion is that of indulgence. "I will drown myself in drink, or drugs, or delinquency. I can forget myself for a little while in my escapades, in my dreams, and my delusions." The results of this type of rebellion are the prodigal son, skid row, and the boredom of a luxury hotel. Another road of rebellion is the way of the stoic. "I can be my own God. I can defy the power of the stars. I can be the master of my soul." Then there are those who seek to escape from reality! They become the dropouts. They lose themselves through conformity. They pretend to be someone else. They wear a mask. To wear a disguise to a party may be innocent fun, but to compel oneself to wear it in broad daylight is another thing.

III. *Answer to Rebellion.* There is a thin line of difference between adventure and daring on the one hand and unfruitful rebellion on the other. Rebellion can be a noble thing. It is noble for youth to be adventurous and daring. Jesus revolted against tradition and custom in His day. He refused to treat people of other races with pride, hatred, and contempt. He ate with sinners and publicans. He refused to adopt old outward customs that were meaningless. He couldn't be a hypocrite. However, it is one thing to revolt against custom and tradition, and it is another to revolt against justice, righteousness, and temperance. Sometimes it is wisdom to rebel and other times it is foolishness. True rebellion is creative, rather than destructive. If youth can choose the truth and move on to higher and nobler things, then to rebel is a wonderful thing.

If youth can discover the will of God and the eternal things and give themselves to them, then youth will not fling themselves in mere selfish and reckless collusion with the old, and with God Himself. The youth who will accomplish the most in our world today are those who reach up to God for life, light, and leadership.

The love of David followed after Absalom. He felt that some day that love would overtake his son. We hear the great cry of David in the room above the gate as the curtain is lifted, and the news comes that Absalom has been killed in the battle. This love is so perfect in purity, unflagging in purpose, and invincible in appeal. Hear the great king say, "O Absalom, my son, my son, would God I could have died for thee!" I wonder if Absalom really knew his father loved him like that. If Absalom could have heard it, he might have come home.

Conclusion. Today, we should listen for the voice of God, "My son, I have died for you." The Absalom spirit of our hearts should hear it. There is an old story of the couple who were engaged to be married. Just before the wedding day, the bride jilted the groom and ran away with another man. It broke his heart so that he could never go with another woman. A few years later she returned to the community, having been deserted and broken by her lover. Everyone expected her old fiancé to jeer and say, "Serves her right for what she did to me." However, to their amazement, he went to her and professed he still loved her and would forgive all. She could not believe him. So great was her shame and sorrow that she could not comprehend that such love was still possible. He tried again and

again to convince her, but his words were impotent. One day she was driving through town in her buggy. Something frightened her horse and it started to run away. Her life was in danger, and the former fiancé, seeing the situation, ran out and brought the horse under control. In so doing, he was severely injured, but as the woman took his head in her arms, he managed to say weakly, "Maggie, don't you believe me now? I do love you." In the same way God spoke of His forgiving love, but sinful men did not believe it, and so, in the fullness of time, He came in human form. He flung Himself into the midst of our runaway world and in so doing was badly mangled, even killed on a cross. But does not that very act say to us, "Won't you believe Me now? I do love you."

This is the story of the Gospel. This is the love of God that reaches out to draw the Absalom spirit to Himself. The answer to rebellion is the cross.

WEDNESDAY EVENING, MAY 8

TITLE: "The Bible Speaks to Our Condition"

SCRIPTURE READING: Romans 11.

Introduction. Romans 9-11 is a passage that is difficult for the modern casual reader to understand. This passage demands a knowledge of the historical situation in which the writer wrote if one would even begin to understand and interpret this passage correctly. Paul was writing to the Christian community in the city of Rome where a large

Jewish community had been for about 200 years. Some of these Jewish people had been converted to Christianity, but the overwhelming majority of the believers were Gentiles. As time went by, Gentiles greatly outnumbered Jewish converts. This gave rise to questions concerning the place that the Jewish people now occupied in the purpose of God.

Paul registers the great concern of his heart for the conversion of his kinsmen according to the flesh (Rom. 9:1-4; 10:1-3).

In this passage Paul discusses how

that the Jewish people in trying to obtain righteousness by the law rather than through faith have disqualified themselves to be the instrument of God for evangelizing the world.

This entire passage deals with God's mercy and the mystery of God's dealings with men. Daily, we should study the Scriptures that we might better understand God's plans for our life.

I. *God's Dealings With Man Are Always Based on His Grace* (11:5, 6). In the Book of Romans, Paul emphasizes that God in grace approaches man in his need. God does not deal with man on the basis of the merit or the achievements of man.

II. *Man Responds to God Through Faith* (11:20, 23). Through faith we receive a "faith-righteousness" rather than a "law-righteousness." The Jewish people were seeking to pursue and obtain righteousness by keeping the law. Paul affirms repeatedly on the basis of the experience of Abraham (Rom. 4) and the teaching of the prophets that men obtain justification (a condition of acceptance before God) on the basis of their faith rather than on the basis of their keeping the law of Moses.

III. *There Is Hope for Israel Through Faith in the Messiah* (11:12, 14, 15). The people of Israel had excluded themselves from the redemptive program of God because of their unbelief in the promises and provisions of God. This was their record through history. It came to a crowning climax in their rejection of Jesus Christ as the Messiah.

In the heart of God, there continues to be a hope for the redemption of Israel through faith in the Messiah. This chapter opens with the question, "Hath God cast away his people?" With a strong negative, the apostle declares that they continue to be in the scope of God's loving redemptive concern.

The present-day church has not faced up to its responsibility and opportunity at the point of evangelizing those who make up modern-day Judaism. The Jews of today need to be pointed to the Messiah through whom they can experience justification and obtain the righteousness of faith.

IV. *Humility, Rather Than Conceit, Should Characterize Christians* (11:18). It is possible that some of the Gentile Christians in Rome were boastful and proud of their privileged position in the program of God. Paul rebuked this attitude of conceit and encourages an attitude of humility and gratitude for the privilege of being in God's great redemptive program.

V. *God's Ways Are Above Human Understanding* (11:33-36). There will always be some things that are mysterious and impossible for human beings to understand concerning the work of God. He is the eternal One, and we are creatures of the day. He has all knowledge and we see only little fractions of truth.

Instead of questioning the judgments of God, we should respond to our opportunities for worship and witness day by day in the confidence that the good Lord will bring all things to a wonderful consummation.

Conclusion. God has been so good to us. He wants to continue to be gracious to us. Let us go out into this day and in every day as His messengers and as His servants, rejoicing in His goodness.

SUNDAY MORNING, MAY 12 (Mother's Day)

TITLE: "Christ in Your Home"

TEXT: "And again he entered into Capernaum after some days; and it was noised that he was in the house" (Mark 2:1).

SCRIPTURE READING: Mark 2:1-12.

HYMNS: "Have Faith in God," McKinney. "O Blessed Day of Motherhood," McGregor. "Faith of Our Mothers," Patten.

OFFERTORY PRAYER:

Our Father, on this special day we would pause to thank Thee for Thy wonderful gifts to us through our mothers. Help us to be mindful that every good and perfect gift is from Thee. Thou hast been most generous toward us. Today, as we give our tithes and offerings, help us to be grateful for Thy great love toward us in the giving of Thy Son in our place on the cross for our sins. In Jesus' name. Amen.

Introduction. The Jesus of history wants to be the Christ of our present-day experience. If we would experience the benevolent and powerful presence of Jesus Christ, we must let the Christ who once lived, died on the cross, conquered death to live again, come to live where we live life today.

We can let this living Christ speak to us from the mountain side as He did in the past.

As Christ spoke to His disciples while on board ship in the midst of a storm, so we can let Him speak to us in the storms that threaten us.

As His disciples listened to Him in the Temple, so we need to listen to Him when we go to the place dedicated to prayer and worship.

The Christ would speak to us in dialogue as individuals as He did during His ministry if we will but put ourselves in the middle of these passages as recorded in the New Testament.

Today, on this day called Mother's Day, let us listen to Him and look at Him while visiting in a home. It is possible that these words which were spoken and the event described took place in the home of Simon Peter. He made a visit to the home of Peter (Mark 1:29-31). While there he ministered to Peter's mother-in-law. He brought healing to one who was sick and in pain. The Christ specializes in bringing healing into the home. He is eager to bring relief from pain and suffering. Is there need for healing and health and relief in your home?

I. *Invite the Christ to Come Into Your Home.* We can be safe in assuming that our Lord entered the home of Simon Peter by invitation. He was welcome there.

It is possible that the events surrounding the healing of the man sick with a palsy took place while Jesus was in the home of Simon

141

Peter. However, it could have been another home. Again, we can be safe in assuming that Jesus was in this home by a specific invitation.

A. The entire family should invite Jesus Christ into the home. This is the ideal.

B. Many times Jesus enters the home because of the invitation of one individual. It may be the wife. It could be the husband. In many instances, a child comes to have faith in Jesus Christ. By means of dwelling in one individual heart, the Christ comes to live within a house; and by means of that individual's Christian testimony, a companion can experience conversion, a parent can receive the gift of faith, children can come to know the Lord Jesus Christ.

C. On this Mother's Day, every mother would be wise to extend a personal invitation to Jesus Christ to come and live within her own heart and live within her own home.

II. *Christ Carries on a Spiritual Conversation in the Home* (Mark 2:2). In the last phrase of verse 2, we read, "And he preached the word unto them." This phrase could leave a false impression. The word which is translated "preached" is not the word which refers to a proclamation or an official announcement. It is not the word which refers to evangelism and announcing the good news. Rather, it is the word which means "to speak, talk, to converse." It literally means that our Lord carried on a conversation with the people in the house concerning spiritual matters.

Those of us who are in the home should recognize that it is possible for the living Christ to so dwell within us that in our conversations we can discuss spiritual things and encourage the faith of each other and experience the presence of the living Christ as we do so.

We must not labor under the impression that the living Christ is limited to the place of public worship and to the altar dedicated to Him.

We would be exceedingly wise in the home if we would give the Christ an opportunity to converse with us. Some suggestions are offered.

A. We should engage in a sincere prayer of thanksgiving at the table before meals.

B. We should memorize verses of Scripture that contain great truths about God, and these should be repeated from time to time so that they can be written on the walls of our memory.

C. We can read selected passages from the Bible and discuss the meaning of these passages within the family circle.

D. We can sing a familiar hymn on appropriate occasions.

E. We can pray together in a family circle with hands joined from time to time.

F. We can read or tell a bedtime Bible story to children.

G. We can encourage private, personal Bible study on a day-by-day basis on the part of each member of the family.

The Christ will join in these times

of conversation and dialogue if we will but let Him.

III. *The Christ Will Encourage Hope While in the Home.* There were many who came to the home in Capernaum where Jesus was. It was impossible to conceal His presence in the home. If we let Him live within our home today, His presence will affect us and the results will become known to those about us. It is possible that many will be drawn to the house in which Christ dwells as is described by the passage of Scripture which we have read today.

A. Some came to see Jesus out of mere curiosity.

B. Many sought to get in because they needed the help which Jesus could give. His very presence was a basis for hope. Some of them were hoping for a revolution against the tyranny of Rome. Others came because they felt a great need for a fresh and loving word from God.

C. There were four men who came bringing a friend, hoping for the return of his health, happiness, usefulness and productiveness.

D. The helpless one was brought on a palette for the return of that which he had lost.

When Christ is permitted to dwell in a home, He imparts hope for something better in the heart of all who live within that home.

IV. *Christ Announced Forgiveness While He Was in the Home* (Mark 2:5).

A. Jesus met the man's spirit-ual need before giving attention to his physical need.

1. The two needs may have been vitally related.

2. Jesus recognized the spiritual need of the man to be of primary importance.

3. In other instances Jesus met the physical need as if it were of primary importance.

B. Unforsaken and unforgiven sin always creates pain and sickness. Sin is a cheater and a robber. Sin separates man from his highest and best self. It literally cripples him and trips him up from becoming what he is capable of being.

C. Christ specializes in forgiving sin.

1. Christ deals with us in mercy and love as well as power.

2. When Christ forgives, He removes the pain created by our alienation from Him.

3. When Christ forgives, He restores a warm relationship with the sinner.

It could be that the greatest need in your home is the need for forgiveness. Do mother and father need to forgive each other for some act or attitude of unkindness? Do parents need to have a forgiving attitude toward children who have disappointed them and perhaps disobeyed them?

Forgiveness that is full and free and forever can bring about health and happiness that nothing else can bring.

Conclusion. Christ revealed who He was in the home. He revealed that He was the Son of man; actually He was the unique messenger of God. He was the promised One of God. He was the Lamb of God who came to take away our sins. He was and is the Lord over all. In this passage He assumed the role of God in forgiving sin. He made illness and pain disappear as if it did not exist.

Christ can make a great difference in your heart and home. He would communicate with you day by day. He would encourage hope and enable you to meet the crises and responsibilities of life with courage. He will deal with your sin problem. You must make Him Lord of all if you would know life in its fullness and in its beauty.

Invite Him to make His home in your heart. He comes seeking entrance into your heart. He will bring heaven into your life in the here and now. He will take you to heaven in the hereafter. It all depends on your decision to invite Him into your heart and into your home.

SUNDAY EVENING, MAY 12

TITLE: "The Teenager and War"

TEXT: "And Abner said to Joab, 'Let the young men arise and play before us.' And Joab said, 'Let them arise'" (2 Sam. 2:14, RSV).

SCRIPTURE READING: 2 Samuel 2:8-14.

Introduction. War is hell! Visit the war cemeteries of the world and see for yourself. Gaze upon the white crosses at the Battlefield of Gettysburg and feel a great sigh of sadness. Go to the National Cemetery at Washington, D. C. and see there the casualties of war. Go to Flanders Field and see the poppies growing between the crosses row upon row. I visited Europe following World War II and saw the rubble and the destruction. I saw what the bombs did in Mannheim and Frankfort, Germany, and I said, "War is hell."

In my text we find these words, "And Abner said to Joab, 'Let the young men arise and play before us.' And Joab said, 'Let them arise.' " It is the young men, who have little or nothing to do with the precipitating of war, who have to bear the brunt of the fighting. There was a time when those who fought the wars, suffered the most, but we live in a day when civil population, the women and children do the most suffering. War seems to have lost its power to protect the innocent. Now it often destroys the innocent.

Why do men fight wars? Listen to James 4:1: "Is it not your passions that are at war in your members?" (RSV). Men refuse to reason it out and therefore they have to fight it out.

I. *Three Attitudes Toward War.*

A. Holy War—the attitude that it has been willed by God. In the Old Testament God seemed to send His people out to fight their battles and destroy their enemies. Many wars of history have been fought as holy wars. In the

Crusades the monks and the priests went up and down the land crying, "God wills it. Deliver Jerusalem from the pagans."

B. The second attitude is that of a just war. The idea is that war is evil, but that it's a lesser evil. People have felt a compulsion to defend the nation against barbarians, to defend a Christian nation against the pagans. All theologians have recognized war as evil, but sometimes the lesser evil. It is a lesser evil than a godless tyranny, than a totalitarian state. As one man said, "I'd rather die on my feet than live on my knees." Having seen the evils of Hitler and the mass murder of six million Jews, I'm sure that some of us have felt that war, under certain circumstances, is justified.

C. But the third attitude is that of rejection. According to some historians the early Christians were overwhelmingly pacifists. We find no writer who condones war during the first few centuries after Christ lived. One has given four reasons why the early Christians were pacifists:

1. The early return of our Lord.

2. They felt no compulsion to fight.

3. They saw no difference in killing privately or corporately.

4. As followers of the Prince of Peace, they felt they should have no part in the bloody business of war. We see then a higher revelation of God in Christ. We find more of the will of God in Jesus Christ.

II. *Today a Major War Would Be Great Evil.* For the first time, there is the possibility of complete annihilation. When the tumult subsides, this planet of ours will be an irrevocable inferno of radioactive debris.

There is a new word in the language of the militarist—"overkill!" Do you realize that we have enough bombs in our stock pile of nuclear bombs to overkill the whole world many times? Of course, we admit once is enough. But can you sense the great danger that we face? The ABC warfare is even more horrifying. "A" stands for the atomic bomb. There is a certain quickness in death from it. "B" stands for the bacteriological danger. Poison the waters and the air, and this is a horrible death. "C" is the chemical warfare. The Massachusetts Institute of Technology says that the fallout shelter is absolutely no good in protecting from the all-out ABC warfare. Further, Walter Lippman says: "If there is an all-out war, the first casualty will be democracy." One hundred million people will die. The world will look for a strong-arm leader. There may be a remnant that will survive, and start a new order, a new civilization.

Someone asked Einstein about the weapons of World War III. He said, "I don't know, but I'll tell you the weapons for the one after that will be stones, arrows, and clubs." Yes, when the bombs of World War III hit, this beautiful earth will become a swirling hell of death.

III. *This Throws a Different Light Upon the Concept of War.* I believe the whole thrust of the Christian message should be to work for peace. We need to sit at the feet of the Prince of Peace, and learn of Him. I do not believe that Jesus

Christ would approve of warfare. You say, "Well, didn't He drive out the tax collectors from the Temple, and use force upon them?" He took a whip of small cords and He drove out the sheep and the oxen, but there is no evidence that He used such physical violence on any person. Jesus Christ is one who overcomes evil with good, hatred by love, and the world by a cross. Jesus said, "My kingdom is not of this world, else would my servants fight" (Matt. 18:36).

There is a verse in the New Testament that says, "And when they saw the . . . soldiers, they stopped beating Paul" (Acts 18:32, RSV). Military power can be used to protect the innocent. But the time has come when the innocent suffer with the guilty. Sometimes women and children do the most suffering. To compare war to killing a mad dog is a false analogy. In war the mad dog is not the only one killed. Millions of innocent youth and innocent people are slaughtered. Further, the prophets visioned world peace. Isaiah and Micah saw people beating "their swords into plowshares, and their spears into pruning hooks." In Matthew 26:52, Jesus said, "All who take the sword will perish by the sword" (RSV). In the Book of Acts we find the Christians defying governments to do the will of God and saying, "We must obey God rather than men" (Acts 5:29, RSV). Now there is no clear teaching "against war" in the New Testament, but the whole direction of the New Testament is toward

peace. Reconciliation is at the heart of the Christian message. When Jesus spoke of "peacemakers," He spoke to them as individuals, but it must not end there. If it does, it ends.

Conclusion. What shall we do? We must be more, as a church, than a feeble echo of the military. We must be more than just enemies of the Communists. There is a place for those who work for peace. There is a place for reconciliation. I still believe that there is a place and purpose for the United Nations. I believe that we should increase the social and political contacts with all nations. The more we come to know each other, the greater friendships are formed, and the greater opportunity we have for living together in peace. I believe there may come the possibility of multilateral disarmament. I believe we must learn how to live together. There should come the acceptance of co-existence. I believe that Christian people of the world should work together with Jesus Christ, our Lord, in bringing peace to this earth. I don't believe that this universe is an affair of chance. I believe that there is a mind behind our lives here, meaning in them, purpose running through them, and destiny running ahead of them so we can have confidence and hope. Such a situation as we face today calls us to have great faith in almighty God, and to believe that He will work together with us in bringing in His kingdom.

TITLE: "The Bible Speaks to Our Condition"

SCRIPTURE READING: 1 Corinthians 2.

Introduction. In the chapter for devotional study today, we find worldly wisdom and the work of the Holy Spirit in sharp contrast. Reference to wisdom appears in six verses of the chapter, and the work of the Holy Spirit is referred to in seven verses. The word "wisdom" is used in a variety of different ways. It does not mean the same thing each time it occurs. In some instances it refers to the strivings of man as he approaches life from a common sense standpoint without any assistance from the Holy Spirit. In other instances, this word is used to refer to God's plan and purpose of salvation in and through Jesus Christ.

I. *Christ at the Very Center* (2:2). Paul was determined to exalt Jesus Christ at the expense of all other efforts and objectives. In a crucified and risen Savior, man had a revelation of God's love, power, and purpose. Christ crucified must be at the very center rather than on the circumference of our life and ministry.

II. *The Wisdom of This Age* (2:1, 4, 6, 13). Do you live solely by the principles of common sense, or are you open to the possibility of walking by faith in the promises of God? The wisdom of this age is merely man's interpretation of God and life unaided by the Holy Spirit. The mind of man is subject to deception by others and even by self-deception. We must be open to God's revelation of Himself through Jesus Christ as the Holy Spirit guides.

III. *The Work of the Holy Spirit.* The chapter of the Word of God which we should search diligently this day speaks most dramatically of the work which the Holy Spirit wants to do in the heart of the individual Christian and in the life of the congregation.

A. The Holy Spirit makes effective the giving of our Christian testimony (2:4, 5).

B. The Holy Spirit reveals the rich spiritual gifts that God has bestowed upon us (2:9-13). Verse 9 is often used as a reference to what God has provided in heaven. In reality, it is talking about what God has provided for us in the present. Rich relationships and inexhaustible resources are available right now to the child of God who by faith will follow our Lord in devoted service.

C. The Holy Spirit makes it possible for us to understand the mind of Christ (2:16b). The natural man does not understand the things of God because they can be grasped only by those who have been born of the Spirit and who are open to the guidance of the Holy Spirit (2:14).

If we would truly become Christlike in spirit and action, we must become like Christ in our thoughts.

Conclusion. As we give ourselves day by day to a reverent, responsive study of God's Holy Word, the Holy Spirit will guide us and teach us the things of God so that we can think the very thoughts of Christ (John 14:26; 16:13-15).

To neglect a daily reading of God's Holy Word is to deprive ourselves of the privilege of becoming better acquainted with our living and loving Lord.

TITLE: "The Value of a Good Name"

TEXT: "A good name is rather to be chosen than great riches, and loving favour rather than silver and gold" (Prov. 22:1).

SCRIPTURE READING: Exodus 20:7; 1 Timothy 6:1.

HYMNS: "O Worship the King," Grant. "Jesus Is All the World to Me," Thompson. "Take the Name of Jesus With You," Baxter.

OFFERTORY PRAYER:

Holy, heavenly Father, today we would thank You for life. We would thank You for opportunities and responsibilities. We would praise You for Your goodness to us in every area of life.

We come during this hour of worship to offer ourselves for ministries of mercy that will bring glory to Your name and release Your blessings into the lives of others. We bring our tithes and love offerings as an indication of our desire that all of life be dedicated to You. In Jesus' name. Amen.

Introduction. In modern times a family name means little more than just the name which designates us as individuals who live at a certain place at a certain time. Such has not always been the case. In Biblical days great stress was placed upon the names of individuals and places. The name of a person provided insight into his character and into his life. Perhaps both our secular life and our spiritual life would be greatly enriched if a greater emphasis was placed today upon the value and the significance of a good name. A person's name really stands for his person, his character, his reputation, his integrity.

Throughout the Scriptures men were warned against using the name of God carelessly. To use His name was to involve Him in either their conversation or their activity. God did not want to be misrepresented by the careless use of His name.

A family should be vitally concerned about its good name. Rich indeed are the children who receive a good name from their parents. The value of one's name should be maintained at all times.

It would be helpful if we would recognize and respond properly to the names which have been bestowed upon us as the children of God and as the servants of the Lord Jesus. In the New Testament we find at least five names or titles that are applied to us which we should bear with gratitude, dignity, and honor.

I. *We are Called "Believers" Because of Our Faith.* It is by faith that we respond to the love of God as revealed in the person of Jesus Christ. Because of our faith, God justifies us—declares us righteous and gives to us a position of acceptance in His presence. We do not find acceptance in the presence of God on the basis of our keeping the law or on the basis of our moral perfection. It is by faith that we please God, and it is by faith that we achieve significant goals in the Christian life.

If we would wear this title of "believer" with honor, we must exercise faith and grow a great faith.

II. *We Are Called "Brothers" Be-*

cause of Our Love. The new birth produces a spiritual infant who becomes a member of the family of God. We become brothers and sisters of each other in the family of God. As brothers and sisters, we should love each other sincerely and steadfastly. We should rejoice with those who rejoice and weep with those who weep. We should make a positive, creative contribution toward the welfare of others within the family. We are under obligation to be especially gracious and kind toward those who are of the household of faith (Gal. 6:9, 10).

Let us respond to the brotherhood of faith with a persistent, unbreakable spirit of goodwill.

III. *We Are Called "Disciples" Because of Our Learning and Knowledge.* The disciples of our Lord were His followers. They listened to His teachings. They were enrolled in His school. They recognized their need for the new truths that He was seeking to communicate.

To be a true disciple, we must sit at the feet of Jesus Christ and recognize Him as heaven's infallible and authoritative teacher. We are not only to hear, but we are to heed His teachings and commandments.

We can never become Christlike in conduct until we become Christlike in our thinking. We must let the mind of Jesus Christ become our mind.

To be a disciple is to accept a discipline. The word disciple and discipline have the same root meaning. To be a disciple, we must let the way of Christ become our way.

IV. *We Are Called "Saints" Because of Our Holiness.* There are some who think of saints as being unearthly heavenly creatures who have achieved a degree of perfection that has permitted them to enter heaven on the basis of their own merit. This is a non-Biblical concept. To be a saint is to be a dedicated one. It means to belong to, to be set apart to the purposes of God. The New Testament uses the word "saint" to refer to all believers, to all converts, to all of the children of God. We are not our own, we have been bought with a price. We belong to God. We need to face up to the divine ownership and recognize our Savior's lordship. As saints, we have been called to be saintly both in spirit and in conduct.

V. *We Are Called Christians Because of Our Spirit and Because of Our Works* (Acts 11:26). We should not use the term, Christian, as a synonym for a believer or for a disciple or even for a brother. Ideally we would bestow the title, Christian, only upon those who have let the mind of Christ so take possession of them that the Spirit of Christ permeated all that they said and did.

To be genuinely Christian is to be Christlike

    . . . in our attitudes
    . . . in our affections
    . . . in our ambitions
    . . . in our actions

Conclusion. The Bible bestows many good names upon us. With the help of the Holy Spirit and with the guidance that we can find in the Word of God, it is possible for us to wear each of these good names with honor and with dignity. By so doing, we bring glory to the name of our God and we obtain a good name for ourselves.

149

TITLE: "The Teenager and Drink"

TEXT: "Wine is a mocker, strong drink is raging: and whosoever is deceived thereby is not wise" (Prov. 20:1).

SCRIPTURE READING: Proverbs 23:19-31.

Introduction. One of the most serious problems facing American youth is drinking. The situation is alarming. It is frightening. We face a crisis. Alcohol is a dangerous enemy of the youth, of the home, and of the nation. In a California community, a teenager gave a drinking party while his parents were away from home. The officer who was called to calm the disturbance was beaten to death by the teenagers. In Ocean City, Maryland, 2,000 yelling, screaming, fighting teenagers had a wild beach party. They grew louder and noisier as the night wore on. The police finally broke it up with tear gas and police dogs. Even in old days, when people used and drank wine, it soon became a problem. Proverbs 23:29-31 speaks of this.

I. *Alcohol Is a Dangerous Enemy of Youth.*

A. The first reason is because alcoholism has become the No. 1 killer. It is listed as the No. 4 killer in America, preceded only by heart disease, cancer, and tuberculosis. But, should we include the deaths and tragedies triggered by alcohol, it would become the No. 1 killer, the No. 1 menace, the No. 1 health hazard in this nation. Dr. Andrew Ivey, the foremost authority, perhaps, in America, on alcohol, says that almost half the fatal automobile accidents are due to drink. In a study made by the *Saturday Evening Post* a few years ago, it was found that in the past two years drinking and drunken teenage drivers have accounted for forty percent of the highway fatalities. Put a drinking person behind the wheel of an automobile, and you have a potentially dangerous killer on the highway.

B. There is the danger of addiction to alcohol. Dr. Ivey says that alcohol is a habit-forming, craving-producing, addiction-producing drug. He states that there are now 5,400,000 alcoholics. Considering them and their families, there are 25,000,000 Americans now affected by alcoholism. One out of every seven people will go down as a victim of alcohol. Two-thirds of the alcoholics begin drinking while in high school. So I say, it is about as safe for youth to play Russian roulette as it is for them to drink.

C. Drinking causes juvenile problems. A U.S. district judge, Luther Youngdahl, summed it up well, "Alcoholism is one of the most devastating factors contributing to juvenile delinquency." From the editorial pages of the Long Beach Press comes this word, "A fifteen-year-old girl was arrested for drunkenness. Her mother finally came to get her at the juvenile court, and looked startled and said, 'I'm amazed. Why, I thought I had taught her to drink like a lady.' "

D. Drinking causes law enforcement problems. DD—drunk and disorderly—is the most common item on the police blotter.

E. Drink is related to mental and physical illness. It is related to poverty. It is related to broken homes. It is related to crime, unemployment, immorality, misery, tragedy, and death! We can say, then, that alcohol is at the root of most, and the ally of all, the evils that infest our society. Think what alcohol does to you! The doctors say, "Drinking impairs reason, will, self-control, judgment, physical skill, and endurance." It removes inhibitions and weakens social controls, which in translation means that when you drink, you lose control of your thinking and your standard of values. I have never been able to be amused at the antics of one who is under the influence of drink. It is always sad to me. I feel like saying with Shakespeare, "Oh, God, that men should put an enemy in their mouths to steal away their brain, that we should for pleasure and applause transform ourselves into beasts."

II. *Why Do People Drink?* There must be some value in it! Surely, 60,000,000 people can't be wrong!

A. The average American Christian is no longer tempted toward Puritanism. He has joined the world. He lives in an affluent society, likes leisure time, and wants to enjoy all the good things of life. Thus, with leisure on his hands, and the desire to keep up with the Joneses, the average American has begun to drink to add pleasure to life. It has become a part of the social pattern!

B. Dr. Ivey says there are three reasons why people drink:

1. The desire to be sociable.

2. It tastes good.

3. It makes one feel good. As one said, "I take it to relax, to get along with people, and to calm my nerves."

Dr. Ivey sums it up, "Thus, alcohol gives temporary relief from worry, abolishes mental tension, disfigures difficulties, relieves a feeling of inferiority, makes a weak person feel strong, an ignorant person feel smart, a poor person feel rich, and an oppressed person feel free." People drink then for immediate thrills and excitement. To have a big time!

C. Here is another reason: people drink to escape the pressures of something in their experience, in themselves, or in their surroundings, possibly to escape pain, or failure, or boredom, or frustration, or fear, or guilt. In every congregation, I suppose, there are varied reactions to drink. Some are struggling with problems, some enjoy drinking socially, some feel it necessary to drink for business or health reasons, but some are violently opposed to drink. Now, I do not want to preach at you or condemn you. I want you to reason together with me about some reasons why it is smarter not to drink.

III. *What Shall We Do?* To drink or not to drink is the question. In the light of the facts, every person must decide for himself. I think we should have a compassionate understanding for those who feel that it is right for them to drink. I fear that sometimes the nagging, self-righteous, condemnatory attitude of good people makes drinking problems worse in some folk. Not drinking does not make you a fine Christian! I have known many church people who would not touch a drop but were hateful, mean, cruel, self-righteous, and critical.

A. What is the Christian view of drink? The teaching of Christ emphasizes the sacredness of human personality. Anything which blights and destroys human personality is opposed to the Gospel of Christ. I wish you could sit where I sit and see what drink does to people's lives, homes, and children! I believe people should regard total abstinence as an essential part of our witness to the faith. When we remember the compassionate Great Physician, Jesus Christ, and His love for people, we know that He would not condone what liquor is doing to the people of this nation. I believe Jesus Christ would take His stand against it.

B. You and I should accept responsibility for living up to our highest and best. We should face reality. There is something noble about self-control.

C. The use of alcohol violates the Christian principle that we are each our brother's keeper. We are stewards of our influence. He who uses alcohol may, by his example, lay a stumbling block in the path of a brother, and thus contribute to the destruction of another person. The influence of personal example is a sacred trust. For a Christian, the use of intoxicating liquors is a fundamental moral question which must be answered in the light of the Gospel of Jesus Christ. Turn to Habakkuk 2:15.

D. Remember that your body is a temple for the dwelling place of the Holy Spirit. The Bible says that if anyone destroys God's temple, God will destroy him, for God's temple is holy, and that temple you are. It's a frightening thing to be a temple of God. We are to keep it holy. We are to live so that we will not desecrate the body. No greater sorrow can come than the realization that one has destroyed the temple of his life. "If your hand or your foot cause you to sin, cut it off, and throw it from you." There is nothing about a hand or a foot in itself that requires it to be cut off, but if gangrene is present, the entire body is in danger and amputation saves life. If drinking affects your body, your life, your integrity, if it endangers your home, then cast it from you!

Conclusion. Are you one who has tried and failed, or whose heart has been broken by some problem related to drink? Remember the power of Jesus Christ to forgive and to redeem and to restore. There's always hope as long as we have faith in God.

WEDNESDAY EVENING, MAY 22

TITLE: "The Bible Speaks to Our Condition"

SCRIPTURE READING: 1 Corinthians 9.

Introduction. Paul's epistle to the Corinthians deals with problems that perplex the fellowship of the Church. By its very nature, the epistle is instructive and corrective in nature. Evidently, this church had written to Paul concerning certain questions and problems that distressed them. Paul seeks to answer these questions one by one as he writes this epistle.

I. *Paul's Reply to Criticism* (9:1-17). As we read between the lines and examine the questions that Paul raises and answers, we discover that he had experienced severe criticism from someone in Corinth.

Kindly, logically, and firmly he sought to reply to this criticism of his apostleship and his authority as an authentic teacher and servant of God. He defends his right to participate in many privileges which he had voluntarily denied himself for the sake of the Gospel. Paul was determined to not let any personal privilege or right serve to hinder the advance of the Gospel (9:12b). Paul had denied himself at the point of receiving financial support from those to whom he ministered lest this become a hindrance to the Gospel (9:13-15).

II. *For the Advance of the Gospel* (9:19-23). Paul's consuming ambition was to proclaim the good news of God's love to as many different people as he possibly could. He adapted both his conduct and his presentation of the good news to various classes and conditions so as to effectively communicate to them the truth of God's love, be they Jews, Gentile converts to Judaism, or pagans.

Great changes would take place in our lives and in the lives of those about us if we had this compelling compassion that caused us to always think in terms of helping others come to know the Lord Jesus.

III. *Voluntary Self-Discipline Is Essential* (9:24-27). The apostle was familiar with the great athletic events of his day. He uses athletic terminology to describe the voluntary self-discipline which is essential if the servants of Christ would be effective. We should run like members of a track team so as to win the approval of our Lord.

Instead of acting like a boxer who swings wild haymakers, we should fight to win in the battle with evil.

Paul declares that the individual must keep himself under rigid discipline lest the evil within him, and the evil about him, so affect his life as to be disqualified to participate in the great race.

In verse 29 the apostle is not thinking in terms of losing his salvation, but in terms of losing the privilege of being an effective servant for the Lord. He is determined that he will not disqualify himself as an effective communicator of the good news of God's love.

Conclusion. We must not let criticism discourage and defeat us. Criticism is bound to come.

We must adapt the message of the good news to meet the unique needs of each individual to whom we seek to communicate. Personal, voluntary self-discipline will always be essential for the person who wants to be a genuine follower of the Lord Jesus Christ.

TITLE: "A Proper Love for Self"

TEXT: "Thou shalt love thy neighbour as thyself" (Matt. 22:39b).

SCRIPTURE READING: Matthew 22:35-39.

HYMNS: "Love Divine, All Loves Excelling," Wesley. "O Love of God Most Full," Clute. "More Love to Thee," Prentiss.

OFFERTORY PRAYER:

Gracious God, help us to be conscious always of the fact that we are but stewards of Thy grace. Help us to be good managers of that which Thou hast entrusted to our care. Help us this day to bring a tithe and an offering that would indicate the sincerity of our love and a deep concern that all of the world might hear the Gospel of Thy redeeming love through the missionary outreach of the Church. For in the name of our Lord we pray. Amen.

Introduction. If we would seek to condense into capsule form the total duty of man to God and the total duty of man to man, we would find such in these two commandments.

These two commandments are invitations that enlarge, increase, and enrich life rather than being rules that restrict and impoverish life.

One of the greatest truths to be found in these commandments may be missed by the casual reader. The second commandment reveals that the measure of our love for self is the measure of love that we are to express toward our neighbor. It follows that if we do not have a proper love for self, we will have no authentic guideline for loving others as we do ourselves.

If one has a low view of himself, he will have a low view of others.

Those who hate themselves cannot love others.

Those who hate themselves cannot really love God until their hate is dissipated.

Unless a man can come to a proper evaluation of himself, it will be impossible for him to really love God and love others. The best way for a man to come to this estimation of himself is through a discovery of the extent to which God loves him. Do you find it difficult to love God? Do you find it impossible at times to love others? Could it be that this is due to the fact that you have a very low view of yourself?

I. *What Are the Symptoms That Indicate the Lack of a Proper Love for Self?*

A. Do you have a habitual tendency to belittle yourself? This can be a form of self-destruction that indicates a lack of a proper love for self.

B. Do you refuse to believe in your own ability to achieve meaningful goals in life? If one chops himself down, it may indicate that he has a lack of respect for himself.

C. Do you hesitate to attempt that which is new or difficult? If so, is this because of laziness or is it due to a lack of confidence in yourself which in turn is a result of the low esteem in which you hold yourself?

D. Do you reject your real self by attempting to escape through artificial means? Some resort to the use of drugs because they have a very low estimate of themselves. The use of alcoholic beverages is often due to the fact that one is seeking to escape from his concept of reality in which he considers himself to be less than he ought to be.

E. Do you reveal a proper love for yourself by a continuing flight from one place to another and from one situation to another?

F. Suicide may be the ultimate in self-hate. He who commits suicide often is one who has had a very low estimate of himself. He does not love himself. He does not admire his ability. He holds himself in very low esteem as one who is not worthy to continue to exist.

II. *What Are the Factors That Contribute to This Lack of a Proper Love for Self?*

A. Some experience an absence of love in early youth. It is highly important that a child experience the genuine, steadfast love of parents. Children who are raised without parents often come to believe that they were rejected because they were unlovely. To feel unloved does something to a child's sense of self-esteem. This deficiency of affection can lead to mental illness and to various kinds of abnormal and destructive activity.

B. Some are overwhelmed by negative and insulting criticisms during their early formative years.

Parents and teachers need to be very cautious lest they resort to cutting and hurtful criticisms in their efforts to provide guidance for children. Those who consider themselves to be specialists in cutting others down to size, may do far more harm to others than they realize.

Parents and teachers should major on constructive criticism that contains stimulating compliments rather than being specialists at the point of being critical.

C. Some have a low opinion of themselves because of uncomplimentary comparisons with others. This comes about as a result of the individual's failure to recognize himself as a unique creation of individual worth.

Each individual must accept himself as he is and appreciate his strengths without letting his weaknesses destroy his sense of self-confidence and sense of personal worth.

D. Some belittle themselves and even hate themselves because of unresolved guilt. If we would deal with this problem properly, we need to recognize the sinfulness of sin and at the same time acknowledge our personal responsibility for our sin.

We can resolve the guilt that destroys by confessing to God our sin and accepting His forgiveness. God is the God of forgiveness. When God forgives, He holds the sin against us no longer, and He restores a warm relationship.

Perhaps the best way to solve the problem of unresolved guilt is to accept God's forgiveness and then to really forgive ourselves. If God forgives us, then we should forgive ourselves also.

E. We must not forget that the old devil, Satan, is an accuser. The basic meaning of the name Satan is "to accuse." The Bible teaches us that the devil is a liar, a deceiver, and a falsifier. He is in the business of trying to destroy us. Often he destroys us by calling our attention to our own faults, flaws, and failures. If he can destroy our self-confidence and self-respect, he will make midgets out of those whom God wants to be giants.

III. *Suggested Steps for Developing a Proper Love for Self.* If we would love our neighbor as God commands us to, we must have a proper love for self. There is no better place for the individual to develop this proper love for self than within the home circle. The following suggestions are offered for consideration within the home.

A. Recognize God's love for you and find full forgiveness in His offer of salvation through faith in Jesus Christ (John 3:16).

B. Fully forgive yourself. Praise God for His mercy and grace and respond to the truth that when God forgives, God forgets. Accept the truth that Jesus Christ died for your sins. Quit looking back to the failures of the past. Look forward and encourage others to look forward.

C. Evaluate yourself properly. Jesus encouraged His disciples to overcome the agony of anxiety by coming to a proper evaluation of their personal worth in the sight of God (Matt. 6:25, 26).

D. Decide to accept the uniqueness of your own person (Matt. 6:27). You are the only person in existence that is exactly like your-self. Accept yourself. Be at peace with yourself. Do not fret because you are not like someone else.

E. Decide to discipline yourself (Matt. 7:13, 14). In these words our Lord is describing the narrow, disciplined life that leads one to life on its highest plane and to its richest quality. This kind of life comes to those who discipline themselves.

F. Dedicate yourself to the highest and to the best (Matt. 6:33). Many of us live on a low level because we never dedicate ourselves to the highest. Jesus would invite and encourage us to dedicate ourselves to the doing of God's will in life.

He who lives day by day to fulfill the will of God for his personal life and who gives himself in ministries to others will come to have an attitude of appreciation for himself as well as for his Lord and for others.

Conclusion. If we would be able to love others as self, we must first of all love ourselves properly.

We come to a proper evaluation of self as we recognize ourselves to be the objects of God's supreme concern.

God loves you. God really loves you. He gave His son on the cross to reveal the extent of His love for you.

If God loves you to that degree, then you should recognize your own personal worth. As you recognize your worth, you will find yourself recognizing the worth of others also

TITLE: "The Teenager and Doubt"

TEXT: "And said unto him, Art thou he that should come, or do we look for another?" (Matt. 11:3).

SCRIPTURE READING: Matthew 11:1-11.

Introduction. A figure clothed in camel's hair looks through the bars of the window of his cell. John the Baptist is in the desert prison of Machaerus. As he stands there, tall and strong, the wavy locks of his hair lie about his broad shoulders. His dark eyes flash with the spirit of a man who has known the freedom of the out-of-doors. His firm, drawn lips speak for the fearless heart of a man who was sure of his mission and would never compromise with evil. His hands grasp the prison bars, and he asks: "Why should my life's work be suddenly stopped at the end of six months of calling men to repent? Why am I in prison when I have work to do for God?"

He walks back and forth in his cell and questions keep coming: "When will my disciples return with a message from Christ? I must be sure."

Early that morning he had sent his disciples to Jesus to ask, "Art thou the coming One, or shall we look for another?"

I. *The Struggle With Doubt.*

A. If you have doubted, you are in good company. The great Christians of all the ages have had their doubts, too.

John the Baptist doubted.

The psalmist doubted.

We live in an age of skepticism. There are many honest doubters. If you have doubts, I wish to speak to you today. Most of us have known the agony of doubt. Thomas à Kempis said, "I have never known anyone so religious that he had not felt at some time a withdrawing of grace, a decreasing zeal."

A great northern preacher entitles a sermon, "The Importance of Doubting Our Doubts." He says that the capacity to doubt is one of man's noblest powers. It has fostered much of the progress in today's world. Honest doubt, ministers spiritual growth. It helps us outgrow our old concepts. Sometimes it is pulling down the old house of faith in order that we might build a bigger and stronger house.

B. We need not be ashamed of our doubt any more than we need be ashamed of growing pains of adolescence. There is faith in honest doubt—that is the essential message of the Book of Job—the moving story of a righteous and Godly man who suffered cruel calamities.

C. The message of the Bible is, "Don't be ashamed of your doubt. Welcome it." You not only have the capacity to doubt, you have the duty to doubt if you would grow into an understanding of God that will meet the needs of your life and the life of the world in this "changing century." Do not repress your doubts. Throw them out into the open, and face them.

In the Bible the great believers were the great doubters. The agony of doubt is no time to throw away the Bible, or turn our backs on the Church. Stay close to God and the resources of the Christian faith. Doubts may be the means of a deeper dedication, a greater understanding, a stronger devotion.

II. *The Source of Doubt.*

A. As John the Baptist walked back and forth in his cell, he remembered so vividly why he was there in the prison. Herod Antipas, that fox, was living in adultery with his brother's wife. John felt called of God to go to the palace and proclaim a message of condemnation. Standing before them, he pointed the finger of God in their faces. He denounced their sin. It was a sin against love, home, and society. It was a sin against the Almighty. He called for them to repent.

Now, he was a prisoner because of his message. Why did Jesus not come and free him? Why did He not come to answer his questions? How long must John wait? In his perplexity, he was asking, "Why were those who lived in wickedness, who mocked at God, who lived in immorality, allowed to openly jeer at his prophecies of their destruction?"

No wonder questions began to form in John's mind.

Have questions come to your mind?

B. What is the source of doubt?

1. Disappointment with our lot in life may cause doubt. You may have wanted one thing, and you have had to settle for another. Maybe you have asked, "Where am I getting in my life? I try so hard, and seem to get no results." Now, you have begun to doubt the meaning and purpose of life.

2. Disillusionment also causes doubt. Like John, you may have been disillusioned with the way of Christ. You wanted Him to come in judgment, in wrath, in condemnation. You wanted Him to send fire from heaven. One thing is certain: The man who waits for savage wrath will always be disappointed in Jesus. The one who waits for things to happen in the dramatic and the cataclysmic ways will usually be disillusioned. It is only as we wait for God to work in love that we see Him accomplishing His purpose and plan.

3. Discouragement is another source of doubt. Do you feel discouraged with the way things are going? Sometimes we put too much confidence in our feelings and our assurance fluctuates. Sometimes we feel good, and sometimes we feel bad. Feelings are unrealiable like the weather. I like what one man said, "Sometimes I'm up, sometimes I'm down, but I'm leaning on the bosom of the Lord."

III. *The Solution to Doubt.*

A. Evening has come at Machaerus. The soldiers enter John's cell. They taunt him as they bring him his evening meal of pork and wine. Jestingly they set it before him. He looks at them and asks, "Why do you jest with one who has set himself under vow to God? Have you no respect for a prophet?"

Not far away, in the city of Jerusalem, in the palace of Herod, that fox, the royal feast has begun. At the midnight hour, the feast reaches its climax. They call for a dance from Salome. The demand grows. "Give us Salome," they shout. Herod demands that she dance, and as Salome moves about the floor, she charms the company of the revelers. "Dance, Salome, dance!"

She dances and Herod is enthralled. Foolhardily, he promises her whatever she would ask. Salome hesitates. Again, he promises whatever she would ask, and pledges it with an oath. She whispers to her mother. Her mother whispers to her. In frenzied curiosity the revelers wait her request. Then she speaks, and her voice carries throughout the room, "I want the head of John the Baptist on a silver platter!" A silence falls like death upon the banquet hall. Herod is horrified.

B. Now, what will happen to John? We see him waiting in the desert prison. We wonder if he will die before the answer comes to his doubts. In the middle of the night, the disciples of John hurriedly return to Machaerus, bearing a strange message.

They enter his cell. "What did He say?" John demands. "Is He the Messiah? Deliver me from these doubts, these fears!" The disciples reply, "We arrived early in the morning with your message. He heard us gladly. Then He asked us to stay with Him that day. We heard Him speak. We saw Him heal the sick, feed the hungry, and cleanse the lepers. At the close of the day He called us and said, "Go, tell John the things you have seen and heard.""

"What did He mean, John?"

John replied, "He is the Messiah."

"How do you know?"

"His works tell us who He is. The things you saw Him do tell us that He is the Son of God."

His words tell us, too. No one has ever spoken like this. His life tells us who He is. No one has ever lived like He lived. No one has ever demonstrated such love. John's doubts were resolved as he waited for the Lord to reveal Himself.

C. Doubts are always resolved as we wait on Christ to reveal the glory of God.

God always comes. Victory is assured to those who wait. The Lord God invades, intrudes. He breaks through to reveal Himself to man in need. See the end of the thing.

The trouble is that people are always leaving the theater before the show is over. Leaving the theater they never see the end of the play, nor hear the benediction. Sometimes even the actors throw up their hands and leave before the curtain falls. Judas did and so do we.

We emerge victorious only as we wait upon God to show Himself.

Conclusion. Do you have doubts? Keep doing the very best you know right where you are. Keep faithful. Keep trusting. Keep following. Keep serving. God will reveal Himself.

George Matheson, a young Scottish preacher, was once so beset with doubts that he wanted to give up the ministry. His friends counseled him to go on living up to the best that was in him, just as if he still believed. Matheson held on, and became one of Scotland's greatest preachers. Believing when we can't see is what makes faith, faith!

"This is the victory that overcomes the world, even our faith."

Faith is the way to victory over sin, suffering, sorrow, and skepticism.

TITLE: "The Bible Speaks to Our Condition".

SCRIPTURE READING: 1 Corinthians 16.

Introduction. It is interesting to note the rather sharp contrast between what Paul has been discussing in this epistle and what he now begins to discuss in chapter 16. First Corinthians 15 is the classic passage in the New Testament having to do with the resurrection of Christ and the resurrection of the saints. Immediately following this tremendous passage, Paul makes a very practical suggestion.

I. *Now Concerning the Collection* (1 Cor. 16:1-4). This passage contains one of Paul's four different references to a generous offering for the poor saints in Jerusalem (Rom. 15:25-29; 2 Cor. 8:9; Gal. 2:10).

These followers of our Lord were encouraged to contribute on a regular, systematic, individual, proportionate basis.

Would God speak to us on the basis of this passage and tell us that we should bring our generous offerings to the church on every Lord's day on a voluntary basis and in proportion to our income? It is interesting to note that nowhere in the Scriptures is a portion less than the tithe mentioned.

I. *Concern for Christian Friends* (1 Cor. 16:10-12). Paul was vitally concerned about the welfare of Timothy and Apollos, his co-laborers and fellow missionaries. He encourages the church at Corinth to extend to them Christian hospitality and every possible assistance.

Our Lord would have us to cooperate and participate with those who are advancing His work.

III. *Practical Suggestions* (1 Cor. 16:13, 14). Five imperatives are given and God-like love is to characterize all that we do.

The badge of Christian discipleship is love, understood as a persistent, unbreakable spirit of good will.

IV. *Christian Greetings* (1 Cor. 16:19-24). Paul closes his epistle with Christian greetings to friends in Corinth. His prayer for them is that they might experience the grace of the Lord Jesus, and that they might be assured of His continuing love.

Conclusion. Commendation, complaints, correction, counsel, and comfort come to us through Paul's epistle to the Corinthians. Let us listen as our Lord speaks to us as we study this wonderful book.

SUGGESTED PREACHING PROGRAM
FOR THE MONTH OF JUNE

Sunday Mornings

The suggested theme for the morning messages is "Faith for Frightening Times."

Sunday Evenings

Continue with the theme "The Teenager: His Problems and His Potential."

Wednesday Evenings

Continue the program of encouraging the reading of a chapter a day from the Word of God with the theme "The Bible Speaks to Our Condition."

The theme verse for the month of June is "This book of the law shall not depart out of thy mouth, but thou shalt meditate therein day and night, that thou mayest observe to do according to all that is written therein: for then thou shalt make thy way prosperous, and then thou shalt have good success" (Josh. 1:8).

SUNDAY MORNING, JUNE 2

TITLE: "The Authority for Faith: the Bible"

TEXT: "And that from a child thou hast known the holy Scriptures, which are able to make thee wise unto salvation through faith which is in Christ Jesus. All Scripture is given by inspiration of God, and is profitable for doctrine, for reproof, for correction, for instruction in righteousness: That the man of God may be perfect, throughly furnished unto all good works" (2 Tim. 3:15-17).

SCRIPTURE READING: 2 Timothy 3.

HYMNS: "Break Thou the Bread of Life," Lathbury. "Holy Bible, Book Divine," Burton. "Wonderful Words of Life," Bliss.

OFFERTORY PRAYER:

Our Father, we thank Thee for all the blessings of life. We thank Thee for faith which is Thy gift to us. We know that we have faith because Thou hast approached us, not because we have found Thee.

And, Father, sometimes we are frightened by life. The times in which we live are difficult times. The demands of faith sometimes seem more than we can meet. But then we realize that Thy grace is sufficient for every need. And then we remember that faith in Thee can overcome all obstacles.

So, our Father, take the things that we give to Thee this morning. Use them to Thy glory. And give to us a greater faith so that we will be able to live courageously in these frightening times. In Jesus' name we pray. Amen.

Introduction. The need of our day is the need of faith. We need an intelligent faith that can face the realities of life and still be anchored to the reality of God and His love and care for us. There is a faith that is possible, a faith that is sufficient for frightening times.

What is the authority for this faith? It is the Bible. The Bible is the revealed word of God to us. Only in the Bible can we know of God's character and work. Only in the Bible can we read of God's acts among us.

The editor of a well-known London newspaper once sent a letter of inquiry to one hundred important men—peer, member of Parliament, university professor, author, merchant—a very varied list. The inquiry was: "Suppose you were sent to prison for three years and could take only three books with you, which three would you choose? Please state them in order of their importance."

Out of the replies, ninety-eight put the Bible first on their list!

Few of these men were keen about religion, many were not even church-goers; others were agnostics or atheists. Yet they knew that no other book could give them cheer and comfort and help in dark and difficult days. (Robert G. Lee, *The Bible and Prayer*, Nashville: The Broadman Press, 1950, pp. 8, 9.)

Why was this? In an article in the June, 1955, *Coronet*, entertainer Eddie Cantor said: "It is not surprising that almost every all-time best-seller list includes the Bible. As its readers know, and as I discovered so many years ago, the Bible is not just a book of the month—it is the book of life, eternal, unchanging, ever-dependable" (p. 148).

Because of this very fact the Bible is our authority for faith. We know that faith can be true because we know the Bible is true. Listen to Bernard Ramm: "The Bible is not the authority for the Christian because it was written by religious geniuses. Nor is it the Christian's authority because it has been pragmatically verified through the centuries, nor because it inspires great religious experience. The Bible is binding upon the Christian because it is part of the organism of divine revelation. It is a divine revelation in written form in various literary genres.

"The Bible is authoritative because it is the Word of God (that is, it is part of the organism of revelation) and for no other reason" (Bernard Ramm, *The Pattern of Religious Authority*, Grand Rapids: Wm. B. Eerdmans Publishing Co., 1957, p. 38).

This is our authority for faith: the Bible. We can know God and have faith in God through the revelation of Himself which is given in the Bible.

I. *The Bible Is the Authority for Faith Because of Its Inspiration.* The word inspiration means "God-breathed." Verse 16 states: "All scripture is given by inspiration of God. . . ." All the Scriptures were written by men who have been inspired, breathed into by God. Of course, Paul was writing about the Old Testament Scriptures at this point. At the time of this writing the New Testament had not been completely written and collected. But if what Paul claimed for the Old Testament was true it is surely true for the New Testament Scriptures too.

We must confess that we do not know exactly how God went about inspiring the men who wrote the Scriptures. We know that they recorded the acts of God. And we know, too, that they used their own personalities and vocabularies in doing it.

God acted among us. That we know. The Holy Spirit then inspired someone to record these acts of God. The Holy Spirit also illumines these records. God still speaks to us from out of the pages of the Bible. So it seems to be a process of revelation, inspiration, and illumination.

We must also consider the fact that the Scriptures still stand as authority. Repeated attacks have been made on the Bible but it still stands

162

and God still speaks through it. Only inspiration can account for this.

II. *The Bible Is the Authority for Faith Because of Its Importance.* In verse 16 the assertion is made that the Scripture is profitable. This ought to mean something to this materialistic culture of ours. The Word of God has profit for us; it is useful; it is important to our lives. Notice how.

A. It is important for the teaching of doctrine. The Bible must be the source of our doctrine. All the doctrine or teaching to which we subscribe must be tested against God's Word as revealed in the Bible. What we believe and how we live are tied closely together.

We cannot expect to find all the answers clearly outlined for us. If the explicit answer for every social question of every age were contained in the Bible it would soon be outdated. In the Bible we find the principles that guide all who believe in God no matter what century it is. The particular problems might change; the principles of God do not change.

B. It is important for conviction. "Reproof" here does not mean faultfinding so much as it means conviction. In the Bible we find the conviction of our sins.

C. It is important for correction. The Bible must correct our understanding and our obedience. The *Amplified New Testament* translates it as: "For correction of errors and discipline in obedience. . . ." The real meaning of this is that all theories, all theologies, and all ethical teachings are to be tested by the teaching of the Bible.

D. It is important for instruction in righteousness. This could be understood as "training in good living." There is no other place to learn the meaning of righteousness than from Him who is righteous— God as revealed in Jesus Christ.

III. *The Bible Is the Authority for Faith Because of Its Intent.*

1. It has the intent of salvation (vs. 15). Through the Bible we can come to salvation. A colporteur was caught one night by brigands in a forest in Sicily. He was held up at the point of a revolver. He was ordered to light a fire and to burn his books. He lit the fire, and then asked if he might read a little from each book before he dropped it in the flames. He read the twenty-third psalm from one; the story of the Good Samaritan from another; from another the Sermon on the Mount; from another 1 Corinthians 13. At the end of each reading the brigand said: "That's a good book; we won't burn that one; give it to me." In the end not a book was burned. The brigand left the colporteur and went off into the darkness with the books. Years later that same man turned up again. This time he was a Christian minister, and it was to the reading of the books that he attributed the change (William Barclay, *The Letters to Timothy, Titus, and Philemon,* "Daily Study Bible," Philadelphia: Westminster Press, 1960, p. 231).

2. It has the intent of equipping for service (vs. 17). After a person has been led to salvation through the Scriptures that is not all

of life. The Lord also intends for the Christian to serve Him. And the Scriptures will completely equip for Christian service.

Conclusion. In these frightening times we can have faith in God. The authority for faith is the Bible. It leads us to God.

SUNDAY EVENING, JUNE 2

TITLE: "The Teenager and Fleshly Lust"

TEXT: "Flee also youthful lusts" (2 Tim. 2:22).

SCRIPTURE READING: 1 Peter 2:11; 2 Timothy 2:22; 1 John 2:16; Matthew 5:28.

Introduction. The other day I read what someone had written about youth: "There is little doubt that the present generation of young men and women is in serious moral difficulty. Compared with the generations preceding, they have shunned discipline and a willingness to excel in their studies. Many give little or no thought to the serious issues of life. Common modesty and decency in manners and dress apparently are things of the past. The fact that evil is called good while good is called evil seems to be of small concern to them. Student groups indulge in wild orgies of self-gratification. . . ." Do you know when those words were written? They were written by Aristophanes more than 400 years before Christ. This simply says that teenagers through all the ages have struggled with the problem of fleshly lust.

I. *The Struggle With the Problem*

A. Consider certain Scriptures: Peter said, "Abstain from fleshly lust." In 2 Timothy 2:22 Paul said, "Flee also youthful lusts." And in Romans 13:14 we read, "Make not provision for the flesh, to fulfil the lusts thereof." Jesus told us not to look on a woman "to lust after her."

B. There's been a revolutionary change in the public attitude toward sex. The frankness of discussion today is amazing. You find it in the literature, in the dramas, and the theaters. The trend in modern dress is another illustration of the revolution. The rise in illegitimate births is another illustration of the growing problem. Three hundred thousand illegitimate births were reported in a recent year. If you add those not reported, we wonder what the proportion would be.

C. Another evidence of the revolutionary thinking is the breakdown in the sacredness of the marriage relationship. It used to be that only the movie actors had several wives or husbands. Now it is spread to the government, to the supreme court, and even to ministers.

D. The problem of fleshly lust is real. Jesus spoke of lust in a look. He warned about looking upon a woman with lust. John warned about the "lust of the eye." The Bible speaks of "evil imaginations." Crimes of all kinds have come from evil imagination. Anything that incites evil thoughts, whether it is a picture, or a movie, or a book, is dangerous.

164

II. *Wrong View of the Problem.*

A. It is wrong to think that premarital relations do not hinder, but rather help the adjustment in the physical realm. The Bible teaches us that "whoso commiteth adultery . . . lacketh understanding" (Prov. 6:32). The Bible teaches that adultery is wrong. It is unworthy. It is false. It is frustrating. Read the sordid story of Tamar and Prince Ammon in the Old Testament. The prince in the court of David seduced a young girl and thought he had gotten away with it. Many modern novels might end here, but not the Bible. It tells the story of the next day. It says very bluntly, "The hatred with which he hated her was greater than the love wherewith he had loved her" (2 Sam. 13:15). It is the old story, as old as human nature, that such an experience becomes, sooner or later, terrible self-hatred and a hatred of others.

B. It is wrong to think that the physical side of life has nothing to do with the rest of the personality. The Bible does not separate the physical from the spiritual. The word for soul in the Old Testament "nephesh," meaning a union of body and spirit. This teaching saved Christianity from two early evils:

1. That the body is bad, so try to get rid of it with its desires and demands.

2. That the things of the body are indifferent, that they have nothing to do with the spirit. The thought that you can be cultured with the mind, and yet in things of the body be utterly debased and immoral is wrong.

C. It is wrong to think that the suppression of this natural desire is psychologically dangerous and can do emotional and even mental harm to the persons involved. Paul knew that this was a problem that all people faced and urged that Christians keep their lives honorable and clean. This was important for the world of that day was rife with immorality. Lust was given almost unbridled expression. It made it all the more imperative that Christians should show that they were different from the pagans, that they were followers of Christ. So the Apostle Paul, writing to the Christians in Thessalonica, laid stress on the necessity that they remember and obey the will of God, "even your sanctification, that ye should abstain from fornication" (1 Thess. 4:3). One eminent psychiatrist says that the basic findings about sex in psychoanalysis agrees with the fundamental Christian view!

D. It is wrong to think that love covers all things. It is wrong to think that if two people love each other, everything is all right. These concepts are utterly wrong, unchristian and tremendously dangerous to the moral well being and the salvation of mankind.

II. *What Is the Christian View?*

A. Recognize God as Creator. In the first chapter of Genesis, we read, "In the beginning God created—male and female created he them," and God saw everything that He had made and "behold, it was good." Thus, we believe that the physical side of life is good, not bad. There is nothing dirty or ugly or sinful in the physical side of life in itself. It is man who misuses, abuses, and perverts that which God meant for good. To the Corinthians, Paul said, "Know ye not that your body is the temple of the Holy Ghost . . . therefore glorify God in your body" (1 Cor. 6:19, 20). Recognize the sacredness of life.

B. Wholesome discipline of the body. J. Wallace Hamilton, in his helpful book, *Ride the Wild Horses,* uses an interesting analogy in comparing basic human instincts to a wild stallion that must be broken. He says that some use the theory of self-assertion, by letting the wild horse run, and by giving free rein to the natural instincts. Others go to the opposite extreme, with self-rejection. Instead of eliminating the rider, and throwing the reins over the horse's head for him to run free, they would eliminate the horse. This is like trying to get rid of your headache by cutting off your head. The Bible teaches that there is power in the discipline of the body. Like a river without banks, the wrong expression of this natural desire can get out of bounds, creating a swamp which becomes a breeding place for disease and misery. Kept within the confining banks of God's laws and love, it can be a mighty force for man's individual happiness as well as for the well-being of society and the strengthening of family life. Young people, by yourself the temptations of the twentieth century can be overwhelming. With God's

help, there is no temptation that you cannot handle. Many a young man or woman has found himself or herself in the situation Joseph found himself as depicted in the thirty-ninth chapter of Genesis. The Bible is very plain in describing the real, live bedroom scene. Joseph was handsome and good looking, and after a time his master's wife cast her eyes upon Joseph, and said, "Lie with me." You remember the outcome? Joseph didn't answer, "I'm afraid I might get caught." His whole refusal was rooted in his faith. "How then can I do this great wickedness, and sin against God?" (Gen. 39:9). This is the secret and this can be your success. Remember, you are not your own—you belong to God.

Conclusion. But what if there has been failure? What if the horse does run wild? What if this surging stream of desire does break out of its banks? What then? What is needed is to come back to God. Adultery, fornication, and perversion can be forgiven. To the woman caught in adultery, Jesus said, "Neither do I condemn thee: go, and sin no more" (John 8:11). We are not told what happened, but I have the feeling that she went away determined to live up to her highest and best from that hour. As she came face to face with the living Christ, she found a new way for her life. You, too, can climb from the low road to the high road.

WEDNESDAY EVENING, JUNE 5

TITLE: "The Bible Speaks to Our Condition"

SCRIPTURE READING: 2 Corinthians 7.

Introduction. When God commissioned Joshua with the task of leading the children of Israel into the Promised Land, He insisted that Joshua follow divine instructions

"This book of the law shall not depart out of thy mouth; but thou shalt meditate therein day and night, that thou mayest observe to do according to all that is written therein: for then thou shalt make thy way prosperous, and then thou shalt have good success" (Josh. 1:8). This is the only occasion where the word "success" appears in the King James version of the Bible. The thought is repeated on many occasions, but the word "success" is used only in this one verse. It is interesting to note that success is promised to those who daily give heed to the Word of God.

Let us let God speak to us from 2 Corinthians 7.

I. *The Promises of God* (7:1).

Paul has just completed a challenge to the Corinthian Christians to separate themselves from evil and to dedicate themselves to a faithful relationship with God. He bases this appeal on the precious promises of God (2 Cor. 6:17, 18). This promise is a condensation of the many exceeding great and precious promises of God.

We should give careful attention to the Word of God that we might discover God's great promises for the encouragement of our faith, the deepening of our love, and the enrichment of our service and ministry.

II. *The Joy of Restored Fellowship* (7:2-4).

When one reads 1 and 2 Corinthians, he is impressed with the corrective nature of these two epistles. There were some strained relationships between the apostle and some of the leaders in the Corinthian church. The Corinthian believers were immature and continued to harbor many of the attitudes and ambitions associated with their pre-conversion life. Some of them resented Paul's authority. They were upset because of his rebukes and his efforts to lead them to conform in both thought and conduct to the mind of Jesus Christ. Some of them had attacked his apostleship and his authority.

In these verses, Paul expresses joy over a great improvement in their fellowship. He does this because finally they have reacted positively and properly to his rebuke and correction. A restoration of fellowship always produces joy.

III. *The Comfort of God* (7:6-16).

A. The coming of Titus (7:6, 13). Titus had been to Corinth and had learned of the change in their attitude toward Paul and the Lord's good will. He brought news of this to Paul. This served to comfort and strengthen Paul in the midst of his tribulations.

B. Comfort from the church (7:7-13). Paul was greatly encouraged because of the response of the church to his message which had taken the form of a rebuke and a correction. He felt that he had been vindicated.

Paul had suffered greatly as a result of their misunderstanding of him. It was exceedingly difficult for him to truly be God's servant and their minister. This should comfort us when life proves to be difficult and painful in the present. The good news from the church was really the comfort of God to the heart of the apostle.

C. The comfort of accepting correction (7:8-12). Paul had strongly rebuked them. His rebuke had produced sorrow and remorse that led to repentance rather than to despair and hostility. Their sorrow had been a godly kind of sorrow that led to repentance, cleansing, and health.

The Corinthian Christians experienced the comfort and the joy of being cleansed, corrected, and in harmony with God and with His servant, the Apostle Paul.

Conclusion. There is a sorrow and a remorse that leads to despair and to destruction. This type of a sorrow and a remorse should be avoided at all costs.

If God's message speaks a rebuke to us, let us respond properly in order that we might experience joy and peace in the present.

SUNDAY MORNING, JUNE 9

TITLE: "The Basis for Faith: God"

TEXT: "Tell ye, and bring them near; yea, let them take counsel together: who hath declared this from ancient time? who hath told it from that time? have not I the LORD? and there is no God else beside me; a just God and a Saviour; there is none beside me. Look unto me, and be ye saved, all the ends of the earth: for I am God, and there is none else" (Isa. 45:21, 22).

SCRIPTURE READING: Isaiah 45: 20-25.

HYMNS: "Immortal, Invisible," Smith. "A Mighty Fortress Is Our God," Luther. "To God Be the Glory," Crosby.

OFFERTORY PRAYER:

Our Father, we come to Thee this day with a full realization and a full recognition of what Thou art and what we are. We acknowledge that Thou art our Creator and the giver of all good gifts. We understand that we are creatures: sinful, rebellious, disobedient, but seeking Thee and Thy face.

Forgive us of our sins, our Father. Help us to be strong in the face of the adversities and the disappointments that we face each day. Help us to know Thy grace, Thy strength, and Thy guidance in every moment of life. Grant us the awareness of both the power and the presence of Thy Holy Spirit.

We come at this time to return to Thee a portion of what Thou hast given us. Help us to give from love and as a response to Thy grace. Thou hast not withheld any good gift from us. Help us not to withhold our time, talents, or treasure from Thee. But, rather, may we give with the liberality of love that Thou hast shown to us. In Jesus' name we pray. Amen.

Introduction. In his book, *The New Shape of American Religion,* Martin E. Marty accused the American people of having a "faith in faith." He indicated that in the revival of interest in religion many people had not put their faith in God but in faith itself. But is this the proper basis for faith? If you are to have faith should it not be based on something more objective something more real than just the act of faith? The basis for faith is God.

In these frightening times we can have faith because this faith is based on God. Isaiah the prophet expressed the reason that faith must be based on God and on nothing else: there is nothing or no one else.

The Bible does not argue for the existence of God. To the Biblical writers the existence of God was a self-evident fact. The Hebrews of the Old Testament were concerned with the character and activity of God. They knew the character and activity of God by what He had done among them.

The opening words of the Bible are: "In the beginning God. . . ." And this sets the stage for all else that follows. Because God is from the beginning, is the creator and sustainer of the world, and is the Savior of the world we can have faith in Him. Rather than trying to prove God the Bible records for us the acts of God. It declares for us God's majesty and power. His presence and will are made known. The Bible is the authority for our faith. God is the basis for our faith.

I. *God Is the Basis for Faith Because of Reality.* Do we know that there is a God? We certainly do. We have not seen Him but we have felt His presence. We have not touched Him but He has touched our lives. We have not heard His voice speak audibly but we have heard the still small voice speak to the depths of our souls. God cannot be measured by the mathematician, or analyzed by the chemist, or even conjured by the philosopher. But any person who reaches out in faith can know that God is. This is the reality of God.

How do we know there is a God?

Surely the Bible tells us; surely creation shouts it to the universe; but we can know decisively because we have known Him. We know because we are known. God is personal, loving, and seeking. This is the reality of our lives, and this is the basis for our faith.

II. *God Is the Basis for Faith Because of Revelation.* What do we know about God? Revelation includes not only how we know God but also what we know about God. Everything we know about God has been revealed to us by God Himself. He has made Himself known to us through the testimony of His creation, through the words of Scripture, and through our experiences with Him. The final and complete revelation of God is in Jesus Christ. What do we know about God?

A. The natural attributes of God.

1. God is all present: the omnipresence of God. God is present everywhere. But more important to faith is the Biblical emphasis that God is present at particular places. After Jacob's dream at Bethel he said, "Surely the LORD is in this place; and I knew it not" (Gen. 28:16).

2. God is all knowing: the omniscience of God. God knows everything. But God also knows everyone. God's knowledge is particular, personal and redemptive.

3. God is all powerful: the omnipotence of God. God can do anything that power can do. Personally, it is important to know that God has the power to save. God's greatest demonstration of power was in the cross and resurrection.

God has the redemptive power to remake any life.

B. The moral attributes of God.

1. God is righteous. God conforms to the norm of right. But God Himself is that norm. God requires righteousness of us. But God gives the righteousness that He requires. All that is right and good is found in God.

2. God is holy. Holiness basically means "separate." God is separate and distinct from man. There is a matter of mystery about God that we will never comprehend.

3. God is love. The basic characteristic of God is love. God has shown His love to us in many and varied ways.

III. *God Is the Basis for Faith Because of Relationships.* How are we related to God? J. S. Whale has said, "The fundamental question is this: How do we pass from abstract argument about God to living awareness of God?" (J. S. Whale, *Christian Doctrine*, London: Fontana Books, 1957, p. 29).

Our relationship with God is one of faith. This is the faith with an adequate basis: faith rested securely in God.

God loves us. And God seeks us. From the time that God walked through the Garden of Eden shouting, "Adam . . . Where art thou?" (Gen. 3:9) to the cross where Jesus said, "Father, forgive them; for they know not what they do" (Luke 23:34) to the last chapter of Revelation where these words are found, "And the Spirit and the bride say, Come. And let him that heareth say, Come . . . And let him that is athirst come. And whosoever will, let him take the water of life freely" (Rev. 22:17), the Bible is the story of God's search for man. Even in the midst of our sin and rebellion against God He loves us and seeks us. We can be related to God through faith and commitment.

A college student touched with skepticism talked with an older, wiser minister one day. He expressed his doubts about God and the Bible. To explain what he considered the contradictions of the Bible he mentioned the reference that "God is love" and that "God is a consuming fire." How were they to be reconciled? The preacher stopped in the lovely garden path where they were walking and pointed to a beautiful flower that bloomed. They agreed that it owed its beauty to the sun. Then they noticed a flower that had been pulled and it was wilting and curled. That, too, was due to the sun. Then the minister stated that the same sun could feed and nourish or wither and kill. It depended on the relationship to it. And it is that way with God. When we are rightly related to God we have His strength, His love, His salvation. When we are not rightly related to Him we know His judgment. By faith we can know God.

Conclusion. God is the basis for our faith. Were there no God we would have no faith. But there is a God. And we can know Him through faith. This carries us through frightening times.

TITLE: "The Teenager and Marriage"

TEXT: "What therefore God hath joined together, let not man put asunder" (Matt. 19:6b).

SCRIPTURE READING: Matthew 19:1-12.

Introduction. The American society is encouraging early marriage. Many times we push our children into early dating and mating. I read of a couple who married so young, that the guests threw pablum instead of rice! The marriage picture is not a clear one and I hope I do not add to the confusion. In Hollywood, a child went to school and was registering. They asked him if he had any brothers or sisters. "No," he said, "I don't have any brothers or sisters, but I have three mamas by my first papa, and four papas by my second mama!" Ours is a kind of sad, mixed-up world.

This subject of marriage is of interest to all of us, for 90% of the people of our society get married. I do not come to speak as one who knows any of the answers, but I hope I do know some of the problems. There is the problem of unhappiness in marriage. David Mace, one of the leading sociologists in the United States, says 20% of the families living together are definitely unhappy. Another 35% of our families are not entirely happy. The average married couple in America, then, has less than a fifty per cent chance of being happy, and the unhappiest people in the world are those who are unhappy at home.

The breakdown of the home has become a "number one" problem in our nation. I do not fear that my country will fall from without, but I do fear disintegration from within. "If the foundations be destroyed, what can the righteous do?" Teenage marriages are adding to the problem. The divorce rate among teenage marriages is twice as high as marriages between older couples. One out of every two teenage marriages ends in divorce. Some of the hardships of the teenage marriage start these teenagers on a life of crime. The war situation has increased the problem. There are many dropouts in school on account of teenage marriages. Teenagers need to give serious consideration to marriage, for anything so important, anything that is to last for a lifetime, "till death shall you part," demands thoughtful and prayerful consideration.

I. *Stoplights on the Road to Marriage.*

A. If you are marrying this person to reform him, stop right now! If he drinks, or is dishonest, is impure, is deceitful, he gambles, lies before marriage, likely as not he will after marriage. The way to be sure is to know that he's the right kind of person before you marry him. It is not so much finding the right person as it is being the right person anyway.

B. If you have the feeling that "if this marriage doesn't work, we can always get a divorce," please stop right now! Don't get married. Jesus said, "Marriage is forever!" The psychologists of America are saying, "It is harder for a child to lose a parent by divorce than it is by death!" There are emotional entanglements they never recover from. Don't hurt one of these little ones.

C. Another stoplight is, do you have the counsel and consent of your parents? The old custom was that the groom had to ask the bride's father. This may no longer be proper, but it is always proper to seek the approval of the families. Isaac's father helped him find a wife. He did a good job, for he found for him Rebekah, and it was love at first sight. Samson fell in love with a girl of the Philistines. His parents pled with him not to marry her, but they finally gave in and Samson married her, only to bring heartache, misery, and tragedy into his life. It is wise to seek the counsel and the consent of parents before marriage.

D. Have you sought the will of God? Have you prayed about this? If it lies beyond prayer, then stop, do not proceed. John the Baptist told Herod, who had taken another man's wife, "It is not lawful for you to have her." What about the will of God? Have you prayed until God has given you a green light?

II. *Caution Lights on the Road to Marriage.* Give serious consideration before you proceed. Here are some danger signs:

A. The first danger signal is that of a mixed marriage, one denomination marrying a person of another. We readily admit there are many perils in a Catholic-Protestant marriage.

B. A second danger sign is marriage with an unbeliever. 2 Corinthians 6:14 gives a warning about this matter. "Be not unequally yoked together with unbelievers." However, Paul was not giving the will of God, but his own advice and opinion. He goes on to say that the believing wife may be able, through her influence, to bring the unbelieving husband to Christ. Marriage with an unbeliever is a caution light.

C. Consider before you marry. "Is this the real thing, or one phase in the period of courtship?" A great marriage counselor and pastor has said, "Most young people think they are in love at least four or five times before they find the real thing."

It is possible, perhaps, to love as sincerely at thirteen as at twenty, but not with the same discernment. Wait until you are old enough to fall in love intelligently, maturely, and permanently. Youth has its infatuations, its transient flames, its momentary crushes. But these are but rungs in the ladder by which we climb upward toward the emotional and spiritual maturity necessary to build a home.

Relationships of young men and women today are undoubtedly the freest of any period of history. It is a wise young person who does not allow every passing fancy, every infatuation, to become too highly emotionalized in physical caresses.

D. Another caution light is "Are you willing to assume the responsibilities that marriage demands?" There are floors to be swept, beds to be made, clothes to be ironed, children to be cared for and endless meals to be prepared Are you ready for some trials Some hard work? Are you ready young man, to provide for a family The Bible says, "If any [man] provide not for his own . . . he is worse than an infidel" (1 Tim 5:8).

III. *Green Lights on the Road t*

Marriage. How can you know you are ready for marriage?

A. Marriage counselors have suggested the following questions: Are you from similar backgrounds? Are you mentally and socially congenial? Do you share a common faith? Are you mutually proud of each other? Do you get along with the families involved? Do you come from happy homes yourselves? Do you share a common vocational interest? Do you measure up in the matter of Christian character—not given to drinking, lying, cheating, profanity, gambling, etc.? Have you passed your twentieth birthday? If your answer to these questions is "Yes," you may have a green light.

B. But here are some questions to ask.

1. Can you sincerely respect this prospective partner? Do you respect this person socially? Intellectually? Physically? This includes pride of vocation.

2. Is he or she emotionally mature? What kind of a disposition does he have? Does he sulk? Does he pout? Is she a neurotic? Can you get along with each other? A reasonable congeniality is essential to a happy marriage. If you can't get along before marriage, don't think it will be easier after you get married. You may think you know this person, but you never know a person until you have lived with him.

Are you old enough to get married? The ideal age is 23 for the boy and 21 for the girl, but the emotional age is most important. Mature people are responsible, adaptable, flexible, and unselfish. Most quarrels over money, in-laws, recreation, or religion that wreck marriages are not over these particular things. The real cause is immaturity. It is because two people have not grown up. There are AM personalities and PM personalities. Some are up at 6:00 AM, singing and buzzing around, and yet go to bed with the chickens. Others stay up all night and want to sleep all day!

Some real adjustments have to be made. But maybe the spiritual adjustments, in the wake of great personal loss, are the greatest.

A young couple earnestly prayed for a child. In due time, when a beautiful baby girl arrived, their joy was boundless. But the passing hours revealed that the infant heart was impaired, and the fragile thread of life would soon break altogether. It was a tragic, bitter adjustment for two young people to make. They met their disappointment with Christian grace. Can you adjust to making decisions independent of family and friends? Are you willing to cut loose from mother's apron strings, and dad's pocketbook?

3. You have a green light if these things are right, and if this partner is thoroughly Christian. This question really underlies all others. Now, to be a church member is not enough. But to seriously follow Jesus Christ gives strength to marriage like nothing else will.

Conclusion. I have known brides and grooms who thought it didn't matter whether their mate had any religion or not, but then the children came. Then you see anxiety increase. You want these little ones to be brought up where there is hope and faith and love.

Most men feel somewhat like

Lord Byron did when he said, "Much as I hate bigotry, I think it is a thousand times more pardonable in a woman than irreligion."

But, in the marriage relationship, at least, this is also true of men. Many women suffer insecurity and loneliness because the one who walks by their side does not know God.

If you are not a Christian, you are not ready for marriage. You are not ready for parenthood. You are not ready for your life's vocation. You are not ready for tragedy and sorrow. You are not ready for life. You are not ready for death. You are not ready for the judgment of God. Will you give your life to our Lord? Will you trust Him?

WEDNESDAY EVENING, JUNE 12

TITLE: "The Bible Speaks to Our Condition"

SCRIPTURE READING: Galatians 1.

Introduction. Paul writes to the churches in Galatia that he might give them the message of the Lord. As we read this chapter today, let us let God speak to our hearts.

Paul begins this epistle with a doxology of joy and praise for what God had done for him and them in the person of Jesus Christ. He has recognized and responded to the truth that the death of Jesus Christ was intended to deliver us from the penalty of our sins as well as from the power of evil in this present world (1:4). The death of Jesus Christ and His redemptive purpose was in line with the will of our Father God.

I. *The Danger of Departing From the Gospel* (1:6-9). Paul was greatly disturbed because the believers in Galatia had departed from the Gospel of grace. They had listened to false teachers who had added to the Gospel and had thus perverted the Gospel. Paul warned them against the great danger of adding

to the Gospel the requirement that one must also keep the law in order to secure a position of acceptance before God.

We need to recognize and respond to the fact that we are saved, not because we are good, but because God is a God of grace. Our position of acceptance before the Father God is not determined by our merit or obedience. We find acceptance before Him on the basis of our faith in Jesus Christ who died for our sins. We must beware lest we depart from this pure Gospel of grace.

II. *Seeking to Please Christ* (1:10). Paul's supreme desire was to please Jesus Christ at all times. This desire took precedence over his desire to have the approval of men.

Because it is basic to our human nature to desire human approval, we must beware lest this desire take precedence over our need to please Jesus Christ.

III. *The Need for Personal Experience With God* (1:11-17). In reply to the charge of some that he had received his authority from the apostles in Jerusalem, Paul affirmed that his message was a direct revelation from Jesus Christ. The truth that he preached was based on personal experience with Jesus Christ. His message and his authority were by divine authority based on personal experience with God.

Conclusion. How deep is your personal experience with God? Have you let the truth of God's Word become the authoritative guideline for your thoughts and your ambitions?

It's wonderful to have a good pastor who can give you guidance. It is very profitable to have parents who set before you the right example. Each person needs a faith that is personal and genuine growing out of a personal experience with Jesus Christ. Such can be possible if we will let God speak to us day by day through His Word.

SUNDAY MORNING, JUNE 16

TITLE: "The Object of Faith: Jesus Christ"

TEXT: "Let this mind be in you, which was also in Christ Jesus: Who, being in the form of God, thought it not robbery to be equal with God: But made himself of no reputation, and took upon him the form of a servant, and was made in the likeness of men: And being found in fashion as a man, he humbled himself, and became obedient unto death, even the death of the cross. Wherefore God also hath highly exalted him, and given him a name which is above every name: That at the name of Jesus every knee should bow, of things in heaven, and things in earth, and things under the earth; And that every tongue should confess that Jesus Christ is Lord, to the glory of God the Father" (Phil. 2:5-11).

SCRIPTURE READING: Philippians 2.

HYMNS: "Jesus, the Very Thought of Thee," Bernard of Clairvaux. "All Hail the Power of Jesus' Name," Perronet. "Blessed Redeemer," Christiansen.

OFFERTORY PRAYER:

Our Father, we come to Thee today thankful for the bountifulness of Thy mercy, grateful for Thy love and grace, and aware of our sins and failure.

We ask that Thy love would be made known to us, that Thy grace would be realized by us, and that Thy forgiveness would be received by us.

When we think of Jesus Christ, Thy Son and our Savior, we are all but overcome by Thy goodness. We praise Thee for Jesus Christ. And we open ourselves to Him that we might know Him personally, that we might be filled with His love, and that we might follow Him in all of life.

We pray that Thou wouldst accept our gifts and bless them to Thy service.

In Jesus' name. Amen.

Introduction. I once knew a prison chaplain who did not surrender to the ministry until rather late in life. He was already married and operated a laundry business. When the Lord called him to the ministry he sold his business and moved to another city to begin his college studies.

He had a Jewish friend in his home city who was a laundry supply salesman. When the friend heard of his impending move he visited with him and asked if he could be of any help. Since he had just sold his business he had no financial needs at the time. So he told his friend, "I need a new Bible. My Bible is worn out. If you want to, you can buy me a new Bible." And he did. And throughout this man's ministry he has supplied him with Bibles.

The friend asked the minister, "Tell me one thing. Why did you do this? Why did you leave an established business and submit yourself and your family to long years of schooling? Why did you leave your friends and home to move to a place where you knew no one?" This was his answer: "It was all because of a man. I met a man named Jesus who saved my soul and my life. I owe everything to Him. When He called me to serve Him there was nothing else I could do."

Jesus Christ is the object of our faith. We have an authority for faith in the Bible. We have a basis for faith because God is and seeks to draw us into a relationship with Him. And we have an object for our faith in Jesus Christ. This can give validity to faith for frightening times.

Nowhere in the Bible is the object of our faith presented more clearly than in Philippians 2:5-11. These verses come about as close as any in the Bible to a systematic statement about the person of Jesus Christ. And it is interesting to note that they were not written as a theological statement but as an illustration. They are found in the midst of an exhortation to unity. The apostle is calling for these people to have the same attitude as did Jesus Christ.

But why discuss the person of Christ? There is no part of our faith more practical than that which expresses what we believe about Jesus. Christ is central to our faith. What we believe about the person of Christ will determine what we believe about the nature of salvation and the cause for conduct.

Faith for these frightening times must be centered in Jesus Christ. He is the object of our faith.

I. *Christ Is the Object of Our Faith Because of His Pre-existence* (vv. 5, 6). Pre-existence means that Christ existed before He was born on this earth. He existed as God before He existed as man. He had a home in heaven before He had a home in Bethlehem. We cannot explain exactly how this happened; it is a mystery of faith.

A. The fact of His pre-existence. In verse 6 "being" can be translated "existing." Throughout all eternity Jesus had existed.

The butterfly can perhaps serve as an illustration of this. The butterfly first existed as a caterpillar. Then he spun a cocoon and after a while emerged from this as a beautiful butterfly. He had first existed as a caterpillar, he then existed as a butterfly. Yet he was the same being in both states. So it is with Jesus. He first existed as God. Then He existed as man. He was the same being in both forms of existence.

B. The manner of His pre-existence

1. He existed in the form of God

2. He existed on an equality with God. Jesus shared in the glories and prerogatives of deity. These He put aside when He came to earth.

C. The attitude that possessed His mind. Jesus was willing to renounce His rights, privileges and claims as God on behalf of sinful humanity. He did not count this as something to be selfishly grasped to Himself.

E. Stanley Jones once told of a little boy who stood before a picture of his absent father. He then turned to his mother and said wistfully, "I wish Father would step out of the picture." And that is what God did at Bethlehem. God stepped out of the picture into the human scene when Jesus Christ was born.

II. *Christ Is the Object of Our Faith Because of His Incarnation* (vv. 7, 8). Incarnation is a word that means the clothing, or the state of being clothed with flesh. When we speak of *the* Incarnation we are referring to the Incarnation of Christ—the clothing of God in human flesh when God became a man in Jesus.

A. The reality of the Incarnation. When the Scripture says that Jesus "made himself of no reputation" it means that He emptied Himself. He emptied Himself of the visible glories and prerogatives of deity, the outward manifestations of deity.

In relation to God He became a servant. Traditionally Christians have interpreted the "Suffering Servant" passages of Isaiah as referring to Jesus.

Jesus became a man. Being "in the likeness of man" was more than just an appearance. He was a real man. Jesus was not just man; He was *a* man.

It was as man that the New Testament believers first encountered Christ. They did not immediately know that He was God. Look at Hebrews 2:17, 18 and 4:14-16. This was a real man who was also God.

B. The aim of the Incarnation.

1. Identification. In the Incarnation God identified Himself with man. He could have a sympathetic heart with man because He knew what men felt. For the gulf to be bridged between God and man God would have to become a man—man could never become God.

2. Redemption. Jesus Christ was obedient; He was obedient even to death on the cross. The extent of God's love can be seen in the extent of Christ's obedience. Only by His death on the cross could there be atonement for our sin.

It was James Denny who observed that if one were to jump in the water to rescue another when nothing was wrong it would be an act of folly. But if one were drowning and then another jumped in, swam to him, and rescued him it would be an act of love. This Christ did for us on the cross.

III. *Christ Is the Object of Our Faith Because of His Exaltation* (vv. 9-11).

A. Christ is exalted because of His redemptive deed. "Wherefore"

(v. 9) refers to what immediately preceded: the redemptive deed of Christ on the cross.

B. The exaltation of Christ is absolute. The exaltation of Christ is unqualified. It is universal. Even if all persons do not recognize Jesus as Lord now, at some time they will.

This means that He is to be the absolute Lord of every area of life. There is no part of the life or will that can be reserved from Him.

The demand of Jesus is for this absolute Lordship of every area of life. There is no part of the life or will that can be reserved from Him.

The demand of Jesus is for this absolute lordship to be now. The reason that we are to make Jesus the absolute Lord of our lives is because He is the incarnate God and He does redeem us from our sin.

Conclusion. James S. Stewart has said that Christianity's greatest need is a rediscovery of Christianity as a vital relationship to a living Christ. Christ is the object of our faith. Through faith in Him we can have life eternal. This relationship with God through Christ gives us faith for frightening times.

SUNDAY EVENING, JUNE 16

TITLE: "The Teenager and Jesus"

TEXT: "And Jesus increased in wisdom and stature, and in favour with God and man" (Luke 2:52).

SCRIPTURE READING: Luke 2: 52; Mark 6:3; Luke 4:16.

Introduction. I believe that Jesus Christ, who walked in the flesh through Galilee 1900 years ago, is accessible to us today. There are many ways of making Jesus real. Some make their vital contact through worship. Others through prayer. Some through fellowship. Some through ministry to people. Another way of making Jesus real is to study His earthly life. With John Ruskin we can be present as if in body at each recorded event in the life of the Redeemer. Let us look at Jesus today and look, and look, and look, until He becomes gloriously real to us. Look at Jesus as a teen-ager. There are some things we know about His early years.

I. *Think of His Life in the Home.* I'm thinking of the boy who came to his pastor and said, "Was Jesus ever a little boy like me?" There was a time when Jesus was a boy. The Book of Hebrews says He learned obedience as a son. The childhood of Jesus was probably a time of great happiness as He grew up wondering at the beauty of His Father's world, loving all, and beloved of all, playing among the shavings, roaming the hills, carrying wood, drawing water, rejoicing in childhood games and pranks, getting His feet wet, misplacing Joseph's tools, attending the village school, stamering out His first verses of Hebrew Scripture, picking flowers in the woods, watching the glories of the sunset, and being startled at the mystery of the dawn. He was a human, happy, normal boy. He learned respect for His parents during those years. Joseph must have been a wonderful father. Barclay tells us that Jesus called God "Father," but in Gethsemane, in the midst of great struggle, He called Him, "Abba." We are told in Romans 8 and Galatians 4 that we can call God "Abba." Now Abba is the word by which a little Jewish boy calls his father in the home circle. If you go to Jerusalem today, in any Jewish home, you'll hear the shout, "Abba, Abba!" ringing through the house—a little boy calling his father. The word Abba would be translated "Daddy." That is the name Jesus gave to God. What a compliment to Joseph! That is where Jesus got His idea of fatherhood. A monument is erected to Joseph when Jesus taught us to pray, "Our Father, which art in heaven. . . ." He could never have been taught that God is like a father unless Joseph had been a wonderful man. Also, Jesus learned the importance of worship in the home. The New Testament speaks of this ". . . as was his custom, he went in to the synagogue on the sabbath day. . . ." Now, worship is a habit, but it must be more than a habit.

We know also that Jesus had four brothers and two sisters. They would not always agree. Tempers would flare. There would be arguments. There would be misunderstandings. You may have problems at home—Jesus did! Even Jesus was a problem child as He baffled His parents. Most scholars speculate that Joseph must have died when Jesus was about thirteen, leaving Him to be a big brother. He learned responsibility. He learned to care for a widowed mother and younger children, for He was the oldest. The home life of Jesus should challenge us to make our homes centers of faith, love, and prayer.

II. *Think of His Education in the School.* The Bible says that Jesus grew "in wisdom and stature, and in favour with God and man." His mental development is stressed. This literally means He became full of wisdom. When He was a boy at age fifteen He started to the village school in Nazareth. A village teacher in Nazareth taught the boy who was going to have more impact on history than any other person ever had. We'll never know the teacher's name, but he taught the boy who was the Son of God. In those days, of course, they didn't have any books. Everything had to be hand written on scrolls which were very expensive. Nobody could possess one for his own. Therefore, if you were going to learn anything, you had to learn it by heart.

The foundation stone of all Jewish education was the Old Testament. From early childhood, Jesus, like all Jewish children, would be brought up in the atmosphere of Genesis, Deuteronomy, Psalms, Isaiah, and Jeremiah. Long hours of His growing youth must have been given to pouring over the sacred page.

He grew up in Nazareth, a little village of prosperous plainsmen and sheep raisers, but it was a crossroads of that ancient world. The roads that led to Egypt, to Damascus, to Syria, and the Far East all ran through Nazareth. Therefore, caravans and merchantmen came through this little village. Roman soldiers were there. He knew about riots in the streets and the clashing of swords. He was educated in a town where His eyes and ears were open to the farthest corners of the world. He lived in a time of tumult and strife.

In John 7:15 we find the people

marveled at His teaching saying, "How knoweth this man letters, having never learned?" They mean He had never studied in their schools, yet He possessed that which their schools could not give Him. The essence of distilled wisdom was evident in His simple stories. Jesus Christ encourages inquiry. He was always questioning His disciples, trying to bring them to the light. We grow through intellectual struggle. Such learning was a part of the early years of Christ.

III. *Think of His Work in the Carpenter's Shop.* In Mark 6:3 we hear people ask, "Is not this the carpenter, the son of Mary?" In the carpenter's shop we see Jesus earning His living by exhausting labor, and carrying with Him that burden which lines the face and weighs upon the heart—the burden of responsibility for the welfare of other people. The Greek word for carpenter is "tekton." Now this word pictures more than a simple carpenter. It actually has in it the idea of "craftsman," "the master of the tools." He was a builder. We see Him making tables, chests, yokes and fitting door frames in houses. We see Him planing wood, melting glue, hammering nails. He was a craftsman. There's a legend which tells us that He made the best ox yokes in the whole of Galilee, and that people beat a track to the door of Jesus of Nazareth to buy the ox yokes that He made. In those days they had trade signs, and it has been suggested that over Jesus' carpenter shop, there was a sentence, "My yokes fit well." Jesus was a working man. He knew some of our labor problems. Jesus puts a glory in our common life. He makes the most humble task meaningful and signifi-

cant. Devoted skill and labor went into those Nazareth yokes, plows, tables, and chests. They were rendered as an offering to God. Toil has been hallowed forever because of Him. There is no division of the cities, parks, streets, slums, schools, progress and improvement in our I believe Jesus can be identified with sacred if performed unto the Lord. sacred and the secular. All work is hospitals, and colleges.

Do you suppose He ever felt restricted by His circumstance—having to earn bread for a widowed mother and her children? Do you suppose He ever asked, "Why do I have to stay in this carpenter shop when I long to preach and to teach and to minister?" I have wondered at times why certain things have happened in my life. God helps a man find fulfillment in his work, even when he has to wait for the fulfilling of his will.

IV. *Think of His Sense of Mission.* You remember when Jesus was lost and Mary and Joseph finally found Him in the Temple. He said, as a twelve-year-old boy, "Wist ye not (that literally means, 'Do you not understand, Mother') that I must be about my Father's business?" Here we see the dawning of a higher allegiance. There was a gradual unfolding of God's will, but even in those early years Jesus felt God had something for Him. There's an old legend that one night He was tired after a long day's work, and He arose and stretched Himself, and as He did, the shadow of his arms and body formed a cross on the wall, and He whispered "The cross!" Even as a teenager Jesus had an amazing awareness of God, of God's plan, and God's will.

Conclusion. A sense of mission often comes early. God speaks to the hearts of youth. "Remember now thy Creator, in the days of thy youth." Jesus Christ, through a larger goal, found the key to a larger life.

Relate your life to the world in which you live. The happiest people as you respond to the voice of God. goal for life? Life takes on meaning will of His Father. What of your Jesus Christ set His face to do the are those who find ways to serve.

WEDNESDAY EVENING, JUNE 19

TITLE: "The Bible Speaks to Our Condition"

SCRIPTURE READING: Ephesians 2.

Introduction. The chapter for today's careful study and prayerful meditation emphasizes God's wonderful grace toward sinners. God's grace has been defined as "What man needs, but what he does not deserve." "Grace" is probably the greatest word in the New Testament. It is a word which contains God's love, mercy, kindness, forgiveness, generosity—all in motion toward the undeserving sinner.

I. *The Believer Is Resurrected From the Dead* (2:1-5). While we look forward to the resurrection from the grave, we can presently rejoice in a resurrection from spiritual death because of God's grace. In the conversion experience, God gave life to us who were dead in trespasses and sins. We did not possess the divine life that comes to us in the miracle of the new birth. We can rejoice in that we have been raised from the dead.

II. *The Display of the Riches of God's Grace* (2:6-10). Each convert is an exhibition of the miracle of God's grace. Paul declares that in the future ages the exceeding riches of God's grace through Christ Jesus will be demonstrated and disclosed in heavenly places. We can be sure that when God puts something on exhibit it will be glorious. We can rejoice in anticipation of what is in store for us through faith in Christ Jesus.

This chapter contains one of the great passages of the New Testament on the grace of God as being the source and the basis for our salvation (Eph. 2:8, 9). Our salvation from the penalty of sin is not due to human merit or achievement. We are saved by the pure grace of God plus nothing. We receive this salvation through the channel of faith, and even our faith is the gift of God.

III. *God's Poems* (2:10). The word "workmanship" comes from the Greek word "poiema," meaning "that which has been made—a work" or "a poetical work" or "a poem." Hence it is clear that we are God's poems. The word implies artisanship and craftmanship. Paul is declaring that we are God's harmonious, beautiful, lovely creations through faith in Christ Jesus.

IV. *The Past Contrasted With the Present* (2:11-22). Paul is writing to Gentile converts who previously were without Christ and were alien from the commonwealth of Israel.

They were strangers from the covenants of promise, having no hope and without God and the world. In the present, in Christ Jesus they are now "insiders" as far as God's great redemptive activity is concerned.

It is the plan and purpose of God that both Jews and Gentiles compose "one body" in the plan and purpose of God (2:16).

Gentile believers are no longer strangers and foreigners but are fellow citizens with the saints and are members of the very household of God (2:19). Gentile believers can rejoice in the privilege of being a part of God's chosen people through whom He would bless the world if they will but have faith and be faithful to His purpose for them.

Conclusion. God, by means of His Spirit, is eager to dwell in the midst of us and not only bless us but through us bless the world. We must beware lest we like national Israel of old distrust our Lord and follow a pathway of disobedience rather than obedience. We have been saved by the grace of God with a redemptive purpose in mind. We have been saved to serve. We have been saved by God's grace in order that through us others might experience salvation.

SUNDAY MORNING, JUNE 23

TITLE: "An Example of Faith" (Father's Day)

TEXT: "So Jesus came again into Cana of Galilee, where he made the water wine. And there was a certain nobleman, whose son was sick at Capernaum. When he heard that Jesus was come out of Judea into Galilee, he went unto him, and he sought him that he would come down, and heal his son: for he was at the point of death. Then said Jesus unto him, Except ye see signs and wonders, ye will not believe. The nobleman saith unto him, Sir, come down ere my child die. Jesus saith unto him, Go thy way; thy son liveth. And the man believed the word that Jesus had spoken unto him, and he went his way. And as he was now going down, his servants met him, and told him, saying, Thy son liveth. Then inquired he of them the hour when he began to amend. And they said unto him, Yesterday at the seventh hour the fever left him. So the father knew that it was at the same hour, in the which Jesus said unto him, Thy son liveth: and himself believed, and his whole house" (John 4:46-53).

SCRIPTURE READING: John 4: 46-53.

HYMNS: "Faith of Our Fathers," Faber. "Have Faith in God," McKinney. "Faith Is the Victory," Yates.

OFFERTORY PRAYER:

Our Father, on this day when we think particularly of fathers and their influence on our lives we are grateful that we can call Thee "Father." And we are grateful that Thou art indeed our father through faith. As a father Thou art interested in our best development, our proper growth, and our abiding relationship with Thee. Help us to achieve these things by Thy grace.

We are thankful for all the blessings Thou hast seen fit to bestow upon us. Make us aware of their source. And make us responsive to Thy Spirit.

We come now to show tangible proof of our gratitude, our love, and our faith. Please accept these gifts. Bless them to Thy use. And bless each one who gives.

This we pray in the name of Jesus, Thy Son and our Savior. Amen.

Introduction. My father died in 1965. I am convinced that the greatest legacy that he left was a legacy of faith. He was not a minister; he was a deacon who took his Christian faith very seriously. He did not leave vast land holdings; he did not leave huge insurance policies; he did not leave large blocks of stocks. But he did leave a legacy of faith that would always challenge and inspire each one of us. A father's faith lives forever in the minds and lives of his children.

There are times when a father's faith makes requests of the Lord in the interest of his family. This was the turn of faith of the unnamed nobleman in John 4. He had evidently heard of the miracles that Jesus had performed at other places. Then when he learned that Jesus was only twenty or twenty-five miles from his home he rushed to Him to ask Him to heal his sick son. At the outset his faith was only that Jesus could work a miracle and save his son's life. But under the skillful hand of Jesus his faith developed more completely.

When we seek faith for frighten-

ing times we need an example of faith. We need to know that in his own experience at least one other person has expressed faith. And on Father's Day there is no better place to turn for an example of faith than to a father's faith. Faith is the greatest legacy a father can leave his family. For an example of faith look to a father's faith.

I. *As an Example of Faith a Father's Faith Approaches the Lord.*

A. The approach of faith requests God's help. In all honesty it must be admitted that at the beginning the nobleman's faith was not spiritually motivated. It was the faith growing out of a desperate attempt for help. From the agony of his heart he asked Jesus to go to Capernaum to heal his son. But the significant thing is that "he besought him." He did make an approach to Jesus.

Our approach to Christ for help may not always be properly motivated. But God can take an imperfect approach and turn it into a perfect blessing.

B. The approach of faith believes God's power. This man did not know all about Jesus. But he did have confidence in His power.

Belief in the power of God may be the greatest ally that we have in life. Moses believed the power of God in the face of seemingly unconquerable obstacles. But Moses through God's power led the children of Israel out of Egypt.

C. The approach of faith accepts God's opportunities. After hearing the nobleman's plea Jesus said to him, "Go thy way; thy son liveth" (v. 50). Jesus knew that the man wanted a miracle, the healing of his son, but He gave him an opportunity for faith.

In faith opportunity does knock twice and more. Repeatedly God has given to us opportunities for faith. We must accept the opportunity that God has given to us and exercise faith.

II. *As an Example of Faith a Father's Faith Experiences Growth.* This incident shows an amazing growth of faith. Notice how faith can grow.

A. Faith begins at the miracle level (v. 48). At first this father only wanted a miracle. He would believe if Jesus would heal his son.

Jesus chided those who would not believe without a sign. This is the lowest level of faith. This is the faith that must have proof through a visible sign or a miracle. The faith that demands a guarantee is really no faith.

B. Faith advances to the "believe at His word" level (v. 50). The faith that can accept Jesus at His word is a higher level of faith.

This does not always involve a full understanding of what has happened or will happen. Likely the father thought that Jesus knew by some intuitive knowledge that the son was better.

But it all turns on the faithfulness of Jesus. We can accept the promises of Jesus, we can believe His word, we can simply take Him at His word because He is trustworthy. Calvin Coolidge's father told of a characteristic that his son took with him when he became president of the United States. His father said that often when he had to go to town he would leave certain instructions with Calvin Coolidge about things that ought to be done before he returned. And, he said, he never at any time when he returned looked to see if these things had been done. He knew without looking that they would be done because he knew that he could rely absolutely on his son Calvin to do them. And Jesus is just that trustworthy.

C. Faith reaches its height in simple belief in Jesus (v. 53). When one believes Jesus he has reached the pinnacle of faith. Isn't it strange that the height of faith is where faith should really start?

Faith reaches its climactic moment when one trusts Jesus completely as Lord and Savior.

III. *As an Example of Faith a Father's Faith Enjoys Victory.*

A. The victory of faith is in the act of God's promise. Faith reached its victory when Jesus did what He said He would do: He healed the boy. Jesus was faithful to His word. At the same hour that Jesus said the boy was healed He began to improve.

In 1941, when General Douglas MacArthur left the Philippine Islands after the fall of Corregidor to the Japanese, he made the promise, "I shall return." When he waded ashore with the attacking troops in 1944 as the battle to regain the Philippine Islands reached the invasion stage he proclaimed, "I have returned." He had brought fulfillment to his promise. And so does God fulfill the promises He has made.

B. The victory of faith is the realization of spiritual gifts. Jesus had to convince the troubled nobleman that the most valuable thing He had to give was not physical healing but spiritual strength that comes from God. This is the best gift that He could give to any of His children.

C. The victory of faith is as a guide to God. Verse 53 indicates that not only did this nobleman believe Jesus but also his whole house. Because of a father's faith a whole family came to know faith in God through Jesus Christ.

No matter what else a father may have provided he has not really supported his family until he has served as a guide to God for them.

In the Hebrew tradition a father served as a representative of God in leading the family in worship. Much of the Hebrew worship is centered in family worship in the home. A modern father may not understand his role as a representative of God, but he can surely be a guide to God. Through his faith, through his participation in worship, through the sharing of his faith in God a father can guide his family to God.

Conclusion. A father's faith serves as a stirring example of faith for frightening times. This father was frightened. His son, perhaps an only son, was at the point of death. In faith he turned to Jesus.

SUNDAY EVENING, JUNE 23

TITLE: "The Teenager and the Will of God"

TEXT: "And I said, What shall I do, Lord?" (Acts 22:10a).

SCRIPTURE READING: Acts 22:1-14.

Introduction. I shall never forget the night I bowed my head before God and said, "Lord, Thy will be done in my life." I cannot describe the joys that flooded my soul. I think this is the most thrilling experience of life. It is, in the phraseology of Churchill, "our finest hour."

Paul tells that one day he was walking down the Damascus Road, and suddenly a great light shown round about him, and he fell to the ground. He heard the voice of God asking, "Why persecutest thou me?" A little later, he surrendered and cried out, "What wilt thou have me

to do, Lord?" Paul had been rebelling against God. He had been kicking against the traces. But now he yielded his life to the will of God. This was his concept of salvation. As we follow Paul on his great missionary journeys, we notice that it was always "the will of God be done." One time Paul wanted to go to Bithynia. The Spirit of God said, "No, go to Troas." He went on in the face of hardships, dangers, beatings, stonings, and imprisonments. The great apostle went on preaching the Gospel from city to city.

Paul was greatly successful in his missionary endeavors. What was the secret of his success? I believe it was that he lived in the center of God's will. In the place of God's will, there is guidance, there is joy, there is power.

Living there enables you to be silent when criticized, humble when praised, and patient when ignored.

Paul's concept of God's will involves three things:

I. *God's Will Involves a Plan for Every Life.*

A. Paul cried out, "What shall I do, Lord?" Paul felt that God had something for him to do. He describes how Ananias came and placed his hands upon his head and said, "The God of our fathers hath chosen thee, that thou shouldest know his will." In spite of his past life, God had a place in His will for Paul.

You recall that Horace Bushnell, the famous preacher of the last century, had a great sermon entitled, "Every Man's Life a Plan of God." As an artist has a plan in his mind for the portrait he is to paint before he takes up the brush, as a potter has a plan in his heart before he takes up the clay, as the sculptor has a plan before he takes up his trowel, so God had a plan in His heart for your life and mine before we were ever born.

God has a place for every life.

Dr. Marshall Craig, pastor of the Gaston Avenue Baptist Church in Dallas for many years, tells of speaking in a series of services at the university chapel. He gave the invitation, pleading with young men and women to lay their lives, their all, upon the altar. They began to come. The president of the student body, some of the football players, campus leaders, beautiful girls, many came, sincerely, honestly, giving themselves to Christ. Then he saw a strange thing. Far back toward the rear of the auditorium, he saw a boy start down the aisle toward the front, and that boy was crawling on his hands and knees.

Dr. Craig turned to the university president who said, "It is all right, sir. The boy is one of our students who is a hopeless cripple, and the only way he can get around is on his hands and knees."

Dr. Craig waited at the altar for him. He leaned down, and the young man looked up at the great preacher and said, "Sir, you said God had a place for a man. I know God has a place for these athletes, these campus leaders. But tell me, sir, does God have a place for a wreck like me?"

Dr. Craig spoke through tears to say, "Son, God has been waiting for a wreck like you."

Whoever you are, whatever you have been, God has a place for you, a plan for your life. As every instrument has a place in the great orchestra, as every star has a place in the heavens, as every flower has a place in the flower garden, so every person has a place in the great plan of God.

B. It is wrong to think that God has a will for the missionary, the preacher, the educational director, the music director, etc., but the butcher, the baker, the candlestick maker, this, "vulgar group," God has nothing for them. They will have to get along the best they can. No, God has a plan for every life.

Would you have the greatest thrill of your life? Would you experience the highest joy? Would you live at your highest and best? Would you be successful in your work?

Then, find God's will. Fit into it. And fulfill it.

II. *God's Will Involves Service.*

Paul cried, "What wilt thou have me to *do*?" Ananias gave him the instructions from God: "Thou shalt be his witness."

A. What are you going to do with your life?

1. You can waste it in dissipation and indulgence, in eating, drinking, and being merry.

2. You can spend your life in self-pleasing. You can say, "Leave me alone, God. I'll run my life. Hands off!" You can do this and be a good citizen and a good neighbor, but there will still be something lacking.

3. You can dedicate your life to the service of humanity. Any concept of salvation which minimizes service is wrong. Salvation and works are so vitally related that they cannot be separated. "Faith without works is dead." Paul interpreted the will of God in the realm of service.

B. What is God's will for us? It is clear that we are to love God and to love people. We are to minister to the needy, the suffering, the poor, the diseased. We are to reconcile people to God and to their fellow men. We are to be instruments of healing and blessing and life to the world.

I believe we can know God's will for our lives. We can find God's will through reason, through the counsel of friends, through conscience, by reading the biographies of great men, by the study of our talents and our abilities, through prayer and communion with God. Most of all, we know His will by what the Quakers call "inner light," the impulse of the heart.

The will of God, if it means anything, involves a life of service.

Here is our missionary impulse, our evangelistic motive. It is God's will that if we have the Gospel, if we know the good news, then we must share it with the peoples of the earth who do not have it.

Too many of us have taken a seat on the sidelines. We have become spectators, sitting in the box seats of comfort and complacency. God calls us to come down, out of the gallery, and fight the good fight of faith, run the race set before us, serve Him with all our hearts.

C. God may be calling you. It may be to preach. It may be to be a missionary, or a nurse. It may be to do some special, definite Christian work. It may be to sing in the choir or to visit the sick and the needy.

But we know that God's will is that every one who names His name be a faithful witness, serve Him, bring other people to Him wherever we are, whatever we do.

III. *God's Will Involves Pleasing God.*

A. "What shall I do, Lord?" he asked. He was really saying, "Tell me what You want me to do, Lord, and I will get busy doing it."

Pleasing the Lord was the deepest desire of his life. He said, "This one thing I do, forgetting those things which are behind, and reaching forth unto those things which are before, I press toward the mark for the prize of the high calling of God in Christ Jesus" (Phil. 3:14).

Every step he took was taken in the will of God. From the very first day when he was stricken down on the Damascus Road by a light from heaven, by the outpouring of the Spirit of God, until forty years later when he was killed for his faith, it was always the will of God be done.

A little while before his death in Rome, he said once again, "I am now ready to be offered, and the time of my departure is at hand. I have fought a good fight, I have finished my course, I have kept the faith," Paul kept his face turned toward the will of God.

B. What is the direction of your life? God's will is never revealed to us all at once, but one step at a time. If you follow the light you have today, more will be given you tomorrow. "In all thy ways acknowledge him, and he shall direct thy paths" (Prov. 3:6).

Conclusion. Are you ready and willing to yield your life, whatever it costs? Wherever it leads?

The highest, the holiest, the happiest calling in all the world is the call to do His will. He calls you to accept Christ as your personal Savior.

Will you turn to Him? Will you do God's will?

WEDNESDAY EVENING, JUNE 26

TITLE: "The Bible Speaks to Our Condition"

SCRIPTURE READING: Philippians 3.

Introduction. God will speak words of guidance to us through His Word as He did to Joshua in ancient days if we will meditate upon His teachings and open our heart so as to receive His counsel.

Paul's note of joy with which this chapter begins is all the more significant when we remember that this epistle was written from a prison cell. Paul was waiting to be tried before the judgment seat of Caesar. The outcome of that judicial experience was unknown at the moment. Despite the discomfort of imprisonment and the humiliation that must have been associated with this, the Apostle Paul was able to rejoice in the Lord and to encourage others to rejoice in Him. Today, let us rejoice in the Lord.

I. *A Warning Against False Teaching* (3:2-9, 17-19). It is interesting to note the corrective nature of many sections of Paul's epistles. It is also interesting to note how much space he gave to warning his beloved friends against the peril of being misled by false teachers.

Paul was vitally concerned that the disciples of our Lord in Philippi not be misled by those who were insisting that one found a position of acceptance before God on the basis of his obedience to the law of Moses.

Paul affirms that he has repudiated all claims of righteousness on the basis of the law in order that he might have the righteousness that comes through faith in Jesus Christ alone. As he compares the two forms of righteousness, he declares that the righteousness that comes by keeping the law is of no more value than garbage as compared with the righteousness that comes through faith in Jesus Christ.

Are you solidly resting in the grace of God through faith in Christ Jesus, or are you trying to earn a position of favor in the presence of God because of your own achievement? May God grant to each of us the faith that will enable us to re-

pond to and rejoice in the righ-
ousness that comes through faith
lus no human merit at all.

II. *Experiential Knowledge of
Christ Jesus* (3:10-12). The Apos-
e Paul had been a disciple of Jesus
Christ for many years. He had an
utstanding reputation as a mission-
ry, as an evangelist, and as a theo-
ogian. Even though this was true, he
till had a deep desire to enter into
richer experiential knowledge of
esus Christ.

There are some folk with whom
ou can get fully acquainted in a
hort time. Once you come to know
hese folk, you have no desire for a
eeper experiential acquaintance
ith them. Such is not the case with
esus Christ. The more we get to
now Him, the more we want to
now Him. We want to have both a
eeper and a higher experience with
esus Christ.

This knowledge of Christ comes
hrough a devotional and responsive
udy of His Word. It comes
hrough transforming prayer experi-
nces. It comes through implicit
ust in His promises. It comes as
e give full obedience to His com-
ands.

May it be that each of us will
ave a growing knowledge of our
ord Jesus.

III. *The Power of a Compelling
Purpose* (3:13, 14). Most of us
drift aimlessly through life. We
never clearly define our goals and
objectives. Consequently, we waste
our energy because of the absence
of clear priorities for the use of our
energy.

Paul's compelling motive was to
fully experience and achieve that
for which the Lord had called him.
Like an athlete running in a race to
win a prize, Paul was pressing
toward the mark in order that he
might fully achieve God's high call
for his life.

God has a high call for each of
us. We would be exceedingly wise if
we were to lift our eyes to discover
His high call and then without res-
ervation give ourselves continually
to that quest.

Conclusion. The chapter for today's experience with God closes
with a reminder of the fact that believers are citizens of heaven and
that their habits and ambitions
should conform to their heavenly
citizenship (3:20). Paul looks forward to the time at the consumation
of the ages when the body of our
humiliation shall be transformed
into the likeness of the body of the
glorified Christ (3:21).

SUNDAY MORNING, JUNE 30

TITLE: "The Outreach of
Faith: the Christian Life"

TEXT: "For we are the circumcision, which worship God in
the spirit, and rejoice in Christ
Jesus, and have no confidence in
the flesh" (Phil. 3:3).

SCRIPTURE READING: Philippians 3.

HYMNS: "When We Walk With
the Lord," Sammis. "More Like
the Master," Gabriel. "Take My
Life and Let It Be,' Havergal.

OFFERTORY PRAYER:

Our Father, we thank Thee for the blessings of life which Thou hast so richly given us this past week.

We praise the name of Jesus Christ for the salvation which we have through Him.

We commit ourselves more completely to Thee and to Thy will. We would pray that Thou wouldst show us the paths that we should take, the decisions that we should make, and the stubborn areas of our own wills that we should break.

As we consider the life that Thou hast called us to live, the Christian life, we would ask for Thy strength in living it. And we would pray that through our lives Thou shouldst indeed have a testimony of grace. Help us to be both witnesses and ministers. Fill us with Thy Spirit that we could live for Thee.

Take now the gifts that we bring. These gifts are material expressions of the life that we have already given to Thee. Use these gifts for Thy glory. And use our lives in Thy will.

In Jesus' name we pray, and for His sake. Amen.

Introduction. John A. Mackay, former president of Princeton Theological Seminary, in his book about South America entitled *That Other America*, tells of an interesting interview with a full-blooded Peruvian Indian. This man had a Ph.D. degree from a leading university in the United States; he was an authority in pre-Incan civilization. He knew both personally and academically what had happened to the culture of his people. The question he asked was this: "Can religion change a person?"

This is a tremendously important the assumption that religion can question. Evidently we operate on change a person. We gather at least once a week for worship. We spend vast sums of money on places of worship. We send people all around the world to try to win people to Christ. Yet sometimes this haunting question lurks in the background. The problem is that we have seen too many people whom religion has evidently not changed.

This is not the type of question that can be answered with a glib word. It is a question that can best be answered by illustration. True you can point out those who were supposedly failures of faith. But on the other hand you can point out others who are veritable walking trophies of grace. A cynical white man one time asked the black man who had been the personal servant of General Robert E. Lee, "Do you believe there is a God?" And the black man, then old and bent, replied very simply, "Yes, sir. I knew Mr. Lee."

Yes, religion can change a person. It has done so. A vital faith in Jesus Christ is the greatest force in the world.

This response to God through Christ in faith we call the Christian Life. Christian life is not only begun by faith, it is lived by faith. Faith for frightening times has an outreach: the Christian life.

Tucked away in the third chapter of Philippians the third verse gives what one New Testament scholar has called "one of the clearest, most concise statements describing Christian found in the Bible." Paul identified the true believers in God to the Philippian Christians. The marks are spiritual rather than physical. This one verse gives three insights into why the Christian life is the outreach of faith.

I. *The Christian Life Is the Outreach of Faith Since It Is a Life of Response to God.* Notice that Paul identified the true people of God as those who "worship God in the spirit. . . ." Jesus taught us that God is Spirit and that those who worship God must worship Him both in spirit and in truth (John 4:24).

A. This frees worship. This means that God is not bound nor contained. Worship can be conducted any place where a person meets God.

This also frees the form of worship. To be a true experience of worship it does not have to follow set patterns. Jesus promised: "For where two or three are gathered together in my name, there am I in the midst of them" (Matt. 18:20). We can worship God by the leading of the Spirit of God. This is a distinctive ritual: the leadership of the Holy Spirit in the life of men leading them to God.

B. This defines worship. What is worship but response to God? We meet God face to face in worship. In the services of a church, in a moment of prayer, during the reading of the Bible, we meet God. And when we meet God we are to respond in repentance and faith. This is true worship. It is not just keeping the forms of worship but is a response to God.

The person who does not join in worship is committing what Elton Trueblood called "the angelic fallacy." He makes the mistake of thinking that he is an angel when in reality he is a man who desperately needs to meet God in worship.

From the worship that is the response to God will flow the results of the Christian life: mission, witness, Bible study, ministry. But it all comes about in response to God. And we do not respond to God if we do not worship God.

II. *The Christian Life Is the Outreach of Faith Since It Is a Life of Commitment to Jesus Christ.*

A. Commitment to Christ is the means of salvation. Commitment to Christ is the essence of the Christian life. One cannot enter the Christian life until he has first met Christ and has committed his life to Him in faith.

This removes all source of pride. If salvation were attained by our merits or our goodness or by our efforts then we could have room for pride. But the Scripture plainly teaches that salvation is the gift of God's grace. And since it is by God's grace there is no place for pride. Our rejoicing can be in nothing else but Jesus and His salvation.

B. Commitment to Christ is the means of Christian growth. The Christian life is to be a life of growth. It is growth in grace. And the way we grow is through commitment to Christ.

Hawthorne's legend of the Great Stone Face reminds us of this. The boy Ernest would look longingly at the great stone face on the side of the mountain. It was a strong, kind, honorable face that thrilled the heart of this boy. There was a legend that some day a man would appear who would look like the Great Stone Face. Through all his childhood, and even after he be-

191

came a man, Ernest kept looking at the great face and for the man who was like it. One day, when the people were discussing the legend, someone suddenly cried out, "Behold, behold, Ernest is himself the likeness of the Great Stone Face." By committing our lives to Jesus and looking to Him we can grow to be like Him.

III. *The Christian Life Is the Outreach of Faith Since It Is a Life of Continual Faith in God.* The response of faith is a continual response of faith in God. Paul designated the ones of the true covenant as those who "have no confidence in the flesh." This means that our confidence or faith cannot be on outward privileges, such as who we are, what we have done, or where we came from, but only in God.

The Christian life is wholly a life of faith. It is not just the faith of a moment but the faith of a lifetime that matters. Remember the battle cry of Martin Luther? "The just shall live by faith," he proclaimed. In Romans 1:17 where these words are found the full quotation is: "For therein is the righteousness of God revealed from faith to faith: as

it is written, The just shall live by faith." "From faith to faith"—from one level of faith to another we are to live.

Faith is a growth process. The faith that is had at the time Christ is accepted as Savior should not be the faith that is held after years as a Christian. Faith should grow, mature, and strengthen.

If the Christian life is a life of continuous faith then some things will have to be removed. In 1 Peter 2:1-3 some suggestions are given about things that must be removed from our lives. One can hardly grow in faith while his life is burdened with these elements that should be stripped away.

In humility we approach God and ask for the renewal of strength, the forgiveness of sin, the cleansing of life and the firming up of faith. Our confidences can only be in God.

Conclusion. These are frightening times. But God has not called us to fear but to faith. The faith that we have in God is sufficient for us to meet any problem in the time in which we live. The outreach of faith is the Christian life. In faith we live, witness, and minister for God.

SUNDAY EVENING, JUNE 30

TITLE: "The Teenager and Prayer"

TEXT: "But thou, when thou prayest, enter into thy closet, and when thou hast shut thy door, pray to thy Father which is in secret; and thy Father which seeth in secret shall reward thee openly" (Matt. 6:6).

SCRIPTURE READING: Matthew 6:1-15.

Introduction. In the words of our text our Lord assumed that His disciples would pray. It was natural for Him to assume that the children of God would desire communion and fellowship with God. The need for guidance as well as the need for

192

forgiveness leads one to desire the help of God.

I. *Prayer Is a Privilege.* Some people think of prayer as a duty, and it is. Some people think of prayer as a stewardship, and it is. Some people think of prayer as a necessity, and it is.

Real prayer is a priceless privilege. By means of prayer we talk to the eternal, loving Father. Real prayer is more than a monologue. It is also listening for the still small voice of the God who loves us with a perfect love and with perfect wisdom.

II. *Prayer Is a Private Affair.* "Enter into thy closet, and when thou hast shut thy door. . . ."

Jesus did insist that the conversation of a child with the Father and the Father with the child be a private and confidential conversation. Perhaps He was insisting in these words that we go apart to a secret place where we could shut out all distractions and interruptions.

Jesus is not forbidding public prayer or united prayer with these words. He is simply declaring that we have the privilege of a private audience with our Father God. The inexperienced teenager can enjoy this privilege as well as the sainted pastor, evangelist or veteran missionary.

III. *Prayer Is a Personal Experience.* ". . . pray to thy Father. . . ." We are not to approach God as one of a vast multitude who can clamor with many voices for His attention. God is personal. He inclines His ear to each of us as if we were the only person in existence.

We appreciate Him on a very personal basis: the parent-child relationship. Here Jesus does not suggest that we approach Him as an almighty God or an eternal God, or the high and holy king of the universe. As needy children, we are to approach our Father God in prayer on a very personal basis.

IV. *Prayer Can Be a Most Productive Experience.* ". . . thy Father which seeth in secret shall reward thee."

Indeed prayer can be a most profitable experience. When we pray with a reverent, trusting, submissive attitude, God reveals Himself to us as the loving Father who is always present with purposes of grace, mercy, and guidance. This is perhaps the greatest reward that comes to the one praying following the initial plea for pardon from sin and acceptance into the family of God.

In the prayer experience, God lets us see ourselves. We see our need for forgiveness. We see our need for cleansing. We see our need for guidance. We see our place in the plan and purpose of God. This provides the guidance that is so desperately needed.

In the prayer experience the Father also opens our eyes to see the need of others. He would speak to us and give us instructions concerning the work that He wants us to do.

Conclusion. Real prayer is a privilege. It is a private and personal experience with God. It can be a most productive experience. It should be a personal experience in the life of each teenager as well as an adult.

We should not be content with the great prayer experiences of the past. We should not look forward wistfully to a mountaintop experience at an undetermined date in the future. Instead we should enter into the closet and have dialogue with the heavenly Father day by day.

SUGGESTED PREACHING PROGRAM FOR THE MONTH OF JULY

Sunday Mornings

Man has always had a problem with sin and with sins. The theme for a series of topical sermons which deals with this timeless problem faced by man is "The Sins Which Damage and Destroy." This series is introduced with a consideration of "man's plight as a sinner."

Sunday Evenings

A series of topical sermons dealing with the theme, "The Great Christian Virtues." Another good theme for this series would be, "The Fruit of the Spirit," as listed by Paul in Galatians 5:22, 23.

Wednesday Evenings

Continue with the theme, "The Bible Speaks to Our Condition."

The theme verse for July is "Study to shew thyself approved unto God, a workman that needeth not to be ashamed, rightly dividing the word of truth" (2 Tim. 2:15).

WEDNESDAY EVENING, JULY 3

TITLE: "The Bible Speaks to our Condition"

SCRIPTURE READING: 1 Thessalonians 2.

Introduction. The words of our chapter for today are addressed to beloved friends in the city of Thessalonica where Paul had had a very brief but significant missionary ministry (Acts 17:1-10).

I. *Boldness After Suffering* (2:1, 2). Paul had suffered great pain for the sake of the Gospel in Philippi. This did not dissuade him or intimidate him from continuing to preach the Gospel when he arrived in Thessalonica. His example should challenge us to be faithful to our Lord in the face of possible misunderstanding and hardship, and in some instances, persecution.

II. *Trustees of the Gospel* (2:4). Paul felt that he had been entrusted by the Lord with the good news of the Gospel for the benefit of both Jews and Gentiles. The only manner in which he could be faithful to his trusteeship was by communicating the good news.

Each follower of Christ is a trustee of the Gospel. We prove to be worthy trustees as we try to give the good news to as many as we possibly can.

III. *The Worthy Walk of Children* (2:12). Paul seeks to persuade the disciples in Thessalonica to walk worthy of their new relationship to God as father and child. He describes the manner of his walk and work among them as an example for them to follow. He speaks of loving them as a nurse would cher-

194

ish her children and as a father loves and comforts his children.

If we wear the name of the Lord, we should remember that there are responsibilities that go along with this privilege.

IV. *The Power of the Word of God* (2:13, 14). These people in Thessalonica had received the Word of God and had permitted the Word to produce a powerful effect in their lives (1:9, 10). When the Word of God is received into the heart, as the authoritative Word of God, it produces a dynamic transformation. It changes our thoughts and it affects our emotions, and it changes our choices.

As we prayerfully and responsively read a chapter a day, let us accept it as the truth of God for our lives.

V. *The Hindrances of Satan* (2: 18). Satan stood in the pathway of Paul to hinder him all of the way. Satan had tried to hinder our Lord as He faced His redemptive mission.

Satan will attempt to hinder each of us each day. He will hinder us from the experience of worship if we permit him to do so. He will seek to hinder us from giving a witness. He will attempt to hinder us in all of our work for God.

Our only hope of overcoming his hindrances is through the strength and power that comes through prayer and faith in our Lord (Eph. 6:10-18).

VI. *The Joy of the Faithful Witness* (2:19, 20). Paul looked forward to the time of the Second Coming of the Lord Jesus Christ. Each convert was a source of joy and happiness to his heart.

Each of us should face the question, "Have I been instrumental in helping someone come to know Jesus Christ?"

Conclusion. Did you let God speak to your heart as you read through this chapter? Perhaps His message will come through more clearly and more authoritatively if you will read it again.

SUNDAY MORNING, JULY 7

TITLE: "Man's Plight As Sinner"

TEXT: "If we say that we have no sin, we deceive ourselves, and the truth is not in us" (1 John 1:8).

SCRIPTURE READING: Romans 1:18-25.

HYMNS: "Christ Receiveth Sinful Men," Neumeister. "Amazing Grace," Newton. "Love Lifted Me," Rowe.

OFFERTORY PRAYER:

Dear Father, in our unworthiness Thou didst redeem us. In our disobedience and faithlessness Thou hast forgiven. Now, dear Lord, take that which is the fruit of our labors and bless it to higher use. Cleanse the stain of sin so often marring our gifts and grant Thy Spirit to reign in us, through Jesus Christ our Lord. Amen.

Introduction. If we compare our

case with other animals, we see how hard it is to be a human being. In the first place, we have to stand upright, a feat for which we are not completely adapted. In addition to this awkward situation, we have to think, and we feel something within us constraining us to act rightly. When we try to do good, we find evil up against us. Now we have to think harder for we are perplexed by the presence of something that we neither understand nor know why it should be there at all.

The age-old problem so often wrestled with in man's mind and reflected on at length in the Scriptures is the raising of the lowly animal creature, man, into fellowship with the divine. How are the "sons of men" to become the "sons of God"? This caused greater problems than the divine relationship to "lower" life, because the matter of the "will of man" came into the picture. The higher the ambition God held for man, the greater became the problem introduced by man's free will. In order to form character in man, God had to take terrible risks. He had to leave man the choice of good or evil. That was man's great opportunity; that was man's occasion for falling.

The Bible attributes man's sin to his willful abuse of his God-given freedom of choosing the basic course and character of his life. Paul, in writing the Roman Christians, outlines the truth concerning man's plight as sinner in careful analysis (Rom. 1:18-25).

I. *The Seriousness of Sin.*

A. Concerned with the total being of man.

1. Not just with the flesh or material.

2. Not only a mental condition.

3. It is in the heart of man, at the very center of selfhood.

B. The New Testament's appraisal of sin in man.

1. Sin in the "flesh" describes living apart from God (2 Cor. 1:17; 10:2; Rom. 8:4, 5, 13).

2. Sin in "your bodies" means sin in your personal being (Rom. 6:12, 13; 12:1).

3. Sin in the "soul" is also referring to one's self or person. The soul or person sinning "shall die" is a warning to the total person. (Use in Acts 2:41 or 3:23.)

Sin is serious for it involves the total man. Man does not have in himself strength to solve his problem. His whole being is adversely affected. Sin has invaded his thinking, his will, his sense of values, his natural responses, and his relationships.

II. *Slavery to Sin.*

A. In man's expressions of self-will, he loses his freedom.

1. From trusting God to self trust.

2. From obeying God to self assertion.

3. From serving God to slavery of sin.

B. In sinning, man brings community to be under dominion of sin (Rom. 6:6; 7:24).

C. Sin snatches and exercises lordship over man (Rom. 6:14; 7:17; Gal. 3:22).

Living is described as serving either "good" or "evil." Man's acts have repercussions beyond the sensations that he momentarily feels. His acts are testimonies for God or for Satan. The constant plea of the New Testament is for man to "serve God" and thus find the liberation for which man was created. When sin is served, man's true destiny is denied, his created role is forfeited, and he falls under the bondage of sin and death.

III. *The Surrender to Sin.* Man's surrender of his relation of "sonship" to God brings into light his personal responsibility or guilt.

A. The Bible holds man guilty for his own sin.

1. Not responsibility of past generations (Deut. 24:16; Ezek. 18: 2-4).

2. Man responsible for action of group if he is a part.

B. Man is guilty for the environment he helps create.

1. We speak of my country, our city, my home.

2. No man lives to himself; living is influencing.

3. Man faces his sin alone.

Conclusion. Man's problem is sin. He may have many problems in life, such as problems in his finiteness, fate, and function. He is plagued with involvement in the material aspect of his life and by his ignorance. When all is said, man's plight, however, is one of sin. The Bible holds man guilty in his sin. Man—and man alone—stands responsible and stands in total solitude to face his sin. To meet this condition, there came the "Good News." When man is willing to admit that sin is his own and his alone, there is a Savior to bear it. ". . . Christ Jesus came into the world to save sinners . . ." (1 Tim. 1:15).

SUNDAY EVENING, JULY 7

TITLE: "Salvation and Its Fruits"

TEXT: "The fruit of the spirit is love, joy, peace, longsuffering, gentleness, goodness, faith, meekness, temperance: against such there is no law" (Gal. 5:22, 23).

SCRIPTURE READING: Hebrews 2:1-4, 9-12.

Introduction. Man has for so many years concerned himself with the question of "Who is God?" that he has forgotten another important question, "Who am I?" Now there are some who answer the question quickly: "I" am merely the train of thoughts and feelings and emotions that, like an Aeolian harp, played on by the wind of sensation, react to my environment. My conviction goes beyond that. Selfhood is a person, separated from all other persons, and remaining always the same being whatever changes may take place around me. I am a self

197

conscious of itself. That constitutes man.

Within this self there occur some very positive notions. I find myself saying, "I ought to do certain things," or "I ought not to do other things." The mystery of this authoritative utterance of the self within me demands my attention. What is the "I ought" that I feel?

Paul says it is "the law [of God] written in their hearts" (Rom. 2: 15). John suggested it was "the true Light, which lighteth every man that cometh into the world" (John 1:9). Whatever the feeling that requires response, it is in this that I differ from other animals. It is in this that I find my relationship to my Creator. So it is that out of inner struggle, out of the warfare within the soul, there comes peace.

Man's cumulative acts of bad choices and good choices through the years have come to complicate our "soul struggle." It has become such a mess that two thousand years ago a man complained, "For the good that I would I do not: but the evil which I would not, that I do" (Rom. 7:19). Right into the middle of this dilemma the God who "in former times . . . in fragmentary and varied fashion" spoke through the prophets "in this the final age he has spoken to us in the Son . . ." (Heb. 1:1, 2, NEB). Now His Son's message is, "Come unto me, all ye that labour and are heavy laden, and I will give you rest" (Matt. 11:28). This is our salvation. This we can not miss.

I. *No Escape,* "if we neglect [that] . . . which at the first began to be spoken by the Lord" (Heb. 2:3).

A. Salvation for each individual.

1. He may "come boldly unto the throne of grace" (Heb. 4:16).

2. He may "reason together saith the Lord" concerning sin and its removal (Isa. 1:18).

3. He may be saved "by grace through faith" (Eph. 2:8).

4. He may find a creative force in grace. "I laboured more abundantly than they all" (1 Cor. 15:10).

B. Salvation from God.

1. "Election"—the purpose and initiative of God in salvation.

2. "Calling"—shows God's choice of man prior to man's choosing God.

3. The seeking God. ". . . the son of man is come to seek and to save that which was lost" (Luke 19: 10). "We love him, because he first loved us" (1 John 4:19).

II. *No Glory,* if we refuse suffering, for "he by the grace of God should taste death for every man" (Heb. 2:9).

A. Dying to live. "Except a corn of wheat fall into the ground and die, it abideth alone; but if it die, it bringeth forth much fruit" (John 12:24).

B. Dying to self. Paul often set before the people the fact of Christ's dying as a challenge for self-denial. "While we were yet sinners, Christ died for us" (Rom. 5:8). "It is Christ that died, yea rather, that is risen again . . . who also maketh intercession for us"

(Rom. 8:34). "Whether we live therefore, or die, we are the Lord's" (Rom. 14:8).

C. Our glory.

1. "Christ in you, the hope of glory" (Col. 1:27).

2. ". . . we beheld his glory . . ." (John 1:14).

3. ". . . all have sinned, and come short of the glory of God" (Rom. 3:23).

4. ". . . like as Christ was raised up from the dead by the glory of the father, even so we also should walk in newness of life" (Rom. 6:4).

5. "And that he might make known the riches of his glory on the vessels of mercy, which he had afore prepared unto glory" (Rom. 9:23).

6. ". . . whatsoever ye do, do all to the glory of God" (1 Cor. 10:31).

7. " . . . my tribulations for you, which is your glory" (Eph. 3:13).

8. ". . . every tongue should confess that Jesus Christ is Lord, to the glory of God the father" (Phil. 2:11).

III. *No Fellowship*, if we resist His "bringing many sons unto glory" (Heb. 2:10).

The great apostle prayed that the Ephesians would be strengthened to understand "with all the saints" the love of Christ and in so doing be filled with the fullness of God (Eph. 3:18). The Bible is the record of God in Christ saving man by creating a new fellowship of persons who will serve under the Lordship of Christ. It is in this fellowship of believers that the message of reconciliation takes meaning and is passed to successive generations.

A. Fellowship in the preaching of the Gospel. Witness—"For we preach not ourselves, but Christ Jesus the Lord; and ourselves your servants for Jesus' sake" (2 Cor. 4:5).

B. Fellowship—in the matter of "giving and receiving" (Phil. 4:15).

C. Fellowship in the sharing of the Lord's Supper (Acts 2:42). Paul's emphasis as he writes the Corinthians is upon the oneness of Christ's body that is proclaimed in the Lord's Supper. The Supper is to proclaim the body of Christ, not the broken body. Breaking bread suggests that many partake of one loaf not that one loaf is broken into many pieces. It is fellowship in Christ, not credentials for partaking, that is Paul's concern.

Conclusion. Salvation is a gift of God. By man it is not earned, merited, or deserved. It is a relationship with Christ offering man redemption from bondage, forgiveness for guilt, reconciliation for estrangement, and a renewal for the marred image of God. This glorious salvation and the fruit it bears in our lives will demand our interest for the next seven Sundays. Do you know the fruits of the Spirit?

TITLE: "The Bible Speaks to Our Condition"

SCRIPTURE READING: 1 Timothy 1.

Introduction. A careful study of God's Word with a heart open to receive God's instructions can guide us toward the abundant life.

Paul's epistle to Timothy is addressed to one who was very dear to him. He considered Timothy to be his own son in the faith and in the ministry. He greets him and wishes for him three great blessings from God the Father and from the Lord Jesus Christ—grace, mercy, and peace. There could be no greater blessings from God than these. These blessings are offered to each of us through faith in and faithfulness to the Lord Jesus Christ.

I. *A Warning Concerning False Teachings* (1:3-11). The Apostle Paul charges Timothy to correct and bring back some of those who had been diverted from the way of truth into falsehood by false teachings. He emphasizes the importance of being correct in our beliefs. He warns us against becoming involved in needless inquiries and unprofitable controversies. Even the law of God can be studied with unworthy motives, and it can be interpreted in such a way as to confuse and to mislead.

Each of us needs to accept responsibility for the correctness of our beliefs, for our actions are the results of what we deeply believe.

II. *Gratitude for the Faith of Christ* (1:12). While we should be grateful for the faith that we have in Christ, Paul was rejoicing because of the faith which Christ had put in him.

How many of us are aware of the faith which Christ has in us? He has entrusted into our care and custody and use the precious Gospel. He has given to us the story of His love as expressed in His death, resurrection and living presence. He depends upon us to share this Good News with a needy world. He has put great confidence in us. We should not disappoint Him.

III. *An Example of the Scope of God's Grace* (1:13-17). Paul considers himself an example of the extent to which God's grace goes in its effort to rescue a sinner from the waste and ruin of sin. He had been a blasphemer and a persecutor and had given his consent to the death of Stephen. Even a sinner of this extent is still an object of God's love. God deals with sinners on the basis of His own wonderful grace.

The example of Saul's being saved should encourage us to believe that any sinner in our community can be touched and redeemed by the grace of our great and good God. Paul is an illustration of the extent of that grace. While we have not sinned as Paul did, each of us is also an illustration of the extent of God's grace.

IV. *The Weapons of Our Spiritual Warfare* (1:18-20). Paul's son in the faith, Timothy, faced some difficulties as he sought to be a true servant of the Lord Jesus. The Apostle Paul urges upon him that he live by the principle of faith, and, at the same time, that he guard the purity of his own conscience. He gives illustrations of men who have forsaken the way of faith, and who did not listen to the voice of their own conscience. They had brought about the destruction of their own testimony and their usefulness to the Lord.

Conclusion. If Timothy needed to be encouraged to walk by faith and to live by the dictates of a pure, clean conscience, it follows that each of us should approach life with all of its perplexities and its uncertainties with faith in God for divine leadership and for a determination to never violate our conscience as it is illuminated by the indwelling Spirit.

SUNDAY MORNING, JULY 14

TITLE: "The Sin of Pride"

TEXT: "When pride cometh, then cometh shame: but with the lowly is wisdom" (Prov. 11:2).

SCRIPTURE READING: Daniel 5: 17-22.

HYMNS: "Though Your Sins Be As Scarlet," Crosby. "I Lay My Sins On Jesus," Bonar. "I Am Resolved," Hartsough.

OFFERTORY PRAYER:

Our God and Father, giver of all perfect gifts and supplier of our every need, grant us the wisdom to be humble. When we would bring our offerings, let us recognize Thy offer. When we would bless Thy name, help us to receive Thy benediction. For the manifold riches provided in Christ Jesus, we thank Thee. For an opportunity to share in proclaiming His name, we are grateful. For it is in His name we pray. Amen.

Introduction. Pride is the first sin of which we have any knowledge. Through pride the angels fell. So it was with our first parents, for in the garden the tempter whispered, "Ye shall be as gods" (Gen. 3:5). The danger of this sin and its destructive results are echoed through the Biblical writers.

"The fear of the LORD is to hate evil: *pride,* and arrogancy . . ." (Prov. 8:13).

"Therefore *pride* compasseth them about as a chain; violence covereth them as a garment" (Ps. 73:6).

". . . out of the heart of men, proceed evil thoughts . . . an evil eye, blasphemy, *pride,* foolishness: All these evil things come from within, and defile the man" (Mark 7:21-23).

"For all that is in the world, the lust of the flesh, and the lust of the eyes, and the *pride* of life, is not of the Father, but is of the world" (1 John 2:16).

It is our task to search into the subtlety of damaging sins, to expose the manner in which they beset us, and to make ineffective their attack on character's bastion. The essence of sin is selfishness. Pride is the inordinate assertion of self.

Our text is the natural development of pride in our lives. How conscious we are that (1) "When pride cometh," (2) "then cometh shame," (3) "but with the lowly is wisdom." In the example of Belshazzar we can identify our struggle with pride.

I. *When Pride Cometh.*

A. The Latins saw pride as "aiming at that above."

1. This is not mere desire to improve; it is the drive to rule or ruin.

2. One may excel without excessive pride. There is the learned man who is wise, recognizes his wisdom, and is extremely humbled by it.

There is the morally clean young woman who refuses bad company and in deep gratitude thanks God for His cleansing.

3. We have to remember that when the charge of "pride" is made, both the accuser and the accused are judged.

4. The Scriptures demand: ". . . God resisteth the proud, but giveth grace unto the humble" (James 4:6). "Wherefore come out from among them, and be ye separate" (2 Cor. 6:17).

B. Pride holds in itself the element of falsehood.

1. The claim for merit not possessed.

2. The hate for those who estimate us at true worth.

3. Our false estimate of ourselves is the mark of pride. "[Love] suffereth long, and is kind; [love] envieth not; [love] vaunteth not itself, is not puffed up" (1 Cor. 13:4).

II. *Then Cometh Shame.* There are many kinds of pride: that within which desperately drives its victims to take every advantage; that without which manifests itself in appearance and possessions.

A. Speech betrays pride.

1. Discussion topic centered on self.

2. One who labors to convince others of his superiority when transparent vanity makes of him a laughingstock.

3. Boastfulness leads to exaggeration and on to falsehood.

Many find it hard to speak the truth about self.

Everything that happens to me is wonderful because of who I am.

While we blow, others say, "You can't believe a word he says."

B. Sources of shameful pride.

1. In the gifts of nature. "Be not wise in thine own eyes . . ." (Prov. 3:7).

"And he [the Lord] said to me, My grace is sufficient for thee: for my strength is made perfect in weakness" (2 Cor. 12:9).

"Favor is deceitful, and beauty is vain . . ." (Prov. 31:30).

2. In the gifts of fortune. "Bless the LORD, O my soul: and forget not all his benefits" (Ps. 103:2).

". . . thou art waxen fat, thou art grown thick, thou art covered with fatness; then he forsook God which made him . . ." (Deut. 32:15).

". . . beware of covetousness: for a man's life consisteth not in the abundance of the things which he possesseth" (Luke 12:15).

3. In the spiritual gifts. "Do ye

look on things after the outward appearance?" (2 Cor. 10:7).

"But he that glorieth, let him glory in the Lord" (2 Cor. 10:17).

"I tell you, this man [publican] went down to his house justified rather than the other; for every one that exalteth himself shall be abased; and he that humbleth himself shall be exalted" (Luke 18:14).

"For by grace are ye saved through faith; and that not of yourselves . . ." (Eph. 2:8).

III. *With the Lowly Is Wisdom.* Pride, even in the spiritual realm, renders progress impossible. When our lives are full of the sense of personal merit, there is no room for love. Throughout the Biblical account and especially in the life of Jesus, we are reminded that true greatness consists of service.

A. God removed pride from His kings.

1. Saul said at the time of his selection: "Am not I a Benjamite, of the smallest of the tribes . . . my family the least of all the families. . . . wherefore then speakest thou so to me?" (1 Sam. 9:21).

2. The Lord said to Samuel in the selecting of David: "Look not on his countenance, or on the height of his stature; . . . for the LORD seeth not as man seeth; for man looketh on the outward appearance, but the LORD looketh on the heart" (1 Sam. 16:7).

3. Solomon prayed when selected: "O LORD my God, thou hast made thy servant king . . . and I am but a little child: I know not how to go out or come in" (1 Kings 3:7).

B. The role of Savior was one of humility. "He is despised and rejected of men . . . he was despised, and we esteemed him not" (Isa. 53:3).

". . . he hath no form nor comeliness; and when we shall see him, there is no beauty that we should desire him" (Isa. 53:2).

"Take my yoke upon you, and learn of me; for I am meek and lowly in heart . . ." (Matt. 11:29).

"For ye know the grace of our Lord Jesus Christ, that, though he was rich, yet for your sakes he became poor . . ." (2 Cor. 8:9).

Conclusion. The sin of pride has its cure in the encounter with Christ. One cannot kneel with the animals in Bethlehem or sit with the publicans in Jerusalem or dine with the fishermen of Galilee and retain pride. Certainly it is difficult to stand beside a cross and glory in anything within ourselves. God forbid that I should glory save in that cross.

SUNDAY EVENING, JULY 14

TITLE: "Love: Complete Living"

TEXT: "And above all these things put on charity [love], which is the bond of perfectness" (Col. 3:14).

SCRIPTURE READING: 1 John 4:16-21.

Introduction. When one decides to preach on love, where does he start? Just to read the marvelous Scriptures on love would fill the hour. The minds of hundreds of Christian writers have been set aflame in dealing with the immensity of the subject. Their works are so compelling that once committed, the volume is hard to put down. Dr. James Moffatt, in his *Love in the New Testament*, fills three hundred and twenty-two pages of teaching and inspiration. There are works by Edwards, Roberson, Coates, Dodd, Menzies, and dozens of others translating, commenting, and in general probing the depths and eminence of love.

I am restricting myself to the consideration of love as a fruit of salvation or as a trait of Christian character. Much of my interest will be in the life that emerges when under the mastery of love. To the student of Greek, I might say that *agapē* not *philia*, *erōs*, nor *storgē* is my chief interest. It is the attitude that a man comes to have toward others after establishing a living relationship with Christ. Love is a fruit of salvation when it is growing and ever mellowing to accomodate others' needs. Life is full and complete when living the "Christ way" becomes natural, the warp and woof of daily decision making.

I. *Christian Life Is to Walk in Love.*

A. Each Christian life a spring. ". . . Jesus stood and cried, saying, If any man thirst, let him come unto me, and drink. He that believeth on me, as the scripture hath said, out of his belly [inner life] shall flow rivers of living water" (John 7:37, 38). "But whosoever drinketh of the water that I shall give him shall never thirst; but the water that I shall give him shall be in him a well of water springing up into everlasting life" (John 4:14).

B. Love like a coat to put on. "And above all these things put on [be clothed in] charity . . ." (Col. 3:14). Love conditions for the day-to-day disposition in the same way that Paul called for the "whole armor" to meet temptation.

C. Love of Christ identifies our walk. ". . . walk in love, as Christ also hath loved us . . ." (Eph. 5:2). "He that loveth his brother abideth in the light, and there is none occasion of stumbling in him" (1 John 2:10).

II. *Christian Purpose Is to Serve in Love.*

A. All our equipment made effective in love. ". . . tongues of men and of angels . . . become as sounding brass, or a tinkling cymbal" (1 Cor. 13:1). ". . . gift of prophecy, and understand all mysteries, and all knowledge . . . all faith . . . I am nothing" (1 Cor. 13:2). ". . . bestow all my goods to feed the poor . . . give my body to be burned . . . profiteth me nothing" (1 Cor. 13:3).

B. Love not directed only to loveable. ". . . I say unto you, Love your enemies, bless them that curse you, do good to them that hate you . . . That ye may be the children of your Father which is in heaven . . ." (Matt. 5:44, 45).

C. "Let all your things [living] be done with charity [love] (1 Cor. 16:14).

III. *Christian Strength Is Unity in Love.*

A. Love was to be the distinguishing mark of the Christian. "By this shall all men know that ye are my disciples, if ye have love one to another" (John 13:35). It was not subscribing to a doctrinal position, or attending church, or even being baptized that proved them Christian; it was and is a zeal for the welfare of men, a trust in men and a love for men.

1. The cry of business you can not trust.

2. Listen: "He that loveth his brother abideth in the light" (1 John 2:10). It is he, not the cynic, who really sees into men's character.

3. In the long run the man who loves and trusts is right, because love and trust create what they believe.

4. No man can go on betraying a trust which is constantly renewed.

B. Christians are "knit together in love" (Col. 2:2).

1. Solution to race problems.

2. If your love is not expanding, you are not growing as Christian.

C. The span of Christian love. "And the Lord make you to increase and abound in love one toward another, and toward all men,

even as we do toward you . . ." (1 Thess. 3:12).

IV. *Christian Love Is Fruit of the Spirit.*

A. As the disciples found the teaching of Jesus difficult and said, ". . . This is an hard saying; who can hear it?" (John 6:60), we find teaching on Christian love hard.

1. Not human achievement— fruit of the Spirit.

2. Love possible only in Christ.

B. When Christ is born in a life, Christian love begins to flow.

Conclusion. "And these were his gifts: some to be apostles, some prophets, some evangelists, some pastors and teachers, to equip God's people for work in his service, to the building up of the body of Christ. So shall we all at last attain to the unity inherent in our faith and our knowledge of the Son of God—to mature manhood, measured by nothing less than the full stature of Christ. We are no longer to be children, tossed by the waves and whirled about by every fresh gust of teaching, dupes of crafty rogues and their deceitful schemes. No, let us speak the truth in love; so shall we fully grow up into Christ. He is the head, and on him the whole body depends. Bonded and knit together by every constituent joint, the whole frame grows through the due activity of each part, and builds itself up in love" (Eph. 4:11-16, NEB).

TITLE: "The Bible Speaks to Our Condition"

SCRIPTURE READING: 2 Timothy 2.

Introduction. In the chapter for today the Apostle Paul is expressing a fatherly concern for his son in the ministry. The content of this chapter is filled with practical suggestions for one who faces great difficulty in rendering a significant ministry to the people for the Lord. Each of us can read this chapter and make personal applications.

I. *Paul Encourages a Willingness to Suffer* (2:1-14). He encourages Timothy to find strength in the grace that is in Christ Jesus. He points out that achieving success always involves self-discipline and the overcoming of difficulties. He uses a number of illustrations to strengthen his suggestion.

A. The example of a good soldier (2:3, 4).

B. The example of an athlete (2:5).

C. The example of a hard-working farmer (2:6).

D. We are to remember the example of Christ (2:8).

E. Paul reminds him of the sufferings involved in his own personal imprisonment.
Paul endured suffering in order that others might experience salvation. We should be willing to suffer for the same purpose.

II. *Paul Warns Against Foolish Disputes* (2:14-19, 23-26). Paul points out that there are many controversies that are always raging. To participate in these controversies can color one's personality and affect his ministry. He encourages Timothy to avoid a reputation for being a disputer in foolish controversies. In contrast he encourages him to be a diligent student so that he can rightly divide the word of truth and present it to his hearers in a spirit of gentleness and meekness.

III. *Paul Issues a Challenge to Disciplined Living* (2:20-22). Paul points out in specific terms that one must exercise a voluntary discipline if he would become a chosen vessel in the hands of the Lord accepted for every good work. There must be great negatives in the life of the Christian as well as a positive seeking that which is good.

Conclusion. Each of us can profit from Paul's suggestions to Timothy. The Holy Spirit will speak to us if we read this chapter with an open, responsive heart.

TITLE: "The Sin of Greed"

TEXT: "He that is greedy of gain troubleth his own house; but he that hateth gifts shall live" (Prov. 15:27).

SCRIPTURE READING: 1 Timothy 6:6-10.

HYMNS: "Give of Your Best to the Master," Grose. "I Surrender All," Van Deventer. "Take My Life, and Let It Be," Havergal.

OFFERTORY PRAYER:

We tremble in Thy presence, dear Father, for we have not come to master our possessions. The things of the world are too much with us, and too often they influence our thinking. Receive this gift that we bring. It represents a freedom that we find in Thee. Father, we are free only as we commit to Thee our concerns, our possessions. Accept this our offering, and accept all that we are for Thine own usage, and for Thy sake. Amen.

Introduction. In the history of man, the sin of greed has played a conspicuous and evil role. A high percentage of wrongs and heinous crimes are due to the inordinate greed of gain. "So are the ways of every one that is greedy of gain . . ." (Prov. 1:19). Greed is seen as a force corroding the hearts of men, spoiling family happiness, and setting people in conflict. Jesus pointed out the terrible dangers in greed as He related the story of "the soils." "And these are they which are sown among thorns; such as hear the word, and the cares of this world, and the deceitfulness of riches, and the lusts of other things entering in, choke the word, and it becometh unfruitful" (Mark 4:18, 19). Surely much of the value of loving God with the whole heart is that it leaves no place for greed to take root. The combination of our text from Proverbs and from 1 Timothy teaches us (1) the gain in contentment, (2) the trouble in one's own house, and (3) the living beyond bribes.

I. *Gain in Contentment.* Paul encourages young Timothy by writing that "godliness with contentment is great gain." What need to hear this today when men are ever conscious of stock holdings, real estate holdings, and position holdings! When we consider inflation, deflation, rate of growth, what is the market value of contentment? Over against this contentment, Paul lists "the love of money is the root of all evil." After all allowances have been made in translation, and it has been noted that the text reads "love of money" not "money," that correctly it is "a root" not "the root," Paul is possibly saying that every kind of evil at one time or another springs from this root. Certainly the words are referring to the widespread evil which money promotes.

A. Wealth in satisfaction.

1. My father often said, "There are two ways to be wealthy: earn a sufficient amount, or learn to be satisfied with less."

2. Often what we give in life is more significant and adds to happiness more than what we get.

B. Health is related to contentment.

1. Was John pronouncing our doom as paupers when he wrote: ". . . I wish above all things that thou mayest prosper and be in health, even as thy soul prospereth" (3 John 2)?

2. Paul noted that those not spiritually in accord "are weak and sickly among you, and many sleep" (1 Cor. 11:30).

II. *Trouble in One's Own House.*

A. Inhumanity springs from one's desire to possess that belonging to another.

1. Lust of one country for soil of another has often let loose war and pillage on the innocent.

2. In every age the powerful, under the sway of greed, plunder and oppress the weak.

3. In our contemporary society, some pad jobs to cheat employers. Some employers take advantage of local conditions and rob employees.

4. Love of money has begotten the courage of the highjacker, sharpened the ingenuity of the thief, and put a knife in the hand of the murderer. For thirty pieces of silver, Judas sold his Lord.

B. One's inner being is destroyed by greed.

1. Sordid sins that greed daily brings.

a. Merchant to adulterate his goods.

b. Clerk to put his hand in the till.

c. Salesman to lie for a sale.

2. The unpardonable sin of the twentieth century is poverty.

a. Men making haste to be rich; if they succeed, everything is forgiven.

b. Gates of highest society swing open to the man with gold, and he is not asked how he came by it.

c. One responsible for another's death while intoxicated is sent to prison if poor, to high office if wealthy.

C. Offspring of greed is gambling. The desire to get money is at the bottom of gambling. One wants to get without investing time and effort.

III. *Living Beyond Bribes.* "He that despises bribes shall live," said the sage of Israel. Today one wonders how many are ". . . dead while she liveth" (1 Tim. 5:6). We are wrong to assume that money is evil. There is the creative use and the resulting blessedness when one's greed is mastered and money is rightly used. These convictions can arm us against greed.

A. Know there are better things than money.

1. The blessings of good health.

2. A keen intelligence.

3. A sympathetic heart.

4. A clear consience.

B. Know that money is not an end in itself, only a means.

1. What would you do with great wealth?

2. What are you doing with what you have?

C. Know that wealth can not be kept forever.

1. It is a trust. Parable of the talents.

2. "Lay not up for yourselves treasures upon earth, where moth and rust doth corrupt, and where thieves break through and steal" (Matt. 6:19).

Conclusion. In the life of Jesus we see two basic concerns relative to the material: (1) that man be free from the tyranny of things and (2) that he be concerned over the needs of his brother. Our true attitude toward God is reflected in our attitude toward our brothers. We are to "seek . . . first the kingdom of God, and his righteousness; and all these things shall be added . . ." (Matt. 6:33). If we master things, then we will not be mastered by greed. The key, Jesus said, is "Do not be anxious [don't go to pieces] about your life, what you shall eat or what you shall drink, nor about your body, what you shall put on" (Matt. 6:25, RSV). The alternate to worrying over things and falling victim to greed is trust in God. Jesus challenges us never to use our materials to divide persons when we may use them to unite (Luke 16:19-31).

SUNDAY EVENING, JULY 21

TITLE: "Joy: Radiant Living"

TEXT: "These things have I spoken unto you, that my joy might remain in you, and that your joy might be full" (John 15:11).

SCRIPTURE READING: Luke 15: 3-7

Introduction. The common denominator of the Christian Church is joy. This is not surprising to the faithful Bible reader, for in the New Testament we encounter more than one hundred and thirty times the mention of joy or rejoicing. The early church did not characterize itself so much in organizational structure or doctrinal exactness as it did in an atmosphere of joy. It is a tragic commentary on the contemporary church that, in a world which is far less antagonistic toward our faith, we should see less evidence of joy in our fellowship. This fact probably accounts for the growing indifference toward church affiliation. Who wants to heap additional discord on the burden he is already bearing? Until "rejoicing in the Lord" again becomes an essential part of our religious exercises, we are not going to be very attractive to saints or sinners. I can think of a dozen places to go to commiserate and each with greater comfort than a church pew. Interesting how it is that Jesus Christ can be proclaimed in such gloom each week when in God's introduction of Him it was with such joy (Luke 1:58; 2:10).

Today, let us look at joy in the New Testament. Truly this was the tie that bound the early Christians into a distinct life-style. This was the dynamic that gave power to their witness. Joy was the force that made possible the fact that ". . . they were all with one accord in one place" (Acts 2:1). Christian joy is seen to be the means by which man is introduced, reconciled, and given to the service of God.

I. *The Means of Introduction.*

A. The coming of a Savior.

1. Joy in angels' message (Luke 2:10).

2. Joy in wise men (Matt. 2:10).

B. The teachings of Jesus.

1. Rejoice even in persecution (Matt. 5:12).

2. Rejoice when the lost is found (Luke 15:9, 32).

C. The believing in Jesus.

1. The faith and baptism of the Ethiopian eunuch (Acts 8:39).

2. The little man Zacchaeus invited Jesus to his home (Luke 19:6).

II. *The Means of Reconciliation.*

A. The fulfilling of joy in unity. "Fulfil ye my joy, that ye be likeminded, having the same love, being of one accord, of one mind. . . . Let this mind be in you, which was also in Christ Jesus" (Phil. 2:2, 5). "But I rejoiced in the Lord greatly, that now at the last your care of me hath flourished again . . ." (Phil. 4:10).

B. In conditioning for the "kingdom." Paul's concern for the Colossians would cause him to pray for them that "ye might walk worthy of the Lord" and "be fruitful in every good work," and "increasing in the knowledge of God," "strengthened with all might . . . with joyfulness" (Col. 1:10, 11). Paul warns the Romans, "Let not then your good be evil spoken of: for the kingdom of God is not meat and drink; but righteousness, and peace, and joy. . . ." (Rom. 14:16, 17). "Let us therefore follow after the things which make for peace, and things wherewith one may edify another" (Rom 14:19). Paul seems to be pointing out that when joy reigns, men are not offended, and reconciliation can be more easily effected.

C. Jesus describes a generation of those refusing reconciliation as children arguing over games. " 'How can I describe the people of this generation? What are they like? They are like children sitting in the market-place and shouting at each other:

" 'We piped for you and you would not dance.'

" 'We wept and wailed, and you would not mourn.' For John the Baptist came neither eating bread nor drinking wine, and you say 'He is possessed.' The Son of Man came eating and drinking, and you say, 'Look at him! a glutton and a drinker, a friend of tax-gatherers and sinners!' And yet God's wisdom is proved right by all who are her children' " (Luke 7:31-35, NEB).

III. *The Means of Service.*

A. Joy supercedes laws.

1. Stooped woman healed. "And when he [Jesus] had said

these things, all his adversaries were ashamed; and all the people rejoiced . . ." (Luke 13:17).

2. Man with withered hand. ". . . Wherefore it is lawful to do well on the sabbath days" (Matt. 12: 12).

B. Joy accompanies progress.

1. When evil spirits were controlled by disciples (Luke 10:17).

2. Paul comforted by the progress of the Thessalonians. ". . . for all the joy wherewith we joy for your sakes . . ." (1 Thess. 3:9).

3. Even a purpose for Paul to live. ". . . I know that I shall abide and continue with you all for your furtherance and joy of faith" (Phil. 1:25).

4. "No greater joy can I have than this, to hear that my children follow the truth" (3 John 4, RSV).

C. Joy is the mission.

1. ". . . who for the joy that was set before him endured the cross, despising the same, and is set down at the right hand of the throne of God" (Heb. 12:2).

2. "My brethren, count it all joy when ye fall into divers temptations" (James 1:2).

3. ". . . I trust to come unto you, and speak face to face, that our joy may be full" (2 John 12).

4. "But none of these things move me, neither count I my life dear unto myself, so that I might finish my course with joy . . ." (Acts 20:24).

Conclusion. To the Christian, joy is an inner condition that comes through and flavors the atmosphere of his life. It does not come, nor is it cultivated, by favorable winds. This joy is ever on the surface as Paul demands, "Rejoice in the Lord alway . . ." (Phil. 4:4). There is the occasion of joy in tribuation or joy in suffering. Such joy is possible, for it comes with Christ. If one must suffer for his relationship to Christ, he is still sustained by His Spirit.

Jesus comforted His disciples as He approached the cross, "And ye now therefore have sorrow: but I will see you again, and your heart shall rejoice, and your *joy* no man taketh from you" (John 16:22).

"Now unto him that is able to keep you from falling, and to present you faultless before the presence of his glory with exceeding joy, to the only wise God our Saviour, be glory and majesty, dominion and power, both now and ever. Amen" (Jude 24, 25).

WEDNESDAY EVENING, JULY 24

TITLE: "The Bible Speaks to Our Condition."

SCRIPTURE READING: Hebrews 1.

Introduction. In these Wednesday evening Bible studies, we have been seeking to emphasize the fact that the Bible speaks to our condition. The opening verses of the chapter for this day provide us with a dramatic statement of the truth that God has been seeking to communicate His love and purpose to men through the ages.

The writer of the Book of Hebrews is trying to illustrate the fact that God's final and supreme word comes to us in and through Jesus Christ. He addresses himself to Hebrew Christians who are recent converts from Judaism. In Judaism they had thought of the prophets and the angels as the mediums through whom the message of God was communicated to men (Heb. 1:1, 4). He will seek to demonstrate through this book that Christ is superior to the prophets, the angels, the Mosaic law, and the Levitical priesthood. He will encourage these new converts to look to and to listen to Jesus Christ as God's authentic and supreme messenger to the hearts of men.

I. *Christ Is Superior to the Prophets* (1:1-3).

A. Christ is the exact image of God (1:3a). The original glory of God belongs to Him.

B. Christ is the appointed heir of all things (1:2b). Christ is the goal toward which everything moves.

C. Christ is the creative instrument by which God created the worlds (1:2c).

D. Christ is the sustainer of the universe (1:3b).

E. Christ is our redeemer "having himself purged our sins" (1:3c).

F. Christ is our priest, king (1:3d).

II. *Christ Is Superior to the Angels* (1:4-14). In the Old Testament God often communicated with men by means of angelic messengers. The scriptural writer seeks to emphasize the truth that Christ is superior to the angelic messengers in the following manner:

A. The angels are described as the servants of God (1:7) as well as the servants of the heirs of salvation (1:4). The Christ is described and declared to be the very Son of God.

B. The Christ is superior to the angels in that He is the object of angelic worship (1:6).

C. The Christ is superior to the angels in that upon Him has been bestowed kingly sovereignty in the kingdom of God (1:8).

D. The Christ is superior to the angels in that He is the anointed one of God, selected and equipped to be our Redeemer (1:9).

E. The Christ is superior to the angels in the same manner in which the Creator is superior to His creation (1:10).

F. The Christ is superior to the angels in that He is eternal and superior to all created things and beings (1:11-13).

Conclusion. While the angels were mediums of communication, the Christ is the actual communication of God to the hearts and lives of men. Let us listen to the message of the prophets, the priests, and the psalmist. Let us learn from the patriarchs and from all persons with whom God has dealt. Let us bow in worship before the Christ as Redeemer and Savior. Let us make Him the Lord of our very life this day.

212

TITLE: "The Sin of Sensuality"

TEXT: "For to be carnally minded is death; but to be spiritually minded is life and peace" (Rom. 8:6).

SCRIPTURE READING: Romans 1:18-32.

HYMNS: "Whiter Than Snow," Nicholson. "Grace Greater Than Our Sin," Johnston. "Though Your Sins Be As Scarlet," Crosby.

OFFERTORY PRAYER:

In lovingkindness Thou hast come, O Lord, to redeem us from ourselves. We are tempted daily to keep ourselves from Thee and spend ourselves in lesser causes. Our dissipation of life is ever a shame to us. Our waste of things leaves us ever in want. Today we come to invest in Thy kingdom. Use, we pray Thee, this gift and our love that Thy purposes be accomplished. Amen.

Introduction. Sensuality, or licentiousness, is sin against the seventh commandment—"Thou shalt not commit adultery" (Exod. 20:14). It is difficult to speak on this subject—so much so that I would find it embarrassing if I were to read our Scripture lesson in Romans from the Greek, using a less staid translation than that of King James' time. On such subjects, I often feel the less said, the better. Silence is sometimes more eloquent than speech. Certainly the reticence in which this sin is shrouded is the severest of all condemnation. I feel as Paul that sins of this kind are so loathsome that "it is a shame even to speak of those things" (Eph. 5:12).

Of necessity, the Bible is not silent on our subject. From Sinai to Calvary one hears the thunder against unchastity and impurity. Not only in the Word is God's judgment against sensuality heard, but "the wrath of God is revealed from heaven . . ." (Rom. 1:18). "Therefore thou art inexcusable, O man . . ." (Rom. 2:1). The sin of sensuality is a threat to the hightest earthly relationship. In our social order it is essential to guard that relationship, the family, upon which all others are built. The very unity of mankind grows out of the unity of husband and wife. It is our purpose to examine the strata of society and see in each case the damaging sin of sensuality.

I. *The Individual's Problem of Carnality.*

A. The contribution of the Book of Proverbs:

1. Is intended as a handbook for life's journey.

2. Treats no other sin with such amplitude and repetition.

3. Depicts lasciviousness as the way of death.

B. Contemporary conditions.

1. Abundance of facts known to all presses responsibility on pulpit for speaking firmly and fearlessly.

2. If we play ignorant, we give temptation a cruel advantage, for the force of temptation often lies in surprise.

3. Even in our schools, attempts are made to corrupt minds.

4. Young men face assault on their virtue from most unlikely quarters.

5. Young women warned that their ruin may come by the very persons from whom they should receive protection.

6. Danger of kindling by my words the very fire we wish to quench, but there is an instinct in healthy minds which tells them what is said on this subject proceeds from moral earnestness.

C. Our basic problem is in "thoughts."

1. "Whosoever looketh upon a woman to lust after her hath committed adultery already in his heart" (Matt. 5:28).

2. How dangerous when licentious thoughts form a part of the pleasure of existence.

3. The subjects which dig the brain channels flow most easily in the daily current of thoughts.

4. The life of dreams is invaded by the habit.

5. Our defense against the tyranny of foul imagination is preoccupation with healthy subjects.

II. *Unchastity and the Family.*

A. Sacredness of motherhood and childhood pointed out in the divine institution of Marriage.

1. Character may be judged by one's attitude toward God's institutions.

2. One is reminded of Joseph's great respect for chastity, "How then can I do this great wickedness, and sin against God?" (Gen. 39:9).

B. Appetites not given to us merely for indulgence; there is also the purpose of restraint.

1. One becomes a man by mastering impulses.

2. If the rule of chastity seems harsh, remember it guards the most perfect flower of human happiness.

III. *Unrestraint in Society.*

A. The sin of sensuality involves another soul.

1. Foolish argument that carnality is native to man—libertinism.

2. Society is a union of families. Any sin which blights the marriage relation and destroys the family is an enemy of society.

3. The adulterer is an enemy of the state.

B. "Righteousness exalteth a nation: but sin is a reproach to any people" (Prov. 14:34).

C. "Let us walk honestly, as in the day; not in rioting and drunkenness, not in chambering and wantonness, not in strife and envying" (Rom. 13:13).

Conclusion. A message on sensuality is difficult to bring in a society where profligacy reigns. It may seem as trifling as a snowflake in the gutter. We must be reminded that enough snowflakes can beautify the winter world about us. God's Word speaks often and sure, and He does have concern for our conduct. In spite of changes in customs and differing styles, the apostle's words ring true to our better selves, "Know ye not that ye are the temple of God, and that the spirit of God dwelleth in you? If any man defile the temple of God, him shall God destroy . . ." (1 Cor. 3:16, 17).

SUNDAY EVENING, JULY 28

TITLE: "Peace: Superlative Living"

TEXT: "And the peace of God, which passeth all understanding, shall keep your hearts and minds through Christ Jesus" (Phil. 4:7).

SCRIPTURE READING: Psalm 4.

Introduction. When Jesus said, "Peace I leave with you, my peace I give unto you: not as the world giveth, give I unto you . . ." (John 14:27), He was not speaking of the absence of war. As a matter of fact, He had spoken earlier that His disciples would face terrible circumstances because of Him. " 'Brother will betray brother to death, and the father his child; children will turn against their parents and send them to their death. All will hate you for your allegiance to me; but the man who holds out to the end will be saved' " (Matt. 10:21, 22, NEB). In the Bible peace is not used primarily to describe circumstances but to indicate the perfection of relationships. Jesus could leave His disciples in a world antagonistic to them, yet in a relationship to Himself that is "my peace." This right relationship, so described as "peace," may exist between man and man, country and country, country and God, or man and God.

Our chief concern is to study peace, the fruit of the Spirit, and see it as the foundation of superlative living. How do we attain this peace? From what source does it come to us? When does it bring us to know superlative living? "Let him eschew evil, and do good; let him seek peace, and ensue it" (1 Pet. 3:11).

I. *The Attainment of Peace.*

A. As a result of good will.

1. The Hebrews greet with "Peace" [Shalom]. The idea was a wishing or desire for the welfare of the one greeted. To say, "Shalom," was in a sense uttering a prayer on the other's behalf.

2. God, in conveying His promise to Abram, concluded that the height of His blessing would bring him "to thy fathers in peace" (Gen. 15:15).

3. In Abimelech's and Phichol's visit to Isaac, there was recognition that God had blessed Isaac. The relationship between the three was described, ". . . and they departed from him in peace" (Gen. 26:31).

B. As the obtaining of tranquility.

1. When Judah and his brothers were deeply worried at finding money in their grain sacks, Joseph said, "Peace be to you, fear not . . ." (Gen. 43:23).

2. When Jethro taught Moses how to organize his judges, he assured Moses, "If thou shalt do this thing, and God command thee so, then thou shalt be able to endure, and all this people shall also go to their place in peace" (Exod. 18:23).

3. Among the rewards promised by God to a faithful people, there was, "And I will give peace in the land, and ye shall lie down, and none shall make you afraid . . ." (Lev. 26:6).

C. As the blessing of friendship.

1. God offered special friendship to the young man Phinehas for his courage in slaying the arrogant Israelite and the Midianitish woman. God stopped the plague and ordered Moses to give His message, "Behold, I give unto him [Phinehas] my covenant of peace" (Num. 25:12).

2. The unfriendly act of the Ammonite and the Moabite disqualified for ten generations their relationship with the Israelites. God ordered, "Thou shalt not seek their peace . . ." (Deut. 23:6).

3. In spite of the trickery of the Gibeonites, Joshua held by his "peace made with them" which was a league to let them live (Josh. 9:15).

II. *The Source of Peace.*

A. Beyond human intrigue—from God.

1. ". . . which passeth all understanding . . ." (Phil. 4:7).

2. The Danites requesting Micah to seek counsel of God receive the assurance of, ". . . Go in peace . . . the LORD is your way" (Judg. 18:6).

3. Solomon required the death of Joab even while he held the horns of the altar. This brought " . . . upon his throne, shall there be peace for ever from the LORD" (1 Kings 2:33).

B. Beyond human merit—gift of Christ.

1. In introducing the Comforter and as a farewell gesture, Jesus offers, ". . . my peace I give unto you" (John 14:27).

2. "These things I have spoken unto you, that in me ye might have peace . . ." (John 16:33).

3. "Peace be unto you"—in the closed room (John 20:19); with the sending of His disciples (John 20:21); Thomas with them (John 20:26).

C. Beyond reason with belief and trust.

1. "Who will render to every man according to his deeds: . . . glory, honour, and peace, to every man that worketh good . . ." (Rom. 2:6, 10).

2. "Now the God of hope fill you with all joy and peace in believing . . ." (Rom. 15:13).

3. "By faith" Rahab is described as receiving the spies "with peace" (Heb. 11:31).

4. In the breaking down of the "middle wall of partition" Jesus "is our peace, who hath made both one . . ." (Eph. 2:14).

III. *The Consummation of Peace.*

A. In the establishing of brotherhood.

1. "There is neither Jew nor Greek, there is neither bond nor free, there is neither male nor female: for ye are all one in Christ Jesus" (Gal. 3:28).

2. "Even the righteousness of God which is by faith of Jesus Christ unto all and upon all them that believe: for there is no difference" (Rom. 3:22).

3. "Follow peace with all men, and holiness, without which no man shall see the Lord" (Heb. 12:14).

4. ". . . be diligent that ye may be found of him in peace . . ." (2 Pet. 3:14).

B. In reconciliation with God.

1. "For it pleased the Father that in him [Jesus] should all fulness dwell; And, having made peace through the blood of his cross, by him to reconcile all things unto himself" (Col. 1:19, 20).

2. "Therefore being justified by faith, we have peace with God through our Lord Jesus Christ" (Rom. 5:1).

Conclusion. The Christian life at its highest ebb is described as peace. No question need continue in our minds as to our acquiring this peace. God is truly "the God of Peace," and to know Him is to have peace. In the same urgency that we seek the Father's face in prayer, we are to seek His peace. Paul offers the suggestion that in revealing to others our willingness to accept less than our due and in the practice of serenity and thanksgiving, a marvelous thing will happen. The peace of God will mount a guard for patrolling the perimeters of our hearts and minds (Phil. 4:5-7). This is indeed that which passes all human understanding: it is of the Lord.

WEDNESDAY EVENING, JULY 31

TITLE: "The Bible Speaks to Our Condition"

SCRIPTURE READING: Hebrews 8.

Introduction. The chapter for today's prayerful meditation and study comes from the middle of a section of the Book of Hebrews that deals with Christ as the High Priest of the new covenant. Emphasis is placed upon the fact that He is the mediator of a covenant which is superior to the old covenant.

The Book of Hebrews will appear to be deep and difficult to the casual reader who has no knowledge of the Old Testament background that provides the framework for the message which the writer is trying tians. An effort is being put forth to to communicate to Hebrew Christreveal that God's final revelation of Himself and God's complete provisions for His children are to be found in Jesus Christ rather than in the old rituals of worship and the sacrifices of the Levitical priesthood. A knowledge of the Old Testament is essential for a full understanding of this New Testament book.

This particular section of the Book of Hebrews is emphasizing the high priestly ministry of Jesus Christ. A priest was a mediator or a go-between. The priest was a bridge-builder between man and God.

The writer has declared that Christ is a merciful and faithful High Priest (Heb. 2:17, 18). Christ is also a sinless but compassionate High Priest (4:4-16). Christ is our living and eternal High Priest who makes intercession for us (7:22-28).

I. *Christ Is the Mediator of a Better Covenant* (8:1-6). The scriptural writer is comparing the Levitical priesthood and the old tabernacle with the present priesthood of Christ in the new tabernacle which is heaven itself (cf. Heb. 9:11, 12). Instead of ministering in a tabernacle built by the priest according to the instructions of Moses, Christ Jesus has entered into heaven itself which is indeed the Holy of Holies. He goes not with the blood of animal sacrifices, but with His own precious blood as a sacrifice of atonement for the sins of believers. His priestly ministry on our behalf is superior to the priestly ministry known under the old covenant in the old tabernacle.

II. *The Nature of the New Covenant* (8:7-13). The writer speaks of a new covenant which supersedes the old covenant between God and Israel. The new covenant is said to be better than the old covenant because it is established upon better promises. Notice these.

"I will make a new covenant with the house of Israel and with the house of Judah" (8:8).

"I will put my laws into their mind, and write them in their hearts" (8:10b).

"I will be to them a God, and they shall be to me a people" (8:10c).

"I will be merciful to their unrighteousness" (8:12a).

"Their sins and their iniquities will I remember no more" (8:12b).

The giving of this new covenant had been predicted by the prophets (Isa. 59:21; Jer. 31:31-34; Ezek. 36:25, 26).

The people of God had repeatedly broken and violated the old covenant. It had proved to be ineffective. The new covenant will be both new and different in a number of respects.

A. It will be new in quality in that it is based on better promises to God's people.

B. It will be new in scope in that it will unite both the house of Israel and the house of Judah which had been separated for hundreds of years.

C. It will be new in its universality. "For all shall know me, from the least to the greatest."

D. It will be new in its inwardness. "I will put my laws into their mind, and write them in their hearts."

E. It will be new in that it will really effect forgiveness (8:12).

Conclusion. In Jesus Christ God has offered and initiated a new covenant relationship with those who are willing to trust Jesus Christ as Lord and Savior. This new covenant will be inward, personal and spiritual. It provides an inward cleansing through the blood of Jesus Christ that soothes the conscience. It offers a high moral standard to challenge the will of God's children. It offers a divine fellowship with God that can satisfy the deepest hunger of the spirit of man.

SUGGESTED PREACHING PROGRAM FOR THE MONTH OF AUGUST

Sunday Mornings

Continue and conclude the series using the theme, "The Sins Which Damage and Destroy." Be certain to focus attention on the Savior who can deliver us from the sins which damage and destroy.

Sunday Evenings

Continue and conclude the topical sermons using the theme, "The Great Christian Virtues." Make certain that each message praises the God of glory who revealed Himself in Jesus Christ and who works by means of the Holy Spirit to make these virtues real in our lives. Only the Holy Spirit can produce "the fruit of the Spirit."

Wednesday Evenings

Continue with the theme, "The Bible Speaks to Our Condition."

The theme verse for August is "For the word of God is quick, and powerful, and sharper than any two-edged sword, piercing even to the dividing asunder of soul and spirit, and of the joints and marrow, and is a discerner of the thoughts and intents of the heart" (Heb. 4:12).

SUNDAY MORNING, AUGUST 4

TITLE: "The Sin of Envy"

TEXT: "For wrath killeth the foolish man, and envy slayeth the silly one" (Job 5:2).

SCRIPTURE READING: Genesis 4:1-10.

HYMNS: "Ye Must Be Born Again," Sleeper. "Depth of Mercy! Can There Be," Wesley. "God Calling Yet! Shall I Not Hear?" Borthwick.

OFFERTORY PRAYER:

Dear Father, our help in all ages and our strength in all circumstances, help us in this day of rapid change. We are so prone to lose sight of the harbor lights, and our vision ever falls short of Thy possibilities. The token of our love that we bring today is less because our faith is weak. Take this gift, we pray Thee, and break it as the five loaves to meet many needs, in Jesus' name. Amen.

Introduction. Can one be of such sweet disposition as to say anything good about envy? Many of those most skillful with pen have aptly described its blight. To Shakespeare it was "green sickness," to Churton

219

Collins "the sincerest form of flattery," and to Ambrose Bierce "emulation adapted to the meanest capacity." Biblical writers have shown equal distaste for the sin of envy. "A sound heart is the life of the flesh: but *envy* the rottenness of the bones" (Prov. 14:30). "Wrath is cruel, and anger is outrageous; but who is able to stand before *envy?*" (Prov. 27:4). "And even as they did not like to retain God in their knowledge, God gave them over to a reprobate mind, to do those things which are not convenient; being filled with all unrighteousness . . . full of *envy* . . ." (Rom. 1:28, 29). It is apparent that we are dealing with a damaging sin whose impact reaches beyond the realm of social distaste. No wonder that many early writers would call it a "deadly sin." Envy is no less a deadly tool of Satan in our more sophisticated contemporary times.

I. *A Sin That Brings Grief When Others Prosper.*

A. Judas Iscariot's problem was not his poor lot in life—it was that others had a better lot.

B. Selfishness is the poisonous ingredient in envy.

1. We hurt when another rises or rejoice in his fall.

2. Sadly true that many find secret satisfaction in the misfortune of friends.

C. Envy and emulation—both excited by another's good.

1. Envy produces a sense of depression.

2. Emulation gives feeling of admiration.

3. Emulation may desire to excel but not for the sake of putting another down.

4. The difference essentially is that envy is ill-humored while emulation is good-humored.

II. *A Sin That Steals Love From Character.*

A. Crimes authored by envy.

1. Murder of Abel. Cain could not tolerate Abel's acceptable offering when his own was rejected.

2. Early Church's persecutions and martyrdoms.

B. Worst sins of the tongue are products of envy.

1. Disparaging remarks about others.

2. Spirit of gossip: He is a wonderful person *but . . .*
Why should humiliation of another afford us gratification?

C. Fear reigns in our hearts lest another attain honor we can not reach.

1. Sickness comes because others are happy.

2. Envy is its own punishment

3. Listen closely to political speeches and hear how often envy speaks.

4. How often envy destroys relationships: family, race.

III. *A Sin That Attracts the Strong.*

A. Many "isms" today use people's proneness to envy for their propaganda.

1. Honorable institutions, even the Church, can fall under the spell of envy.

2. Removing envy solves most class problems.

B. World leaders have been affected by envy.

1. Alexander the Great permitted no praise for his generals because it detracted from him.

2. Attitude of Nero.

3. Envy often occurs with limited knowledge. If we knew all about the wealthy man or the talented person, we might covet his position less.

IV. *A Sin That Has a Remedy.*

A. Count your blessings.

1. The envious are always comparing their lot with the more fortunate. Try contrasting with the less fortunate.

2. What a different person I was after an extended visit to the Crippled Children's Hospital.

B. Learn to love excellence for its own sake.

1. It is not so important who plays lovely music so long as the right note be sounded.

2. Sign above my desk, "What wonderful things are wrought for God when we work without concern for who gets the credit."
This can keep envy down in your life.

Conclusion. God has put a "For Rent" sign on the universe. It is yours for the appreciation of it. The bird sings as sweetly for the pauper as for the prince. Water quenches the thirst of the vagabond as readily as for the tycoon. If we keep our hearts right, the world is ours. I had never owned a foot of land but found much delight in hiking through the woods. The owner approached me once saying, "It pleases me to see you so enjoy my woodland. How I wish I could enjoy it as you do." I was so glad that he owned the land but also grateful for the capacity to appreciate what God had given to me.
John the Baptist set the stage for all to conquer envy. Upon seeing his followers turn from him to Jesus, he was heard to say, "He must increase, but I must decrease" (John 3:30).

SUNDAY EVENING, AUGUST 4

TITLE: "Patience: Reconciled Living"

TEXT: "Better is the end of a thing than the beginning thereof: and the patient in spirit is better than the proud in spirit" (Eccl. 7:8).

SCRIPTURE READING: Romans 5:3-6.

Introduction. The idea of *patience* in the New Testament is usually in reference to attitude toward people, not things or events. James was very concerned about our patience with each other. He saw the need so greatly that we are to, "Count it all joy when ye fall into divers temptations; knowing this, that the trying of your faith worketh patience. But let patience have her perfect work, that ye may be perfect and entire, wanting nothing" (Jas. 1:2-4). The concept of patience is also found in the description of God's attitude toward man. This ". . . riches of his goodness and forbearance and longsuffering . . ." (Rom. 2:4) which Paul writes of is to be copied by the believer. To Timothy he writes ". . . that in me first Jesus Christ might shew forth all longsuffering, for a pattern to them which should hereafter believe on him to life everlasting" (1 Tim. 1:16).

Reconciled living is reflecting the forgiving, forbearing, patient attitude which God has shown toward us to those with whom we have associations. It is living in a security that rests upon the acceptance of "Vengeance is mine; I will repay, saith the Lord" (Rom. 12:19).

I. *The Discipline of Patience.*

A. It is to control anger.

1. "The discretion of a man deferreth his anger; and it is his glory to pass over a transgression" (Prov. 19:11).

2. Old saying, "Only value of anger is to put the curve in a cat's back."

3. As a requirement for bishops, ". . . but [be] patient, not a brawler . . ." (1 Tim. 3:3).

B. It is a teacher of humility.

1. When the most severe tests come, and the disciples would be most tempted to strike back. Jesus said, ". . . there shall not an hair of your head perish. In your patience possess ye your souls" (Luke 21:18, 19).

2. To insure that "the ministry be not blamed; but in all things approving ourselves as the ministers of God, in much patience, in afflictions, in necessities, in distresses, in stripes, in imprisonments . . ." (2 Cor. 6:3-5).

3. "For ye have need of patience, that, after ye have done the will of God, ye might receive the promise" (Heb. 10:36).

C. It is the meeting place for minds.

1. "Grudge not one against another . . . take, my brethren, the prophets, who have spoken in the name of the Lord, for an example of suffering affliction, and of patience" (Jas. 5:9, 10).

2. Even the church at Ephesus, who had left her first love, had a chance in that she "hast borne, and hast patience . . ." (Rev. 2:3).

II. *The Creativity in Patience.*

A. Forgiveness is possible.

1. Forgiveness that is not creative is license.

2. The God who made a covenant with Moses on Sinai is described as ". . . merciful and gracious, longsuffering, and abundant in goodness and truth" (Exod. 34:6).

3. God's patience pictured as ". . . longsuffering to us-ward, not willing that any should perish, but that all should come to repentance" (2 Pet. 3:9).

B. Wisdom is born.

1. Man is small; he is in a hurry. God is great; He has the ages. He can be patient.

2. Of Bezaleel Moses said that God had prepared him for the tedious work with gold and silver, "he hath filled him with the spirit of God, in wisdom . . ." (Exod. 35: 31).

3. "With the ancient is wisdom; and in length of days understanding" (Job 12:12).

4. "He that is slow to wrath is of great understanding: but he that is hasty of spirit exalteth folly" (Prov. 14:29).

C. True leadership emerges.

1. "A wrathful man stirreth up strife: but he that is slow to anger appeaseth strife" (Prov. 15:18).

2. "He that is slow to anger is better than the mighty; and he that ruleth his spirit than he that taketh a city" (Prov. 16:32).

3. Elihu's words, "I said, Days should speak, and multitude of years should teach wisdom" (Job 32:7).

II. *Our God-Likeness in Patience.*

A. Expression "sons of God" implies likeness is desired.

1. ". . . let us run with patience the race that is set before us, looking unto Jesus the author . . ." (Heb. 12:1).

2. "Ye have heard of the patience of Job, and have seen the end of the Lord; that the Lord is very pitiful, and of tender mercy" (James 5:11).

B. ". . . the longsuffering of our Lord is salvation . . ." (2 Pet. 3:15).

1. Persistence in soul-winning needed.

2. Love until love works patience.

C. Reconciled to God in Christ.

1. "And you, that were sometime alienated and enemies in your mind by wicked works, yet now hath he reconciled" (Col. 1:21).

2. Even the two natures within us are brought together in Christ, ". . . that he might reconcile both unto God in one body by the cross, having slain the enmity thereby . . ." (Eph. 2:16).

3. "All things are of God, who hath reconciled us to himself by Jesus Christ, and hath given to us the ministry of reconciliation; to wit, that God was in Christ, reconciling the world unto himself" (2 Cor. 5:18, 19).

4. "Now then we are ambassadors for Christ, as though God did beseech you by us: we pray you in Christ's stead, be ye reconciled to God" (2 Cor. 5:20).

Conclusion. Living described as patient—or as I have chosen to call it "reconciled"—does not imply a negative reaction to happenings. It is not a grim wait until everything works out satisfactorily. It is positive. It is a trust that keeps hope alive as one labors under a difficult situation. It is faith in people, in what they can become when rightly related to God. Of all the fruits of salvation, patience is the greatest virtue. In it one shares so closely with the God we have known, the God who keeps loving man in spite of his sin, who ever probes the con-

science of man even as hearts are hardened, who with outstretched arms beckons when man continues to reject.

Waiting with God, waiting with an expecting faith, waiting when others give up, waiting in joy, knowing that dawn comes and that the darkest hour precedes its light—that is patience; that is a reconciled life.

WEDNESDAY EVENING, AUGUST 7

TITLE: "The Bible Speaks to Our Condition"

SCRIPTURE READING: James 2.

Introduction. The theme of the Book of James is the practice of pure religion. Chapter 2 deals with the practice of pure religion in our relationship to our fellowman.

I. *The Practice of Pure Religion Does Not Express Itself in Snobbery* (2:1-13).

A. The command against snobbery (2:1).

B. An illustration of the snobbery that is forbidden (2:2, 3).

C. The application and warning against snobbery (2:4-13).

1. Snobbery shows a divided allegiance to the Lord (2:4a).

2. Snobbery reveals evil motives in the heart (2:4b).

3. Snobbery dishonors the poor (2:5-7).

4. Snobbery violates the royal law of love (2:8-13).

II. *The Practice of Pure Religion Issues in Loving Obedience* (2:14-

26).

The world about us issues the command, "Show me your faith." Even our Father God says to us, "Show Me your faith."

All scriptural writers are in agreement that salvation is by God's grace through faith rather than by human achievement. All Biblical writers are in agreement that good works are the fruit of a genuine salvation experience.

This chapter, which emphasizes the place of works in the life of the believer, is not conflicting with other passages of Scripture. It is contrasting a genuine faith with a spurious faith. It is declaring that the faith which is genuine is a living experience that produces gracious, loving works in the life of the believer.

A. A genuine faith is more than a mere *profession* of faith (2:14-17).

The faith which has nothing but words to prove its existence is a dead faith. The faith which is genuine will have works as well as words to prove its existence.

B. A genuine faith is more than an acceptance of a creed (2:18-20). James points out that even the demons give mental assent to the existence of God. One must do more than believe about God to have a genuine faith in God (Heb. 11:6).

C. Illustrations of genuine faith and pure religion (2:21-26).

1. The sacrifice of Abraham (2:21-24).

2. The great risk of Rahab as she exposed herself to the possibility of execution in order to provide service for the spies (2:25, 26).

Conclusion. Let each of us examine the faith that we claim. Is it genuine? Is it real? Does it express itself by a genuine practice of the royal law of love toward the poor and the unfortunate as well as the rich and the privileged?

Is our faith an inward experience that produces obedience to God and loving service to others? If it is, let us rejoice. If it isn't, then we need to seek Jesus Christ as our own Lord and Savior that ours might be a genuine experience with God.

SUNDAY MORNING, AUGUST 11

TITLE: "The Sin of Appetite"

TEXT: ". . . there are many whose way of life makes them enemies of the cross of Christ. They are heading for destruction, appetite is their god, and they glory in their shame. Their minds are set on earthly things" (Phil. 3:18, 19, NEB).

SCRIPTURE READING: Proverbs 13:18-25.

HYMNS: "God of Grace and God of Glory," Fosdick. "A Charge to Keep I Have," Wesley. "Rise Up, O Men of God," Merrill.

OFFERTORY PRAYER:

Dear Lord and Father of mankind, forgive our foolish ways. We set our hearts on things that perish and waste our strength in grieving at their loss. In poor judgment and excessive appetites we prostitute Thy precious gifts.

Forgive us for what we are. As we invest ourselves in Thy will, we recognize what we may become in Thee. Dear heavenly Father, accept our humble gifts and ourselves. Transform us in Thy power to make us useable, through Jesus Christ our Lord. Amen.

Introduction. Because of appetite's necessary role in the economy of life, we are reluctant to think of its function as sin. Of course, it is not its use but its abuse wherein sin lies. It is usually recognized that man experiences appetite in three distinct ways: hunger, thirst, and sex. Since the matter of sexual appetite was considered in the message on sensuality, today we will give attention to hunger and thirst.

Biblical writers were alert to the sin of appetite and frequently pointed to it as the basis of other evils. Job, in castigating the hypocrites and their "tabernacles of bribery," writes, "They conceive mischief, and bring forth vanity, and their belly [appetite] prepareth deceit" (Job 15:35). Proverbs, in similar fashion, when pointing out the way of transgressors, testifies, "The righteous eateth to the satisfying of his soul: but the belly [appetite] of the wicked shall want" (Prov. 13:25). The New Testament is equally sharp in its scorn of the gluttonous. In his counseling words to young Titus, Paul acknowledges his familiarity with the uncouth citizens of Crete. He quotes a Cretan prophet as saying, "The Cretans are always liars, evil beasts, slow bellies [uncontrolled appetites]" (Titus 1:12). This proclivity toward food and drink caused Paul to press Titus to "rebuke them sharply" (Titus 1:13). Paul also makes a connection between "them which cause divisions" and those having predilection to excesses. "For they that are such serve not our Lord Jesus Christ but their own belly . . ." (Rom 16:18). He warns the Philippians, "Mark them which walk so . . . they are enemies of the cross of Christ; whose end is destruction, whose God is their belly, and whose glory is in their shame, who mind earthly things" (Phil. 3:17-19). The extreme interest shown appetite today would convince us that little heed is given to Biblical exhortation; therefore, words on the sin of appetite are most needful and appropriate.

I. *Consider Eating and Drinking.*

A. Time and energy of much of the population used to provide food.

1. Hunger called the mainspring of the human machine.

2. Fortunate that means of supplying appetite of thirst less costly.

B. God's favor on us in that the satisfying of appetite is accompanied with pleasure.

1. To what extent pleasure is to prompt the filling of appetite must be measured with all results considered.

2. Labor is often the means of more appreciation for sustenance.

II. *The Sin of Gluttony.*

A. Special message to fat clergymen. The libidinous attitude toward plate and cup often brings ineffectiveness and even death to many of the cloth.

B. Sickening experience of seeing savage eat. Supply of food is attained after long intervals. When opportunity comes, they stuff themselves to the point of discomfort.

C. Ancient Rome held her carnivals of gluttony.

D. Even today children—and often adults—need assistance in gauging proper food intake.

III. *The Sin of Drunkenness.*

A. Many who can control the appetite of hunger fail with appetite of thirst.

B. In our world there is expansion in the use of intoxicants.

1. Every act of drunkenness is sin.

2. Surrender of rational thinking to drink.

3. Drunkenness promotes other sins: immorality, anger, loss of self-control.

4. Not surprising that Paul advises against keeping company with a drunkard (1 Cor. 5:11).

5. When listing those who are eliminated from the "kingdom of God," drunkards follow thieves and covetous on the list (1 Cor. 6:10).

C. Drunkard's home is a proverb for misery.

Conclusion. How often we see the image of God (that is, the glory of manhood) dragged through the muck of sin because of appetite's abuse. What shame when the pleasures of controlled eating and drinking are dashed with the insatiability of drunkenness and gluttony. How beautiful the words of Paul reminding us, ". . . the earth is the Lord's. and the fulness thereof . . . whether therefore ye eat, or drink, or whatsoever ye do, do all to the glory of God" (1 Cor. 10:26, 31).

SUNDAY EVENING, AUGUST 11

TITLE: "Kindness: Sensitive Living"

TEXT: "Put on therefore, as the elect of God, holy and beloved, bowels of mercies, kindness, humbleness of mind, meekness, longsuffering" (Col. 3:12).

SCRIPTURE READING: Ephesians 4:25-32.

Introduction. An anonymous writer has pointed out, "The ministry of kindness is a ministry which may be achieved by all men, rich and poor, learned and illiterate. Brilliance of mind and capacity for deep thinking have rendered great service to humanity, but by themselves they are impotent to dry a tear or mend a broken heart." Kindness made its most noticeable impact in the coming of Christ and in the lives of His early followers. One often feels that today's greatest loss is that the Christian Church has devoted more time in creating and preserving dogma than in practicing kindness.

Kindness is of God. In our message we will trace the evidence of God's kindness throughout the Biblical record and relate it to what the Christian life is to be. As we discover the kindness of God in action, drawing men to Himself in sacrificial love, we understand the challenge to us for sensitive living. Blessed are we when we get a grasp of Paul's depth of experience with his Lord. "Let love be without dissimulation. Abhor that which is evil; cleave to that which is good. Be kindly affectioned one to another with brotherly love . . ." (Rom. 12: 9, 10).

Sensitive living for the Christian is practicing ". . . whatsoever ye would that men should do to you, do ye even so to them . . ." (Matt. 7:12). and then going a step further. It also means acting toward others in the same spirit that God has acted toward us.

I. *Kindness of God in the Old Testament.*

A. Deserving of our thanks.

1. He answered prayer of the fearful: ". . . for he hath shewed me his marvellous kindness in a strong city" (Ps. 31:21).

2. The redeemed of the Lord should say so, ". . . for he is good: for his mercy [kindness] endureth for ever" (Ps. 107:1).

3. In prison Jeremiah is addressed by the Lord, "Call unto me, and I will answer thee, and shew thee great and mighty things . . ." (Jer. 33:3). "Praise the LORD of hosts: for the LORD is good: for his mercy [kindness] endureth for ever . . ." (Jer. 33:11).

B. Has effect on our relationships.

1. In fellowship with each other. Jonathan and David: "And thou shalt not only while yet I live shew me the kindness of the LORD, that I die not" (1 Sam. 20:14). Naomi to daughters-in-law: "Go, return each to her mother's house: the LORD deal kindly with you, as ye have dealt with the dead, and with me" (Ruth 1:8). David to men of Jabesh-gilead: "And now the LORD shew kindness and truth unto you: and I also will requite you this kindness, because ye have done this thing" (2 Sam. 2:6).

2. In association with God. Zion and the Lord: "For a small moment have I forsaken thee; but with great mercies will I gather thee. In a little wrath I hid my face from thee for a moment; but with everlasting kindness will I have mercy on thee . . ." (Isa. 54:7, 8). Zion to avert destruction: "And rend your heart, and not your garments, and turn unto the LORD your God; for

he is gracious and merciful, slow to anger, and of great kindness . . ." (Joel 2:13).

C. To be seen around us.

1. In the material world. "Truth shall spring out of the earth . . . the LORD shall give that which is good; and our land shall yield her increase" (Ps. 85:11, 12).

2. In God's hand in victory. "They shall abundantly utter the memory of thy great goodness, and shall sing of thy righteousness. The LORD is gracious, and full of compassion; slow to anger, and of great mercy" (Ps. 145:7, 8).

3. In God's concern for the poor and to those of faith. "But I am poor and needy; yet the Lord thinketh upon me: thou art my help and my deliverer . . ." (Ps. 40:17). "O taste and see that the LORD is good: blessed is the man that trusteth in him" (Ps. 34:8).

II. *Kindness of God in the New Testament.*

A. It is directed toward all. "That in the ages to come he might shew the exceeding riches of his grace in his kindness toward us through Christ Jesus" (Eph. 2:7). "But love ye your enemies, and do good, and lend, hoping for nothing again; and your reward shall be great, and ye shall be the children of the Highest: for he is kind unto the unthankful and to the evil" (Luke 6:35).

B. It is for man's salvation. "Or despisest thou the riches of his goodness and forbearance and long-suffering; not knowing that the goodness of God leadeth thee to repentance?" (Rom. 2:4). "But after that the kindness and love of God our Saviour toward man appeared, not by works of righteousness which we have done, but according to his mercy he saved us, by the washing of regeneration, and renewing of the Holy Ghost" (Titus 3:4, 5).

III. *Kindness of God in Christian Experience.*

A. It is a "fruit of the Spirit," an essential part of mature Christian living.

1. Peter points out that by means of "precious promises" we might be partakers of the divine nature.

By giving all diligence, he directs that we add to faith "virtue; and to virtue knowledge; and to knowledge temperance; and to temperance patience; and to patience godliness; and to godliness brotherly kindness . . ." (2 Pet. 1:5-7).

2. Paul held kindness as among the things which "approve" as the minister of God. He lists the order as "pureness, by knowledge, by longsuffering, by kindness, by the Holy Ghost, by love unfeigned" (2 Cor. 6:6).

B. It is a pattern for growth.

1. In prayer, give attention to others. "And forgive us our debts, as we forgive our debtors" (Matt. 6:12).

"For if ye forgive men their trespasses, your heavenly Father will also forgive you" (Matt. 6:14).

2. Bitterness, wrath, anger, clamor, and evil speaking are to be put away. These are replaced by: "be ye kind one to another, tenderhearted, forgiving one another . . ." (Eph. 4:31, 32).

3. In Paul's exhortation of love as the height of Christian graces, he describes such love when he writes, "love suffereth long, and is kind . . ." (1 Cor. 13:4).

Conclusion. Matthew records in his eleventh chapter a series of colorful accounts of our Lord's activities. There is in the one chapter the commanding of the twelve, preaching in the cities, the encounter with John's disciples, the evaluation of John's ministry, a denunciation of the present generation, an upbraiding of the cities, a tender prayer to the Father, and a touching invitation to all who labor and are heavy laden. In this invitation we catch a hurried view of the secret of sensitive living. Jesus is saying, "Take my yoke upon you, and learn of me; for I am meek and lowly in heart: and ye shall find rest unto your souls. For my yoke is easy [kind] . . ." (Matt. 11:29, 30). The marvelous message is that when Christ enters the heart of man and conditions that heart to a sensitive response to His will, He also monitors the load to be pulled, the yoke to be worn. "My yoke is properly fitted," said Jesus. We can come to Him in perfect trust. If, in His love, our hearts are rendered sensitive, in His kindness our yokes are lovingly fitted.

TITLE: "The Bible Speaks to Our Condition"

SCRIPTURE READING: 1 Peter 4.

Introduction. The Apostle Peter writes out of personal experience to assist Jewish believers who had been scattered abroad as they faced the possibility and the agonizing problem of undeserved suffering because of their faith.

I. *The Example of the Sufferings of Christ* (1 Pet. 4:1, 2, 12-15, 19). In order to encourage those who were experiencing the agony of undeserved suffering, Peter points out how that Christ suffered in the flesh that He might be our Redeemer and Savior.

He tries to give them some assistance in order that they might avoid suffering the due results of illegal or immoral activities. He points out that there is a difference between suffering for righteousness' sake and suffering for evil (1 Pet. 3:13-17).

II. *Guidelines for Living on the Edge of Eternity* (1 Pet. 4:7a). Peter could have been referring to the end of the age which will be consumated by the Second Coming of Jesus Christ. He could have been thinking about the possibility of their annihilation as a group by persecution and martyrdom. He provides some guidelines for proper conduct for believers as they live on the very edge of eternity.

A. He encourages them to determine to be at their very best, "Be ye therefore sober" (4:7b).

B. He encourages them to maintain constant communication with God (4:7c).

C. The practice of genuine love toward each other is always important (4:8).

D. Love will render practical assistance to those in need (4:9). There were no AAA motels in those days. It was absolutely essential that Christians provide hospitality to each other as they traveled or as they fled from persecution.

E. Each one is to make responsible use of the spiritual gifts that have been bestowed upon him (4:10, 11).

1. The ministry of words (4: 11a).

2. The ministry of works (4: 11b).

Conclusion. This chapter comes to a conclusion with a challenge to the effect that the followers of Christ face the future with faith and with a determination to do God's will in all circumstances and at all times.

Do we have the kind of a relationship with Jesus Christ that would stabilize and sustain us in the midst of terrible, undeserved suffering? Surely it would not be selfish for us to pray for deliverance from such, but we need to examine the nature of our faith to make sure that it is genuine, because suffering could be our lot in the future.

The practice of the guidelines that Peter suggested would be helpful toward building the kind of a faith that would be needed in case the individual Christian found himself in the midst of sufferings which he did not merit.

TITLE: "The Sin of Anger"

TEXT: "Be not hasty in thy spirit to be angry: for anger resteth in the bosom of fools" (Eccl. 7:9).

SCRIPTURE READING: Matthew 5:21-24.

HYMNS: "O Brother Man," Whittier. "I Am Praying for You," Cluff. "I Heard the Voice of Jesus Say," Bonar.

OFFERTORY PRAYER:

My dear Father, forgive me when I speak hasty words to my brothers. I consider so little when others seem wrong and judge so quickly when I don't understand. The gift I bring today does not equal the wrong of which I am conscious. I do not have enough to pay my debt of injustices toward others. Receive this offering, I pray, as token of my love and acknowledgment of Thy goodness. Make it a blessing to others, and strengthen me in giving, I pray, in Jesus' name. Amen.

Introduction. It seems strange that at a time when we are afraid of being emotional we have turned out to be overly so. Emotionalism is rampant, and most of it is self-disruptive. A generation afraid of emotion ends up subscribing to the thing it fears. We have tried to suppress emotions that are an essential part of us and find only that our attempts at elimination end in complexes. We can not set our emotions aside; we can only direct them to higher purposes.

We consider anger for our message today. It is basically an instinct of self-protection. To describe it one would say: a sudden heating of the blood, the flushing of the face, with speech forcible and action swift and sure. Anger is not unlike some sort of military equipment which nature has provided to repel wrong. Paul's direction to "be ye angry and sin not" (Eph. 4:26) implies that there is an anger that is not sin. Perhaps our capacity to love the good determines our capacity to hate the evil. Of this we can be sure: it is our virtue, not our pride, that is to be lashed into a rage. There is a difference. One is connected with higher ends, thus constructive; the other is concerned with a wounded self, thus destructive. We face this message with the full awareness that there is both righteous and unrighteous anger. The excellence of character depends on a sensitivity of honor latent beneath the outward aspect of civility. We know that to be completely blind to insult and injury is evidence of an inferior being. Jesus was observed as He "looked round about on them with anger, being grieved for the hardness of their hearts . . ." (Mark 3:5).

I. *Anger Has a Direction in Flow.*

A. It may be directed against permissible objects.

1. Injustice and cruel foolishness.

2. Woman slain on the street before men who were not moved.

3. Easy toleration of evil is more truthfully called treason or dishonor.

4. Pride and selfishness turn to anger when not appeased.

231

B. Sin in anger seen when directed:

1. Toward trivial differences.

2. Toward personal inconveniences.

3. Toward others asserting their rights.

4. Toward over-consideration of our own merits.

II. *Anger Has a Depth of Flow.*

A. The expression may be out of proportion with the cause.

1. Husband's outbreak of anger over burned toast.

2. Cain's slaying of brother when his offering was not accepted.

3. Action of Joseph's brothers when he received new cloak.

B. Excessive anger destroys.

1. Cause of ulcer problem.

2. Poisoning by ill will.

3. Often anger is permitted to become hatred.

III. *Anger Has a Channel of Flow.*

A. Cause of profane language is anger in the wrong channel.

1. Disgust in hearing a maddened brain vent anger with profanity.

2. Could Simon Peter have cursed and denied his Lord apart from anger and fear?

B. Violent acts induced by anger.

1. "He that hateth his brother is in darkness . . . because that darkness hath blinded his eyes" (1 John 2:11).

2. Inflicting a blow in frenzy.

3. Danger is surrendering to a passion.

IV. *Anger Has a Tempo in Flow.*

A. Temper is the chronic disposition to anger.

1. The closing days of King Saul.

2. Who can justify acrimony?

3. Even David with his asperity listened to the calm reasoning of Abigail.

B. Temper springs more quickly in familiar territory.

1. Anger the sin of the home.

2. Anger in the Church. Much of the temper habit begins within the circle that favorably reacts to it. One's temper may rise, but the expression of it is usually by habit. The paroxysm is a much-practiced expression of temper.

Conclusion. Expression of anger is a triumph of the lower nature over the better life. It is righteous if on account of what is done to others and not a grudge on account of what happens to one's self. We have to be very careful, for the mind plays tricks on itself; it has been known to clothe its personal resentments in garments of righteous and religious indignation so they will pass inspection with our religious self. Many a fight for principle is only a fighting for personal pique and pride.

TITLE: "Faithfulness: Immutable Living"

TEXT: "Moreover it is required in stewards, that a man be found faithful" (1 Cor. 4:2).

SCRIPTURE READING: Luke 12: 42-48.

Introduction. The difference between the Christian man and the irreligious man is not that one has faith while the other has none, but rather it is that their faiths rest in different things. For the irreligious, seeing is believing. He has seen man's weakness and trades upon it; he has seen the efficacy of material force and relies on it; he has seen the power of finances and makes use of it. There is another who believes in goodness of others and works for it; he trusts in the efficacy of sacrifice and suffers for it; he hopes for the vindication of righteousness and waits for it. With him, all life is guided by a confidence in things hoped for, and each act is a testing of things not seen. Thus, the basic difference between men is not to be sought in their theological opinions but in the object of their practical trust.

When Paul came to write of faith as he listed the fruits of the Spirit, he was writing of ethical virtues. His interest was not so much in our relationship to God as it was our affiliation with our fellow man. As indicated by the RSV, Paul's concern is faithfulness; it is the trait of character that may be described as reliability or loyalty. Paul is describing the Christian in whom there is no swerving in his fidelity to Christ. This quality of reliability and trustworthiness is unchanging, invariable, and thus worthy of the name of "immutable living." Our message traces the Biblical account of faithfulness in God, our Savior, the Word itself, and the Christian life.

I. *A Faithful God.*

A. Viewpoint of the Old Testament writers.

1. "Know then that the LORD your God is God, the faithful God; with those who love him and keep his commandments he keeps covenant and faith for a thousand generations" (Deut. 7:9, NEB).

2. The psalmist observes, "All thy commandments are faithful . . ." (Ps. 119:86), and "Thy testimonies that thou hast commanded are righteous and very faithful" (Ps. 119:138).

3. Isaiah, in outlining the mission of Jehovah's servant, asserts, ". . . Kings shall see and arise, princes also shall worship, because of the LORD that is faithful . . ." (Isa. 49:7).

B. Testimonies from the New Covenant.

1. When observing the withered fig tree, Jesus directs His disciples, ". . . Have faith in God" (Mark 11: 22).

2. Paul affirms, "Faithful is he that calleth you, who also will do it" (1 Thess. 5:24). In his second epistle to the same Christians, he writes, ". . . the Lord is faithful, who shall stablish you, and keep you from evil" (2 Thess. 3:3).

3. In a most practical way Paul points out that ". . . God is faithful,

who will not suffer you to be tempted above that ye are able . . ." (1 Cor. 10:13).

4. John declares that "God is light . . ." "If we confess our sins, he is faithful and just to forgive us our sins, and to cleanse us from all unrighteousness" (1 John 1:9).

II. *Jesus Is a Faithful Savior.*

A. An example to be followed.

1. One cannot believe that he has faith in Jesus if he continues to have respect of persons (Jas. 2:1). Jesus is the example of humility in that He showed no unfair partiality.

2. ". . . Christ also suffered for us, leaving us an example, that ye should follow his steps" (1 Pet. 2:21).

B. A witness for pointing to God.

1. When compared with Moses, Jesus was as a son, Moses as a servant. "Christ Jesus; who was faithful to him that appointed him . . ." (Heb. 3:1, 2).

2. "But I have greater witness than that of John: for the works which the Father hath given me to finish, the same works that I do, bear witness of me, that the Father hath sent me" (John 5:36).

3. John introduces his Revelation as from "Jesus Christ, who is the faithful witness" (Rev. 1:5).

III. *The Scriptures Are the Faithful Word.* Biblical writers affirm that the truth which they reveal is completely trustworthy. Paul labored at one point to show that a particular idea was his and not equal with those received of the Lord. "That which I speak, I speak it not after the Lord . . ." (2 Cor. 11:17). The special occasions where there is notice of the "faithful word" are worthy of our attention.

A. To be a good bishop one must, among the other qualities, be one "holding fast the faithful word . . ." (Titus 1:9).

B. To Timothy Paul punctuates the fact that "Jesus came into the world to save sinners"; by saying, "This is a faithful saying and worthy of all acceptation . . ." (1 Tim. 1:15).

C. John closes his Revelation with caution for those who may "add unto these things" or "shall take away from the words" (Rev. 22:18,19).

IV. *The Christian Life Is a Life of Faithfulness.*

A. Loyalty to Christ.

1. An identity in His death and life. "I am crucified with Christ: nevertheless I live; yet not I, but Christ liveth in me: and the life which I now live in the flesh I live by the faith of the Son of God, who loved me, and gave himself for me" (Gal. 2:20).

2. It is recorded that Stephen, "full of faith and power," did many miracles. At his death Luke records, "And they stoned Stephen, calling upon God, and saying, Lord Jesus, receive my spirit" (Acts 7:59).

3. The responsibility of the

ministry must be placed in loyal hands. "And the things that thou hast heard of me among many witnesses, the same commit thou to faithful men, who shall be able to teach others also" (2 Tim. 2:2).

B. Faith, the foundation of life.

1. Paul asserts that he is not ashamed of the Gospel of Christ, "For therein is the righteousness of God revealed from faith to faith . . . The just shall live by faith" (Rom. 1:17).

2. Jesus asked the question to fearful disciples, "Why are ye so fearful? how is it that ye have no faith?" (Mark 4:40).

3. Just before speaking a parable "unto certain which trusted in themselves" Jesus asked a question, " . . . when the son of man cometh, shall he find faith on the earth?" (Luke 18:8).

Conclusion. In a world that changes daily, among a people whose chief fad is change, "Let us hold fast the profession of our faith without wavering; (for he is faithful that promised)" (Heb. 10:23).

Christian faith has learned to trust in the love of God. That love often makes stern demands; what it bids will seem impossible; it may seem outrageous; we see no evidence of forces working toward the goal to which it points. If we really trust God, He will strengthen us to live by confidence in what we hope for and in the perpetual testing of forces we can not see. In faithfulness we can come to know the sustaining strength of ". . . so great a cloud of witnesses . . ." that compass us.

WEDNESDAY EVENING, AUGUST 21

TITLE: "The Bible Speaks to Our Condition"

SCRIPTURE READING: 1 John 3.

Introduction. John writes his epistle with many purposes in mind. He reveals these in a number of different places. One of his primary motives is to provide assurance of salvation to those who have put their faith and trust in Jesus Christ as Lord and Savior (1 John 5:13).

The chapter through which we would let God speak to our hearts today is one of the great chapters of the New Testament. It speaks concerning the fact, the nature, the obligations, and the basis for our assurance of divine sonship.

I. *The Unbelievable Privilege of Divine Sonship* (3:1, 2). John, the apostle of love, stands in amazement before the wonder of the privilege of being a child of God through faith in Christ Jesus. He also recognizes that his present experience of this wonderful truth is only partial. He looks forward to the final revelation of Jesus Christ at the end of the ages for the full revelation of what God has provided for those who love Him.

II. *The Nature of Our Divine Sonship* (3:3-10).

A. Our sonship is spiritual rather than natural (3:9). We become the children of God by a new creation in the spiritual birth. We are the creatures of God by physical birth and the children of God by spiritual birth. We become the sons of God through faith in Christ Jesus (Gal. 3:26).

B. The new birth results in righteousness (3:3-9). John was dealing with a serious error that threatened the very existence of early Christianity. According to gnostic beliefs, one entered into a relationship with God through knowledge rather than through faith and commitment. Christianity insisted that God was a moral God who required moral conduct on the part of the children of God. John warns the followers of Christ against the erroneous beliefs of the gnostics who taught that man's conduct did not in any manner affect his relationship with God or his service to God.

C. The new birth produces obedience (3:22-24a). To really know God through faith in Jesus Christ is to experience a divine change within the heart that causes the child of God to want to give himself to God in loving obedience at all times.

III. *The Obligations of Divine Sonship* (3:11-24). There are certain obligations that go along with the privilege of being the children of God. Toward God these obligations are faith and obedience. Toward our brothers our obligation could be listed as follows:

A. To love (3:11-16). This love is a persistent unbreakable spirit of goodwill toward the objects of our love.

B. A spirit of generosity toward the need of others (3:17-19). The love which does not find expression in practical deeds of kindness is no genuine love.

IV. *The Basis of Our Assurance of Divine Sonship.* In this chapter there are at least three bases for our assurance of divine sonship.

A. The testimony of scripture (3:1, 2).

B. Our love for the brethren (3:14). This is a subjective measurement by which we can examine our own heart. If we find love for the people of God in our heart, then this is an additional basis for our believing that we are indeed the children of God.

C. The witness of the indwelling spirit (3:24b).

Conclusion. We should rejoice in the glad consciousness of being the children of God. We should respond with full commitment to the development of and the expression of the new life that has come to us through faith in Christ Jesus.

As we live a life of faith and faithfulness, love and generosity, others will become convinced that we are indeed the children of our heavenly Father.

TITLE: "The Sin of Laziness"

TEXT: "The way of the slothful man is as an hedge of thorns: but the way of the righteous is made plain" (Prov. 15:19).

SCRIPTURE READING: Hebrews 6:7-12.

HYMNS: "O Master Workman of the Race," Stocking. "To the Work," Crosby. "Ready," Palmer.

OFFERTORY PRAYER:

Dear Father, we see the work of Thy hands in all the world about us. How we rejoice and praise Thee that we may be a part of Thy creation. Now, dear Lord, continue in us Thy creation. Remake our hearts, cleanse our hands, and mold our minds. In our giving today, we give ourselves. Use us, we pray Thee, for Thy purposes, and keep us to Thyself, through Jesus Christ. Amen.

Introduction. I have never been of the persuasion that as a hard-and-fast rule "history repeats itself." In a most striking manner, however, we often see repetitions. Today we see in many of our contemporaries a repetition of the spirit prevalent during the close of the eighteenth and beginning of the nineteenth century. This spirit was manifested in an outbreak of literature throughout Europe which was filled with disgust with the world, life, and everything in it. Perhaps if Goethe and Lord Byron had known honest labor they could have worked out some of their hypochondria instead of reflecting it through their writing.

The whole file of "hippies," "yippies," and "protestors" might march right out of existence if honest labor were required for livelihood. Indeed, the sin of laziness is a damaging sin and deserves our attention.

I. *Man's Character Is Conditioned in Work.*

A. Work is not a curse placed on Adam. "And the LORD God took the man, and put him into the garden of Eden to dress it and keep it" (Gen. 2:15). This was before Adam's disobedience and prior to the curse pronounced in Genesis 3:17.

B. Work is a commandment of God. "Six days shalt thou labour, and do all thy work" (Exod. 20:9). This commandment was given along with "Remember the Sabbath day, to keep it holy." The will of God for man is that he should work. Work and worship complement each other. He who never works is never fitted for worship. If one never pauses to worship, he is not capable of work. God's commandment is clear in declaring that man fulfills his right relationship to God only as he becomes a worker and a worshiper.

C. Jesus points to God's nature as a worker.

1. After healing on the Sabbath, Jesus said, "My father worketh hitherto, and I work" (John 5:17).

2. Upon being questioned about a blind man, Jesus said, ". . . I must work the works of him that sent me, while it is day . . . " (John 9:4).

3. Jesus identified Himself by

working. ". . . the works that I do in my Father's name, they bear witness of me" (John 10:25).

4. Jesus was worthy of trust because of work. "If I do not the works of my Father, believe me not" (John 10:37).

II. *The Church's Purpose Realized in Serving.*

A. Sloth, the Church's greatest enemy.

1. Ministers beset by dilatoriness and remissness.

2. In laggardness, a spiritual numbness steals over people.

B. Faith gets "ingrown" concern, limited to anxiety about its own welfare, and it becomes dreary and morbid.

C. Neglect of worship in lethargy.

1. Spirit of gratitude dies.

2. Challenge of outreach disappears.

D. Spirit of missions is attitude of work.

III. *Human Destiny Is Related to Serving.*

A. Parable of talents: "I was afraid, and went and hid my talent . . . Thou wicked and slothful servant . . . take therefore the talent from him . . . For unto every one that hath shall be given, and he shall have abundance; but from him that hath not [not work] shall be taken away even that which he hath" (Matt. 25:25-29).

B. God's promises realized in serving. "That ye be not slothful, but followers of them who through faith and patience inherit the promises" (Heb. 6:12). "If any man will do his will, he shall know of the doctrine . . ." (John 7:17).

C. Entering the kingdom is service.

1. "Verily I say unto you, Inasmuch as ye did it not to one of the least of these . . . and these shall go away into everlasting punishment" (Matt. 25:45, 46).

2. "Who then is a faithful and wise servant . . . whom his Lord when he cometh shall find so doing" (Matt. 24:45, 46).

3. Parable of the laborers. "For the kingdom of heaven is like unto a man that is an householder, which went out early in the morning to hire labourers . . ." (Matt. 20:1).

Conclusion. The thought that an ideal world is one without labor is not Biblical. Labor is a necessary part of our world and a necessary condition for happiness. There is a period in youth when there comes recoil from the conventional and contempt for patterns. When this tendency is coupled with the energy lost in growing, indolence comes easily. Sometimes it takes less effort to criticize; so the world has never been short on young critics. One recognizes that young eyes see with greater clearness and many times can discern the noble and the base. Great good can come from noble discontent. But merely to criticize and do nothing (not work) wrecks character. It sours the temper and produces a spirit of discontent toward both man and God.

TITLE: "Meekness: Self-Controlled Living"

TEXT: "But sanctify the Lord God in your hearts: and be ready always to give an answer to every man that asketh you a reason of the hope that is in you with meekness and fear" (1 Pet. 3:15).

SCRIPTURE READING: Ephesians 4:1-7.

Introduction. In dealing with an age-worn problem, that of evildoers prospering in a world where the righteous suffer, the psalmist concludes, "But the meek shall inherit the earth; and shall delight themselves in the abundance of peace" (Ps. 37:11). His argument is that judgment is often hasty, that one discovers the justice of the moral order when taking a longer view. Violence has never, and can never, inherit the earth. History bears testimony that it is meekness which prevails.

I have described this meekness as self-controlled living. I do not equate meekness with humility nor is there an element of weakness in it. The Bible points to one, "The man Moses was very meek, above all the men which were upon the face of the earth" (Num. 12:3). This quality being described in Moses certainly was not weakness nor mere humility. His character trait described as meekness was his faith in God's purpose for His people and trust in his fellow men that they would turn to God. A meek man sees himself as God's tool to be used in causes beyond himself, and he sees his contemporaries as possible instruments of God. He will not fret at personal inconveniences or rejections. In an attitude of self-effacement he directs his energies toward the higher goal, the will of God. Controlling self is the greatest task of kingdom service; it demands of us meekness. Let us consider the message of the Hebrews as they speak of the meek before God. Let us review meekness in the life of Christians and listen to the words of Jesus on meekness.

I. *Standing of the Meek Before God.*

A. Seven times the psalmist points to the meek:

1. 22:26: they shall eat and be satisfied; they shall praise the Lord; their heart shall live forever.

2. 25:9: God will guide in judgment; He will teach them His way.

3. 37:11: they shall inherit the earth; they shall delight themselves in peace.

4. 45:4: in majesty ride prosperously.

5. 76:9: God arose to judgment to save them.

6. 147:6: the Lord lifted them up; He cast the wicked down.

7. 149:4: God will beautify them with salvation.

B. Meekness, a basis of special relationship.

1. By seeking the Lord, "it may be ye [the meek] shall be hid in the day of the LORD's anger" (Zeph. 2:3).

2. God will not turn away punishment for those who "turn aside the way of the meek" (Amos 2:7).

3. Among the glories for Jerusalem, "The meek also shall increase their joy in the LORD . . ." (Isa. 29:19).

C. Special message for the meek.

1. "The Spirit of the Lord GOD is upon me; because the LORD hath anointed me to preach good tidings unto the meek . . ." (Isa. 61:1).

2. The rod out of the stem of Jesse. The Spirit of the Lord shall be upon him. "With righteousness shall he judge the poor, and reprove with equity for the meek of the earth . . ." (Isa. 11:4).

II. *Meekness in the Christian Life.* Dr. William Barclay has beautiful insight into meekness in the Christian life as he shows the association of other words used with meekness in the New Testament. (William Barclay, *Flesh and Spirit,* Abingdon Press, Nashville [1962], pp. 115-118.) He divides the words as those "keeping company" and those "contrasting."

A. The companion words of meekness.

1. Meekness and *love.* To face the problem in the church, Paul proposed to go to them. He poses the question ". . . shall I come unto you with a rod, or in love, and in the spirit of meekness?" (1 Cor. 4:21).

2. Meekness and *gentleness.* As an encouragement to godliness, Paul

encourages, "To speak evil of no man, to be no brawlers, but gentle, shewing all meekness unto all men" (Titus 3:2).

3. Meekness and *lowliness.* To be marks of the Christian vocation. ". . . walk worthy of the vocation wherewith ye are called, with all lowliness and meekness . . ." (Eph. 4:1, 2).

B. Words contrasted with meekness.

1. Previously noted: chastening rod or meekness (1 Cor. 4:21).

2. Previously noted: brawling or meekness (Titus 3:2).

C. Meekness as essential for Christian life.

1. Spirit in which one learns. "Wherefore lay apart all filthiness and superfluity of naughtiness, and receive with meekness the engrafted word, which is able to save your souls" (Jas. 1:21).

2. Spirit in which discipline is exercised. "Brethren, if a man be overtaken in a fault, ye which are spiritual, restore such an one in the spirit of meekness . . ." (Gal. 6:1).

3. Spirit in which opposition is to be met. "In meekness instructing those that oppose themselves; if God peradventure will give them repentance to the acknowledging of the truth" (2 Tim. 2:25).

4. Spirit of Christian witness. "But sanctify the Lord God in your hearts: and be ready always to give an answer to every man that asketh you a reason of the hope that is in

you, with meekness and fear" (1 Pet. 3:15).

5. Spirit to prevail in whole life. "But let it be the hidden man of the heart, in that which is not corruptible, even the ornament of a meek and quiet spirit, which is in the sight of God of great price" (1 Pet. 3:4).

III. *Jesus and Meekness.*

A. Pronouncement of teaching. "Blessed are the meek: for they shall inherit the earth" (Matt. 5:5). "Thy King cometh unto thee, meek . . ." (Matt. 21:5).

B. Explanation of Himself. When inviting others to take His yoke and learn of Him: ". . . for I am meek and lowly in heart . . ." (Matt. 11:29).

C. Paul's description of Christ. "Now I Paul myself beseech you by the meekness and gentleness of Christ . . ." (2 Cor. 10:1).

Conclusion. The more attention we give to the fruits of the Spirit, the more conscious we become that their attainment comes with the help of God. That is strikingly true in the matter of self-control. We can control self only when God's control is effective. Changing circumstances and personalities are too much for us. We can be meek only as the passions of our lives are subject to our Master's Spirit. We can know the Christian virtues only by committing ourselves to Christ.

WEDNESDAY EVENING, AUGUST 28

TITLE: "The Bible Speaks to Our Condition"

SCRIPTURE READING: Revelation 2.

Introduction. To read this chapter is to experience the cutting edge of the living Word of God. "For the word of God is alive and active. It cuts more keenly than any two-edged sword, piercing as far as the place where life and spirit, joints and marrow, divide. It sifts the purposes and thoughts of the heart" (Heb. 4:12, NEB).
Revelation, chapter 2, contains four of the letters which the living Lord dictated to be sent to churches in Asia Minor. Through these last written communications from our Lord to individual churches, we can learn much today.

In each of these individual epistles which were to be circulated among all of the churches, our Lord first of all identifies Himself. He does so by using one of the descriptive phrases applied to Him in Revelation 1.

I. *The Christ: I Know Thy Works* (2:1, 9, 13, 19). The Christ with whom we have to do is the Christ who has complete knowledge concerning both our visible actions and our invisible attitudes. He knows all about us. From His piercing, penetrating eye nothing is concealed. This thought can be shocking, but also can be comforting. This thought can be challenging and stimulating.

II. *The Christ Offers Commendation.* In each of these four verses, our living Lord speaks words of commendation to each of the churches. He saw that which was good about them and calls attention to it. He was complimentary of that which deserved His commendation. It can be comforting to know that our Lord will always look for that which is best in us first. He is more eager to commend than to rebuke.

III. *The Living Christ Offers Some Complaints.* Our Lord offers complaints against each of these four churches with the exception of Smyrna. He offers no complaint against them. But concerning Ephesus, he charges them with having lost their first love (2:4). The church at Pergamos was tolerant toward false doctrine, inappropriate worship activities and immorality (2:14, 15). Thyatira was also tolerant toward false teachings and immorality (2:20, 21).

In severe terms, our living and loving Lord speaks words of complaint to these churches upon whom He is depending to publish the good news of God's love and to demonstrate a new quality of life in these areas where there were so many that needed salvation.

IV. *The Living Christ Offers Counsel to His Churches.* To the church at Ephesus, he urged upon them that they remember and repent (2:5).

The church at Smyrna was encouraged to be faithful to the point of death (2:10).

The church at Pergamos was urged to repent (2:16).

The church at Thyatira had been given an opportunity to repent, and it seems as if judgment was already on its way (2:21-23).

Those who have been faithful are encouraged to "hold fast till I come" (2:25).

Conclusion. Without exception each of these letters to the churches of Asia Minor closes with the refrain, "He that hath an ear, let him hear what the Spirit saith unto the churches" (1:7, 11, 17, 29; 3:6, 13, 22).

It would appear from these words that our Lord would have us to read His book with hearing ears. It would appear that He is insistent that we listen for the voice of the Spirit that dwells within. It would appear that we must look upon prayer as a dialogue rather than a monologue and let God speak to our condition day by day and week by week.

God promised Joshua that if he would listen and heed and obey, then he would walk the highway to success and prosperity. It follows that if we would give proper attention to the instructions of our Lord and daily do His good will, then His blessings will be upon us and in turn we will be a blessing to others. Let us let God's Word serve as a surgical knife to cut out of our minds and hearts and lives those attitudes and ambitions that are displeasing to our Lord. Let us listen to His counsels in order that we might hear His words of commendation.

SUGGESTED PREACHING PROGRAM FOR THE MONTH OF SEPTEMBER

Sunday Mornings

The five suggested messages are based on some of the great parables which fell from the lips of our Savior. A good theme would be, "Our Lord Continues to Speak Through Parables." These messages will speak words of warning as well words of inspiration to God's people.

Sunday Evenings

The suggested theme for the evening messages is, "The God With Whom We Have to Do." The messages are doctrinal in nature and practical in objective.

Wednesday Evenings

If the program of reading a chapter a day has been followed, the New Testament will be completed during the month of September. Continuing with the theme, "The Bible Speaks to Our Condition," certain great chapters from the New Testament are selected for use for the Wednesday evening services.

The theme verse for the month is, "Thou wilt shew me the path of life: in thy presence is fulness of joy; at thy right hand there are pleasures for ever more" (Ps. 16: 11).

SUNDAY MORNING, SEPTEMBER 1

TITLE: "The Vitality of the Kingdom"

TEXT: "If any man have ears to hear, let him hear" (Mark 4: 23).

SCRIPTURE READING: Matthew 13:1-8, 18-23; Mark 4:26-29.

HYMNS: "Praise Him, Praise Him," Crosby. "I'll Go Where You Want Me to Go," Brown. "Bringing in the Sheaves," Shaw.

OFFERTORY PRAYER:

Holy Father, today we would thank Thee for all of those whom Thou didst use in bringing to us the knowledge of Jesus Christ, the Savior. Today we would offer ourselves as communicators of the old, old story that others might come to experience Thy love and Thy mercy. Accept and bless these tithes and offerings in such a manner as to tell the old, old story of Jesus and Thy love. Amen.

Introduction. "Jesus came into Galilee, preaching the gospel of the kingdom of God, And saying, The time is fulfilled, and the kingdom of God is at hand: repent ye, and believe the gospel" (Mark 1:14, 15). In the parallel passage in Matthew "kingdom of heaven" is used for "kingdom of God." The terms seem to be synonymous. Perhaps heaven was used for God by some because of the Jewish reverential fear lest by the very pronounciation of the name of God one might profane it. Even today we hear men pray, "May heaven grant. . . ." What they really mean is, "May God who is in heaven grant. . . ."

The word "kingdom" as used by Jesus is not to denote a national, political, or geographical entity. It is better translated "rule" or "reign."

In reality, all that Jesus teaches is helpful in understanding the kingdom of God; that is, the reign of God and especially the principles and methods by which He deals with men. In a special way He used stories to illustrate truth. The word translated "parable" means "to throw alongside." These stories thrown alongside spiritual truth are called parables. Many of the more than fifty parables of Jesus begin: "So is the kingdom of God (or heaven)," which means that the story which He will tell will illustrate one or more of the principles by which God deals with men.

In Matthew 13, Mark 4, and Luke 8 are recorded the first great group of parables which Jesus spoke to the multitudes from a boat in the Sea of Galilee. How many parables Jesus spoke on that day we cannot know. (See Mark 4:33.) We are grateful for those which the evangelists have recorded, and we shall use them in this series of messages. Eight of these parables fall into four sets of twin parables. The first set consists of "The Parable of the Sower" (Matt. 13:3-8, 18-23; Mark 4:3-9, 13-20; Luke 8:5-8, 11-18), and "The Parable of the Seed Growing of Itself" (Mark 4:26-29). These parables emphasize "The Vitality of the Kingdom."

I. *The Parable of the Sower.* A sower sows his seed. He is scattering it by hand. Whether the seed will germinate and grow depends upon the kind of ground upon which it falls. The sower is primarily Jesus; but also, anyone who preaches the Word. "The seed is the word of God" (Luke 8:11). The people who hear the Gospel are as varied as are the soils of Palestine.

A. Some seeds fell by the wayside (Matt. 13:4, 19). These seeds fell on the road or the path. The birds ate some of them. The wind blew others away. The seeds had no chance to take root. This kind of soil represents the Gospel-hardened man. He has failed to respond for so long that he has lost the power to respond. An arm which is bound to one's body for weeks will become so weak that it can't be used. The muscles will have atrophied. There is also an atrophy of soul to the one who repeatedly fails to respond to the Gospel. Unless God sends some tragedy to plow a furrow of mercy down his hard heart there is little hope for this man to respond to the Gospel. Sometimes God does exactly that.

A young Christian mother had just given birth to her first child. The attending physician thought that all was well with both mother and child. Then there was a sudden, unexpected reversal of her condition. She died within a couple of days. It seemed a case of unrelieved tragedy. What could the preacher say at the funeral service to justify the ways of God to men in such tragedy? A few weeks after that the father of the deceased mother came to the pastor's office. He said, "I have been a hardhearted, stubborn sinner. God took my daughter to wake me up. I want you to know that I have become a Christian, but it took my daughter's death to do it." Who can rightly read God's providences? It may well be when the Christian husband, the Christian wife, and the Christian father meet in heaven, never more to part, that all will join in giving praise to God who can bring good out of evil. There is profit in tragedy that causes one to meet life earnestly.

B. Some seed fell on the stony places (Matt. 13:5, 6, 20, 21). The picture is that of a very thin layer of soil over a rocky ledge. The seed germinated quickly because it was near the surface, but having no root quickly withered in the hot sun. This soil represents the shallow person who upon sudden impulse decides to be a Christian; but he has not counted the cost. It has not been a life-long commitment. He has no intention of loyalty to Jesus Christ through persecution. Quickly come, quickly go! Jesus bids those who would be His disciples to count the cost and be willing to pay it. (See Luke 9:57-62 and Matt. 10:32-42.)

C. Some seed fell among thorns (Matt. 13:7, 22). This seems to be ground which was already latent with thorn seeds. As the good seed grew, the thorns grew also, and choked out the good seed. This represents the man of divided loyalties. "The cares of this world," and "the deceitfulness of riches" must be weeded out if the Gospel seed is to bear fruit. This man would like to put Christ first, but he is not willing to do so. Jesus said, "No man can serve two masters: for either he will hate the one, and love the other; or else he will hold to the one, and despise the other. Ye cannot serve God and mammon" (Matt. 6:24). One who makes earthly treasures the end of life is foolish. Jesus, Himself, says so: "So is he that layeth up treasure for himself, and is not rich toward God" (Luke 12:21).

D. Some seed fell on good ground (Matt. 13:8, 23). The good seed fell into the good ground which had been prepared for it. It germinated, grew, and brought forth good fruit. This is the purpose both of seed and of soil. God has made us in His own image. He has made us spiritual beings with the capacity for fellowship with Him. He has done everything necessary to breach the barrier caused by our sins. He convicts of sin and invites to salvation. When one accepts the grace of God offered in Jesus Christ and is saved, it is as good seed sown in good ground.

Every saved person is not equally fruitful, but a saved soul "beareth fruit, and bringeth forth, some an hundredfold, some sixty, some thirty" (Matt. 13:23).

II. *The Parable of the Seed Growing of Itself* (Mark 4:26-29).

A. The wonderful correspondence of seed and soil illustrates that the Gospel and sinful man are made for each other. The eye is made for seeing; God has also made the light by which one sees. The ear is made for hearing; the sound waves are adapted for one's hearing. The seed and the soil are made for each other. The Gospel is adapted for the needs of sinful man.

B. There is tremendous vitality in the seed. It germinates and pushes itself through the soil with mysterious force. The seed grows, "he knoweth not how" (Mark 4:27). God's saving power is very mysterious.

C. The plant grows in orderly fashion "first the blade, then the ear, after that the full corn in the ear" (Mark 4:28). Paul said, "I have planted, Apollos watered; but God gave the increase" (1 Cor. 3:6).

When the Gospel is planted faithfully God will give the harvest.

Conclusion. No earthly story can completely illustrate spiritual truth. The soils of life do not in every way parallel the soils of nature. There is little hope that the rocky soil can become good soil. The soils of Palestine do not have free will. They are not responsive to the Spirit of God. However, the hearts of men who are represented by these soils can change. Rocky soil of the heart can become good soil. A hardened heart can be convicted. A life choked with care can repen. The shallow, impulsive follower can consider and come to a deeper loyalty. In fact, that is what these parables are about. Hearing is urgent, important business. We are responsible for how we hear and heed the Gospel. "If any man have ears to hear, let him hear" (Mark 4:23). "Take heed therefore how ye hear: for whosoever hath, to him shall be given; and whosoever hath not, from him shall be taken even that which he seemeth to have" (Luke 8:18).

SUNDAY EVENING, SEPTEMBER 1

TITLE: "In the Beginning God"

TEXT: "In the beginning God created the heaven and the earth" (Gen. 1:1).

SCRIPTURE READING: Genesis 1:1-2:3.

Introduction. The Bible begins with the words, "In the beginning God" (Gen. 1:1). The gospel written by the Apostle John begins with these words, "In the beginning was the Word, and the Word was with God, and the Word was God. The same was in the beginning with God" (John 1:1, 2). Someone has said: "The Bible begins and ends with God." The Bible does not seek to define God, nor does it present an array of arguments to prove that there is a God. It simply announces that there is a God. The words "in the beginning" in Genesis 1:1 are out of regular Hebrew order. The words stand first in the sentence when normally they would come at the end. This arrangement in the sentence emphasizes the absolute fact of creation, that nothing existed before God.

Men's concepts of God vary. Some think of Him as only a concept of the mind. Some think of Him only in anthropomorphic terms. Some think of Him as a long-whiskered, white-headed, doting grandfather. Some think of Him as a remote diety who is too far away to be interested in human affairs. Some think of Him as a celestial computor who has all the facts. Some think of Him as a tranquilizer who is to be used in an hour of tension, turmoil, anxiety, or death. Some think of Him as an opiate, a narcotic. Apart from the Biblical revelation men are sure to get a distorted concept of God.

Let us consider what the Bible has to teach concerning God.

I. *God Is a Person.*

A. God is a real person. He is not a mere idea or concept but a reality. He exists. He is self-existent. He lives. He is a person who possesses all the qualities attributed to personality—intelligence, self-determination and moral consciousness.

B. God is a spiritual person. Jesus said: "God is a Spirit; and they that worship him must worship him in spirit and in truth" (John 4:24). What is the meaning of this verse? It evidently means that the essence of His being is spirit rather than matter. God does not have a body; He is not material. He is not limited as is matter. The Bible does speak of God as having hands, feet, arms, mouth, eyes, and wings. These are anthropomorphic adaptions to enable us to understand God. To make our understanding of God still clearer, we have the incarnation of God in Jesus (John 1:14; 14:9). He is a spiritual person.

C. God is a triune person. The word "trinity" is not found in the Bible. Tertullian of the second century used it to express the truth taught about God as a triune person. The trinity of God was revealed to man by God. God has revealed Himself to man as God, the Father; God, the Son; God, the Holy Spirit. All three manifestations of God are found at the baptism of Jesus.

II. *God Is Absolute.*

A. God is self-existent. When we speak of God as absolute we mean that He is not dependent on anything outside of Himself. He is not dependent on the world; the world is dependent on God. God can exist without the world but the world cannot exist without God. He has the source of His being in Himself. He is not dependent on the world for life and being.

B. God is one. There is one absolute, self-existent being and that one is God. God in His being is undivided and indivisible. This truth is taught in both the Old Testament and the New Testament. It is a fundamental truth of God's Word.

The fact that God reveals Himself as Father, Son and Holy Spirit must not be construed to teach tritheism, or the doctrine of three gods. The fact that God is one, or monotheism, excludes polytheism and idolatry. There is only one true God. In the New Testament the one true God is revealed to men by Jesus Christ.

C. God is omnipresent. God is not limited by space and time. He is present everywhere in space and time. God is accessible to all at all times and in all places (Ps. 139:7-12).

D. God is omniscient. By omniscience we mean that God is all-knowing, has all knowledge. Since God is omnipresent, He knows everything simultaneously. God even knows beforehand.

E. God is omnipotent. He is all-powerful. God has power to do anything that is not inconsistent with His nature, character, and purpose (Gen. 17:1; 18:14). The only limitations on God's power are self-imposed (Gen. 18:25).

III. *God Is Moral.* Moral consciousness is an essential element in personality and God is a moral person. Consider four moral attributes of God.

A. God is holy. The word "holy" means to separate, to set apart, to cut off. God is holy in the sense that He is separated or distinguished from the finite, and created. He transcends finite things. His ways and thoughts are not man's but are higher than those of man (Isa. 55:8, 9). Isaiah saw the character of God as holy (Isa. 6:1-4). God's character is holy and man's character is imperfect. His goodness is more than that of man. Everything about God is excellent. His character is perfect. He is holy.

B. God is righteous. God's character is upright. In Him is no evil. John, the apostle, expressed the righteousness of God when he said: "God is light" (1 John 1:5). In God there is no darkness. He is free from anything evil. Dr. W. T. Conner said: "He is not only free from evil, he is opposed to the evil. All the energy of his being is set against sin. He put himself against sin and for the right" (W. T. Conner, *Revelation and God*, Broadman Press: Nashville, Tennessee, 1936, p. 247).

C. God is love. John, the apostle said "God is love" (1 John 4:8). The love of God is difficult to define. Dr. E. Y. Mullins defines love "as the self-imparting quality in the divine nature which leads God to seek the highest good and the most complete possession of his creatures. Love in its highest form is a relation between intelligent, moral, and free beings. God's love seeks to awaken a responsive love of man to God. In its final form love between God and man will mean their complete and unrestrained self-giving to each other, and the complete possession of each by the other" (E. Y. Mullins, *The Christian Religion In Its Doctrinal Expression,* Broadman Press: Nashville, Tennessee, 1917, p. 236).

Dr. W. T. Conner describes the qualities of God's love as intelligent, benevolent, righteous, self-giving, and demanding man's love. Love belongs to the very nature of God.

D. God is truth. He is truth personified. He is the source and ground of all truth. He is the basis of all human knowledge. If we reject God, we lose all criteria of truth (Isa. 38:18). All facets of truth are grounded in God.

IV. *God Is at Work.*

A. God was at work when He created the world. The Bible points out that the origin of the world is the creative work of God (Gen. 1:1; Col. 1:16; Heb. 11:3). The how and when of creation are not as important as the fact that God did it in His own way.

B. God is at work preserving the world. God not only made all things, but He upholds all things and controls all things (Col. 1:16, 17; Heb. 1:3).

C. God is at work seeking to save sinners. "For the Son of man is come to seek and to save that which was lost" (Luke 19:10). "For by grace are ye saved through faith; and that not of yourselves: it is the gift of God: not of works, lest any man should boast" (Eph. 2:8, 9). "Therefore if any man be in Christ, he is a new creature (creation): old things are passed away; behold, all things are become new" (2 Cor. 5:17).

Conclusion. "In the beginning God" (Gen. 1:1) and throughout all time and eternity God! Believe in Him today!

TITLE: "The Bible Speaks to Our Condition"

SCRIPTURE READING: Revelation 9.

Introduction. The Book of Revelation has been neglected, misunderstood, pitifully mistreated, and grossly perverted. It stands uniquely alone in the New Testament.

It is a book of prophecy which utilizes apocalyptic literature as its medium of communicating the message of God to the hearts of men.

This book cannot be properly understood or interpreted without a knowledge of the historical situation out of which it comes.

The chapter for study today is but a fragment of a larger section of the book which proclaims the judgments of God upon the Roman Empire (Rev. 8 and 9). Following the opening of the seventh seal, there are seven angels with seven trumpets to proclaim the judgment of God (8:1, 2). He proclaims the judgment of God upon the land (8:6, 7), on the sea (8:8, 9), on the fresh water (8:10, 11), on the heavenly bodies (8:12).

I. *The Terrible Locust Plague* (9:1-12). As we read of this terrible plague, let us remember that the author is using apocalyptic language and that he is speaking in symbolic language in which he is seeking to communicate a great truth. The details of apocalyptic literature must be understood as symbolic rather than literal.

II. *The Army From the East* (9:13-19). The sixth angel sounds the trumpet and John sees a vision of a horrible army from the East invading the land. It is possible that this is a reference to invasion by the Parthians who inflicted great damage upon the Roman Empire.

It is interesting to note in this series of visions that there are fifteen cases of destruction or judgment upon the people, and in twelve of these instances the extent of suffering is limited to "one third." This is indicative of the fact that while the judgment and the suffering were to be severe, it was a limited judgment upon those who were rebelling against God.

III. *The Refusal to Repent* (9:20, 21). The last two verses of this chapter reveal the purpose behind the judgments that are to befall the Roman Empire. In spite of all of the judgments of God, men refuse to forsake their idol worship and turn to the true and the living God.

Conclusion. Repentance involves a basic change of mind toward God, toward sin, toward self, toward others, toward things. Genuine repentance is accepting God's viewpoint concerning all things and then building one's life upon that basis.

Let us be open at all times to God's good way so that judgment will not come upon us.

TITLE: "The Enemy of the Kingdom"

TEXT: "An enemy hath done this" (Matt. 13:28).

SCRIPTURE READING: Matthew 13:24-30, 36-43, 47-50.

HYMN: "Breathe On Me," Hatch. "Nothing Between," Tindley. "Yield Not to Temptation," Palmer.

OFFERTORY PRAYER:

Heavenly Father, today our hearts would thank Thee for the abundance of Thy grace toward us. We would praise Thee with our lips. We would glorify Thee with our lives. We would proclaim Thy salvation to all peoples throughout the world. As an indication of our desire that others might know of Thy grace we bring our tithes and offerings for the advancement of the work of Thy kingdom. Bless these offerings to that purpose. In Jesus' name. Amen.

Introduction. In some way the kingdom of God (that is, the reign or rule of God) will be illustrated by the following story. A man sowed good wheat seed in his field, but, while he and other good men were sleeping, an enemy came and sowed tares. The tares were a kind of darnel or bastard wheat which looked like wheat but the grains were black and poisonous. These tares were not discovered until the grain began to form. The servants were surprised. They asked the householder, "Did you not sow good seed?" "Yes." "Then how do you account for these tares?" The house-holder replied, "An enemy hath done this."

One wonders if this cheap, despicable act was an actual occurrence of which Jesus had knowledge.

What can be done about it? The servants suggest that they pull out the tares. The householder knows that this is impracticable. The tares looked so much like wheat that mistakes would be made and wheat would be uprooted also. Again the roots would be so intertwined that in pulling up the tares much wheat would be uprooted. The householder had a better plan. "Let both grow until the harvest: and in the time of harvest I will say to the reapers, Gather ye together first the tares, and bind them in bundles to burn them: but gather the wheat into my barn" (v. 30).

Happily in Matthew 13:36-43 we have recorded our Lord's own interpretation of this parable. The one sowing the good seed is the Son of man. Jesus is the sower. The field in which He sows is the world. He sows good seed which are sons of the kingdom or saved persons. He expects them to be seed for the Gospel which will multiply many other saved people. The devil is the one sowing the tares which are the sons of the evil one or unsaved people.

I. *The Perplexing Problem of Evil in the World.* Now if this is God's world and He sows good seed why should there be sons of the evil one? Why should there be lying, stealing, cheating, murder, war, etc. in God's world? "Master, didst thou not sow good seed?"

A. Jesus recognizes sin as a reality. It is a fact. Tares are in with the wheat. Tares are not immature wheat. They are noxious weeds.

They are fit only for destruction. Hear Dr. George A. Buttrick:

"To regard evil as illusory solves no problems. A God who, eager to create children of His love, confronts them with a good and evil choice and so fills His universe with danger, is a God who by that act fills our minds with dismaying questions. But a God who suffers His children to live under illusions is not a winsome substitute! A world of real good and real evil does at least provide the setting for heroic character, but a world in which every one is victimized by false impressions is a mad world in very truth. Jesus says of the choking weeds of life: 'I do not account for them, but they are the work of an "enemy" ' " (George A. Buttrick, *The Parables of Jesus,* Harper and Row: New York, 1928, p. 66).

B. Jesus recognizes sin as the work of an enemy. God with great courage of love has made man "in his own image," which among other things carries the power of moral choice. One may accept the grace of God and become a son of the kingdom; one may reject the grace of God and become a son of the devil. This power of choice which places man above the animal creation is both a precious and a perilous possession. Character would be impossible without moral choice. Yet the same moral choice which opens heaven can be used to open hell. "Sin is enmity against God."

II. *What Are God's Servants to Do?* Some are willing to rush out and try forcibly to pull up the tares. History is filled with examples of those who in the name of Christ have been willing to root out the evil with the sword, but Jesus says otherwise.

Wheat and tares look so much alike that no mortal can possibly draw the dividing line. "Man looketh on the outward appearance, but the LORD looketh on the heart" (1 Sam. 16: 7). We have no doubt but that God can indicate at this very moment the lost or the saved condition of every person living on earth, but only God can. He alone knows all of the facts including the motives which give moral quality to the actions. Our responsibility as servants of God is not to persecute others. "Judge not, that ye be not judged" (Matt. 7:1). Certainly, in trying to gather up tares we would gather wheat with the tares and leave tares with the wheat.

The servants of Christ are to speak "the truth in love" (Eph. 4: 15). "But ye shall receive power, after that the Holy Ghost is come upon you: and ye shall be witnesses unto me both in Jerusalem, and in all Judea, and in Samaria, and unto the uttermost part of the earth" (Acts 1:8). The weapon for that witness is not the sword of temporal power but rather "the sword of the Spirit, which is the word of God" (Eph. 6:17). In the natural world there was no way by which tares could become wheat. In the spiritual world, however, sons of the devil can become sons of God through faith in Jesus Christ.

III. *God's Judgment Is Certain.* At the time of harvest the tares and the wheat will be harvested with no difficulty in separation. The wheat without exception will be in the barn. The tares without exception will be destroyed by burning. The Son of man Himself will through His messengers do the harvesting. Not one saved will be among the unsaved; not one unsaved will be among the saved. The saved will shine forth as the sun in the kingdom of their Father. The unsaved will know anguish.

The Parable of the Net spoken later that same day emphasizes the same truth. It presents the familiar picture in the New Testament of the fisherman casting his net. The net draws in of every kind of fish. The fisherman divided the good fish from the bad. He kept the good and cast the bad away. So at the end of the age all will be judged. The angels as God's messengers will effect the separation as easily as fishermen sort fish.

The wheat is gathered into the barn (v. 30); the good fish are gathered into vessels (v. 48); then shall the righteous shine forth as the sun in the kingdom of their Father (v. 43). The wheat, the fish, the saved are valuable unto their owners. These and countless other figures of speech in Scripture enhance the joy of salvation both to the believer and to the Lord. Their variety should warn against an insistence upon too literal an interpretation.

The tares are bound in bundles for burning (v. 30); the bad fish are cast away (v. 48); the wicked are cast into the furnace of fire where there shall be wailing and gnashing of teeth (vv. 42, 49). These and other images are used of the sad fate of the wicked. Their variety should warn against acceptance with crude literalism, but the awful spiritual truth depicted by them must be accepted with all seriousness.

Conclusion. God will be the final judge. He will not make any mistakes. There will be no idle arguments about the hypocrisies of others. "So then every one of us shall give account of himself to God" (Rom. 14:12). But God as judge does not desire to pronounce the sentence of death, "not willing that any should perish, but that all should come to repentance" (2 Pet. 3:9). In love He approaches sinful man with the offer of forgiveness and salvation.

In the spiritual realm tares can become wheat; bad fish can become good fish; wicked men can become righteous. If God seems to delay His judgment, Paul suggests that mercy may be the reason: "And thinkest thou this, O man, that judgest them which do such things, and doest the same, that thou shalt escape the judgment of God? Or despisest thou the riches of his goodness and forbearance and longsuffering; not knowing that the goodness of God leadeth thee to repentance? But after thy hardness and impenitent heart treasurest up unto thyself wrath against the day of wrath and revelation of the righteous judgment of God" (Rom. 2:3-5). "Now then we are ambassadors for Christ, as though God did beseech you by us: we pray you in Christ's stead, be ye reconciled to God" (2 Cor. 5:20). "Behold, now is the accepted time; behold, now is the day of salvation" (2 Cor. 6:2).

TITLE: "How to Have the Guidance of God"

TEXT: "And he said, "O LORD God of my master Abraham, I pray thee, send me good speed this day, and shew kindness unto my master Abraham. Behold, I stand here by the well of water; and the daughters of the men of the city come out to draw water: And let it come to pass, that the damsel to whom I shall say, Let down thy pitcher, I pray thee, that I may drink; and she shall say, Drink, and I will give thy camels drink also; let the same be she that thou hast appointed for thy servant Isaac; and thereby shall I know that thou hast shewed kindness unto my master" (Gen. 24:12-14).

SCRIPTURE READING: Genesis 24:1-33, 57-67.

Introduction. Sarah, Abraham's wife, lived to be 147 years of age. She died forty years after the birth of Isaac. To Isaac the death of his mother, Sarah, was a very great personal loss. Although he was forty years of age at the time of her death, he had always lived at home, had been the recipient of his mother's love and devotion, and was the subject of her constant hope and prayer.

Abraham, Isaac's father, made plans with his chief servant to secure a wife for his lonesome son. The faithful servant made the journey requested by Abraham and brought Rebekah to Isaac without Isaac's approval or disapproval. The selection of Rebekah for Isaac was the custom of that day but it also reveals the meekness and acquiesence of Isaac. Abraham and his servant did a good job in selecting Rebekah for Isaac. The Bible portrays her as a kind, gracious, beautiful, and charming woman.

The beautiful story as told in Genesis 24 reveals to us how we can have the guidance of God in daily matters. Let us deduct these important and instructive guidelines from the story.

I. *To Have the Guidance of God We must Realize that We Have Been Sent on a Mission.* "But thou shalt go unto my country, and to my kindred, and take a wife unto my son Isaac" (Gen. 24:4). The thought of a bride for Isaac originated in the mind and heart of Abraham. It was the outcome of his love for his son. Abraham chose his eldest servant for the task of selecting a bride for Isaac, and the servant set out to accomplish the task his master had given to him.

All of us have tasks to perform in life. In fact, God has a purpose for every life. To put it more succinctly, God has a purpose for you. If we are to perform His will, our tasks in life, we must know what it is for us and have the guidance of God in doing it.

II. *To Have the Guidance of God We must Be "in the Way"* (Gen. 24:27). Being "in the way" the God of heaven will lead us. Being "in the way" means having our feet in the path God approves. Being "in the way" involves doing what God wants us to do. Being "in the way" means being involved in the task set out for us.

Jesus enunciated this great principle when He said: "If any man will do his will, he shall know of the doctrine, whether it be of God, or whether I speak of myself" (John 7:17).

III. *To Have the Guidance of God We Must Ask for It*. It is clearly evident that Abraham's servant asked for and got the guidance of God in finding Isaac a bride. His task was more than that of obeying his master Abraham; the task of finding a wife for Isaac became his evident delight. What a grand privilege it was to secure a bride for Isaac, his master's son. He gave himself to the task when he asked God to guide him. The Bible teaches: "Ask, and it shall be given you; seek, and ye shall find; knock, and it shall be opened unto you" (Matt. 7:7). "If ye abide in me, and my words abide in you, ye shall ask what ye will, and it shall be done unto you" (John 15:7).

God's guidance is yours for the asking. God's will and the accomplishment of His will is through the privilege of prayer.

IV. *To Have the Guidance of God We Must Expect It*. Abraham's servant prayed earnestly that God would guide him. He had said: "And let it come to pass, that the damsel to whom I shall say, Let down thy pitcher, I pray thee, that I may drink; and she shall say, Drink, and I will give thy camels drink also: let the same be she that thou hast appointed for thy servant Isaac; and thereby shall I know that thou hast shewed kindness unto my master" (Gen. 24:14).

The servant had prayed thus and now he expected an answer to his prayer. He was prepared to accept God's answer and to accept whomever God appointed. He prayed, expected and answered and left it all in God's hands.

We will have the guidance of God when we pray and expect an answer to our praying. We must not say, "O, Lord, guide me," when all the time we mean, "Let me guide Thee."

V. *To Have the Guidance of God We Must Look for It in Other Persons*. "And they called Rebekah, and said unto her, Wilt thou go with this man? And she said, I will go" (Gen. 24:58). The trusted servant could see the guidance of God in Rebekah's answer, in Rebekah's actions. He understood that God had been at work in her life too.

My theology professor used to say: "If God has called you He will tell someone else about it." My experience teaches me that this is true. Often when God speaks to us He speaks to others about us. Often He speaks to us through others. Often we can see His guidance for our lives in the lives of others.

VI. *To Have the Guidance of God We Must Proclaim God's Purpose* (Gen. 24:34-56). The one purpose of the servant was to announce his master's purpose—the will of Abraham. How wonderfully he proclaimed it. He not only proclaimed it but he went on to proclaim the resources of Abraham (v. 35) and the glory of the son (v. 36).

Christians are instruments in the hands of the Holy Spirit to proclaim the greatness of the Father and the glory of Christ, the Son. When we proclaim His will He gives us guidance all the way.

VII. *To Have the Guidance of God We Must Accept It When Given*. What did the servant do when it became evident Rebekah was to become Isaac's bride? He immediately talked with her family, secured per mission to take her to Isaac and proceeded to bring her to him. There he introduced the two to each other. The Bible says, "Isaac . . . took Rebekah, and she became his wife" (Gen. 24:67).

Conclusion. If we seek and follow the guidance of God it will lead to victory. God never commands without providing provisions and guiding us in the way. His grace is sufficient for His will for our lives. Lottie Moon said: "My life is completely God's to direct as He chooses." Let Him give you His guidance now!

WEDNESDAY EVENING, SEPTEMBER 11

TITLE: "The Bible Speaks to Our Condition"

SCRIPTURE READING: Revelation 16.

Introduction. The chapter for today's meditation from this strange and mysterious book at the end of the New Testament gives to us a dramatic picture of the pouring out of the wrath of God upon the enemies of His people. There are seven angels that go forth with seven bowls filled with the wrath of God. The inspired writer uses apocalyptic literature to express the message and we must seek the truth behind the symbolic language.

The historic situation into which the Book of Revelation was written probably requires that we interpret this chapter as being a prophecy of the wrath of God that was going to fall upon the Roman Empire which threatened the very existence of Christianity in that decade. As such, it would have brought encouragement and hope to those who were distressed and in despair.

We probably should interpret this passage as being a demonstration of the wrath of God that has fallen upon the enemies of God's people through the ages. This chapter reveals that God is the eternal foe of those who seek to destroy His people and His work in the world.

By all means we should see this chapter as speaking of the final demonstration of God's wrath upon those who reject Him and blaspheme Him as we come to the end of the age. Man in his unbelief and in his revolt against God will try to throw off the authority and the power of God.

I. *The Second Coming of Christ* (16:15a). In the midst of this chapter which proclaims the wrath of God upon the wicked, there is a clear promise of our Lord's personal return. He describes the manner of His coming as being sudden and unexpected.

II. *A Beatitude* (16:15b). In the midst of this chapter describing the judgment of God upon the wicked, our Lord announces a beatitude upon His disciples who are alert and watchful and responsive to His leadership. One of the primary purposes of this entire book is to assure His disciples of His abiding presence with them in all circumstances and to assure them of His ultimate victory over all adverse circumstances. They are encouraged to always be alert and responsive to their opportunities and responsibilities.

III. *An Encouragement to Purity and Fidelity* (16:15c). Another of the primary purposes of the writer of the Book of Revelation is to encourage the disciples of the Lord to be faithful, even to the point of death. Martyrdom was a real possibility for each one who was loyal to the Lord in those days. Faithfulness is required if they are to please the Lord and if they are to give an effective witness to their contemporaries.

Conclusion. Out of this very strange chapter that deals with both the past and the future, there comes a promise and words of encouragement for those of us who live today. Let's live in a constant expectancy of our Lord's return. Let us be faithful to Him. Let us be ready at any time for His triumphant and victorious return.

SUNDAY MORNING, SEPTEMBER 15

TITLE: "The Growth of the Kingdom"

TEXT: "The kingdom of heaven is like to a grain of mustard seed" (Matt. 13:31).

SCRIPTURE READING: Matthew 13:31-33.

HYMN: "Praise to the Lord, the Almighty," Neander. "Take Time to Be Holy," Longstaff. "Brethren, We Have Met to Worship," Atkins.

OFFERTORY PRAYER:

Our heavenly Father, as we approach the harvest season of the year when men will be reaping the harvest from the fields, we would remind ourselves of Thy bountiful goodness toward us. We would thank Thee for every gift of Thy mercy. As we bring tithes and offerings of the fruits of our labors we would thank Thee for the opportunity to work and the power to get wealth. Help us never to forget that Thou art the giver of every good and perfect gift. Help us to give unto Thee even as Thou hast given unto us, through Jesus Christ our Lord. Amen.

Introduction. Jesus was sure about God. Jesus never doubted God nor His ability to accomplish His purpose. "Have faith in God," He pleads (Mark 11:22). "Ye believe in God, believe also in me" (John 14:1). You do not need to be afraid of the future. It is in God's competent hands.

Jesus had complete confidence in the success of His mission. Even as He faced death it was in terms of victory. He faced the anguish and sorrow of the cross, but never for a moment did the cross represent defeat. Always His death was associated with victory and the accomplishment of the Father's will. "And I, if I be lifted up from the earth, will draw all men unto me" (John 12:32). In the upper room He was confident of the future, "In my Father's house are many mansions: if it were not so, I would have told you. I go to prepare a place for you. And if I go and prepare a place for you, I will come again, and receive you unto myself; that where I am, there ye may be also" (John 14:2, 3). They were not to despair nor faint at tribulation. "In the world ye shall have tribulation; but be of good cheer; I have overcome the world"(John 16:33).

On the cross Jesus was sure of His saving mission. He assured the repentent robber of salvation (Luke 23:43, 44). "It is finished," was a cry of victory. It seems to me that His cry "My God, my God, why hast thou forsaken me?" was also an affirmation of victory. He was beginning to quote the twenty-second psalm and applied it to Himself. "Why" is "for what purpose" and the psalm answered the question. The Messiah suffers in order to be the Savior. "Father, into thy hands I commend my Spirit" was an affirmation of faith.

After the Resurrection Jesus had complete confidence in the world-wide nature of the kingdom of God. The commissions (see Matt. 28:18-20; Luke 24:44-49; Acts 1:8) all assume a world-wide conquest. He will be with them during the Gospel age in the person of the Holy Spirit. He will return at the end of the age in power and great glory. (See Matt. 25:31ff.)

Who of the contemporaries of Jesus could have foreseen that He would be King of an eternal kingdom? He was of humble birth, the son of a carpenter (as the people thought) and of a humble Jewish maiden. He was a teacher who so enraged the religious authorities as to lead to His condemnation and death upon a shameful cross. His followers were few and from the common people. Surely at His death His followers would disperse and His name vanish.

However, to the surprise of everyone except Jesus Himself, His name did not vanish. Rather, "God also hath highly exalted him, and given him a name which is above every name: that at the name of Jesus every knee should bow, of things in heaven, and things in earth, and things under the earth; And that every tongue should confess that Jesus Christ is Lord, to the glory of God the Father" (Phil. 2:9-11).

I. *The Parable of the Mustard Seed* (Matt. 13:31, 32). The unexpected growth of the kingdom of heaven from such humble beginnings to such importance is like the growth of a grain of mustard seed (which was the smallest of the seeds in common use) to become the largest of the herbs, growing to about ten feet in height, becoming a tree—in size rather than in nature—so large that even the birds found shelter in its branches. The mustard seed was proverbial in Jesus' day for something small and relatively insignificant. The emphasis of the parable is upon the fact that a seed so small could grow into a bush so large. Thus did Jesus predict the expansive growth of the kingdom of heaven.

II. *The Parable of the Leaven* (Matt. 13:33). The method by which the kingdom of heaven grows our Lord illustrates by the parable of the leaven. Often as a boy, Jesus had seen His mother take three measures of meal, by which He probably means wheat flour. This was the large quantity needed to bake enough bread to last a large family for several days. The leaven or yeast carefully saved from the last baking was placed in the flour dough. Immediately, quietly, continuously the leaven worked, changing particle after particle of the dough until the whole had been conquered by the yeast.

A. The leaven works silently, inwardly. The kingdom of heaven is the reign of God in the hearts of men. It comes as men yield their hearts to God. Jesus is the King of the kingdom of heaven. God, the Holy Spirit, is in charge of the present Gospel mission of leading men and women, boys and girls to the acceptance of Jesus Christ as Lord and Savior. The Holy Spirit bears witness to the truth as it is revealed in Jesus Christ. (See John 14:16, 17, 26; 15:26.) The Holy Spirit convicts of sin and invites to the acceptance of Jesus Christ. (See John 16:7-14.) The Spirit of God works quietly, powerfully, inwardly. Often great sources of power work quietly. Who hears the light? Electricity? Atomic power? The solar system does not chatter in its course. Love does not make a big noise. God is at work.

B. Leaven works continuously. Whether the housewife thinks about it or not the leaven is continuously at the task. "Behold, he that keepeth Israel shall neither slumber nor sleep" (Ps. 121:4). The divine Potter has His hands in the clay of our humanity seeking to make a vessel of honor. He uses the truth as His weapon. His providences—which may seem to us both good and ill—are to accomplish His purpose.

C. Leaven works by contact. One particle becomes leavened. This particle leavens the next and so particle by particle the leaven relentlessly conquers the dough. It is an apt illustration of the way by which the kingdom of heaven expands. One life is changed by the Spirit of God. He who was dead in trespasses and in sins has been made alive in Christ Jesus. A part of his new life in Christ is the compassionate desire that others might be Christian. He expresses that desire as he bears witness of his faith to someone in whom he is concerned. God uses the witness to help another to come to the truth. Note how the kingdom of heaven began to spread. John the Baptist pointed out Jesus to his disciples. John and Andrew spent the day with Jesus. They were convinced. Andrew "first findeth his own brother Simon, and saith unto him, We have found the Messias, which is, being interpreted, the Christ" (John 1:41). John probably won his brother James. "Jesus ... findeth Philip, and saith unto him, Follow me" (John 1:43). "Philip findeth Nathaniel, and saith unto him, We have found him, of whom Moses in the law, and the prophets, did write, Jesus of Nazareth, the son of Joseph" (John 1:45). And so the kingdom grows. God's method of winning the multitudes seems to be to win them one by one.

D. The leaven works victoriously. It has vitality and power to conquer the dough. We have already learned that a story from nature cannot always parallel spiritual truth, because nature lacks the quality of free will which man has. To interpret "till the whole was leavened" to teach that all men will be saved would be too rigorous an interpretation. The Parable of the Tares and the Parable of the Dragnet as well as other explicit teachings of Jesus teach otherwise. The meal of our human life has the power to resist the leaven. It is true, however, that the leaven of the Gospel will affect every particle in the meal. No person can escape a confrontation with the Gospel.

Conclusion. The triumph of Christ's kingdom is assured. "For he must reign, till he hath put all enemies under his feet" (1 Cor. 15:25). "The kingdoms of this world are become the kingdoms of our Lord, and of his Christ; and he shall reign for ever and ever" (Rev. 11:15). At the end Satan and those who follow him are cast into the bottomless pit. Jesus and those who follow Him live and reign. The purpose of

this Gospel age is not to determine whether Christ or Satan will be victorious. That issue is already settled. The purpose is to determine who will be with Christ in victory and who will be with Satan in defeat.

The Parable of the Mustard Seed assures us that the triumph of Christ will be greater than any of His contemporaries could have imagined. The Parable of the Leaven assures us that God is working quietly, effectively, continuously to add members to Christ's kingdom. Wonder of wonders, He can use us to help Him in this significant work. Let us be willing witnesses for Christ.

SUNDAY EVENING, SEPTEMBER 15

TITLE: "Walking With God"

TEXT: "And Enoch walked with God: and he was not; for God took him" (Gen. 5:24).

SCRIPTURE READING: Genesis 5:21-24.

Introduction. The Bible says "Enoch walked with God." Who was Enoch? The Bible tells us that he was the son of Jared (Gen. 5:18), the father of Methuselah (Gen. 5:21, 22) and the seventh in descent from Adam in the line of Seth (Jude 14). The Bible says he lived 365 years. The brief record of his life is written in the words, "Enoch walked with God: and he was not; for God took him" (Gen. 5:24).

The words "walked with God" denote a devout life lived in close communion with God. The words "and he was not" are explained by Hebrews 11:5, "By faith Enoch was translated that he should not see death; and was not found, because

God had translated him: for before his translation he had this testimony, that he pleased God." The words "lived," "begat" and "died" in Genesis reveal how brief and uniform are our lives.

Enoch was a man who walked with God. Using the story of Enoch's life I want to share with you some pertinent points concerning walking with God.

I. *The Companion of Walking With God.*

A. The companion for life's walk is a divine companion. Paul said: "And what agreement hath the temple of God with idols? for ye are the temple of the living God; as God hath said, I will dwell in them, and walk in them; and I will be their God, and they shall be my people" (2 Cor. 6:16). The agnostic and the skeptic ask, "Where is God?" The Christian, like Enoch, is quietly walking with this divine companion.

B. The companion for life's walk is a close companion. The Bible says, "A friend loveth at all times" (Prov. 17:17) but God is a companion who is near at all times. He makes His abode in the Christian and He walks with him always.

C. The companion for life's walk is a faithful companion. We can trust Him for He is faithful and just. He does not desert us to our foes. He wants to be with us and is preparing a place for us.

II. *The Demands of Walking With God.*

A. Walking with God demands entire surrender. The name "Enoch" means "dedicated, one yielded up to God, to be conformed to God's mind and will." Walking with God demands surrender to God's will. Paul indicated this surrender when he wrote: "And be found in him, not having mine own righteousness, which is of the law, but that which is through the faith of Christ, the righteousness which is of God by faith" (Phil. 3:9).

B. Walking with God demands unbroken fellowship. As Enoch walked with God he had fellowship with God. The two were in perfect agreement. Amos said: "Can two walk together, except they be agreed?" (Amos 3:3). Enoch had good company for the road of life. Walking with God makes the trip of life enjoyable.

C. Walking with God demands continual progress. Walking with God implies progress, it means a growing knowledge of God. The chariot wheels of life never stand still. There is no standing still with

God, no marking time with Him. Each day is a new journey for we have not passed this way before. We journey toward a new country, the upward way, the promised land.

D. Walking with God demands complete separation. Walking with God prohibits indulgence in the sinful pleasures of the world. God is light and those who walk with Him do not walk in darkness. Paul said: "Set your affections on things above, not on things on the earth" (Col. 3:2). The Book of Leviticus says, "Sanctify yourselves therefore, and be ye holy; for I am the LORD your God" (Lev. 20:7).

E. Walking with God demands suffering. Those who walk with God suffer the criticism of the world. Those who walk with God suffer the hatred of the world (John 15:18). Those who walk with God suffer as good soldiers of Jesus Christ (2 Tim. 2:3).

III. *The Manner of Walking With God.*

A. Walking with God means walking by faith. We receive Christ through faith. Paul said: "For ye are all the children of God by faith in Christ Jesus" (Gal. 3:26). Paul said to the Ephesians: "For by grace are ye saved through faith; and that not of yourselves, it is the gift of God: Not of works, lest any man should boast" (Eph. 2:8, 9). We walk by faith in happiness, sorrow, turmoil, and death. It is faith all the way. Without faith it is impossible to please God (Heb. 11:6).

B. Walking with God means not walking in a hypocritical way. We do not walk with faces disfigured but transfigured, not conformed to the rites of men but transformed by the power of God. We do not walk with a pious face but with a pious life. We do not walk with ears opened to idle tales or gossip, but ears opened to the voice of God.

C. Walking with God means walking in truth. Jesus said: "I am the way, the truth, and the life" (John 14:6). John the apostle said: "For I rejoiced greatly, when the brethren came and testified of the truth that is in thee, even as thou walkest in the truth" (3 John 3).

D. Walking with God means a spiritual walk. Paul said: "This I say then, Walk in the spirit, and ye shall not fulfil the lust of the flesh. If we live in the Spirit, let us also walk in the Spirit" (Gal. 5:16, 25).

IV. *The Privileges of Walking With God.*

A. Walking with God assures us of the forgiveness of our sins. John the apostle said: "If we confess our sins, he is faithful and just to forgive us our sins, and to cleanse us from all unrighteousness" (1 John 1:9). Oh, the joy of walking with God on the highway of life and knowing you are forgiven, that you are cleansed (Isa. 35:8, 9)! It certainly is the greatest of all feelings in life.

B. Walking with God assures us of strength day by day. The Lord has promised to be with us always (Matt. 28:20). Paul said: "Notwithstanding the Lord stood with me, and strengthened me; that by me the preaching might be fully known, and that all the Gentiles might hear: and I was delivered out of the mouth of the lion. And the Lord shall deliver me from every evil work, and will preserve me unto his heavenly kingdom, to whom be glory for ever and ever. Amen" (2 Tim. 4:17, 18). As we walk with Him He does give us strength when it is needed!

C. Walking with God assures us of comfort for life's sorrows. Enoch didn't die but I am sure he had sorrows along life's journey. Who doesn't? Many passages of God's Word assures us of comfort for life's sorrows. God is with us and He speaks to us (Ps. 23; John 14:1-6).

D. Walking with God assures us of happiness for life's journey. Walking with God is happiness, true happiness. Paul knew about that joy even in prison and wrote to the Philippians urging them to, "Rejoice in the Lord alway: and again I say, Rejoice" (Phil. 4:4).

Conclusion. Begin today your walk with the Lord Jesus Christ and He will go with you each step of the way.

TITLE: "The Bible Speaks to Our Condition"

SCRIPTURE READING: Matthew 4.

Introduction. Temptation is the universal experience of man. We read in the Bible that God tempted Abraham. We also read, "Let no man say when he is tempted, I am tempted of God: for God cannot be tempted with evil, neither tempteth he any man" (James 1:13). These two references must be studied in their context. God tempted or tested Abraham to bring out the good. God never puts a man to the test to bring out evil. Satan is responsible for this kind of temptation. Occasionally man is responsible for his own temptations when he deliberately exposes himself to that which is dangerous.

The act of being tempted should not be considered as sinful within itself. We read concerning our Lord that He was, "In all points tempted like as we are, yet without sin" (Heb. 4:15). Our Lord conquered temptation and would show us the way to victory.

I. *Victory Over Temptation* (Matt. 4:1-11). Satan tempted our Lord in the area of His natural appetites (4:3, 4), the methods that He would use in His ministry (4:5-7), and the nature and purpose of His mission (4:8-11). Our Lord overcame the temptation of Satan on the basis of His pure manhood and on the basis of His absolute trust and recognition of the authority of God's Word.

Apart from a diligent study and a reliance upon the great truths of God's Word, there is no way for us to have victory over temptation.

Our Lord set for us an example that will point us toward victory over every temptation toward evil.

II. *The Call to Repentance* (Matt. 4:17). The word translated "repent" literally means "to change the mind, to change the attitude, to change one's scale of values." It is a call to accept the mind of God rather than the mind of the natural man. Positively, repentance is a call to a proper attitude toward God, toward self, toward sin, toward others and toward things. It is an invitation to a high, holy, happy way of life.

III. *The Call to Service* (Matt. 4:18-22). Our Lord approached men on the basis of their native endowments, their natural dispositions and the context in which they were living life. He spoke to fishermen in terms of becoming fishers of men. He spoke to farmers in terms of sowing the seed.

He would speak to each of us in the context of where life finds us. He would call us to high, wonderful service to others in the name of our God in the world in which we live.

To truly follow Him involves a forsaking of the nets that would hinder us from being fully committed to Him.

Conclusion. Our Lord went about teaching, preaching, and healing and ministering to those in need. If we would be His true followers, we would find ourselves following His example and ministering as He sought to minister.

TITLE: "The Value of the Kingdom."

TEXT: "The kingdom of heaven is like unto treasure" (Matt. 13:44).

SCRIPTURE READING: Matthew 13:44-46.

HYMNS: "Holy, Holy, Holy," Heber. "Though Your Sins Be As Scarlet," Crosby. "Serve the Lord With Gladness," McKinney.

OFFERTORY PRAYER:

Holy and loving Father, we would approach Thy throne of grace with our best. We would not come before Thee with that which is cheap and shoddy. Out of genuine love and deep gratitude we would offer to Thee the fruits of our labors as an expression of the worship of our hearts. Accept these tithes and offerings as we seek to give ourselves completely unto Thee. In Jesus' name. Amen.

Introduction. These messages are focused on the parables about the kingdom of God which were spoken in one day by Jesus as He preached from a boat. Four sets of twin parables are among those spoken:

The twin parables of the Sower and of the Seed Growing of Itself emphasize "The Vitality of the Kingdom."

The twin parables of the Tares and of the Dragnet emphasize "The Enemy of the Kingdom."

The twin parables of the Mustard Seed and of the Leaven illustrate "The Growth of the Kingdom."

The twin parables of the Hidden Treasure and of the Pearl of Great Price emphasize "The Value of the Kingdom," which is the title of this message.

Like twins these parables are alike. They both emphasize the same great truth that the kingdom of God is more important than anything else in the world; that is, to be right with God, to possess the forgiving grace of God through Jesus Christ, is worth more than everything else.

Like twins there are some differences. The parables show that men come to Christian experience by diverse routes.

I. *The Parable of the Hidden Treasure* (Matt. 13:44). In Jesus' day the finding of buried treasure was not an uncommon occurrence. The ground was the security vault of a people besieged by conquering armies. Even the one-talent man in the parable hid his talent in the earth. He didn't steal it; he didn't waste it; he meant to preserve the precious talent by hiding it in the earth. A man plowing in his field apparently with no thought of finding treasure drove his plowshare deep. The tip struck a strange object. He investigated. There before his eyes was a treasure more valuable than he had ever imagined. He recognized its value. He must possess it at all costs. He covered it to keep others from finding and stealing it. He joyfully and quickly sold all that he had in order to buy that field and in accord with the law of his land claim the treasure as his possession.

II. *The Merchantman Seeking Goodly Pearls.* (Matt. 13:45, 46). Pearls were valued in the New Testament world much as diamonds are today. The merchantman was a drummer who went from place to place buying and selling pearls. He was always looking for pearls of more beautiful color, perfect size, and symmetry of form. One day he discovered a pearl more wonderful than he had imagined. He immediately appraised it as of more value than all of his possessions. He must have it. Quickly he sold his possessions in order to buy that pearl.

III. *Experiences by Which Men Come to Find the True Treasure Are in Many Ways Alike.*

A. The surpassing value of the kingdom. The man in the field realized that he had struck it rich. The connoisseur of pearls knew he had found the ultimate in value. "He that cometh to God must believe that he is, and that he is a rewarder of them that diligently seek him" (Heb. 11:6). What is the treasure? What is the pearl? Is it not to know God as revealed in Jesus Christ? It is to discover that He has forgiven our sins not in part but completely and that He has adopted us as children in the divine family. It is to be right with God. It is to enter the kingdom of God by being born again (John 3:3).

B. One who enters the kingdom of God must come by repentance and faith. He parts with all else to gain it.

1. In the nature of the case there can be no compromise here. For God to compromise on the terms of salvation and allow one to be saved who refuses to renounce sin is a moral impossibility. "Except ye repent, ye shall all likewise perish" (Luke 13:3). The Gospel that is to be preached among all nations is the message of "repentance and remission of sins" (Luke 24:47). Paul sums up the whole Gospel for both Jews and Greeks as "repentance toward God, and faith toward our Lord Jesus Christ" (Acts 20:21).

2. The heart of the Christian experience is that one personally forsakes all in order to give his all in believing faith to the Lord Jesus Christ. Entry into the kingdom of God is not by outward ceremony nor by church membership. Judas was a member of the church but apparently not the kingdom of God. Simon Magus was duly baptized but he was headed for perdition. The robber on the cross was never baptized but Jesus affirmed his salvation.

C. With joy, both men parted with all else to possess the treasure. The normal expression of Christianity is joy. The angels sang in heavenly chorus to announce the Savior's birth. "Jesus came into Galilee, preaching the gospel of the kingdom of God" (Mark 1:14). The Gospel means good news. Christians sing at church. The emphasis on the part of one who has found Jesus is not upon how much he gives up but rather upon how much he has found. Suppose a man contemplating marriage begins to weigh the issue in this way: think of how much I will have to give up; I will have to share my income; I'll not be able to date other girls any more; I'll have to stay home with my wife and not be out with the men as much as I would like; this marriage would surely cramp my freedom. What do we know about this man? We know that he does not know what love is. The man truly in love thinks his intended bride is the most wonderful person in the world, and he counts himself to be truly blessed to be able to endow her with all of his worldly goods.

The normal Christian does not think about what he has given up for Christ. He rejoices in the true riches which he has found in Christ.

For example hear Paul exult in Philippians 3:7-11: "But what things were gain to me, those I counted loss for Christ. Yea doubtless, and I count all things but loss for the excellency of the knowledge of Christ Jesus my Lord: for whom I have suffered the loss of all things, and do count them but dung, that I may win Christ, And be found in him, not having mine own righteousness, which is of the law, but that which is through the faith of Christ, the righteousness which is of God by faith: That I may know him, and the power of his resurrection, and the fellowship of his sufferings, being made conformable unto his death; If by any means I might attain unto the resurrection of the dead."

We "buy" what Jesus gives by being willing to "sell" all lesser values. We gain life by losing it. "Ho, every one that thirsteth, come ye to the waters, and he that hath no money; come ye, buy, and eat; yea, come, buy wine and milk without money and without price" (Isa. 55:1).

IV. *Twins, Even Identical Twins, Have Some Difference.* So do these parables.

The ways by which men come to find the treasure are varied. The man in the field plowing had no thought of finding buried treasure. He was about his daily task. Perhaps his very eagerness to do his work well by plowing deep helped him find the treasure. The merchantman on the other hand was seeking. He had gone from place to place seeking the best. The man in the field was probably a poor man. The merchantman was probably rich, although this is only a conjecture. In any case the providence of God led both to the treasure in his own way.

Conclusion. Every individual's experience in coming to Christ is in some way different from that of others, just as he is different from all others. The Apostle Paul was blinded by the light from heaven and heard the voice of Jesus. It would be false to insist that others must do so to enter the kingdom. Some know exactly the time and place when they found Jesus precious to their souls. As one said to me, "Of course I know when I was saved, I was there." Others of us are not so sure about the time and place when we first loved Jesus. Some crossed over without any great emotional upheaval. It was the reasonable thing to do. Others prayed and agonized until relief came. To insist that one cannot be saved unless he sees the light, has a time and place experience, experiences great emotion is to apply false tests. The true test is: Is Jesus valued above all? Is life gladly yielded to Him? Really the important question is not so much, "When was I saved?" but rather, "Am I saved?" "Is Jesus precious to me now?" The promise is "that whosoever believeth in him shall not perish, but have everlasting life" (John 3:16).

TITLE: "How Does God Speak Today?"

TEXT: "God, who at sundry times and in divers manners spake in time past unto the fathers by the prophets, Hath in these last days spoken unto us by his Son, whom he hath appointed heir of all things, by whom also he made the worlds" (Heb. 1:1, 2).

SCRIPTURE READING: Psalm 19: 1-14; Hebrews 1:1, 2.

Introduction. The question most often asked the minister is "How can I get forgiveness for my sins?" It is the sinner's question! The question most often asked the minister by the Christian is "How can I know God's will for my life?" or "How does God speak today?"

I am thoroughly convinced that God is continually sending out His messages today. He is speaking His will to men. Of course, there are those who doubt that God speaks at all to men today. Joan of Arc was one of the most spectacular military leaders France ever had. As a simple peasant girl, she started her career by getting a French army commander to arrange an interview for her with King Charles VII. When she told him voices were bidding her to become the leader of her nation's armies, the king impatiently replied that if God had any word for France it should come to him as ruler. Joan of Arc assured him that voices did come but he did not hear them because of his failure to pray and listen.

How does God speak today? He speaks to us in many ways. Let us note a few ways God speaks today.

I. *God Speaks Through History.*

My history professor in college said: "History is His-story." A noted historian said: "History is a voice forever sounding across the centuries the laws of right and wrong." Thomas Arnold reviewed the downfall of the great world empires of the past and summed up what had happened by saying, "Down they come, one after another, and all for the lack of righteousness."

God controls the universe by physical and moral laws. Ruthless leaders who seek to rule by military force may find success for a brief time but will in the end perish. Unjust, greedy, selfish men who exploit others for gain may appear successful for a brief spell but they too will soon perish. God has a universal law. It says: "Be not deceived, God is not mocked: for whatsoever a man soweth, that shall he also reap" (Gal. 6:7). Surely, God speaks to us through history for no nation or individual can permanently endure who defies God and His law—His laws!

II. *God Speaks Through Nature.* The writer of Psalm 19 said: "The heavens declare the glory of God; and the firmament sheweth his handiwork" (v. 1). The writer of Romans said: "For the wrath of God is revealed from heaven against all ungodliness and unrighteousness of men, who hold the truth in unrighteousness; Because that which may be known of God is manifest in them; for God hath shewed it unto them. For the invisible things of him from the creation of the world are clearly seen, being understood by the things that are made, even his eternal power and Godhead; so that they are without excuse" (Rom. 1:18-20).

I remember hearing of a Frenchman who had incurred the displeasure of Napoleon and was cast into a dungeon. Forsaken by his family and friends, forgotten by everyone in the outside world, he wrote on the wall of his cell "Nobody cares." One day a green shoot came through a crack in the floor. Each day the Frenchman shared his water with the little green plant. The plant grew and grew toward the small window in the cell and one day the Frenchman found on the plant a beautiful blue flower. As he looked at the beautiful blue flower he scratched away the words, "Nobody cares" and wrote the words, "God cares." God had spoken through nature, through a plant with a blue flower.

III. *God Speaks Through Conscience.* The inner voice, the conscience, does speak. It speaks according to the individual's standard of right and wrong. If the voice of the conscience is ignored the individual is left without a guide. If the voice of conscience is ignored the Christian will be unable to tell the difference between right and wrong.

Let each one of us read God's word, pray, worship, witness, and work that our conscience might guide us aright!

IV. *God Speaks Through Human Instrumentality.* There is no way in which God speaks to us more convincingly than through the lives of others. How often have we heard others say, "I am a Christian because I saw Christ in you." No wonder the Bible says, "he that winneth souls is wise" (Prov. 11:30). When we witness God speaks through us to others. Paul said: "Ye are our epistle written in our hearts, known and read of all men" (2 Cor. 3:2).

Yes, God speaks through you. You are His human instrument.

V. *God Speaks Through the Bible.* The Bible is the written record of the revelation of God to man. The Bible is God's Word for today, this generation, and for all time. The Bible testifies: "All scripture is given by inspiration of God, and is profitable for doctrine, for reproof, for correction, for instruction in righteousness: That the man of God may be perfect, throughly furnished unto all good works" (2 Tim. 3:15-17).

A young man who had lost his arm in battle was frightened, depressed and disturbed as he began his voyage home. He wondered if he could face his family, face the world, make a living, and be a real man without his right arm. On the verge of panic he opened his Bible and his eyes fell on the words: "If God be for us, who can be against us?" (Rom. 8:31). As he read these words he became aware that God had spoken. He had the divine answer, the answer from heaven. He came home to meet life victoriously and successfully. God had spoken to him through His Word.

VI. *God Speaks Through Prayer.* I once asked my pastor's wife, Mrs. J. D. Grey, concerning her favorite verse in the Bible. Her answer was: "Call upon me, and I will answer thee, and shew thee great and mighty things, which thou knowest not" (Jer. 33:3). Surely this verse contains one of the greatest invitations in the Bible. Jesus said: "Ask, and it shall be given you; seek, and ye shall find; knock, and it shall be opened unto you" (Matt. 7:7). Let the person who desires to hear God speak go to Him in prayer.

Prayer is the means by which God reveals Himself to the individual soul. Spend much time in prayer if you desire to hear the voice of God.

VII. *God Speaks Through His Son Jesus Christ.* The Bible teaches that "God, who at sundry times and in divers manners spoke in time past unto the fathers by the prophets, Hath in these last days spoken to us by his Son" (Heb. 1:1, 2).

Jesus Christ is the apex of God's revelation to man. Jesus Christ is the final revelation of God to man. Jesus Christ is the only adequate revelation of God to man.

A. God speaks through His Son's character.

B. God speaks through His Son's sacrifice.

C. God speaks through His Son's love.

Conclusion. Have you heard God speaking to you? He speaks through history, nature, conscience, human instrumentality, the Bible, prayer, and Jesus Christ His Son. Surrender to Him and follow His voice as He speaks!

WEDNESDAY EVENING, SEPTEMBER 25

TITLE: "The Bible Speaks to Our Condition"

SCRIPTURE READING: Matthew 5.

Introduction. The great chapter from the New Testament which we examine today is the first portion of that section of the Scripture which we know as the Sermon on the Mount. Actually, it is the beginning of the lecture of heaven's infallible teacher. Our Lord was not preaching as such but rather He was teaching (Matt. 5:2; 7:29). In this great chapter our Lord describes the ideal citizen of the kingdom of God with respect to his inner spiritual attitude, his influence, and his superlative conduct.

I. *The Inner Spiritual Attitude of the Ideal Citizen of the Kingdom of God* (5:1-12). In these beatitudes our Lord is giving a portrait of the inner spiritual attitude of an ideal citizen of the kingdom of God. There is a progression from one

beatitude to the other. There is a proper sequence in these beatitudes. The great Christian life grows out of an awareness of spiritual poverty which leads to genuine grief because of sin and the lack of that which would be commendable in the sight of God. These attitudes lead to a spirit of meekness, open-heartedness, a spirit of being teachable and open to the will of God. The meek person is one who hungers and thirsts with a deep intensity to be right with God and to be right with one's fellow man. This ideal citizen is merciful in his relationships toward others and he has an undivided loyalty of heart to his Savior. He becomes a peacemaker. His life is such that it aids others in entering into a peaceful relationship with God and in a condition of peace one with another.

Often the influence of this kind of a person upon those who are adverse to the Gospel will provoke persecution. Our Lord congratulates those who experience this persecution for righteousness and assures them that great is their reward in heaven.

II. *The influence of the Ideal Citizen of the Kingdom of God* (5:13-16). Jesus declares that ideal citizens of the kingdom of God will serve as salt which purifies and preserves from decay and deterioration. They will also serve as light which illuminates and purifies and makes life possible.

Each of us should examine the quality of our commitment to Christ to see if we are serving as the salt of the earth and the light of the world.

III. *The Superior Conduct of the Ideal Citizen of the Kingdom of God.* The ideal citizen of the kingdom of God will seek to fulfill the law by living a life in both mind and spirit that exceeds the legal requirements of the law of the Old Testament. A number of illustrations are used to show the inward nature of the righteousness of the ideal citizen of the kingdom of God as compared with those who sought righteousness by keeping the law of Moses.

A. The actions flowing from the righteous character of the ideal Christian are such as make for universal peace (5:21-26). The true follower of Christ will refrain from disagreeable attitudes which create discord among brethren.

B. The new man in Christ will seek to be characterized by a perfect purity of mind and spirit (5:27-32). He will seek to avoid the thoughts that endanger the sacred relationship of husband and wife. He will banish lust from his mind and from his heart.

C. The speech of the Christian, which is an index to his character, will be absolutely truthful (5:33-37). The follower of Jesus Christ will make no provisions for dishonesty and untruthfulness in his speech.

D. The ideal citizens of the kingdom are those who repudiate the right to retaliate (5:39-42). They refuse to live by the law of the jungle. They choose to live by the law of love. They refrain from returning insult for insult.

E. The ideal citizen will practice universal love toward all men and thus give evidence of his relationship to his heavenly Father (5:43-48).

Conclusion. Our Lord would seek to speak to us through this great chapter in His Word. May the Lord bless us and help us as we seek to listen and follow Him.

SUNDAY MORNING, SEPTEMBER 29

TITLE: "The Relevance of the Kingdom"

TEXT: "Jesus said unto them, Have ye understood all these things?" (Matt. 13:51).

SCRIPTURE READING: Matthew 13:51, 52; 9:14-17.

HYMNS: "Love Divine, All Loves Excelling," Wesley. "May God Depend on You?" Martin.

"O Jesus, I Have Promised," Bode.

Introduction. In these five messages we have used the parables recorded or spoken on one day by Jesus as He sat in a boat by the sea side. The parables have all related to the kingdom of God. To the final parable spoken that day, the Parable of the Householder, we add three similar parables spoken earlier, namely, the Parable of the Children of the Bridechamber, the New Patch on an Old Garment, and the New Wine in Old Wineskins. All of these parables bear on the theme of "The Relevance of the Kingdom."

I. *The Parable of the Householder* (Matt. 13:51, 52). After speaking the parables publicly, Jesus explained them to His disciples privately in the house. Happily, some of these explanations have been recorded. The disciples affirmed that they understood what He had been teaching. A scribe was one who copied the Scriptures. The scribes became familiar with the text. It was a natural step that they should become interpreters and teachers. A "scribe which is instructed unto the kingdom of heaven" would be a scribe or teacher who had become a disciple of Jesus. He now has more to teach than Moses and the Old Scriptures. He has the new insights which Jesus has added. He "is like unto a man that is a householder, which bringeth forth out of his treasure things new and old." The work of a householder is illustrated in the Parable of the Tares. He had the responsibility for the operation of the farm. Old methods which had value would be retained. He must be open to accept new methods which were profitable. The scribe of Moses who now becomes a scribe of the kingdom of God will find much in Moses to retain but he will also adopt the fuller revelation in Jesus Christ.

The disciples of the old continually question the disciples of Jesus and Jesus Himself. "Why do thy disciples transgress the tradition of the elders? for they wash not their hands when they eat bread" (Matt. 15:2). Repeatedly they accused Jesus of not keeping the sabbath day. It was probably at the feast which Matthew had given so that his friends might meet Jesus on a Jewish fast day on which John's disicples and the Pharisees were fasting that the disciples of John came to Jesus saying, "Why do we and the Pharisees fast oft, but thy disciples fast not" (Matt. 9:14)? Really the question is, "Why do Christians not observe the requirement and traditions of Judaism?"

II. *Jesus Replied in Parables to This Challenge* (Matt. 9:15-17).

A. Parable of the Children of the Bridechamber (Matt. 9:15).

Children of the Bridechamber is a term which means the wedding party. A wedding is a time for joy. Fasting is a sign of sorrow. It would be most inappropriate for the wedding party to fast while the bridegroom is with them.

1. The kingdom of God is joy like a wedding. The Gospel is good news. "These things have I spoken unto you, that my joy might remain in you, and that your joy might be full" (John 15:11). "But whosoever drinketh of the water that I shall give him shall never thirst; but the water that I shall give him shall be in him a well of water springing up into everlasting life" (John 4:14). "Looking unto Jesus the author and finisher of our faith; who for the joy that was set before him endured the cross, despising the shame, and is set down at the right hand of the throne of God" (Heb. 12:2). "Likewise, I say unto you, there is joy in the presence of the angels of God over one sinner that repenteth" (Luke 15:10).

2. Fasting is a sign of sadness. It is not appropriate for one in the joy of right relationship with God. Jesus does foretell His death by indicating that the days will come when the bridegroom will be taken away. Fasting would then be appropriate.

Under the Mosaic law only the Day of Atonement was designated as a fast day. The Pharisees had multiplied the fast days. They thought that fasting was meritorious. In the parable, the Pharisee congratulates himself by saying, "I fast twice in the week" (Luke 18:12). Fasting—nor any other ceremony—has any merit per se. Usually, fasting is as out of place for a Christian as it would be at a wedding.

B. Twin Parables Illustrate the Relation of the New to the Old.

1. The Parable of the New Patch on an Old Garment (Matt. 8:1). Most clothes in Jesus' day were made of wool. Wool when first wet shrinks tremendously. It would be most foolish to sew a piece of wool cloth which had not been shrunk on an old garment which was fully shrunk. The patch would shrink and the tear in the garment would be worse than before. Christianity is not a patch on Judaism; it is not a sect of Judaism. This was the issue in the Jerusalem Conference. With reference to the Gentiles "there rose up certain of the sect of the Pharisees which believed, saying, That it was needful to circumcise them, and to command them to keep the law of Moses" (Acts 15:5). Paul and the apostles recognized that this was contrary to the Gospel which teaches that all men whether Jew or Gentile become Christian by faith in Jesus Christ. How wonderful that Paul won a victory for salvation by grace through faith for every man to come directly to God. No one must become a Jew before he becomes a Christian.

2. The Parable of New Wine in Old Wineskins (Matt. 9:17). One not knowing the customs of the day might be misled by the bottles of the common version to think of glass bottles. The reference, of course, is to containers for the wine made from the skins of goats or kids. After a time the skins became hardened and more likely to crack. If the new vintage was put in an old wine skin, the skin would probably

burst when the juice began to ferment. New wine is to be put in new wineskins.

The new Gospel of the kingdom of God is powerful like fermenting wine. The old Judaic wineskins could not hold it. The new Gospel must have new forms. No more are there animal sacrifices. "Behold the Lamb of God, which taketh away the sin of the world" (John 1:29). There is no more need for the observance of the Passover. "For even Christ our passover is sacrificed for us" (1 Cor. 5:7). There is no longer need of temple or holy place. Worship of God according to Jesus is not restricted to special places. "Jesus saith unto her, Woman, believe me, the hour cometh, when ye shall neither in this mountain, nor yet at Jerusalem, worship the Father. Ye worship ye know not what: we know what we worship: for salvation is of the Jews. But the hour cometh, and now is, when the true worshippers shall worship the Father in spirit and in truth: for the Father seeketh such to worship him. God is a Spirit: and they that worship him must worship him in spirit and truth" (John 4:21-24). The distinctions of ceremonially clean or unclean of persons, foods, and vessels is completely gone. (See Matt. 15:1-20.) The distinction between priest and laity is no more. Jesus is the High Priest. He invites every man to be his own priest and to come unto God by him. "The veil of the temple was rent in twain from the top to the bottom" (Matt. 27:51). Jesus has opened the way for every man to come to God.

Conclusion. The Old Covenant has been fulfilled in the New Covenant. The Old Testament as authority has passed away by fulfillment in Jesus. In a wonderful passage, Matthew 5:17-20, Jesus said that "one jot or one tittle shall in no wise pass from the law, till all be fulfilled" (v. 18). He did not say, as some erroneously interpret, that nothing would pass away. He said that nothing would fail to be fulfilled in Him. In the illustrations which follow in Matthew 5:21-48, Jesus makes it clear that nothing of permanent value in the old is lost but all is carried to a higher plane by fulfillment in Him. A bud is fulfilled by becoming a rose. A baby is fulfilled by becoming an adult. Is the bud lost? Is the baby lost? Yes, if you mean they are no more. No, in the sense that they have fulfilled their intended purpose. This has the most important practical bearing. The Old Testament is valuable. It is the history of God's progressive revelation. It contains the prophesies which were fulfilled in Jesus. It has many great insights which abide, but it is an old wineskin, it is an old garment, it is as out of place for the expression of Christian experience as fasting at a wedding. It was good; Christ is better. The final answer to any great question is to be found in Jesus. "All power is given unto me in heaven and in earth" (Matt. 28:18). "For Christ is the end of the law for righteousness to every one that believeth" (Rom. 10:4). "This is my beloved Son, in whom I am well pleased; hear ye him" (Matt. 17:5).

TITLE: "God's Faithful Few"

TEXT: "And the LORD said unto Gideon, By the three hundred men that lapped will I save you, and deliver the Midianites into thine hand; and let all the other people go every man unto his place" (Judg. 7:7).

SCRIPTURE READING: Judges 7: 1-23).

Introduction. For seven long years Israel was troubled by the Midianites who came to destroy the increase of the fields. We read, "And Israel was greatly impoverished because of the Midianites" (Judg. 6:6). So afraid and so impoverished were they that they lived in dens, caves and strongholds (6:2). Why this trouble for seven years? We read, "And the children of Israel did evil in the sight of the LORD; and the LORD delivered them into the hand of Midian seven years" (6:1).

In their anguish they cried to the Lord and He heard their cry. Gideon was called to lead Israel out of their pitiful plight. He issued a call for men and 32,000 responded. God told Gideon that 32,000 were too many because Israel would vaunt themselves against God and claim the victory by their own hand. All of the fearful in the army were told to return home and 22,000 turned back (7:3). The Lord said 10,000 were too many for the army of the Midianites which numbered 120,000 (8: 10). "And the LORD said unto Gideon, The people are yet too many; bring them down unto the water, and I will try them for thee there" (7:4). The sifting of the Lord took place and only 300 were left of the ten thousand. Think of it, a band of 300 men left to fight 120,000 men.

It is always God's faithful few who get the Lord's work done. Seldom do the masses of people serve Him. Let us look further at Gideon and his 300 men, God's faithful few.

I. *God's Faithful Few Are Endowed With Great Assets.*

A. God's faithful few are endowed with a call from the Lord. "And the angel of the Lord appeared unto him, and said unto him, The Lord is with thee, thou mighty man of valor" (6:12). "And the LORD said unto Gideon, By the three hundred men that lapped will I save you, and deliver the Midianites into thine hand" (7:7). No one will do much in this world until he hears the voice of the Lord speaking to him. Our service will be in proportion to our hearing the voice of the Lord.

B. God's faithful few are endowed with faithfulness. The beautiful verse reads, "And they stood every man in his place round about the camp" (7:21). Ponder the results today if every Christian stood in his place. The crying need of the hour is faithfulness. Only those who trust implicitly stand steady and ready.

C. God's faithful few are endowed with confidence in the Lord's help (7:15). It is evident that Gideon felt inadequate for the task the angel of the Lord had assigned to him. He said: "Oh my Lord, wherewith shall I save Israel? behold, my family is poor in Manasseh, and I am the least in my father's house" (6:15). Gideon asked the Lord to show him a sign or two. This the Lord did and he became convinced

273

that the Lord would help him in routing the Midianites.

D. God's faithful few are endowed with humility (6:15).

F. God's faithful few are endowed with obedience (7:17, 18). They were told to follow Gideon's example and they did.

F. God's faithful few are endowed with togetherness and unity. They were as one man with one sword. This is the way to victory. It was so in the day of Gideon and it is so today.

II. *God's Faithful Few Render Great Service.*

A. God's faithful few render great service by undertaking the impossible. Whoever heard of a band of 300 men taking on an army of 120,000? Gideon and the three hundred believed in undertaking the impossible. Some Christians would be shocked and surprised if anything out of the ordinary ever happened to them. They never take on the impossible task for their Lord. These are usually corrupt and spiritually bankrupt.

B. God's faithful few render great service by holding fast to their convictions. Many people hold opinions but few hold fast to their convictions. We are not held by opinions but by convictions. There were only 300 men but "they stood every man in his place" (7:21).

C. God's faithful few render great service by holding the trust committed to them. The task as-

signed Gideon and his 300 men must be performed. The trust in them must not be violated, must not be profaned.

D. God's faithful few render great service by showing us it can be done. Too often the faithless and unbelieving say, "You are asking too much; it can't be done." But the faithful few teach us it can be done.

III. *God's Faithful Few Teach Marvelous Lessons.*

A. God's faithful few teach us that the Lord is active in human history. For seven long years Israel cowed before the Midianites. For seven long years Israel hid in caves, dens, and strongholds. For seven long years their possessions, their food, and their land had been taken over by the Midianites. For seven long years it appeared as if the Lord were dead. But He was not dead. He was at work in answering prayer, in Gideon and 300 men. God is active in human history. History is His-story!

B. God's faithful few teach us that success is not dependent on numbers. Would it be 32,000 or 10,000? No, it would be 300! We do not need to be anxious about counting heads when we are sure we are in God's will and busy about His work! We don't need to count numbers but need to learn how to make numbers count. God's people need not fear being in the minority. God is not dependent on numbers, neither is success!

C. God's faithful few teach us that it is moral influence that counts for Him in this world (8:33-35). It is a tragedy when men turn away from God, His will, His way, His work.

D. God's faithful few teach us that He will use us when we are dedicated to Him. He used Gideon. He used the 300. He didn't use the 31,700. Why? Wasn't it because they were fearful, careless, indifferent and selfish? Wasn't it because they were not dedicated?

Conclusion. Are you one of the faithful few the Lord is using today? How do you classify yourself? Will you become one of the faithful few and let Him accomplish His work through you?

SUGGESTED PREACHING PROGRAM FOR THE MONTH OF OCTOBER

Sunday Mornings

The suggested theme for the morning messages is, "The Great Claims of Our Lord." John's gospel records a number of claims by our Lord in which he used various metaphors to describe his mission and ministry. These messages have an evangelistic objective and they can also encourage the saints.

Sunday Evenings

A series of eight messages based on the Book of Joshua is suggested. The suggested theme is "The Walk and Work of Faith."

Wednesday Evenings

Continuing with the theme, "The Bible Speaks to Our Condition," certain great chapters of the New Testament are used for the mid-week services. The theme verse for the month is, "He that hath an ear, let him hear what the Spirit saith unto the churches" (Rev. 2:29).

WEDNESDAY EVENING, OCTOBER 2

TITLE: "The Bible Speaks to Our Condition"

SCRIPTURE READING: Matthew 6.

Introduction. In this Sermon on the Mount, this lecture by heaven's infallible teacher, we find Him contrasting the righteousness of the ideal citizen of the kingdom of God with the righteousness of the law and with the righteousness of the Scribes and Pharisees.

Each of us needs to sit at the feet of Jesus and listen to these words that fell from His lips. God would speak to our condition today if we will but open our mind and our heart to Him who spoke as man had never spoken before—or since.

I. *The Motive for Kingdom Righteousness* (6:1-18). To Jesus the motive for the righteous conduct of a kingdom citizen was of primary importance. Without the proper motive there could not be proper conduct. In the illustrations which follow, our Lord is contrasting the desire for the approval of God with the desire for the approval of men

275

as a basis for motivation in religious service.

It is important that we examine our motives. Whose approval are we seeking? Where do we get our deepest satisfaction? Are we seeking to please God or are we seeking to please men?

A. True piety and righteousness toward others—alms giving (6:2-4). Some give merely in order to receive the applause of men. If we would be properly motivated, we must give in order to please God and minister to the needs of others. The desire for the approval of men is not a worthy motive for a citizen of the kingdom of heaven as he practices generosity and philanthropy toward the needy.

B. True piety and righteousness toward God—prayer (6:5-15). In these verses our Lord gives authoritative teaching concerning the art of effective praying. The primary thought behind it all concerns the motive that we have when we go into the presence of God in prayer. Jesus is declaring that one can be so deceived as to be motivated by the desire for the approval of men even when he bows to offer his petitions to God. If prayer is to be genuine, it must be a conversation between a needy child to the heavenly Father rather than a speech to be made for the ears and for the applause of men.

C. True piety or righteousness toward self—fasting (6:14-18). In man's personal, private discipline designed to produce genuine piety, he must beware lest he put on a show. Do you read the Bible day by day in order to be able to report to others that you have read all the

way through the Bible? Do you pray in order that you might have the reputation of a person who prays much? Jesus affirmed that the genuine disciple would make no public display of his personal piety with a desire to receive the applause of men. He would encourage us to seek supremely the approval of our heavenly Father. Our motives are of supreme importance.

II. *The Kingdom Attitude Toward Things.* The ideal citizen of the kingdom must be rightly related to the world in which he lives. The Christian is faced with two problems in the light of material things. He is tempted to trust in them or to worry about them. His trust must be in God rather than in material things.

A. Jesus issued a warning against faith in material values (6:19-24). Our Lord sounds some serious warnings against trusting in material things, for material things are perishable and do not have permanent value. They have temporary significance only.

Jesus taught that earthly treasures will master a Christian if he does not master things first. They will master his desires and his affections. If he majors on materialistic values, they will destroy his ability to tell right from wrong so that he cannot trust his conscience. Earthly treasure will master one's will and make a slave out of a man if he gives them primary priority in his life.

B. Jesus encouraged us to trust implicitly in the heavenly Father (6:25-34).

The only genuine alternative to the agony of anxiety is for one to have an implicit faith in the generosity and benevolent faithfulness of the heavenly Father. In these verses our Lord has much to say about the foolishness of a life of worry.

1. Worries are pagan (6:24).

2. Worries are secondary and unworthy (6:25).

3. Worries are useless (6:27).

4. Worries are pagan (6:32).

5. Worries are injurious (6:34).

Conclusion. Instead of living a life of worry, our Lord makes three positive suggestions that can help us overcome the agony of anxiety.

A. He suggests that we evaluate ourselves (6:26). We need to listen to a sermon from the sparrows and to take a lesson from the lilies.

B. He suggests that each of us accept ourselves (6:27). This will relieve a lot of pressure and a lot of anxiety.

C. Jesus suggests that we dedicate ourselves supremely to the kingdom (6:33). This will take our mind and heart off the cares that distress and disturb and that upset. It will give us a proper scale of values and a proper set of priorities for life.

May the Lord give to us hearing ears as we seek to listen to these words from our living Lord.

SUNDAY MORNING, OCTOBER 6

TITLE: "I Am That Bread of Life"

TEXT: "I am that bread of life" (John 6:48).

SCRIPTURE READING: John 6: 5-13, 26, 27, 48-58.

HYMNS: "Guide Me, O Thou Great Jehovah," Williams. "The Lord Is My Shepherd," Montgomery. "He Leadeth Me!" Gilmore.

OFFERTORY PRAYER:

Heavenly Father, from Thy bountiful hand many blessings have come. We thank Thee for life. We are grateful for forgiveness. We rejoice in the opportunity to serve. Thou hast bestowed upon us the privilege of labor and, today, as

an act of worship, we would bring unto Thee the fruit of our toil. Bless these tithes and offerings for a ministry of mercy to the suffering and a ministry of redemption of the lost through Jesus Christ. Amen.

Introduction. Modern psychologists are emphasizing the importance of the person's self-image. It is extremely important what people think of themselves. It may well mean the difference between success and suicide. It is never true humility to have a low self-image, nor is it always arrogance to think well of oneself. Jesus was the ultimate pattern of humility. Yet, He made extravagant claims for Himself. He even claimed to be God in the flesh.

Our message is the first of four based on the self-applied metaphors of Jesus as recorded in John's gospel. A metaphor is a figure of speech denoting literally one thing yet meaning another. We say he is a ball of fire, or she is a cyclone, or he is a wolf. These are metaphors.

Jesus said, "I am . . . bread."

I. *The Need of the Bread* (v. 5). There was no question but that hungry people needed bread. Early in the Bible God said to Adam, "In the sweat of thy face shalt thou eat bread, till thou return unto the ground; for out of it wast thou taken; for dust thou art, and unto dust shalt thou return" (Gen. 3:19). Since then men have needed bread. It is the staff of life. Nothing takes the place of bread.

There is the same basic necessity for the soul. Man is made with a spiritual appetite. He has a built-in hunger of spirit. One scholar has reported that three things have been possessed by every civilization: jails, temples and cemeteries. He observed that this is because all people sin, worship and die. That every civilization has had its temples is evidence of the basic need of men for spiritual bread. It is said that man is incurably religious; this is debatable. But because he is made in the image of God, there is a soul-hunger for bread.

II. *The Identity of the Bread* (v. 48). To people who were informed about temporal bread and who had eaten personal bread, Jesus declared. I am the real bread. He does not just give it. He *is* it. There is a loaf-shaped vacancy in every heart until Jesus comes in to fill it. Jesus attributes to Himself as bread five unique qualities.

A. He has a unique origin (vv. 33, 41, 50). He is the bread which "cometh down from heaven." He came from no earthly oven. He was no ordinary man. His origin was not earthly but heavenly. He was divine. The passover bread had spiritual significance but was earthly in origin. The loaves which our Lord blessed just before this discourse were earthly. They were multiplied by divine miracle but they were originated with men. They came *out* from a boy's lunch basket and not *down* from heaven. Jesus was and is the "bread of heaven."

B. He is living bread (v. 51). He is no packaged loaf. No inert ingredients lie stored in Him awaiting the temporary fancies of men. Moving, speaking, healing, teaching, He lives forever.

C. He is available bread (v. 51b). "If *any* man eat of this bread, he shall live for ever." Any man can afford Jesus, but no man can afford not to have Him. The invitation to eat is "whosoever will let him come." God's prophet asked, "Wherefore do ye spend money for that which is not bread? and your labour for that which satisfieth not? hearken diligently unto me, and eat ye that which is good, and let your soul delight itself in fatness" (Isa. 55:2). This is the operational basis of all missions. This is the optimism of our evangelism. This colors all our theology because our God is "God our Saviour; who will have all men to be saved, and come unto the knowledge of the truth" (1 Tim. 2:3b, 4). As long as there is one person on the earth who has not come to a knowledge of Jesus there is an urgent task for those of us who do know Him.

D. He is preserving bread (v.

51b). "If any man eat of this bread, he shall live for ever." Temporal bread has temporal limits but eternal bread has no limitation except eternity. The fathers ate, even the manna in the wilderness, yet they died. The real bread has a future. Because He lasts forever and comes into us, we last forever. Because He *is* life everlasting, we *have* life everlasting. This does not mean that we "get saved" and forget it. Daily replenishment of our lives is a part of His eternal nature.

E. He is expendable bread (v. 51c). "And the bread that I will give is my flesh, which I will give for the life of the world." As earthly bread does not exist for itself, so Christ does not exist for Himself. Earthly bread is taken, it loses its identity, is transformed into life itself when received and eaten. It is so with heavenly bread. Jesus gave Himself. He was and is expendable.

F. Bread is rejected (v. 66). "From that time many of his disciples went back, and walked no more with him" (John 6:66). In our Lord's parable of the great supper there were many who rejected the feast although the table was spread. The rich young ruler went away from Jesus a pauper because this bread of life was refused. It is unthinkable that a drowning man would refuse rescue or a dying man would refuse medical help. Yet starving men refuse the "bread of heaven."

"You can lead a horse to water, but you cannot make him drink." You can lead hungry men to the Bread of heaven but you cannot make them eat. As the final refusal of earthly food means physical sui-cide, so the refusal of Jesus means suicide of the soul.

III. *The Comparison of the Bread.*

A. Similarities.

1. Both the bread "in the wilderness" and the true Bread came down from heaven. Each was an act of God.

2. Both the breads were and are for personal consumption. One man does not eat bread for another. It is not done by proxy. Each must partake for himself.

3. Both were miracles. The manna of the wilderness was a miracle of God (Exod. 16:11-21). The virgin birth of Jesus was a miracle of God (Luke 1:28-56).

B. Contrasts.

1. The bread given in the wilderness was for the physical body. The true Bread is given for the spiritual body of man.

2. The bread given in the wilderness sustained life temporarily. The true Bread sustains life everlastingly.

3. The bread given in the wilderness was temporary. The true Bread is permanent.

Conclusion. The testimony of millions is that Jesus satisfies. The promises of the Scriptures assure us that Jesus is the Bread of life. Therefore, if we have never received Him, "O taste and see that the LORD is good: blessed is the man that trusteth in him" (Ps. 34:8).

If we have tasted and seen that

He is good, let us share Him with those about us who hunger for spiritual bread that satisfies.

"Blessed are they which do hunger and thirst after righteousness: for they shall be filled" (Matt. 5:6).

SUNDAY EVENING, OCTOBER 6

TITLE: "Conquesting by Faith"

TEXT: ". . . arise, go over this Jordan, . . . you and all this people, into the land which I am giving to them, to the people of Israel. Every place that the sole of your foot will tread upon I have given to you, as I promised to Moses" (Josh. 1:2, 3, RSV).

SCRIPTURE READING: Joshua 1: 1-9.

Introduction. One of the most encouraging books of the Old Testament is the Book of Joshua. Many Christians need this type of encouragement. All of us need to know the power of faith; so that we can be "more than conquerors." God's Word says that "this is the victory that overcomes the world, our faith" (1 John 5:4). We need to know that we can conquer the challenges of the day by faith.

The historical lesson from Joshua is that it is a beautiful illustration of the power of faith, of God's wonderful way of working, and that He does honor faith in His Word.

The living lesson is that Joshua teaches us the key to victorious living in Christ. The principles that Joshua lived by, and by which he was successful and victorious, are the same principles we may live by to be victorious in Christ. The key principle is faith.

Who was Joshua? He was the man whom God used to realize His promise to His people regarding the land of Canaan. He was born as a slave in Egypt, but who experienced the supernatural deliverance from Egypt, the crossing of the Red Sea.

During the second forty years of his life he was a minister to Moses, assisting, leading in battle, and observing the ways of the Lord.

Now he comes to the time of his appointment to the leadership of the people following Moses' death. In Moses was the anticipation of the Promised Land; in Joshua was the realization of it.

He was a man whose heart and life was prepared for this challenge. Numbers 27:18 says he was "a man in whom is the Spirit" (RSV). He was controlled by the Spirit of God. Numbers 32:10-12 says he was a man who wholly followed God in faith. He was victorious and obedient. Deuteronomy 34:9 says he was "full of the spirit of wisdom" (RSV). Joshua can teach us how to conquer by faith.

I. *Faith's Challenge* (Josh. 1:2). Verse 2 indicates it is a challenge from God to accept His Word and act upon it. It is Joshua's greatest challenge, to see what *God* will do! He had already seen God at work in other victorious experiences in Egypt, at the Red Sea, and against Amalek.

He already knew what man could not do. Numbers 13 and 14 record the Kadesh-barnea experience and the bitter consequences of unbelief. And just as Israel suffered these consequences, so does unbelief disqualify us from service and God's success. A life lived according to self is like Israel in the desert wandering for an entire generation. It is a picture of the carnal life of a Christian.

Now God challenges Joshua to go into the land and possess it. It is a challenge to experience the victory God had already given. It is God's commission to him. This is our challenge: to experience the victorious life in Jesus Christ and to experience spiritual conquest in obeying the Lord's commission to us following His Resurrection.

II. *Faith's Assurance* (Josh. 1:5, 9). God not only commands; He also assures fulfillment. His promises are ever ours to accept.

1. There is the promise of divine authority. All of God is behind His Word. God's "I will" is enough! As He commands us to service, so He obligates Himself to see us through (John 15:16; Phil. 1:6).

2. There is the promise of divine faithfulness. Verse 5 states God's promise of His abiding presence, "I will be with thee." This is not just for Joshua, because it is repeated elsewhere in the Bible, especially in Hebrews 13:5. This is God's eternal principle made real through the ministry of the Holy Spirit.

III. *Faith's Appropriation* (Josh. 1:3). As Joshua responded by faith, the promise would be fulfilled in every place that the sole of his foot would tread. Here is the principle of appropriation. He was to claim what God had already given. God promises to give the land, but the

people must possess it. God provides, faith takes. God waited for them to believe His Word and claim the land for themselves. It was legally theirs from the moment God uttered His promise; it was experimentally theirs when they entered the land to possess it.

All of God's provisions are waiting to be claimed today. After we have claimed salvation in Jesus Christ by faith, there are other vast spiritual possessions in Christ we are challenged to claim in faith. When we do, we are wonderfully rich; when we don't, many of the Lord's riches remain unclaimed.

IV. *Faith's Victory* (Josh. 1:5). In verse 2 Joshua is told to "go over this Jordan." In verse 5 he is assured that not any man would be able to stand before him—nothing could stop faith in action. Verse 10 records that Joshua accepts the challenge and moves out according to God's Word. Verse 16 describes the people's response in obedience to God's command through Joshua. Victory is assured in God's Word to Joshua. Something will happen! And the rest of the Book of Joshua tells that story.

V. *Faith's Secret* (Josh. 1:7, 8). Verses 7 and 8 teach that successful living is living by the principles of God's Word. It was God's purpose for Joshua that if he was to be a leader there must be spiritual discipline in his life through the Word of God. There was also to be absolute obedience—obedience to the Word of God, the source of our strength and courage. If we are to experience God's secret to life, we must get into God's Word and meditate upon it, allowing it to do its work in us.

Conclusion. How can you exercise faith today? You can accept God's challenge to you, whatever it is. You have some "land" to conquer. You can believe in Jesus Christ and receive Him as your Savior and Lord. You can believe God will never leave you, nor forsake you. You can believe God has an answer for your problem, your suffering, your circumstance. You can believe God's Word and begin today reading it, memorizing it and meditating upon it.

WEDNESDAY EVENING, OCTOBER 9

TITLE: "The Bible Speaks to Our Condition"

SCRIPTURE READING: Matthew 7.

Introduction. The great chapter from the New Testament through which we would let the Lord speak to us today is the concluding portion of the Sermon on the Mount. We see from the closing verses of this lecture from heaven's infallible teacher that His purpose for us is a life that is stable and satisfying. He was seeking to deliver us from the storms and stresses of life that would destroy and disappoint.

I. *A Warning Against Improper Judgments* (7:1-6). There are some who labor under the impression that our Lord forbade the use of our power to discriminate and to arrive at moral decisions. For Him to do so would have been to deny us the use of one of God's greatest gifts to man.

Our Lord was forbidding improper judgments, snap judgments, superficial judgments, unkind judgments, untrue judgments.

In these words He forbids our reaching a decision and pronouncing a verdict without considering all of the evidence. We must beware of and guard against the snap judgment that places someone else either in a very favorable or a very adverse light. He is suggesting that we treat others and judge others in the same manner and method by which we would want our own case to be considered.

The real focus of attention is upon self-judgment. We could be more critical of ourselves than of others.

II. *The Habit of Prayer Is Encouraged* (7:7-11). It is the habit of prayer that is encouraged. The nature of our loving Father God is the main basis upon which we should have faith in the efficacy of prayer. God is good. He always will be good.

III. *The Golden Rule* (7:12). To practice the Golden Rule is to bring a foretaste of heaven into the present.

IV. *Voluntary Self-Discipline Is Necessary* (7:13, 14). Our Lord believed that one must voluntarily discipline himself if he is to experience fullness of life. Our Lord points out that those who aimlessly drift live a life of mediocrity.

The broad way against which He warns is not so much the road that leads to a hell hereafter as it is the way that leads to a hell in the here and now.

To achieve significantly one must

choose the pathway of voluntary self-discipline and then follow that discipline. This leads to fullness of life in the chosen area of endeavor.

V. *A Warning Against False Teachers* (7:15-20). We must beware of false teachers who come to us claiming to speak authentically for God. We must beware lest we listen to the many different voices in the world that would lead us astray. Each one must do his own listening because each one does his own suffering if he follows a false way of life.

VI. *Profession Plus Practice* (7: 21-23). It takes something more than a pious profession to satisfy the heart of man. It takes something more than mere words to be pleasing to God. We can be sure of the genuineness of our profession only when it leads to a practice of the implications of our profession.

VII. *Life Built Upon a Rock* (7: 24-27). Are we building our life upon the shifting sands of time? Are we mere hearers of the Word? Is our religion merely the religion of our forefathers, or is it really real to us? Do we listen responsively to the words of the Lord Jesus, and do we recognize His Lordship? Only those who both hear and heed can be sure of a stable life when the storms begin to blow.

Conclusion. Jesus was an authoritative teacher. His authority grew out of His unique person, the absolute truthfulness of what He taught, and His purpose of love for us.

Today God wants to speak to our hearts through this portion of His Word. May we have ears to hear.

SUNDAY MORNING, OCTOBER 13

TITLE: "I am the Light of the World"

TEXT: "I am the light of the world" (John 8:12).

SCRIPTURE READING: John 1: 1-9; 8:12.

HYMNS: "The Light of the World Is Jesus," Bliss. "We've a Story to Tell," Nichol. "Rescue the Perishing," Crosby.

OFFERTORY PRAYER:

Our heavenly Father, through the testimony of others we have learned of Thy great love for us. We thank Thee for the gift of salvation. Gratitude compels us to desire to share the good news of Thy love with a lost world. Today we bring our tithes and offerings that the ministry of preaching and teaching and healing and ministering of Jesus Christ might be carried to all parts of the earth. Bless these tithes and offerings. To that purpose we pray in Jesus' name. Amen.

Introduction. Most of us have been taught that the sun is the center of our solar system and thus is the light of the world. The sun is 93,000,000 miles from the earth. If a baby should start flying to the sun when it is born and travel 150 miles per hour, he would be nearly 71 years of age when he arrived. Astronomers estimate the diameter of the sun is 109 times that of the earth. Its output of energy is 70,000 horsepower per square yard per minute. The temperature at its surface is about 10,000° F

But the light of the world is not the sun but the Son. Jesus declared Himself to be such. It was He who made the sun for He was co-existent with the Father in creation. With one bold stroke Jesus declared, "I am the light of the world." Though it is beyond our grasp, let us reach out by faith and try to apprehend some of our Lord's meaning in this self-addressed metaphor of the Master.

Know that,

I. *Light Is Repulsive.* Immediately before Jesus proclaimed He was the light of the world the scribes and Pharisees brought to Him a woman taken in the act of adultery and demanded of Him an opinion of her punishment in the light of Moses' law. Jesus stooped and wrote on the ground. Then He said to them, "He that is without sin among you, let him first cast a stone at her" (John 8:7). Then He wrote again and when he looked up the accusers had fled one by one until only the condemned woman was left. The truth was they did not like the light.

Turn over a log in the woods and the bugs will scurry everywhere, not because they fear you, but because light is repulsive.

Two chapters earlier Jesus had preached the crowd away. This is foreign and unwelcome truth for our day. We want crowd getters. We want to "pack 'em in," while Jesus frequently thinned them out.

The Gospel has always been a stumbling block. Paul declared "But we preach Christ crucified, unto the Jews a stumbling block, and unto the Greeks foolishness" (1 Cor. 1:23).

It was this very quality of the light our Lord so vividly described. "And this is the condemnation, that light is come into the world, and men loved darkness rather than light, because their deeds were evil. For every one that doeth evil hateth the light, neither cometh to the light, lest his deeds should be reproved" (John 3:19, 20).

And because light is repulsive,

II. *Light Is Rejected.* "He was in the world, and the world was made by him, and the world knew him not. He came unto his own, and his own received him not" (John 1:10, 11).

Can one easily think of a conscious dying man refusing a doctor? Can one readily imagine a starving man rejecting bread? Can one comprehend a drowning man refusing rescue, or a freezing man refusing a warm house, or a sinking ship spurning help?

Yet the Light was rejected. He still is by many.

Why?

A. There is the sinful nature of man.

B. There are the deeds of man who lives in darkness.

C. There is the ignorance of man who does not know the blessing of the true light.

D. There is the rule of the prince of darkness, even Satan, in the hearts of unregenerated men.

But woven into the fabric of all this divine truth is the fact that

III. *Light Is Revealing.*

A. The light reveals us to ourselves. We never see ourselves truly until we see ourselves in the context of Christ. In that light Thomas saw himself and cried out, "My Lord and my God" (John 20:28).

In that light the woman of Samaria saw herself and said, "Come, see a man, which told me all things that ever I did" (John 4:29a).

In that light the robber saw himself and asked, "Lord, remember me when thou comest into thy kingdom" (Luke 23:42).

B. The light reveals the identity of Christ to us. The woman at the well saw herself, but she also saw Jesus and identified Him, "Is not this the Christ?" (John 4:29b).

The two who walked the road to Emmaus recognized Him finally in the light of His own revelation.

The light shone and John so recognized Jesus that he declared without hesitation, "Behold the Lamb of God, which taketh away the sin of the world" (John 1:29).

C. The Light reveals the Father. Philip voiced the yearning of many a disciple when he requested, "Lord, shew us the Father" (John 14:8).

Beautifully and blessedly Jesus claimed His own deity when He testified, "He that hath seen me hath seen the Father ... Believe me that I am in the Father, and the Father in me ..." (John 14:9-11).

Clearly the light reveals the Father. Hear him say, "I and my Father are one" (John 10:30).

D. The light reveals the way of salvation. "He that followeth me shall not walk in darkness, but shall have the light of life" (John 8:12).

"I am the way, the truth and the life: no man cometh unto the Father, but by me" (John 14:6).

Never has so much light been thrown on any subject as when the Light of the world shone on His subjects, on Himself, on the Father and on the way of redemption.

IV. *Light Is Refining.* Wherever Jesus has come into the hearts of men there has been a refining, purifying, uplifting influence.

When He came into the demoniac, the evil spirits went out. When He came into the heart of Simon, holy refinement followed. As sunlight purifies, so the Sonlight of God purifies wherever He shines.

V. *The Light Is Regulating.* The ordinary traffic lights which we encounter daily are regulatory. We stop, we go, we use caution, we turn, we observe signs because of the lights. The lights of the airport guide the giant birds of metal through the night to safe landings.

In some comparable way the great Light of Jesus Christ regulates the traffic of life when He is permitted to do so. He tells us when to go, and when to stop. He flashes the warning signals. He guides us through our nights to safe landings.

There is a simple story of a man who drove his team and wagon swiftly and safely on a road through a dark forest. Afterward he was asked how he knew where all the trees were along the road so that he could miss them as he drove the narrow road. He replied that he did not know where they were but he knew where they were not. He added, "I looked up at the opening between the tree tops and knew that if I followed the light above I could be safe." Oh, that men might do so in their spiritual journey!

VI. *The Light Is Reassuring.* There is reassurance in the lights of the city as one comes home. There is comfort in seeing the light in the window of one's own house. The lights of the shore reassure one as the returning ship approaches the harbor. There is reassurance in the presence of the night light in the nursery.

It is so with our Light. We are coming to our heavenly home and the light is shining gloriously there for us. Oh, what reassurance!

Conclusion. The light of the world is Jesus. Let Him reveal yourself, Himself, the Father, and the way of life to you. Let us let Him and His presence refine us and make us pure. Let us permit Him to regulate every mile of the journey. Let us be reassured and encouraged that Christ shines forever for His own.

This Light is for every man. You can have Him. Will you not take Him and let Him shine for you and through you?

SUNDAY EVENING, OCTOBER 13

TITLE: "Crossing the Jordan"

TEXT: "And Joshua rose early in the morning; and they removed from Shittim, and came to Jordan, he and all the children of Israel, and lodged there before they passed over" (Josh. 3:1).

SCRIPTURE READING: Joshua 3.

Introduction. The Book of Joshua is important to everyone who will listen to it. Chapter 1 describes God's challenge to Joshua and His assurances to his faith. Chapter 2 describes the two spies who were sent out to search the land secretly and how God provided for their deliverance through Rahab. Their report is stated in Joshua 2:23 and 24.

Joshua believed that surely it was God's will to cross into the land to possess it, so he wasted no time. Verse 1 indicates that he rose early in the morning and got the nation to begin moving. He moved from Shittim and came to Jordan.

Between them and the land of abundance was the Jordan River.

Humanly speaking, to cross the Jordan was an impossibility. Verse 15 indicates it was a time of overflow; the river was flooding. There were no bridges and only a few fords, and these were impassable at this season. How could they cross with the women, children and baggage?

The historical fact is that the people did cross the flooding Jordan to enter the land. God had a plan and in His power He performed it. What was God's plan to follow? It is fully described step by step in chapter 3 how they were to move when the priests moved the Ark. The priests were to lead the way before the people, and when they came to the Jordan they were to stand still in it. What happened is described in verses 13 through 17.

Why was there such an urgency about this? Why was it necessary to go into the land at this precise time? Why not wait until the river was down and not flooding? There are several answers to these questions. For one thing, it was all God's timing and God's timing is always perfect and right. He specified exactly when it was to be done according to the Scripture. Another thing—it was God's opportunity to demonstrate His power as seen in verse 10. Also, it provided opportunity for faith to be exercised. This challenge helped to develop that quality. And a fourth answer is that it was God's way of magnifying Joshua, and this was very important to the people because Joshua was to be God's instrument for leadership. There are two truths to be shared from this experience.

I. *The Significance of Crossing the Jordan.* For Israel the significance of crossing the Jordan was a definite historical experience in which the people left the desert life to enter into the land of abundance. It was a victory miraculously and divinely given. It was also a step of faith in which God magnified Himself in His plan of conquering the land. It was the commitment of the people to go into the land, enter into the warfare to possess the land and to enjoy its benefits.

For us, "crossing the Jordan" is not symbolic of entering heaven; it is the symbol of the Christian entering into the abundant life God has promised in Jesus Christ. It is not passing into eternity; it illustrates the Christian's passing from one level of Christian experience to another level in the Lord.

Egypt in Israel's life was representative of sin and bondage. The deliverance from Egypt, miraculously, was representative of the salvation —the new birth and spiritual deliverance. The wilderness in the life of Israel was representative of the carnal life of Christians where self-centeredness, defeat, discouragement and unbelief reign. Canaan was representative of the triumph that the

people experienced. It had both conflict and rest, but it also had the abundant life that God had promised. Caanan was representative of the victorious Christian life.

Therefore, the Jordan River crossing is the gateway to the conquering life. It is the experience that leads to the possessing of our spiritual possessions in Christ Jesus. Ephesians 1:3 refers to all the spiritual blessings that we have in heavenly places in Christ. "The crossing" is that moment of victory when we make our lives available to God, to cause us to possess all that truly belongs to us in Jesus Christ. It is that point when self-life and its control ends and the Christ-life begins. It marks the separation between the carnal Christian and a Christ-controlled Christian.

II. *The Secret to Crossing the Jordan.* How are we to do it? For Israel the secret of crossing the Jordan was listening to God's Words and obeying them, as seen in verse 9. It was also by following in faith the Ark of the covenant. This required cleansed lives, as in verse 5, and confidence in God's promises and power, verses 5, 7, and 11.

The secret of it all was the Ark of God. There are ten references to the Ark in chapter 3. According to this chapter it was the key to the victory Israel had over the Jordan River. What was the Ark? It was the most outstanding piece of furniture in the Tabernacle. It represented the presence of God. It contained the two tables of stone on which the law was written by the finger of God, and it represented the awesome power, and holiness and presence of the living God. It resided in the Holy of Holies—God's continual dwelling place with men.

For us it also is a type of the person of the Lord Jesus Christ. On the Ark was a cover of gold called the mercy seat. This mercy seat represents Jesus Christ who was God's propitiation through His blood. Just as the Israelites were to focus their attention on the Ark, so are we to focus attention upon Christ. We are not to focus attention upon our frustrations, circumstances or surroundings, but we are to keep our eyes upon Jesus Christ.

The secret to crossing Jordan, the spiritual victory over the self-life into a Christ-controlled life, is related to three steps to victory. First, we must desire sincerely to be victorious. Joshua 1:16 indicates the people were willing and eager to enter into the land. How about you?

The second step is to confess our sins and be cleansed (cf. 1 John 1: 9). The sins of our lives must be confronted and God's cleansing experienced. The third step is to surrender by faith to Jesus Christ. Jesus Christ is God's plan of victory for us. As the Ark led them to victory, so does Jesus Christ lead us.

Conclusion. It is not God's will for any man to live in Egypt spiritually. He is not willing that any should perish. Neither is it God's will for any Christian to live in the wilderness spiritually, because of all that is related to it—ignorance, unbelief, sin and pride. It *is* God's will to enter into the land of Caanan spiritually, to cross over the Jordan, to experience the power of God in our lives and to make ourselves available to Him now.

WEDNESDAY EVENING, OCTOBER 16

TITLE: "The Bible Speaks to Our condition"

SCRIPTURE READING: Matthew 8.

Introduction. The great chapter through which we would seek to let God speak to us describes the diversity of the ministry of our Lord. He would come today into every type of a situation to minister in mercy and in power. Each of us needs to let Him work in us and through us.

I. *The Cleansing of a Leper* (8: 1-4). The lepers were the untouchables of that day. Everyone else, but especially the leper, was surprised when Jesus reached forth His hand and touched him. Immediately he was cleansed.

Jesus would come into the midst of our situation today and give to us the healing and cleansing touch of His grace and power if we will permit Him to do so.

II. *The Prayer of an Outsider* (8: 5-13). The centurion was no doubt a Gentile. He did not approach our Lord on the basis of his own faithfulness and his own moral merit. He approached our Lord on the basis of our Lord's compassion and power. He had faith to believe that Jesus had the authority to heal disease at a distance. It was not necessary that Jesus place His hand upon a person in order to impart healing. Our Lord was amazed at the greatness of the faith of this outsider.

Let us beware lest we put restrictions upon the disposition of our

288

God to hear and answer the prayers of those who have no relationship to Him except that which His grace permits.

May we be granted the gift of faith, and may we utilize a faith like unto that which the centurion demonstrated.

III. *The Healing of the Sick* (8:14-17). Our Lord was the great healer. He healed all kinds of sickness—of the mind, body and spirit. Let's invite Him to come in as the divine minister and healer in every possible illness today.

IV. *The Priorities of Life* (8:18-23). Our Lord recognized that many men live an unsatisfying life because they do not have the right priorities in their life. Jesus declared that if one would be a true follower of the will of God material things must not have the position of top priority. He also declared that the will of God must also have priority over the claims of family.

V. *What to Do in a Storm* (8:24-27). The storms of life are bound to come upon the life of each individual, each family, and every na-

tion. What will you do when the winds begin to blow and the waves begin to toss the ship of your life? The disciples turned to our Lord with a plea for help.

Even though their faith was feeble, He responded to their plea and commanded the winds to cease their blowing and the waves to cease their tossing.

When Christ is on board the vessel of your life, you will enjoy a degree of safety that is not to be found at any other place or time.

VI. *Do You Love Pigs More Than Men?* (8:28-34). This is a strange incident in the life of our Savior. It gives rise to many questions. It is interesting to note that seemingly the citizens of this city were more concerned about the pigs who had committed "hogicide" than they were for the welfare of the men out of whom the demons had been cast.

Which is more important, pigs or the lives of men in distress?

Conclusion. Surely we can hear the voice of God speaking to our condition through one of these incidents in the life of our Lord, "He that hath ears to hear, let him hear."

SUNDAY MORNING, OCTOBER 20

TITLE: "I Am the Door"

TEXT: "I am the door" (John 10:9).

SCRIPTURE READING: John 10: 1-10.

HYMNS: "Jesus! the Very Thought of Thee," Bernard of Clairvaux. "Saviour, More Than Life," Crosby. "Jesus Saves," Owens.

OFFERTORY PRAYER:
Holy Father, Thy Holy Spirit has come to dwell in our physical bodies to make us holy. Take now the substance of our hands and bless and use it for holy purposes. We pray this in the name of Jesus our Savior. Amen.

Introduction. This is the third metaphor which our Lord employs in His effort toward complete revelation of Himself to His disciples. Types, symbols and figures have always been used of God. But they have been frequently misused by men as they have cited these very figures to support their own pet theories and theological fabrications.

Let us be zealous to see all our Lord sought to reveal, but let us be careful that our zeal does not warp our judgment to the point that we shall read into this figure more than was intended. We may well squeeze all the juice from the fruit, but beyond that our pressure merely brings the flavor of the pith and cover.

I. *Pastorale.* The language of Jesus was more meaningful to the people of Palestine than it is to those who do not live in sheep country today. We are told that many flocks of sheep were brought to one sheepfold and enclosed for the night. Each of these flocks had its own shepherd. Each shepherd would bring his sheep in for the night, and call for them the next morning. Frequently there was one common keeper of all the flocks through the night. It was a preventive measure to guard the sheep against their many enemies.

II. *Pests.* There were the natural predators which were always after the sheep.

Then there were the thieves and robbers. Of these Jesus observed, "The thief cometh not, but for to steal, and to kill, and to destroy" (John 10:10a).

There were also those who came before Jesus; that is, those who claim spiritual priority above Jesus. We must remember that Jesus spoke to the Pharisees (John 9:40).

It has been suggested that these very Pharisees made the simple way of salvation so difficult that they were as those who would "climb up some other way." Jesus may have been saying to them that instead of using the Door, they preferred to use their own ecclesiastical ladders and their own religious inventions. This is likely an apt interpretation. If it is, then let it be observed that then as well as now, there are scarcely any pests as pestiferous as religious ones.

III. *Preeminence.* Jesus declared that He was *the* door.

The Ark had but one door. Dr. George Truett was fond of saying that the big elephant and the little ant both entered through the same door. He would then remind his congregation that the big business man and the small child must come into the kingdom through the same door.

This singularity, this exclusiveness, this monopoly—all of these were packed tersely into the statement of Jesus, "I am the way, the truth, and the life: no man cometh unto the Father, but by me" (John 14:6).

It was this same deep conviction that prompted Peter to declare, "Neither is there salvation in any other: for there is none other name under heaven given among men, whereby we must be saved" (Acts 4:12).

There is perhaps no more fatal heresy than the teaching that Jesus is an optional way of salvation.

He has the exclusive franchise on salvation.

IV. *Porter.* It does not appear to overlabor the figure to suggest that the porter is the Holy Spirit. It is He who makes the door available. It is He who points to the door. He is the divine usher who attends the door. Just as He opens the door He also closes the door. For those enclosed the Holy Spirit guarantees complete safety.

But there is a time when the final offense against the Holy Spirit so grieves Him that He closes the door. And without the doormanship of the Holy Spirit, none may enter for salvation and life.

V. *Promise.*

A. The promise is universal. "If any man" is the condition of the invitation.

B. The promise is sure. "He shall be saved" is the blessed assurance.

C. The promise is for liberty. "He shall go in and out" is the scope of freedom. As the use of earthly doors affords liberty and freedom in that which is beyond these doors, so the access to the divine door brings freedom indeed.

D. The promise is for sustenance. "He shall find pasture" is the guarantee. The Christian is not on cold storage. He is alive, moving, going and coming, always strengthened by the pasture.

VI. *Prescription.* The blessings of the door are suspended on one condition and that one condition is that one "enter in."

Doors are not primarily for decoration, although some are appealing. Their primary purpose is not to bear the name plates or the house numbers.

Doors are for entrance and exit.

Those who were saved from the Flood were those who "entered in" to the Ark. The six cities of refuge (Num. 35) afforded immunity and security to only those who would "enter in." Those who partook of the marriage feast were those who purposed to "enter in." This is the human side of salvation; it involves will, choice and action. We never satisfy our hunger by admiring bread: we eat it. We are not cured by examining and analyzing medicine: we take it.

So it is with the door. Unless we "enter in" it becomes but another wall.

Conclusion. Let us not be overcome by the spiritual pests that plague our way. Let us know, once and for all, that Jesus is the only door; that He is the entrance to salvation and the exit from many of life's perils.

We cannot afford to ignore the courteous, personal work of the Holy Spirit as He presides at the threshold of the door.

May we claim the promises and find salvation, freedom, and sustenance for our souls.

But let us act now!

SUNDAY EVENING, OCTOBER 20

TITLE: "The Triumph of Faith"

TEXT: "Now Jericho was straitly shut up because of the children of Israel: none went out, and none came in. And the LORD said unto Joshua, See, I have given into thine hand Jericho, and the king thereof, and the mighty men of valour" (Josh. 6:1, 2).

SCRIPTURE READING: Joshua 6.

Introduction. Why was Jericho so important? Jericho was the key city to Israel's whole campaign in the land of Canaan. Once that obstacle was removed the armies of Israel could spread out in all directions. Israel could not retreat. Behind them was the Jordan River overflowing its banks, the desert, the Red Sea and Egypt. They had committed themselves to God's Word. Now is the time to begin possessing the land. Jericho stands in the way of possessing what God had promised them and had potentially given them.

Jericho was a strong fortress about three miles in circumference. It was strategically located, guarding all the passes to the interior of Canaan.

The fall of Jericho is a literal fact of history. Joshua is the first book of history to record it as such and describes in details its conquests. Five hundred years later it was referred to when the city was rebuilt. And in New Testament times the fall of Jericho is referred to in the Book of Hebrews. Also, archeology confirms the fall of Jericho. Dr. John Garstang excavated the ruins of Jericho in the 1930s and found pottery and scarab evidence that the city had been destroyed about 1400 B.C., coinciding with Joshua's date. He also found that the walls did actually fall down flat (v. 20). There were double walls fifteen feet apart. The outer wall was six feet thick; the inner wall twelve feet thick. The walls were thirty feet high and were linked together by houses built across the top. The outer walls fell outward, down the hillside dragging the inner wall and houses with it. Verse 24 speaks of the city being burned with fire. Archeologists have concluded there were signs of conflagration and destruction that are very marked.

The fall of Jericho is not only a literal fact of history, it is also a living spiritual lesson. It is an illustration of the triumph of faith. Joshua does not say this pointedly but its evidence is discerned throughout the experience. Hebrews 11:30 definitely states that "by faith the walls of Jericho fell down."

All the forward progress and victories Israel experienced were victories God wrought by faith. Faith is a spiritual principle of life for us all. Faith is trusting God and His Word, relying upon His promises and truth. Romans 4:20, 21 reveals that Abraham's faith was the secret to his life and victories. The world does not understand faith, considering it foolish and illogical. It emphasizes human power in the power of the flesh. But faith rests in the power of God to fulfill His Word.

I. *Faith's Conflicts.* Jericho represents the opposition and conflict that Israel would face in possessing the land. God, however, promised life to them. In possessing the spiritual blessings God has given us we, too, confront spiritual conflicts. In the gospel of John Jesus indicates that the world does not hate its own, but that it does hate Jesus and His followers.

Verse 2 describes the victorious assurance that Israel had. Just as they experienced this assurance so do we have peace through Jesus Christ (John 14:27; 16:33). Faith accepts the reality of conflict and claims God's victory. Christians have conflict with the world, flesh and the devil—all of the invisible forces of the evil world—but Jesus Christ gives victory (Eph. 6).

II. *Faith's Obedience.* Victory over Jericho depended upon the obedience of Israel to God's command. God speaks and Joshua listens, believes, obeys and acts. Victory was dependent upon obedience to the plan of God (vv. 3-5). They were to march around the city each day for six days and seven times on the seventh day. There was to be no noise made except ram's horns. This was God's plan. He didn't tell why; they were merely to obey. Obedience is based on the faith that God is sufficient. It may sound foolish, but we are to trust God to fulfill His purpose.

Faith disciplines itself in the silence that the people experience. There was to be no complaining, no suggesting, no frivolous talk; there was to be utter silence. In other words, keep silent—let God work. Victory is experienced in letting God give us triumph in His way (John 15:5; Phil. 1:6; 4:13).

III. *Faith's Secret.* The key fact of the procession was the Ark of God, as it was when the people crossed the Jordan River victoriously. Eleven times is the Ark of God mentioned in Joshua 6. It means that God was with His people really and undeniably. The supernatural was with them. There is an obvious lack of the supernatural in many churches today. We need to see God at work today. We need Jerichos to challenge our faith, to put us on our knees, to give God an opportunity to demonstrate His power. We need fresh experiences of faith for "the new generation." The secret of faith is trusting Him. *He* is our victory.

IV. *Faith's Patience.* The Israelites were to circle the city thirteen times in seven days, and all during this time the walls of the city were stout and forbidding. God required that they wait on Him and demonstrate

patience in His willingness to work. Possibly He's teaching us some quality that needs to be developed in us; that we are helpless within ourselves, that victory is His. Can you keep on trusting when outward results are not happening? Victory may be just moments away. When it was all accomplished it was all God's victory. They were physically exhausted and what resulted was the working of God's power. Sometimes faith demands that we rest in the Lord and wait patiently for Him.

V. *Faith's Achievement.* This is symbolized in a shout of victory (vv. 16, 20). It came at the close of the last time around the city. During the last time no wall began to crumble, yet every step around the city was a step of the appropriation of faith. The city had to be circled thirteen times before the shout of victory was given. The shout was the outward expression of the people's inward faith in their omnipotent God. The walls were still intact immediately prior to the shout. There was a risk of everything upon God's faithfulness. Then it happened! The city was demolished, burned and cursed. Faith had achieved the victory.

Conclusion. How are we to see God's supernatural power unless we let Him give us a Jericho challenge? What is your Jericho in your spiritual life? Can you trust God to work today as then? God's will is for us to experience victory and power in our lives. Once we cross Jordan, yield ourselves to Him and His will and way, He will give us victory in all our spiritual conflicts, Jericho and spiritual life.

TITLE: "The Bible Speaks to Our Condition"

SCRIPTURE READING: Matthew 17.

Introduction. The great chapter through which we would let our Lord speak to our condition describes one of the truly great experiences in the life of our Lord.

I. *An Experience on a Mountain Top* (Matt. 17:1-8). It is interesting to note that our Lord felt the need to go apart for prayer and communion with God. It is also interesting that He took several intimate friends with Him for this experience of prayer and fellowship with God. It is significant that as He prayed there was an inward transformation that expressed itself in an outward transfiguration of His face.

In this prayer experience, Moses and Elijah came to communicate with Him, and I would assume, to encourage Him as He faced the ordeal of His exodus, His death upon the cross, His Resurrection from the dead, and His Ascension to the Father.

While on the mountain top His disciples heard a voice of identification and commendation from heaven. By this experience they came to a new recognition of His unique person and His divine authority.

It is possible today for us to have experiences with God that bring enlightenment and encouragement as we would walk toward the great crises of our life.

II. *The Suffering in the Valley* (17: 14-21). The tremendous experience on the mountain top was not designed to produce a mystical experience that would provide emotional satisfaction for the disciples. At the bottom of the mountain there is always a suffering, needy world that needs the ministry of those who have been on a mountain top with God.

It is most interesting to note how our Lord responded to the faltering faith of a fearful father as He prayed for a helpless son.

By this experience our Lord would encourage every distressed father and mother to bring their needy children before God's throne of grace for help and for mercy in a time of need.

III. *Jesus Speaks of His Approaching Death* (17:22, 23). The death of Christ upon the cross was no accident in the plan of God. Jesus lived and labored under the burden of calvary long before the cross was ever placed upon His shoulder. His love for us is an unmerited love. His love for us is a sacrifical love. His love for us is a suffering love. With a steadfast, unflinching dedication and determination He moved toward His cross.

Paul prayed that he might know "the fellowship of his sufferings." Most of us try to avoid this knowledge and this experience.

IV. *The Payment of Taxes* (17: 24-27). It is interesting to note that the conclusion of this great chapter, which has said so many significant things about the heart and the life of the Lord of life, would also speak concerning His paying the taxes that were expected from every good citizen of the country.

We have a responsibility toward our country which we fulfill only as we pay our portion of the taxes that are necessary for the functions of government.

Conclusion. May the God of grace and mercy enlarge our hearing capacity to hear what He would have us to hear as we study a great chapter like this.

SUNDAY MORNING, OCTOBER 27

TITLE: "I Am the Way"

TEXT: "I am the way" (John 14:6).

SCRIPTURE READING: John 14: 1-6.

HYMNS: "Joyful, Joyful, We Adore Thee," van Dyke. "Blessed Redeemer," Christiansen. "The Old Rugged Cross," Bennard.

OFFERTORY PRAYER:

Heavenly Father, Thou didst give Thy Son to die upon the cross for us. Thou hast given to us the Holy Spirit to dwell within our hearts. Thou hast given to us eternal life which causes us to hunger after Thee and to love Thee. Today we would give ourselves completely to Thee. Accept our tithes and offerings as tokens of our desire to belong completely to Thee, through Jesus Christ our Lord. Amen.

Introduction. This is another metaphor of the Master which He employed in an effort to communicate to those nearest Him. Webster has defined a metaphor as "the use of a word or phrase literally denoting one kind of object or idea in place of another by way of suggesting a likeness or analogy between them."

To those in darkness Jesus had affirmed—"I am the light."

To the hungry Jesus had declared—"I am the bread."

To the separated He had asserted—"I am the door."

Now, to those so uncertain of where He is going and where they are going He announces—"I am the way."

In the context of our Lord's announcement, let us observe

I. *An Evident Desperation.* "Lord, we know not whither thou goest; and how can we know the way?"

It was no ordinary hour for those about Jesus. The shadows of the cross came closer. The Last Supper had been observed with all its prophetic and unique meaning. Judas had made His historic exit, following the sop, and had arrived or was on His way to suicide. There had been the bold but shallow assurance of Peter, an assurance that would not last long nor prove true. Their plans were shattered. Their hopes were spoiled. Their fondest dreams had suddenly become a frightening nightmare. Their bright and promising future had become quickly a leaden gray. Their leader, on whose presence so much depended and in whose fellowship they so delighted, was going away. The sunshine of certainty yielded to the clouds of uncertainty and doubt.

Thomas voiced the frustration of the group when he said, "Lord, we know not whither thou goest; and how can we know the way?" They are not sure where their leader is going, so they are not sure where they are going. Thy know only that they are going; where and how they do not know. Theirs was a bad outlook. But theirs was a good logic. It just makes good sense that if you do not know where you are going, you don't know how to get there. Routes and roads and maps don't mean much until destinations are fixed.

There is something of this desperation in our world. Men find themselves confronted by enemies, amazed by politics, frightened by knowledge, confused by conflicting ideologies and shaken by human performance.

In desperation millions ask, "How can we know the way?" In the face of such contemporary desperation, let us hear

II. *An Exact Designation.* "I am the way."

It can't be much clearer than that. Although the primary focus was on the cross, the Resurrection and the Ascension of Jesus, a world of truth for this life and the next one is contained in his pungent statement.

A. Jesus is the way to a victorious confrontation of sin. There was no way around the cross. Nor is there any adequate salvation from sin apart from the cross.

B. Jesus is the way of victory over death. He had already told His disciples of His coming death. His assurance was projected to His post-resurrection victory.

C. Jesus is the way of truth. He is the way of truth because He is the truth.

D. Jesus is the way of life. Again, He is the way of life because

He is life. It is not playing with words to affirm that because He is the way of life, He is the way to live, in time and in eternity.

In life's troubles, Jesus is the way.

In personal and social tensions of today, Jesus is the way.

In temptations all around us, Jesus, who was in all points tempted as we are, is the way to live victoriously.

In our tasks, Jesus who came with a sense of sentness to "work the works of him that sent me" is the way to accomplish our work objectives. Our generation has offered a de-personalized way of success. It is not straining the point to declare and to believe that Jesus does not simply have a way: He *is* the way. Here also is

III. *A Declaration That Is Exclusive.* "No man cometh unto the Father but by me."

The acid test of Christian theology is what a man does with Jesus Christ. There is no more dangerous indulgence than to reduce Christ to the equality of others and make Him simply *a* way rather than *the* way.

We are not hesitant to accept absolutes in the natural world. We boast of our open-mindedness, yet we accept the absolutes of physics, chemistry and in all forms of scientific calculations. Yet so many of us are afraid of the divine dogma that Christ is the absolute in spiritual salvation.

To proclaim Christ as an optional way of salvation is to reduce His divinity to mere humanity. And a human Christ cannot lift us from human despair.

The Duke of Wellington was right when he said, "Education without God will fill our world with clever devils." And a salvation without a divine Savior will fill our world with devils, clever or dull.

It was this excellent exclusiveness that Peter preached. "Neither is there salvation in any other: for there is none other name under heaven given among men, whereby we must be saved" (Acts 4:12).

Conclusion. Let us come from life's deepest desperations to Jesus who is the way.

Let us receive Jesus as the clear, simple designation of heaven for earth's afflictions.

Let us be consistent in giving Christ absolute authority and mastery over our lives.

Have you lost your way, dear friend? Hear Him say, "I am the way."

Asked the way to heaven Bishop Wilberforce replied crisply, "Take the first turn to the right and go straight ahead."

If you have not already done so, will you not do it now!

SUNDAY EVENING, OCTOBER 27

TITLE: "How to Lose at Christian Living"

TEXT: "But the children of Israel committed a trespass in the accursed thing . . . Israel hath sinned, and they have also transgressed my covenant which I commanded them . . ." (Josh. 7:1, 11).

SCRIPTURE READING: Joshua 7.

Introduction. Joshua 1 through 6 teach us how to live victoriously; chapter 7 tells us how to lose at Christian living. Chapter 6 closes with a victorious statement; chapter 7 begins by introducing a dark cloud that covers Israel's life.

Verse 1 states that it was a trespass, a breach of faith that affected the whole nation. Verses 2 through 5 describe Israel's defeat by Ai. The people were overwhelmed and their hearts melted and became as water. Verses 6 through 9 record Joshua's prayer, that he fell on his face before the Ark of the Lord until evening, in a crushed and perplexed spirit. Verses 10 through 15 share

God's answer to Joshua. God was not unfaithful; it was Israel who had sinned. Verses 16 through 26 describe how Achan was exposed and punished severely. In this chapter are three lessons shared with us.

I. *The Reality of Defeat in the Christian Life.* As Israel was defeated in its conquest of faith to possess the land, so do we as Christians and churches sometimes experience defeat in the Christian life. Defeat may occur but it is not necessary (1 John 2:1). Victory is always possible in Christ (1 Cor. 10:13).

Defeat may be related to two things according to this chapter. One is presumption (vv. 2 and 3). Because of the fewness of people the children of Israel presumed to gain victory. Their pride was their undoing. A second fact related to defeat is prayerlessness. In this chapter there is no evidence of God's promise of victory, and there is no evidence of prayer like before Jericho. Here is an experience of Joshua praying after defeat rather than before victory. How like our Christian living this is.

II. *The Root Cause of a Defeated Life.* Why am I not experiencing victory in the Christian life? Why do I keep losing? Joshua's reaction was one of resentment as reflected in his prayer. His attitude was that God had failed. Why did God let it happen? The real question is, what is God saying through this experience? When I fail it is not that God is unfaithful; it may be that God is saying something to me through the experience.

God gets to the root cause of the defeat of Israel as well as to our own. There was first a surface problem—something that was visible. Achan had stolen what belonged to God. It is not a trivial thing to steal God's devoted thing. The warning toward this was given in Joshua 6:18, 19. However, the sin was committed. Many of God's people today are guilty before God in taking what belongs to Him in God's tithes and offerings.

The root problem was that Achan's life was built on temporal values. He wanted to live for now rather than for eternity. What he could see was important rather than the unseen.

The root cause is found in verse 11 where the sin is described as a transgression against God's covenant. The root cause of every sin is to live life our way instead of God's. We try to live by our wisdom and reject God's principles. At the base of all our surface problems is resistance to God's way.

III. *The Remedy for Spiritual Defeat.* What is the solution? God's way is the only way—through confession and repentance. Two things must be remembered. One, God truly discovers us. He knows all about us. He instructed Joshua to the very individual responsible—from tribe, to family, to household, to individual. God knows our actions, attitudes, thoughts and motives; nothing escapes His eyes.

The second thing to remember is that the sin problem must be solved. The nation was delivered when the sin was judged and confessed. We experience victory over our sins through Jesus Christ. There is forgiveness for us on the basis of His death on the cross. He is our sacrifice.

We claim this victory over sin and the sins that defeat us through confession (1 John 1:9). To confess is to agree with God that we have sinned, and it is to claim by faith His cleansing and forgiveness because of Christ's death.

Cleansing is also related to repentance, a turning from sin in sorrow of heart to the way God intends for us to live. It also involves making restitution wherever is necessary.

Conclusion. You may do something about your defeated Christian life. One, take a pen and paper and make a list of every known sin in your life which the Holy Spirit brings to your memory. Two, across that list write the wonderful promise of 1 John 1:9. Three, when the list is completed destroy the paper on which it is written. Four, express thanks to the Lord that He has forgiven you. Five, claim by faith God's promise to forgive and cleanse us from all sin.

TITLE: "The Bible Speaks to Our Condition"

SCRIPTURE READING: Matthew 28.

Introduction. The last chapter of Matthew's gospel focuses in upon the Resurrection of the Lord Jesus Christ and the Great Commission which He gave to His disciples to publish to the ends of the earth His redemptive acts and their meaning for the heart of every man.

I. *He Is Risen* (28:1-7). Never did trumpeters sounding ten thousand trumpets speak with greater significance than did the angel when he said, "Fear not ye: for I know that ye seek Jesus, which was crucified. He is not here: for he is risen" (Matt. 28:5, 6).

We have let the truth of the Resurrection of Jesus Christ become so common that it is threadbare. In reality, the overwhelming majority of His followers live somewhere between sundown on Good Friday and before dawn on Easter Sunday. We have not recognized and fully responded to the fact that ours is a living Lord.

II. *Jesus Met Them* (28:9, 10, 16, 17). Over and over again our Lord revealed Himself to His disciples following His conquest of death and the grave. There are at least ten different recorded instances of His appearance to His disciples—to individuals, to small groups, and to over 500 at one time.

Our Lord wants to meet us today in Spirit on life's highway to quiet our fears, to open our minds to divine truth and to encourage us in service. He deserves our faith, and He merits our love.

III. *Sharing the Good News* (28: 18-20a). Our Lord speaks concerning the fact that God has invested Him with authority both in heaven and on earth. This bestowal of authority has been vested upon Him because of His self-denying surrender of Himself to His redemptive mission and His willingness to suffer the agony of calvary (Phil. 2:5-11).

While some have professionalized the Great Commission and applied it only to the clergy, others have internationalized it and they think that it applies only to the work of foreign missionaries.

The real imperative in the Great Commission is found in the phrase translated in the King James Version, "Teach all nations." Jesus is literally saying, "Make disciples." The word translated "go" is a participle with the force of an imperative. It literally means, "In your going about from place to place, make disciples." This includes every disciple of the Lord Jesus Christ. All of us are to be sharers of the good news of both the redemptive acts of Jesus Christ and their significance for the heart need of every man, woman, boy and girl.

IV. *A Wonderful Promise* (28:20b). The great Commission closes with the glowing promise of our Lord to bless with His continuing presence those who give themselves in obedience to His command to share the good news of His love with all men.

As He was with Abraham, Isaac, Moses, Joshua, Jeremiah and others, so will our Lord be with us if we are obedient to Him.

Conclusion. If we would please the crucified but risen living Lord, we must not be silent concerning what He has accomplished and what He has come to mean to us as individuals. May God grant to each of us hearing ears as we listen to these words that fell from the lips of our precious Lord.

SUGGESTED PREACHING PROGRAM FOR THE MONTH OF NOVEMBER

Sunday Mornings

After one has been led to put faith in Jesus Christ as Lord and Savior there is probably no greater service that can be rendered to him than to lead him to become a joyful and sacrificial contributor to the work of God's kingdom. A series of messages emphasizing that it is more blessed to give than to receive can make a great contribution toward spiritual growth and the enlargement of the life of those who have trusted Christ as Savior. Without being flippant, a good theme for this series of messages might be, "Taking the Stew Out of Stewardship."

Sunday Evenings

Continue with the theme, "The Walk and Work of Faith," based on the Book of Joshua.

Wednesday Evenings

Continue with the series, "The Bible Speaks to Our Condition," using selected great chapters from the New Testament. The theme verse for the month is, "Thy word have I hid in mine heart, that I might not sin against thee" (Ps. 119:11).

SUNDAY MORNING, NOVEMBER 3

TITLE: "Can a Man Rob God?"

TEXT: "Bring ye all the tithes into the storehouse that there may be meat in mine house, and prove me now herewith, saith the LORD of hosts, if I will not open you the windows of heaven, and pour you out a blessing, that there shall not be room enough to receive it" (Mal. 3:10).

SCRIPTURE READING: Malachi 3:5-10.

HYMNS: "We Give Thee But Thine Own," How. "Trust, Try and Prove Me," Leech. "All Things Are Thine," Whittier.

OFFERTORY PRAYER:

Our heavenly Father, we recognize that we are always in Your holy presence. Thank You for reminding us every day that You are a God who plans. Now let us follow Your plan by giving Your tithe and our offerings to Your work. In Jesus' name. Amen.

Introduction. How many attend your Sunday school class? For the sake of illustration, let us imagine that ten people attend regularly.

You know all ten of them well and you enjoy studying the Bible with them each Sunday. As far as you can tell, all ten of them are dedicated Christians.

You pick up the morning newspaper and read on the front page that eight of the ten people in your Sunday school class have been jailed for robbery! Would you be alarmed? Of course, you would.

Did you know that far less than two out of ten Christians actually give a tithe (10%) of their income to God's work through their local churches? The Bible calls the non-tither a robber!

I. *The Non-Tither Robs God.*

A. God's wrath is declared upon six categories of evildoers—sorcerers, adulterers, false swearers, oppressors, those who abuse the helpless, and those who do not fear God (Mal. 3:5-7). Such people deserve total destruction but God's grace prevents such destruction. His patience is greater than His wrath.

B. Even God's people stray from His teachings and break their covenants. God bids them return. In the spiritual darkness of their backsliding, many Christians blindly ask, "Wherein shall we return?"

C. Most Christians who are not tithers never think of themselves as robbers who have strayed from God. But Malachi leaves no doubt about this matter. Even though his name may not be entered on the local police ledgers, the non-tithing Christian is guilty of robbery in the worst way (3:8).

II. *The Non-Tither Denies God's Ability to Plan His Universe.* God,

the master planner, has left nothing to chance.

A. The nine planets in our solar system range in distance from the sun of from thirty-six million to about thirty-six hundred miles. Each moves around the sun in exact precision with orbits ranging from 88 days for Mercury to 249 years for Pluto.

B. Our earth, which makes its orbit in 365.25 days, rotates on its axis so accurately that a variation of one second in a hundred years would throw earthly life into unspeakable chaos.

C. It is said that the ink in an ordinary period contains more atoms than there are people in the world.

D. Scientists tell us that each atom contains its own individual solar system perfectly balanced with its protons and neutrons.

E. Recently, scientists have found over thirty more submicroscopic units called "fundamental particles" which exist within the nucleus of the atom. At the Argonne Laboratory near Chicago, a synchrotron with 12.5 billion electron volts has been built to investigate the world of the "particles." A research scientist at this laboratory remarked, "My respect and admiration of God's handiwork grows with every passing day I spend in this lab."

F. A watermelon has an even number of stripes on the rind. There is an even number of segments in every orange and an even number of rows in every ear of corn. Every stalk of wheat has an even number of grains. The waves of the sea roll into the shore at the rate of twenty-six times a minute in all kinds of weather. A limb grows as much as fifty feet from the trunk of a tree with no anchorage except the tree's trunk.

III. *The Non-Tither Denies God's Ability to Provide Salvation for the Lost.*

A. God plans everything. God has proclaimed just one plan of salvation. Paul said, "God was in Christ, reconciling the world unto himself" (2 Cor. 5:19). Simon Peter said of Jesus Christ, "Neither is there salvation in any other: for there is none other name under heaven given among men, whereby we must be saved" (Acts 4:12). "For whosoever shall call upon the name of the Lord shall be saved" (Rom. 10:13).

B. God's missionary plan was expressed by Christ just before His Ascension when He said to His disciples, "Go ye therefore, and teach all nations, baptizing them in the name of the Father, and of the Son, and of the Holy Ghost: teaching them to observe all things whatsoever I have commanded you: and, lo, I am with you alway, even unto the end of the world" (Matt. 28:19, 20).

Conclusion. Would God, who has planned everything in such detail, leave the financial support of His work to chance? Not at all! In the Old Testament, the tithe was considered "holy unto the Lord" (Lev. 27:30). God's people were to pay the tenth of "all the increase" (Deut. 14:22). They were to bring the tithe "into the storehouse" (Mal. 3:10).

SUNDAY EVENING, NOVEMBER 3

TITLE: "Principles for Spiritual Victory"

TEXT: "And the Lord said unto Joshua, Fear not, neither be thou dismayed: take all the people of war with thee, and arise, go up to Ai: see, I have given into thy hand the king of Ai, and his people, and his city, and his land: And thou shalt do to Ai and her king as thou didst unto Jericho and her king: only the spoil thereof, and the cattle thereof, shall ye take for a prey unto yourselves: lay thee an ambush for the city behind it" (Josh. 8:1, 2).

SCRIPTURE READING: Joshua 8: 1-8, 30-35; 9:3-15.

Introduction. The Book of Joshua is a fascinating book, describing how God's people possessed the land He had given them. It is a story of victories and defeat, of intrigue and war, of faith and supernatural power. It is a book of history but it is more than that; it is a book of principles that apply to the Christian life. This even the writer of Hebrews in the New Testament recognized.

Many key events in the life of Israel have spiritual meaning to us in our Christian lives. The children of Israel crossed the Jordan River into the land of Canaan. They experienced God's victory over Jericho. In doing so they experienced the power of conquering faith in following

God's leadership. Then there came unexpected defeat, humiliating defeat. Why? Because there was sin in the camp of Israel. Joshua 7 deals with this particular experience in their history and closes with the sin that caused defeat being punished. What would be next for Joshua and the people? The next chapters describe continuing conquest of the armies of God in possessing the land. Several principles of spiritual victory may be discovered.

I. *Claim God's Victory Over Sin.* The Bible teaches that any victory over sin involves confession, repentance, and restitution. Israel was defeated and sin was exposed. Joshua was humbled in prayer, and in answer God revealed the problem. The sin was confessed, judged and the guilt removed. The nation returned to victory. The only way to experience victory over sin in our lives is found in 1 John 1:9: "If we confess our sins, he is faithful and just to forgive us our sins, and to cleanse us from all unrighteousness."

What does this say to us specifically? Whenever we take what belongs to God we commit a dangerous sin. It may be stealing, covetousness, love of material things or taking the tithe that belongs to God. Whatever it is, if we desire to find spiritual victory from the Lord we must confess our need to God, become honest with Him and experience His spiritual victory in our Christian lives. We must claim God's victory in our lives today.

II. *By Faith Follow God's Directions for Your Life.* For one thing, we are not to let sin defeat us and failure stop us. When God forgives us our sins He is ready to give us directions for victorious living. In Joshua 8:1, after the sin was cleared up, God commanded Joshua to move out to further conquests. There is no need to keep on living our failures and defeats, once forgiven. They are settled in Jesus Christ. Satan tempts us to keep thinking about them, but God commands us to walk in victory. (See Rom. 8:28; Phil. 3:13.)

A second thought—accept God's leading. God gave to Joshua new orders for Ai. God had one plan for Jericho, another for Ai. The Lord does not always work the same way year after year. The method used here was not repeated for any other city or fortress in Canaan. This was God's new plan for Ai. Chapter 8 describes it as an intriguing ambush of the city.

Although God never changes in character and in purpose, He does change His methods. He is not stereotyped in His working. First Corinthians 12 describes the diversities of ministries. God is creative and He wants us to be creative in expressing spiritual freedom. The amazing thing today is how God is blessing so many varied ways in doing His work. There is a freshness being experienced that we have needed for many years. The principle that comes to me is that He will bless any of His people who make themselves available to Him, whether it is the Jesus movement, or the fast growing lay movement in America, or the various types of men and ministries that may be discerned. God gives strategies to those who seek them and who are willing to attempt them by faith. Our goal should be to let the Holy Spirit lead us in the fulfillment of God's purpose.

III. *Be Prepared for Spiritual Conflict.* Chapter 9 describes the deception used by the Gibeonites. There are three lessons to be learned. One, we're tempted to compromise God's principles. Two, we're tempted to live by our wisdom rather than God's. All that was done in chapter 9 was done without the counsel of the Lord. Three, be alert for Satan. The Gibeonites worked like Satan does—deceptively. Satan battles with us in various ways, and we're warned in the Scripture "to be strong in the Lord." Ephesians 6:11 speaks of the wiles of the devil. Second Corinthians 2:11 describes how Satan disguises himself. First Peter 5:8 indicates that Satan is sometimes like a roaring lion seeking whom he may devour. He is doing everything he can to thwart God's purposes through us, but his power was broken two thousand years ago.

We may claim the spiritual victory that God has for us in Jesus Christ.

Conclusion. The Book of Joshua teaches us that God's purpose for our lives is a victorious one. It is His purpose to lead us and to fill us with His power. He knows that we will be faced with conflicts in our Christian lives, and He wants us to be prepared with His counsel of wisdom. We need God's wisdom in our lives. Where can we get it? God's wisdom comes to us from His Word. Proverbs 4:7 says, "Wisdom is the principal thing; therefore get wisdom: and with all thy getting get understanding." Wisdom is looking at life with God's point of view, and understanding is responding to life's situations as God does. If we want to be victorious we must be willing to seek His wisdom and commit ourselves to living according to His way of life.

WEDNESDAY EVENING, NOVEMBER 6

TITLE: "The Bible Speaks to Our Condition"

SCRIPTURE READING: Luke 15.

Introduction. The opening verse in the great chapter for today reveals the strange attraction of Jesus for men of every class and condition. Particularly, those who are normally considered as irreligious were attracted to Him. In some respects this is an indictment against the clergy of today and many of those who consider themselves to be the very best of Christians. This conclusion is reached because there is something about us that repels the sinner rather than attracts him.

Jesus was accused of being a friend of sinners and He gave a beautiful parable made up of three different stories to plead guilty to the charge. There are at least four important truths that come shining through this great chapter.

I. *The Parable of Lost Things.* The entire chapter speaks of lost things—a lost sheep, a lost coin, a lost younger son, and a lost older son who stayed at home. The older son personifies the attitude of the Pharisees and the Scribes toward sinners. He was critical and had no compassion for lost things.

II. *The Parable of God's Sorrow* (15:4, 8, 13). The great God of heaven is not unconcerned about lost things. He suffers like a shepherd with a lost sheep, like a woman with a lost coin, and like a father with a wayward, rebellious, ungrateful son. God's heart is broken because of the lostness of men.

III. *The Parable of God's Struggles* (15:6, 8, 23). God is the God of grace. God sent the Savior to seek and save the sinner.

God goes out searching for the lost sinner like a compassionate-hearted shepherd seeking a lost sheep in the darkness of the midnight. God works to find those who have become lost values like a woman seeking a lost coin. God is like a broken-hearted father who practices generosity toward a son who proves to be unworthy and ungrateful. He grants the son the liberty to go to hell if the son is determined to do so. In the meantime, he builds a stall and feeds a calf so that he will be prepared to provide a banquet feast should the son come to his senses and return home.

IV. *The Parable of God's Joy* (15:6, 10, 22-24, 32). The highest happiness ever known is the happiness of heaven over the safety of those who once were lost. God rejoices over the salvation of a sinner like a shepherd rejoices when he finds a lost sheep; like a distressed woman who finds a lost coin; like a grieving, broken-hearted father when he sees the long lost son returning to the home.

Conclusion. This parable is often called the parable of the prodigal son. In reality, it is the parable of the waiting father who lovingly longs for the return of a foolish, wayward, unworthy son.

There are still many lost over whom God yearns. We can enter into God's sorrow and God's struggle to save. To the degree that we do so, we can enter into God's joy over the salvation of the lost.

SUNDAY MORNING, NOVEMBER 10

TITLE: "Did Jesus Teach Tithing?"

TEXT: "Woe unto you, scribes and Pharisees, hypocrites! for ye pay tithe of mint and anise and cummin, and have omitted the weightier matters of the law, judgment, mercy, and faith: these ought ye to have done, and not to leave the other undone" (Matt. 23:23).

SCRIPTURE READING: Mark 12: 41-44.

HYMNS: "I Gave My Life for Thee," Havergal. "More Love to Thee, O Christ," Prentiss. "My Jesus, I Love Thee," Featherston.

OFFERTORY PRAYER:
Our heavenly Father, we thank You for Your love expressed in Jesus Christ. We praise You for His love which caused Him to hurt for our sins. Now, may Your love for us through Christ constrain us to give until it hurts. In Jesus' name. Amen.

Introduction. Did Jesus tithe? If He did not tithe, surely the Pharisees would have openly criticized

Him as they did when He violated their Sabbath regulations.

Did Jesus teach tithing? Since Jesus must have assumed that the Christian would tithe, He did not spend much time talking about this subject. However, He commended the practice of tithing when He said, "Ye pay tithe of mint and anise and cummin, and have omitted the weightier matters of the law, judgment, mercy, and faith: these ought ye to have done, and not to leave the other undone" (Matt. 23:23).

I. *Jesus Commended Tithing.*

A. Christ commended the Scribes, Pharisees, and hypocrites for tithing but He condemned the motive and manner in which they tithed.

B. The Pharisees were careful to pay the tithe on the smallest of garden herbs—mint, anise, and cummin. They were giving their tithe instead of their lives. What about being just in their dealings with others (judgment)? What about being merciful toward the unfortunates (mercy)? What about loyalty to God and honesty in their business dealings (faith)? They had omitted these, thinking somehow that their tithing would substitute for their unethical practices.

C. Tithing is no back door to dedication. You do not become a better Christian by tithing. Tithing is an outgrowth of dedication—not a substitute for dedication. Paul indicated the proper order for stewardship of possessions when he spoke of the liberal giving of the Macedonian Christians who "first gave their own selves" (2 Cor. 8:5). God gets your money not to get you but God gets your money *when* He gets you! The proper order is self before substance.

II. *Jesus Condemned Impure Tithing Motives.*

Behind the tithing of the Pharisees were impure motives. What should be our motive when we tithe?

A. What about the motive of fear? "I tithe because I am afraid not to tithe," say some well-meaning Christians. Tithing completely motivated by fear leads to the conclusion that God can be "bought off."

B. "I like to pay my way because I just don't like to be a Christian free-loader," says the motive of duty. There is a sense in which tithing is a Christian duty, but tithing wholly motivated by duty reduces Christian stewardship to mere bill paying.

C. What about the motive of self-respect? Some say, "I'll give as much as the next fellow." It *is* surprising that many churches collect more money when more people know who is giving it. Someone has justly claimed that it would be surprising how little might be done in some churches if we did not care who got the credit. Self-respect falls far short of the proper motive for tithing.

D. What about the motive of reward? Does tithing really pay? God certainly promised to protect Israel's crops and make her a delightsome nation. But was God blessing tithing or the spirit that was behind tithing?

Tithing *does* pay—but not always in financial blessings. In fact, some tithers face more hardships than non-tithers. The greatest blessing in tithing is found in the heart of the Christian who knows that he is co-operating in God's plan of the ages for financing the most important work in the world.

E. A pastor went visiting with one of the men in the Married Young Peoples' department of his church. As he climbed into the old car, he noticed that the right, front fender was badly damaged. The young man started the car and pulled away from the church. From the sound of the motor, the pastor noticed that it was badly in need of repair. Before the evening was over, the young man said, "I know this car isn't much. We would have bought a new one before now if we had not decided to tithe this year. We are happy to drive this 'rattle-trap' a few more miles until we feel that we can buy a new one without having to take the payments out of our tithe."

III. *Jesus Conveyed the Proper Motive for Tithing.*

A. Certainly, the elements of fear, duty, self-respect, and blessing are involved in Christian steward-ship. But the underlying motive behind tithing ought to be love. God so loved that He gave (John 3:16).

B. Our love for God and fellow-man will not let us spend God's tithe on a house, a new car, vaca-tion, furniture, bowling ball, tennis racket, rifle, boat, water skis, TV set, stereo, golf clubs, or a new wig. There is nothing wrong with owning these things. But Christian love will let us buy them only after the first fruits of the tithe have been taken from the pay check.

C. God's knowledge of our stewardship means more than the fact that He sees how much we drop into the envelope or offering plate on Sunday. God asks more than, "Did you give today?"

Conclusion. How do you earn your money? Do you work for it? Is your occupation honest? Are you honest within your occupation? Do you hurt others to make your liv-ing? What is your attitude toward your money? Are you depending on money to bring happiness? Would you depend more on God if you did not have as much money as you now have? Are you more dedicated to money-making than your family, health, church, and God? How much of your money do you give to God's work through the storehouse of your local church? How much do you keep for yourself? Do you spend wisely what is left after giving your tithes and offerings?

The tithe is the beginning place in Christian stewardship. Have you be-gun to give yet?

SUNDAY EVENING, NOVEMBER 10

TITLE: "Growing on in Christ"

TEXT: "So Joshua took the whole land, according to all that the LORD said unto Moses; and Joshua gave it for an in-heritance unto Israel according to their divisions by their tribes. And the land rested from war. . . . Now Joshua was old and stricken in years; and the LORD said unto him, Thou art old and stricken in years, and there remaineth yet very much land to be possessed" (Josh. 11:23; 13:1).

SCRIPTURE READING: Joshua 11:23; 13:1; 18:1-5; 14:6-15.

Introduction. The Book of Joshua describes how Israel conquered Canaan by faith. It also shares spiritual lessons on how to conquer the Christian life by faith. Israel had seen God's miracles at work in their crossing the Jordan and in conquering Jericho. They had also seen defeat at Ai, disobedience by Achan, and deceit by the Gibeonites. In it all they were marching on in conquest of the land. But what next?

Their work was not finished. God's will, as revealed to Joshua, was to go over the Jordan and inherit the land which He had sworn to give to their fathers. After Jericho and other experiences Joshua 11 describes what happened. Joshua took all the land and made war a long time. The land was taken according to God's Word. Then in verse 23 it states that the land rested from war. Joshua was going on in the conquest of the land. This is exactly what God wants us to do. Once we have Jesus Christ in our lives and we're committed to His victory in Christian living, He wants us to *grow* on in Christ. We're not to cease maturing in our relationship with Him. Three truths come from this section of Joshua.

I. *God's Rest.* This is described in Joshua 11:23, ". . . and the land rested from war." The Bible speaks of rest when it describes Israel experiencing rest in the conflict and con-

quest of Canaan. Hebrews 4:1, 9 also refers to rest in the Christian life. For the Christian rest is a marvelous reality. It is God's will that we know this rest and experience it. It is not physical rest; it is spiritual rest the Bible is describing. It is rest from turmoil and strain in the Christian life. It is rest from the worry of trials and troubles; it is rest from frustration and discouragement. Jesus described rest in Matthew 11:28-30—the rest of forgiveness of sins and also the rest of submission to Jesus Christ. When we are yoked to Christ we experience life under His control. This is abundant life— rest indeed!

II. *God's Challenge.* This is described in Joshua 13:1 when God said to Joshua that "there remaineth yet very much land to be possessed." So God's challenge came to Joshua to go on to possess the land. There are two words that need emphasizing. One is the word "inheritance," a word used to refer to the land as God's gift to Israel (v. 23). The second word is the word "possess" in verse 1. This was the action Israel was to take to make the land their actual inheritance.

The inheritance was what God provided; possession was that which they took. God gives but we must possess. We must go on to possess all that belongs to us.

The chief lesson for us is that God has the rich spiritual heritage for us in Jesus Christ (Eph. 1:3). God has given spiritual blessings in Christ but we must possess them by faith. God gives by grace; we must claim by faith. The challenge for us then is to grow in Christ, to go on to maturity (Heb. 5:11-14; 6:1; 2 Pet. 3:18).

It is not God's will that we not

grow spiritually, or that we be defeated, fruitless, miserable Christians. He challenges us to grow on in Christ.

III. *Our Response.* What will be our response to the challenge of spiritual growth, or to possess our spiritual heritage in Christ? Two illustrations in Joshua point out two responses that we may make. First, in Joshua 18:1-3 is the attitude of slackness to do what God wills us to do. To be slack refers to slothfulness in Christian growth. The Bible has a lot to say about slothfulness. (See Judg. 18:9; Prov. 10:4; 15:19; 18:9; 21:25; 24:30.)

This is one attitude that we may take toward spiritual growth—being slothful, spiritually lazy toward God. When we have this attitude it prevents appropriating the victorious life and hinders fruitfulness.

The second attitude is found in Joshua 14:6-15, against the background of a noble person named Caleb. He is one of the truly beautiful characters of the Bible. He is referred to in Numbers 14:8, 9, 24 where the qualities of his life are seen. Numbers 32:10-12 describe his faith and his fullness of the Spirit. In this passage he is now eighty-five years old, yet full of daring. He was both physically strong and spiritually courageous. He is facing the greatest challenge of his

lifetime. He was not ready for retirement. The keys to his life are found in Joshua 14:10 where he says, "The LORD hath kept me alive." He had the constant assurance of the presence and power of God. He was constantly walking in the Spirit. Also, in verses 8, 9, 14 it says that he "wholly followed the LORD." He was not concerned about a comparison of himself with others; He wanted God's best for his life.

There was a burning desire in his heart to get into the battle. His one great request was "give me this mountain." He was hungry and thirsty after righteousness and, consequently, he was completely satisfied in his relationship with God.

Conclusion. Growing on in Christ means that we must not be slothful toward the spiritual heritage that God has given to us in Jesus Christ. Rather, we must be spiritually zealous for God to fulfill His ministry through us.

We must claim God's victory in our lives by faith. Let us believe He will give His victory. As Jesus said, "According to your faith be it unto you" (Matt. 9:29), and as Paul said, "I can do all things through Christ which strengthenth me" (Phil. 4:13). Growing on in Christ is the continual step in fulfilling God's purpose for a victorious life.

WEDNESDAY EVENING, NOVEMBER 13

TITLE: "The Bible Speaks to Our Condition"

SCRIPTURE READING: Luke 18.

Introduction. The Bible was not

written merely that we might have a historical record of the past. The Bible is a revelation of God in action, revealing His nature, His purpose and His good will for our lives. On every page, in every incident, in every conversation recorded in Holy Scripture, God would speak to our condition today.

I. *Persistence in Prayer Is Encouraged* (18:1-8). Jesus speaks a parable to the intent that men ought always to pray and not to faint. We must develop the habit of prayer and not break that habit. To neglect this spiritual discipline is to faint and cave in when the times of stress come. A contrast is drawn between an unjust judge who finally grants the plea of a poor widow with the God of heaven who is eager to bless His children.

II. *Beware of Strutting Into God's Presence* (18:9-14). Human nature is deceptive. It is easy for moral man to assume that he merits a position of preference in the presence of a Holy God. The proud Pharisee was filled with conceit even in the presence of God. He went through a ritual which he thought was prayer which in reality was nothing more than a conversation with himself.

The publican, hated and despised by the citizens of his country, feeling cut off from those about him, enjoyed an audience with the eternal God because he came in an attitude of humility, reverence, and confession of sin. He made a plea for pardon and our Lord declares that he received a position of acceptance in the presence of God on the basis of his plea growing out of his faith.

III. *A Lesson From the Children* (18:15-17). Our Lord loved little children. He welcomed them. He prayed for them. He used their open attitude of humility, trust, and willingness to receive truth as a method of teaching great truths to men who stumbled over the simple way of salvation.

IV. *The Worship of Things Material* (18:18-30). The ruler who came to our Lord asking for the way of life ·was a prisoner of perishables. He had wrapped his heart and life around the physical things which he held title to. In reality, things owned and dominated him.

His question to our Lord concerning the way of life revealed the unsatisfied hunger of his soul. He who worships a false god will ultimately be disappointed by the object of his worship.

Jesus perceived the man's real problem and dealt decisively and radically with the man's worship of things material. He was unwilling to repudiate his false god in order to become a follower of Jesus Christ.

V. *The Way to the Cross* (18:31-34). With a steadfast commitment to the will of God, and with an indescribable love for lost men, our Lord moved steadfastly to the cross. He was willing to suffer to glorify God and to bless mankind. To what degree are we willing to spend and be spent in order that our God might be lifted up in the hearts of other men?

VI. *The Gift of Sight* (18:35-43). On the way to His crucifixion, our Lord tarried for a moment that He might bestow the gift of sight to one whose eyes were blind. This incident reveals His infinite compassion and His attention to the personal needs of those about Him.

Conclusion. This chapter speaks words of encouragement and words of warning to each of us. Each of us needs to communicate with God more often. Each of us could be more humble in God's presence. Each of us needs to beware lest we worship things unworthy of worship. God will grant to us sight and insight if we will but trust Him and obey Him.

SUNDAY MORNING, NOVEMBER 17

TITLE: "Investing in Heaven"

TEXTS "Lay not up for yourselves treasures upon earth, where moth and rust doth corrupt, and where thieves break through and steal: But lay up for yourselves treasures in heaven, where neither moth nor rust doth corrupt, and where thieves do not break through nor steal: For where your treasure is, there will your heart be also" (Matt. 6:19-21).

SCRIPTURE READING: Revelation 7:9-17; 11:15.

HYMNS: "O That Will Be Glory," Gabriel. "O They Tell Me of a Home," Alwood. "My Saviour First of All," Crosby.

OFFERTORY PRAYER:

Our heavenly Father, we thank You for the assurance that Your children will dwell with You in heaven forever. While we are on earth, help us to think of heaven. May we give today as though we were laying up treasures in heaven. In Jesus' name. Amen.

Introduction. A little girl, blind from birth, knew the beauties of the earth only from her mother's lips. A noted surgeon performed a successful operation. When the last bandage was removed from her eyes, she ran from the doctor into the arms of her mother. Then, she ran to the window and looked out at the world for the first time. For the first time, the glories of the earth rolled into her vision. She ran to her mother and screamed with joy, "Oh, mama, why didn't you tell me it was so beautiful?" As the mother wiped the tears from her eyes, she said, "Precious child, I tried to tell you."

We read much about heaven in the Book of Revelation. But when we get to heaven, we too will scream with joy, "John, why didn't you tell us it was so beautiful." Perhaps John will say, "I tried to tell you in the last book in the Bible."

What is heaven like? In the last two chapters of the Revelation, John says that heaven is like a tabernacle, a city, and a garden.

I. *Heaven Is Like a Tabernacle* (Rev. 21:1-5).

A. In the Old Testament, the tabernacle was a place of fellowship with God. In heaven, the Christian will fellowship with God in a way that man has never known.

B. John says that in heaven there is "no more sea" (Rev. 21:1). The sea is a symbol of separation (Rev. 4:6). There will be nothing in heaven to separate one from God. John also referred to the tabernacle experience of the Christian in heaven in an earlier part of his book (7:9-17). He pictures Christians of all races standing in God's presence dressed in the white robes

311

of purity with palms in their hands. Soldiers carry spears to war but those who celebrate the victory of battle wave palm branches!

C. The Christian will enjoy heavenly fellowship with God without the distressing presence of grief. John pictures heaven as a place where God is served day and night "in his temple" (7:15). He pictures heaven as a place where there is no hunger nor thirst and where God wipes away the tears.

D. Illustration: After Dr. Wayne Ward, professor of theology at Southern Baptist Theological Seminary, preached a sermon on heaven, a ninety-year-old blind man approached him with these words, "Brother Wayne, I want to *see* you."

He ran his fingers over Dr. Ward's face. Then with tears streaming out of sightless sockets he said, "When I open my eyes for the first time, you know who I will be looking at, don't you?" Dr. Ward said, "Yes, you will be looking at Jesus."

Then, with a cry of joy the blind man said, "Brother Wayne, it is worth being blind for ninety years to know that the first time I open my eyes, I will be looking at Jesus!"

II. *Heaven Is Like a Walled City* (Rev. 21:10-14, 21-27).

A. In Old Testament times, the walled city was the city of protection. In times of trouble, everyone made their way to the walled cities. Heaven is a place of perfect protection!

B. Illustration: A little girl who was spending her first night away from home with a girl friend was heard to cry in the night. The mother of the house went to her bedroom and said tenderly, "Honey, what is the matter? Are you homesick?" The little girl said, "No, I'm here-sick." The Christian often gets sick of living in a world where the threat of war and destruction hang over his head. But he can rest assured that, in heaven, there is perfect protection.

C. A preacher said to a dying pauper, "I am sorry for you!" The poor man said, "Sorry, for me? Just look at the prospects!"

III. *Heaven Is Like a Beautiful Garden* (Rev. 22:1-5).

A. John paints an unforgettable picture of a garden where there is plenty of water and vegetation. In the garden of heaven, everything we need is provided. Heaven is not only like a tabernacle where we have perfect fellowship with God and a city where we have perfect protection, it is also like a garden where we have perfect provision.

B. The drama of redemption in the Bible revolves around three gardens. Man is cast out of the garden of Eden because of sin. In the garden of Gethsemane, man finds his way back to God and forgiveness for sin. In the Garden of heaven, man's redemption from sin is complete!

IV. *Heaven Has Pearly Gates* (Rev. 21:21).

A. But how does one get to heaven? Only through Jesus Christ! John indicated that those who stand before God's throne in heaven stand there because their robes have been made white "in the blood of the Lamb" (Rev. 7:14). John pictures the wall around heaven with twelve tremendous gates and each gate is one huge pearl.

B. A pearl is formed when a piece of foreign matter such as a grain of sand gets into the shell of the oyster. The wounded oyster's body secretes a milky liquid which forms a hard cover around the piece of sand. The oyster is suffering during the whole process. Finally, the hard cover builds up around the piece of painful sand and forces it out of the shell.

C. How wonderful! The entrance to heaven is pictured as pearly gates! We could not walk through the gates of heaven on our own merit. Our entrance to heaven is gained through the suffering of our Lord and Savior, Jesus Christ. Jesus said, "In my father's house are many mansions ... I am the way" (John 14:2, 6).

Conclusion. We *shall* inherit heaven. But what treasures are we laying up there now? A Texas oilman said, "The best way I know to lay up treasures in heaven is to invest my money in people who are going there." Won't heaven be great! Invest your money, time, and talents in your church. It's in the heaven-going business!

SUNDAY EVENING, NOVEMBER 17

TITLE: "The Faithfulness of God"

TEXT: "And, behold, this day I am going the way of all the earth: and ye know in all your hearts and in all your souls, that not one thing hath failed of all the good things which the LORD your God spake concerning you; all are come to pass unto you, and not one thing hath failed thereof" (Josh. 23:14).

SCRIPTURE READING: Joshua 23.

Introduction. In Joshua 23 the great leader of the people of Israel has reached old age and is stricken in years. The final two chapters record his last words to the people. To the end he remained full of faith and full of the Spirit. He knew what it meant to conquer by faith and to possess God's inheritance.

There is one great keynote found in chapter 23. Although the word itself is not used, the truth undergirding all Joshua says in this chapter relates to the faithfulness of God. Some of the verses sound this encouraging note. Verse 3: " . . . for the LORD your God is he that has fought for you." Verse 5: " . . . ye shall possess their land, as the LORD your God hath promised unto you." Verse 10: ". . . the LORD your God, he it is that fighteth for you, as he hath promised you." Verse 14: " . . . not one thing hath failed of all the good things which the LORD your God spake concerning you." What a faithful God Joshua had!

This is one of the great truths of Scripture and life—the faithfulness of God. Numerous times the Bible claims it. Just as Joshua was able to conquer through God's faithfulness, so do we as we live victorious Christian lives. Three words stand out in understanding the faithfulness of God.

I. *Reliance*. Just as Israel conquered the land of Canaan relying upon the faithfulness of God, so may we rely upon His faithfulness for the victorious Christian life. It is utterly impossible for us to rely upon ourselves. We must depend upon His trustworthiness. There are Scriptures that will build our faith regarding the faithfulness of God. One is 1 Corinthians 10:13 where it indicates that God does not allow Christians to be tested beyond His willingness to provide a way of escape. Another is 1 Thessalonians 5:23, 24, where it states that God is faithful to keep us to finish what He has set out to do. There is also 2 Thessalonians 3:3, which states that God is faithful to give us stability and protection against all that is evil. Another is 1 John 1:9, where God is faithful to forgive and cleanse us of all our sins. And still another is Hebrews 10:23 and 11:11, where God is said to be faithful to keep His promises to us. Whatever He has promised He will fulfill.

II. *Responsibility*. Just as there are rewards and assurances, there are warnings and responsibilities. In Joshua 23:7 and 8 the people are warned against becoming like their surroundings. So are we to live a separated life by not copying the world (Rom. 12:1, 2), and by not co-existing with sin (2 Cor. 6:14).

In verse 11 they were to heed themselves and to love God with a deep love. This is not just a human love but it is God's kind of love—an undivided love in our hearts for Him.

III. *Retrogression*. In verses 12 and 13 we are warned that we are not to fail to go on in faith. Turning back was being willing to give up the Canaan life for the old life. It meant to turn against God and His will and live for self will. So the challenge is to keep going forward (Heb. 12:1).

The warning is a very real one because it is possible to retrogress in the Christian life. When we do there are three losses as seen in Joshua 23. One is the loss of power (v. 13). God removes His power when we do not honor Him and His will for our lives. Samson is a testimony to this truth. When we resist the ministry of the Holy Spirit from our lives we experience powerlessness. Therefore, there is an inability to bear fruit. According to John 15 we must abide in Christ if we are to be fruitbearing Christians.

A second loss is the loss of comfort, also found in verse 13, when it refers to snares and traps, scourges and thorns. Israel's enemies would be like all of these to them. When we resist and reject God's principles from our lives, our lives too are filled with all types of conflicts. God does not leave us comfortable. He warns, and probes and pricks our conscience. If the conscience is not troubled then there is danger.

The third loss is the loss of capacity. This is also found in verse 13, when the people were told that they would perish from the land if the rejection continued. When we turn back from God there is a progressive loss of capacity. It may not all happen at once but it is a downward pattern of life (see Ps. 1.)

Conclusion. Reverse this trend of thought from the negative to the positive. Determine in your heart to go forward in Christ instead of backward by relying upon the faithfulness of God. How can this be done? Five things will keep you moving. One, read the Word of God faithfully. Two, pray daily. Three, fellowship with other Christians. Four, witness for Christ. Five, be obedient to God's Spirit in your life.

WEDNESDAY EVENING, NOVEMBER 20

TITLE: "The Bible Speaks to Our Condition'

SCRIPTURE READING: John 1.

Introduction. The gospel of John is the favorite gospel of multiplied millions of followers of the Lord Jesus. John is known as the apostle of love. It is believed by many that he is the apostle who leaned upon the bosom of our Lord on the night when He instituted the Lord's Supper.

The great chapter from the New Testament through which we would let God speak to us today is both profound and simple.

I. *The Eternal One Enters Time* (1:1-14). There is some similarity between this chapter and the first chapter of the Book of Genesis. Genesis 1 speaks of how in the beginning God created the heavens and the earth. John 1 tells us about how the eternal Creator clothed Himself in human flesh and entered time.

The eternal Word of God clothed Himself in human flesh and came to live with and to speak to the hearts and minds of men. John was one of those who had beheld Him with the eyes, felt Him with the hands, and heard Him with the ears. He declared that this Lord had come, "full of grace and truth."

II. *The Witness of John the Baptist*

(1:15-34). John the Baptist was a servant of the Lord whom God appointed to be the forerunner of our Lord Jesus Christ. John came as a voice, as a witness, giving a verbal testimony to those who came in great multitudes to hear his message demanding repentance and proclaiming the early arrival of the Messiah.

Over and over the ministry of John the Baptist is described in terms of giving a witness, giving a testimony, establishing an official record concerning the coming Messiah. Instead of calling attention to himself, we find John directing the attention of his disciples toward Jesus, "Behold the Lamb of God, which taketh away the sin of the world" (John 1:29).

John was careful to give testimony only to what he knew personally about Jesus Christ. Each of us should follow his example. God does not expect us to give anyone's testimony concerning Christ except our own personal testimony.

III. *A Continuing Invitation* (1:35-40). When two of the disciples of John the Baptist followed the Lord Jesus with genuine curiosity, they received a gracious invitation which continues to be relevant for those who want to know more about Jesus Christ. Our Lord spoke to them and said, "Come and see" (1:39). The conversations of that visit would be interesting if we could but listen in.

IV. *The Example of Andrew* (1:41, 42). After Andrew had recognized Jesus as the Messiah, he sought his brother, Simon Peter, in order that he might introduce him to Jesus. Later we find Andrew bringing a lad with his loaves and fishes to Jesus (John 6:8, 9). It was Andrew who brought the Greeks to see Jesus shortly before the end of His ministry (John 12:20-22).

In the three instances in which Andrew is described as being active,

he is described in terms of bringing someone to Jesus.

Conclusion. The eternal One who entered time has reentered eternity and yet He dwells within the hearts of those who have trusted Him as Lord and Savior. We should follow the example of John the Baptist and give our personal testimony to those about us concerning this wonderful Lord. We would be wise if we followed the example of Andrew and bring as many as we can into an acquaintance with the Lord Jesus Christ.

SUNDAY MORNING, NOVEMBER 24

TITLE: "Giving More Than Thanks"

TEXT: "For we shall all stand before the judgment seat of Christ" (Rom. 14:10b).

SCRIPTURE READING: Romans 14:7-12.

HYMNS: "Come, Ye Thankful People, Come," Alford. "Thanksgiving Hymn," McNeely. "Now Thank We All Our God," Rinkart.

OFFERTORY PRAYER:

Our heavenly Father, at this Thanksgiving season we engage in thanks-living. Help us to be thankful. But most of all, help us to act thankful. In Jesus' name. Amen.

Introduction. Daniel Webster once said, "The most serious thought of my life is that I, as an individual, am accountable unto God." Dr. Wernher von Braun, the missile

expert, said that one of the things that gives meaning to his life is the assurance that someday he will stand before God and give an account of his life. In Romans 14:10 Paul says, "We shall all stand before the judgment seat of Christ." Again in the same chapter, verse 12, Paul states, "every one of us shall give account of himself to God."

I. *Total Stewardship Involves the Total Man.*

A. We will give an account to God of how we spend our time. We will be held accountable for how much of our time we gave to witnessing to the lost. We will give an account of how much time we spent in helping those in need and visiting those who were sick. In Ephesians 5:15, 16 we read, "See then that ye walk circumspectly, not as fools, but as wise, redeeming the time, because the days are evil."

B. We shall give an account of how we have used our tongue. ". . .

316

every idle word that men shall speak, they shall give account thereof in the day of judgment" (Matt. 12:36). Every day each of us speaks enough words to fill a book. So much is said that could and should go unsaid. Our gossip, our lies, the hurtful things we have said about another person even if they were true, all these things will be witnesses against us in that day of judgment. We are always to speak in a Christ-like manner. "And to him that ordereth his conversation aright will I shew the salvation of God" (Ps. 50:23). We will give an account of the good and bad that we have spoken.

C. We are all charged with the responsibility of using the talent that we were given by God. Some people can sing beautifully and some can teach. Some can preach and others are given the talent to witness. Some are given the talent of intercessory prayer. We are all given some talent and we will all be held accountable for how we have used the talents we were given.

D. We will give an account of how we have used the opportunities to witness that have opened to us. Some Christians witness whenever the opportunity presents itself. They speak of Christ at the beauty shop. They invite people to come to church while they do their grocery shopping. Some men tell of the love of Christ over their fishing rods and over the campfire at the deer camp. They take every opportunity to use their talent for witnessing. But many do not. Many find themselves talking about anything other than God's work.

II. *Giving Money to God's Work Is*

Thanks Giving. Christian stewardship involves more than just dropping money into the offering plate. It involves our position behind the offering plate, above the offering plate, in the offering plate, and beyond the offering plate.

We are not good stewards until we have fulfilled our responsibility to God in all four of these aspects.

A. Behind the offering plate. God is concerned with how we earn our money. He expects us to work for our money at a legitimate trade. "Six days shalt thou labour, and do all thy work" (Exod. 20:9). " ... if any would not work, neither should he eat" (2 Thess. 3:10). When you consider earning money in a manner that pleases God, ask yourself these questions:

(a) Is it legal? God will not honor money made by gambling, narcotic sales, prostitution, dishonest advertising, and shady business deals even if we give 90% instead of 10%.

(b) Is it helpful? If the money is earned by the sale of obscene material, drugs, alcoholic beverages, and other detrimental products, it will not be pleasing to God.

(c) Is it fair to everyone concerned? One can be in an honest vocation and still be dishonest and unfair.

B. Over the offering plate. God also wants to know if you have the right attitude toward your money. "For the love of money is the root of all evil" (1 Tim. 6:10). Before you can change your attitude toward money, you must ask yourself several questions.

(a) Would I be just as happy without as much money? You must come to the place where you would be willing to take a job even with less pay in order to have time to attend the Lord's house on the Lord's day.

(b) Would I depend upon God more if I didn't have as much money? It is easier to trust God when finances are scarce. As we become more affluent, we depend upon our own resources and have a tendency to depend less upon God.

(c) Do I put money before my God, my church, and my family? Jesus said, "But seek ye first the kingdom of God, and his righteousness; and all these things shall be added unto you" (Matt. 6:33).

C. In the offering plate. As you hold your money, ready to drop it in the offering plate, God asks another question, "Why are you giving this money?" Your gift to God's work should be from a heart of love and a desire to serve Him. It should not be given out of fear or duty. It should not be given to receive reward or praise from men. Jesus rebuked the Pharisees and scribes and said of them, "But all their works they do for to be seen of men ..." (Matt. 23:5). Your tithe and offerings should not be given to make up for failures in other areas of your Christian life. Giving is an outgrowth of dedication, not a substitute for dedication.

The Christian is also accountable for what he puts into the offering plate. When God asks, "How much did you put into the offering plate," He is not talking about dollars but percentage.

God asks for 10% of our earnings. That is the least that we can give. But God desires that we go beyond the tithe as soon as we can. "Upon the first day of the week let every one of you lay by him in store, *as God hath prospered him* ..." (1 Cor. 16:2). If God has prospered you and blessed you to a great extent, then you are to give proportionately as God has blessed you.

D. Beyond the offering plate. Christian stewardship also involves our money and possessions beyond the offering plate. God wants us to be wise stewards of the money that we have left after paying our tithe and giving our offerings. Charles Haddon Spurgeon said, "A fool can make money but it needs a wise man to spend it." It follows that the art of acquiring money is subordinate to the art of using money.

So often the possessions that are left at death cause headaches and heartbreak among the loved ones that remain. With a Christian will you know, before death, exactly how your money will be used after death. Every Christian should pray about this and let God help him decide what percentage of his estate will go to the work of the Lord. A Christian's stewardship of possessions is not over until he has decided here upon this earth before he dies, how his estate will be used after he dies.

Conclusion. We must gather all the facts and information that God has given us concerning stewardship so that we can wisely evaluate our accountability unto God. The stewardship of money is just one part of the total picture of our accountability to God. As we give our money, we need to realize that God looks behind the offering plate, over the offering plate, in the offering plate, and beyond the offering plate. Let's give more than thanks this Thanksgiving!

SUNDAY EVENING, NOVEMBER 24

TITLE: "Victorious Christian Commitment"

TEXT: "And if it seem evil unto you to serve the LORD, choose you this day whom ye will serve; whether the gods which your fathers served that were on the other side of the flood, or the gods of the Amorites, in whose land ye dwell: but as for me and my house, we will serve the LORD" (Josh. 24:15).

SCRIPTURE READING: Joshua 24.

Introduction. Joshua 24:1 describes that awesome scene—all the tribes of Israel, their elders, their heads and their judges, along with Joshua the leader, presented themselves before God. It is the occasion when the respected and loved leader gives his farewell message to the nation. It is a message of God's miraculous works and Joshua's personal commitment. It became a decisive moment for Israel that resulted in continuous victory for years to come. It was an experience in which the Lord was enthroned and self dethroned and victory assured.

This is what the Christian life is all about. There is salvation. The Lord saved Israel from Egyptian bondage and He has saved us from sin's bondage. There is also the abundant life. Just as God promised the abundant land for Israel so He has promised the abundant life for all who are in Jesus Christ. We are also confronted with unbelief and faith; Israel failed to experience the victorious life because of unbelief. So we live in failure, defeat and frustration by trusting in our own efforts to live Christlike. But Israel entered the land by faith and experienced great victories according to Joshua. And it is not God's will that we be defeated; rather, we are to experience daily victory through Jesus Christ our Lord.

Chapter 24 is that moment in the life of Israel that describes the commitment they made that was to continue for years to come. This chapter will give insights on how to go on to continuing victory in the Christian life by means of a victorious Christian commitment. A commitment that is continually victorious does at least two things.

I. *It Rests in God Confidently.* This is described in verses 1 through 13 where God's sufficiency is proclaimed. Great moments in Israel's history are referred to, but all of it is God's doings. It was all unmerited; it was all God's grace. All that we are is also by God's grace, according to Ephesians 2:8-10. All that we are spiritually now is God doing it, according to Philippians 2:13. How is this made real to us? It is by faith. The purpose, and power, and faithfulness of God calls for faith in Him. Just as the Israelites experienced the sufficiency of God by faith, so does every Christian experience victory by faith. We're saved by faith; we walk by faith. By faith we accept God's salvation, and by faith we accept God's victory. The same faith that saves us is the faith that makes us victorious. We do not need any more faith.

II. *The Victorious Christian Commitment Responds to God Decisively.* This is described in verses 14 through 28. Verse 14 begins, "Now therefore. . . ." On the basis of what has been said in the previous verses a commitment is called for. They were to respond, to act, to choose. What are the marks of this response as described in this chapter? The first mark is to fear the Lord—in verse 14. This is not a cringing fear of God but a reverent trust in Him. Fear is an awareness of the presence of God. The first step of wise living is to fear Him. Proverbs 1:7 says, "The fear of the LORD is the beginning of knowledge." Jesus said, "Fear him which is able to destroy both soul and body in hell" (Matt. 10:28). Acts 2:43 says, "And fear came upon every soul." Commitment that is worth anything at all has an element of fear in it, an element of God-consciousness, reverence and trust for Him.

A second response is availability. In verse 14 it says, "Now therefore fear the LORD, and serve him. . . ." The heart of a victorious response is the attitude of making ourselves available to Jesus Christ. It is not our ability that is important but our availability. We're to live the Christian life in the arrangement of the Book of Romans. Romans 1 through 11 describe all that God has done for us. Romans 12 begins by a plea for Christians to yield themselves to God, making possible true service. It is possible to do deeds of service for God without making ourselves available to Him.

Victorious service is allowing God to work through us. We may have been told all our lives to do things for Him, but very few have really told us to first make ourselves available to Him for Him to be and do in us what He desires. When you arrive at this point in your life, then service becomes meaningful and joyful without pressure.

III. *A Decisive Commitment Involves a Cleansed Life.* In verse 14 Joshua challenges the people "to put away the gods which your fathers served on the other side of the flood, and in Egypt." God did not allow His people to worship other gods. They were to turn away from these false gods that could destroy their relationship with *the* God.

Verse 23 says, "Now therefore put away . . . the strange gods which are among you, and incline your heart unto the LORD God of Israel." Anything that inclines your heart away from the Lord is a strange god and it is sinful; it must be put away. Anything in our lives—attitudes, thoughts, actions, habits—that causes us to drift away from God is sinful and must be put away from us. A cleansed life is essential to victory in the Christian life.

IV. *A Mark of a Decisive Commitment Is a Yielded Life.* In verse 15 Joshua says, "Choose you this day whom ye will serve." We cannot be neutral. We must progress or retrogress in our relationship with God. To go on in victory we must choose the Lord. This describes Joshua's yielded life. He first speaks as a person, as a man, as an individual, then he speaks as a father in being willing to become God's spiritual leader for his home. There is no greater combination than this personal life related to the family.

This is life under new management—under God as Lord. Joshua said, "As for me and my house, we will serve the LORD."

Conclusion. A man shared with me the fact that he had wandered for forty years in his Christian life, trusting Jesus only as Savior, but only this year has come to experience the living truth of two additional words—"and Lord." Jesus is both Savior and Lord. Victorious Christian commitment recognizes both.

WEDNESDAY EVENING, NOVEMBER 27

TITLE: "The Bible Speaks to Our Condition"

SCRIPTURE READING: John 10.

Introduction. The great chapter of the New Testament for today has been called the "Good Shepherd" chapter. In these words our Lord used a familiar figure on the scene of that day and time to communicate great truths concerning His relationship to His people and their relationship to Him.

It is said that even though Jesus used the Parable of the Good Shepherd and the sheepfold that some of those to whom He spoke did not understand Him (10:6). One must have hearing ears if he is going to hear the Lord speak authentically to his condition.

I. *The Lord Is the Good Shepherd.* Our Lord describes Himself as the good shepherd who provides for his sheep. He also describes Himself as the door of the sheepfold, and by this symbol He was seeking to communicate the security that He provides for those who hear His voice and who follow His leadership. The good shepherd is described in a number of different ways.

A. He calls his sheep by name (10:3).

B. He leads his sheep (10:3b).

C. He describes His purpose for coming into the world in terms of making possible for His sheep the abundant life (10:10).

D. He lays down His life for the sheep (10:11-18). By laying down His life he reveals not only His love for the sheep but also His love for the Father.

E. He knows His sheep (10:27).

F. He gives His sheep eternal life (10:28).

II. *The Sheep of the Shepherd.*

A. They know the good shepherd (10:14).

B. They hear the shepherd's voice (10:3).

C. The sheep follow the good shepherd (10:4, 27).

D. The sheep refuse to follow a stranger (10:5).

321

Conclusion. There were various reactions to the person and to the ministry of Jesus Christ who described Himself as the Good Shepherd (10:19-21, 31-39). Some repudiated His claims. They refused to examine His works or to consider His words. They rejected Him as a blasphemer.

Because of the testimony of John the Baptist, there were many who responded to Jesus affirmatively and put their faith in Him as the good shepherd who could lead them into the home of the heavenly Father.

Even at this point, our Lord was eager to have all of the sheep in the same fold. Perhaps this is a reference to the conversion of the Gentiles at a later time.

Our Lord came into the world that He might provide forgiveness of sin, new life and the spiritual security that comes as a result of being safe in the hand of our Father God (10:29, 30).

It is wonderful to know the Good Shepherd. As the sheep of His pasture, we should love Him, know Him, hear His voice, follow Him and refuse to follow any strange voice that would lead us astray. May the good Lord grant to us ears to hear His message of comfort for us today.

SUGGESTED PREACHING PROGRAM FOR THE MONTH OF DECEMBER

Sunday Mornings

The suggested theme for the sermons that focus on the coming of Christ is "The True Spirit of Christmas."

Sunday Evenings

The general theme for the suggested messages is "The Missionary Message of Christmas." The obligation of each individual Christian to be a publisher of the Good News is the reoccuring emphasis for the month.

Wednesday Evenings

Continue with "The Great Chapter of the New Testament." The theme verse for the month is, "Thy word have I hid in mine heart, that I might not sin against thee" (Ps. 119:11).

SUNDAY MORNING, DECEMBER 1

TITLE: "They Shall Call His Name Immanuel"

TEXT: "Behold, a virgin shall be with child, and shall bring forth a son, and they shall call his name Emmanuel, which being interpreted is, God with us" (Matt. 1:23).

SCRIPTURE READING: Matthew 1:18-25.

HYMNS: "O Little Town of Bethlehem," Brooks. "Joy to the World," Watts. "O Come, All Ye Faithful," Latin hymn.

OFFERTORY PRAYER:

Our heavenly Father, we thank You for many wonderful names, but today our minds are focused especially on the name Immanuel. The reason we so turn our hearts is because of this season of the year when we place special emphasis on the birth of Jesus. We thank You that You are with us today and all of our lives. Help us to give, conscious of Thy presence, and with the purpose of making Jesus known to others. We pray in Jesus' name. Amen.

Introduction. What is in a name? Most any name one can call will immediately bring to his mind something other than the name and/or person. The name Herod stands for cruelty. The name Alexander stands for conquest. The name Demosthenes stands for eloquence, and Beethoven for music. The name Milton suggests poetry and the name Judas stands for treachery. Other names such as Hitler, Mussolini, and Stalin stand out in the minds of many for barbarity, bestiality, and atheism.

But there is a Name that stands for much more than this. It is the name of the One whose birthday is celebrated at Christmas.

He bears several different names. His name is Jesus and the word itself is a contraction of words meaning Jehovah is helper, thus, the name Jesus means Savior, Redeemer, Comforter, and Friend. His name is Christ, which means Anointed One. His name is teacher, which suggests truth. His name is friend and He sticks closer than a friend.

The name that is being used in this message is "Emmanuel." This name was given by the angel of the Lord (Matt. 1:20-23). It was prophesied by Isaiah (7:14). It is a name that has meaning today. It means that God is in touch with His creation right now.

I. *The Name Immanuel—God With Us—Is the Way God Saves the Sinner.*

A. Every lost sinner is in despair and apart from God's being in reach of him, there is no hope.

The Bible tells us that man hungers and thirsts for righteousness. This is especially true when he is without Christ. This is true because life without Christ is incomplete. A Christless life is one without a compass. It is a life that is unhappy—straying feet and condemning conscious. It is a life that is condemned, lost, and wretched. The soul of the lost sinner cries out for redemption.

B. Every lost sinner has hope in Emmanuel. The presence of God serves as a standard to show one he is a sinner. The presence of God leads one to salvation. When God became a person, it was then He paid the supreme price for the sinner's salvation.

II. *The Name Immanuel—God With Us—Enables Him to Comfort the Sorrowing* (Luke 4:18).

A. Sorrow is universal. It is a common denominator. It is a ground leveler. Sooner or later, each person experiences it one way or the other. The world is full of griefs and graves. The very air seems heavy with farewells. The people of the world are weary and heavy laden.

B. People go about alleviating this sorrow in a number of ways.

They attempt by withdrawal. They withdraw from activity, other people, places and things, but this gives very little, if any, relief. They attempt living in the future. They seek to use activity, but these efforts become futile.

C. In the person Jesus Christ, whose name is Emmanuel, there is real comfort.

His presence provides real compassion. His presence gives comfort and He has the will to comfort.

III. *The Name Immanuel—God With Us—Serves As a Constant Inspiration for His Children.*

A. Servants of God need inspiration and encouragement.

The road seems full of unappreciative people. It seems crowded with criticism. The road of life is difficult. It is demanding, trying, and time-consuming. It is full of doubts and despair. In order for one to continue at his best, there must be strength and inspiration, and it is available.

B. Servants of God find the inspiration in the presence of God—Emmanuel.

"It is God that girdeth me with strength, and maketh my way perfect" (Ps. 18:32). The word "strength" means twisted together and God with man becomes entwined with Him.

When one's life is entwined with God's, there is strength.

IV. *The Name Immanuel—God With Us—Makes Him Present in Time of Death.* Death is cold, dreaded, and universal. It is a deep, dark, uncertain mystery and is feared by many. There is only one light that will continue to burn through the valley of death. It is God, who is light and whose light darkness cannot comprehend. It is Emmanuel (Rev. 21:2-4).

Conclusion. You may anticipate the celebration of Christmas in many different ways, but if you have never experienced the presence and power of Jesus Christ in your life, then give your heart to Him now and you will have your greatest Christmas. It is then you will come to know the true meaning of the name, Emmanuel. It is "God with us."

SUNDAY EVENING, DECEMBER 1

TITLE: "The Contemporary Missionary"

TEXT: "In this work, we work with God" (1 Cor. 3:9, Phillips).

SCRIPTURE READING: 1 Corinthians 3:1-9.

Introduction. As a child of seven years through twelve I received an impression of a "missionary" which was indelible yet insecure. My home church sponsored one of our pioneer missionaries in Brazil, South America. Every three years this man of God would return to his home community and share his experiences in missionary labor. I got the impression from this experience that a missionary was somebody who leaves home, and leaves his home church, and goes far, far away, to come back every three or four years to tell stories about people in strange lands and what God is doing there.

A bit later in my spiritual pilgrimage, I discovered 1 Corinthians 3:1-9. I read this passage anew in J. B. Phillips' translation, "In this work, we work with God." I discovered for the first time that I was included by the grace of God as a missionary.

The professional understanding of a "missionary" is neither Biblical nor practical for our time. God intends mission accomplishment from each redeemed person. Rightly considered, the Word of God teaches that a missionary is a redeemed personality living under the lordship of Christ, on mission in his particular setting.

A Christian, seriously concerned about personal mission, can be moved to commitment by the factors of his personal setting, his sense of sensitivity for others, and his response in commitment to daily leadership of a living loving Lord.

I. *Perception: The Contemporary Missionary Is Perceptive of His Setting.* Paul points to the incompleteness of the concept of "professional missionary." The Corinthian congregation found itself greatly divided by an attempt to determine leadership. Some felt Apollos was the complete missionary; others felt Simon Peter was the divine example; and still others looked backward to their experiences with the Apostle Paul. "In this work, *we* work with God." It is not a matter of professional leadership. It is a matter of associated Christian action. Redeemed persons have diversity of gifts, diversity of available time, diversity of endowment of talent and diversity of economic possessions, but each Christian is on mission in his setting.

The contemporary missionary begins with the inward look. Questions about self, about use of time, about divine endowments, and material resources are appropriate for self-inventory. The early Christians were scattered abroad in a limited world for their time. The Book of Acts wonderfully tells the experience of Christians who were scattered, but who saw themselves perceptively as missionaries.

The contemporary missionary is perceptive of his immediate setting. Urban patterns keep pointing us to the diversity of community, diversity of socio-economic backgrounds, diversity of churches, diversity of life styles, and especially, a great diversity of geographical location. New York City is not Albany, Georgia; Louisville, Kentucky is not Schenectady, New York; and Texarkana, Texas is not Buenos Aires, Argentina. Characteristics of life styles and daily patterns for living are being determined by socio-economic circumstances, the crush of population, and daily human encounter in personal life situations. The modern Christian begins well to be a missionary when he is alert and perceptive of the people who daily surround him, and of their life patterns. What are the needs of people with whom I am cast? What are their problems? What are their hang-ups?

Effective mission service seldom begins by program orientation. The excitement and joy of the Christian life is generated by personal relationships with other people. The contemporary missionary can find a new joy and a delightful partnership with God and other redeemed persons by seeing his immediate setting realistically. Some reside in the inner city of great metropolitan areas. Some are the factory workers, others live behind the desk. Wherever we are, God still says, "You shall be my witness."

II. *Sensitivity: The Contemporary Missionary Is Daily Involved in the Process of Sensitivity.* The last visit of Jesus to Jerusalem is prefaced by an emotional display which produced tears. Luke tells us (Luke 19:41) "And when he was come near, he beheld the city, and wept over it." This is a modern parable of sensitivity. There are many things that Jesus saw in His immediate setting which produced His tears. He saw their false peace; He was perceptive of the failure of the things which produced their insecurity, and sensitive to their human plight.

The tears of Jesus were not tears of failure or emotion. He was able to catch the feeling of people in His immediate setting. Jesus knows what is in man. His sensitivity was alerted at what He saw in the immediate setting of the beloved city of Jerusalem. By personal relationship with others the contemporary missionary will not only see His setting perceptively, He will be consciously sensitive of the human plight of very real persons.

The contemporary missionary will understand the emotions and trauma of real people. In recent years many pastors, some great churches, and too many of the Lord's people have pulled away from any personal commitment to certain kinds of people. Our Lord saw people who had moved too much toward self and ignored others, who were caught in the circumstances of life which produced fear, guilt, inferiority feelings, and hate. The expressions of hostility and bared interpersonal relationships are seldom helpful for either the person or those about him. The contemporary missionary will be sensitive to the problems that produce these behavior patterns in the lives of millions of real persons. He will be sensitive to human need and be alert to relate himself, by the love of God, to those who seek redemptive relationships.

IV. *Commitments: The Contemporary Missionary Will Move Toward Decision in the Challenge of Mission for His Personal Commitment.* The theme of the public ministry and life of our Lord is one that tells the story of God come down to man, as He became man, and gave Himself for what he found in man. Indeed He was a "man for others."

He taught His disciples the art of servanthood, the joyful necessity of giving self away to others. He not only told His disciples this necessity, He demonstrated it by a cross.

When the redeemed person is perceptive of his world, sensitive to the human plight of others, he comes to decision time. Only he can make that decision. The major question at this point is, "Can I be this kind of person?" The contemporary missionary will see himself on mission in his domestic setting. A good place to begin to be a missionary is in our own home and family circle. God seeks dedicated Christian missionaries at the level of parenthood. The business man may see himself on mission in his setting, the tradesman as he plies his trade. The contemporary missionary will see himself on mission where he is and whenever he is involved in personal relationships with others.

Involved in the decision for commitment to personal mission are at least these factors: (1) What is my first loyalty? Who is my Lord? (2) How important, really, is one individual person? (3) I am not really alone on my mission, am I? ("In this work, we work with God. ...") (4) The timeless significance of God's commission to each disciple ("... and ye shall be my witnesses").

Conclusion. The basic task of the contemporary missionary is one that involves an understanding of communication. Basic to providing communication is relationships. There is a creative excitement loose in our world for redeemed personalities under the Lordship of Christ committed to personal mission in their setting. The next door neighbor and his family, the kids in the playground or in the park, the community in which you live (whether inner city, ghetto, or suburbia) will have new significance for the Christian on mission in our time.

WEDNESDAY EVENING, DECEMBER 4

TITLE: "The Bible Speaks to Our Condition"

SCRIPTURE READING: John 14.

Introduction. The words recorded in the chapter for today fell from the lips of our Lord on the night before His crucifixion. This passage of Holy Scripture has spoken to the hearts of multiplied millions of the saints through the centuries bringing comfort and courage for living in difficult times. Surely God will speak to our hearts this day as we prayerfully consider this great chapter from the New Testament.

I. *The Secret of the Untroubled Heart* (14:1-3, 27-31). Our Lord has announced to His disciples that the time for His departure has arrived and that He is returning to the heavenly Father. We can easily imagine how this must have disturbed and distressed them. Our Lord encouraged them to face the future with faith. He encouraged them to believe that the secret of tranquility and inward poise in a time of stress would be found through faith.

A. We must believe His words (14:10). There is no way to face the future with poise and inward peace if we do not trust implicitly in the truthfulness of the words of the Lord Jesus Christ.

B. We must believe in His Works (14:11-14). Our Lord was not only a speaker, He was a worker. He encouraged His disciples to put their faith in Him on the basis of His good works in the name of the Father. He is not a silent, inactive spectator. He worked the works of God while He was here on earth. He declares that He is going to depart and be with the heavenly Father in order that His disciples might be able to do even greater works than He did.

With implicit faith in the words and promises of our Lord, and with confidence in His activity on our behalf, it is possible for us to experience the untroubled heart—inward peace and poise in the midst of circumstances that might otherwise terrify us.

II. *The Revelation of the Heavenly Father* (14:4-11, 20-24). Jesus speaks to His disciples concerning one of the major purposes for His ministry in the world. He declares over and over that He came to reveal the Father. He affirms that He is the only way to the Father (14:6). Men can discover the power of God by studying nature and the physical world about us. Men come to experience God as heavenly Father only through faith in Jesus Christ.

Jesus Christ was more than just the best man who ever lived. He was something more than just a heavenly inspired teacher who lived an unselfish life. Jesus Christ was the eternal God with a human body. If we would come to understand and to know God, we can do so only as we look into the face of Jesus Christ. He is a revelation of the nature and purpose of the loving Father God (14:8-11).

III. *The Promise of the Holy Spirit* (14:12-19, 25-27). Our Lord sought to tranquilize the hearts and to dissolve the fears of His disciples by promising to them "another comforter" who would abide with them forever. There are several significant words in verses 16-18 of this great chapter.

A. The word "another" means "another of the same kind." There is another word that Jesus could have used which means "another of a different kind."

B. The word "comforter" means "one called to walk by the side of." Jesus had walked with them and talked with them for three and a half years. They were distressed at the thought of being deprived of His presence.

C. The Holy Spirit is to abide with them forever. This is in contrast to the three and a half years of the ministry of our Lord.

D. In the phrase, "whom the world cannot receive," Jesus is saying that the Holy Spirit will not be subject to arrest and crucifixion as He is to be arrested and crucified. The word translated "receive" can also mean "to seize," "to arrest." Jesus is declaring that no one will be able to crucify the Holy Spirit because He is invisible and spiritual. He will not be tangible and limited to a human body as the Savior was.

E. The Holy Spirit is to dwell within them. He is to dwell within them permanently. Our Lord declares that He will not leave them desolate and forsaken as if they were orphans. He says, "I will come to you."

Conclusion. This chapter speaks of God the Father, God the Son, and God the Holy Spirit, a perfect unit expressing itself in trinity. God the Father expressed His love through God the Son in a dramatic and unique manner. God continues to manifest Himself through the person of the Holy Spirit who is in the heart of each believer, and who is in the world to impart faith and life to those who will trust the Lord Jesus Christ.

TITLE: "Why the Christ Child?

TEXT: "Therefore the Lord himself shall give you a sign; Behold, a virgin shall conceive, and bear a son, and shall call his name Immanuel" (Isa. 7:14).

SCRIPTURE READING: Isaiah 53: 1-12.

HYMNS: "Hark! the Herald Angels Sing," Wesley. "The First Noel," Old English Carol. "Come, Thou Long-expected Jesus," Wesley.

OFFERTORY PRAYER:

Our heavenly Father, babies have been blessings throughout our lives, but the one baby who has meant more to us than all others is the Christ Child whose birth we commemorate at the Christmas season. We thank You for what He has meant to us as individuals and to all the world. Help us to honor Him with our lives and our gifts, as we pray in Jesus' name. Amen.

Introduction. Most of the major doctrines of Christianity can be found in the Christmas message. Those that are not specifically found are implied. A few examples can illustrate the many. The thought, "God with" is the doctrine of omnipresence. "His name, Immanuel" is the doctrine of justification. The Lord Jesus satisfies the demands of both man and God. "He gave His only begotten son" illustrates His love. The baby Jesus points out the doctrine of humility.

The hymns that are sung around Christmas time are good phrases to help one get the real Christmas message. The hymn, "Hark, the Herald Angels Sing" is being used as the basis of this message.

I. *The Phrases "Jesus, Our Immanuel," and "Veiled in Flesh the God-Head See," Are the Very Center of the Christmas Thought.*

A. Two passages of Scripture (Isa. 7:14 and Matt. 1:23) use the word "Immanuel." This word is a derivative of three Hebrew words—*im* means "with"; *anu* means "us"; *el* means "God." One combines the three and he has the word "Immanuel," which means "God with us."

B. The lesson derived from this thought is most helpful. God is identified with the total self of each person. By being born as a babe, He is identified with the birth of other babes. By living here on earth, He is identified with the normal life of all people. By dying on the cross, He is identified with the death of all. By rising from the grave and ascending to heaven, He is identified with the hope of all.

Second Corinthians 5:21 says, "He hath made him to be sin for us, who knew no sin; that we might be made the righteousness of God in him." This passage shows each sinful person how God is identified with his temptation and sin and how He removes sin.

God is ever present to protect, help, and guide His people.

C. This identity makes the Lord Jesus a just king to reign over His people.

No king can be a good king apart from an identity with his people. But the King of kings who is the Lord Jesus is the perfect King. He

329

knows His people and never makes a mistake in regard to them.

II. *Another Phrase in the Familiar Hymn Is "God and Sinners Reconciled."*

A. This is His mission into the world. The meaning of the word "reconcile" is to reunite, or to cause to be friendly again, or to bring back to harmony. A definition of this nature immediately implies a break, man's break with God. This is man's sin. Sin causes estrangement. The estrangement is on man's part, not God's. The one greatest need of man today is to be brought into harmony with God. His lack of harmony explains the unrest, evil, and problems of the world today.

B. A phrase in the hymn that suggests what happens to man in this reconciling process is, "born to give them second birth."

The gospel of John says, "Ye must be born again" (3:7). This is the making of a new life. A new emphasis on the doctrine of the new birth would be of help in these troubled times.

III. *The Third Phrase Is "Hail the Heaven-Born Prince of Peace."*

A. The Prince of Peace came to establish peace on earth, yet the world seems to be a long way from it. Genuine peace starts with the new birth. It starts with the right relation to God. This is on an individual basis. One person at a time surrenders to Jesus for salvation and becomes a new creature in Christ

Jesus. Then the peace Jesus came to establish on earth will become a reality as a life of righteousness is lived by each of the children of God. Righteousness is right living and peace among people will become a reality when God's people live right.

B. It is the privilege and responsibility of each Christian to join with the angelic host and proclaim.

The only hope of peace is the true reign of God in the hearts of all. This can be done as each person who has been born again conducts himself in a Godly manner. One of the greatest promises in all the Bible is, "If my people, which are called by my name, shall humble themselves, and pray, and seek my face, and turn from their wicked ways; then will I hear from heaven, and will forgive their sin, and will heal their land" (2 Chron. 7:14). This is a firm commitment on God's part to heal a sin-sick world when the world meets the conditions of a righteous, loving God.

Conclusion. Where do you fit into a message of this nature? You need to personally place yourself in the will of God. If you are not a Christian, you need to unashamedly confess Him before men and live for Him.

Christmastime is a time of rededication for all God's children. If you have a tendency to celebrate Christmas in a debauchery sort of way, in a way that is unchristian, then resolve to not do such and make a new commitment of real Christ-like living.

TITLE: "Do We Look for Another?"

TEXT: "Now John sent two of his disciples, and said unto him [Jesus], Art thou he that should come, or do we look for another?" (Matt. 11:2, 3).

SCRIPTURE READING: Matthew 11: 1-6.

Introduction. Life without purpose is an empty shell. A purposeless life is flabby and subject to fluctuation. It is no problem to discover the purpose God gave to all other of His creation. Man has purpose too, but purpose must be discovered and personal commitment be made to the highest reason for life. This message deals with the interplay of relationships between John and Jesus. These men were highly motivated by a realization of purpose. They were in this life for reasons assigned by God!

John knew his mission and fulfilled it. The coming of John into this world is a preface to the coming of Jesus. A boy child was born to Zacharias and Elizabeth. The proud parents suffered a traumatic experience in the loss of speech from the lips of the father. With the coming of the son, and his naming him "John," his speech returned. This couple was dedicated to the things of the temple. The announcement of the coming child was brought to the father by an angel of the Lord. He would be a child promised by the Lord and he would be the one who would announce to the world the Holy One of Israel.

There were no shepherds, no wise men, no bright stars in the East and no heavenly chorus when John came into the world. The child grew and waxed strong in spirit and was in the desert until the day of his appearance to Israel. John was preaching. The echoes of his message rang across Israel. A high moral note was sounded for a follower of Jehovah. He called men to repentance! He insisted that men should bring forth fruits indicating their repentance.

I. *Scene One: John the Baptist and Jesus.* His highest moment had come. It was at the Jordan. John was involved in a baptismal service. He saw Jesus in the crowd. It was time for the great announcement: "Behold, the Lamb of God." John had lived for this minute and for this epochal announcement.

See how he did it! There was no great fanfare. He planned no promotional events or techniques. John stood in the last of the long line of prophets across many years. It was his commission, his task. Other prophets before him had the privilege of saying, "He will come." John had the privilege of shouting, "Here he is!" The one promised by God, looked for by His people is now provided to the world.

John denounced himself in favor of Jesus. "I am not worthy to loose the strings of his shoes." John's purpose was to indicate Jesus as the Messiah of God. He fulfilled his mission. It is not strange that John moves from the scene of history in favor of Jesus.

Later Jesus evaluated the role of John the Baptist in the ranks of the prophets. He was no reed shaken with the wind, a man clothed in soft raiment. He was a prophet of the Lord and Jesus said that there is none greater than John. He was a man on mission and the mission was realized in Jesus.

II. *Scene Two: John in Prison.* John was placed in prison. The walls were high. He was shut off from developments. No reports had come to him as to the activities of Jesus. Often he wondered, "How are things going with Jesus?" "What are His activities?" "What are His methods?" He eagerly waited to hear word of His crowning. That word never came.

Patience sometimes wanes when a man is cut off from friends and his activities are stymied. He sent word through two of his disciples to Jesus: "Are You the one who is to come, or are we to expect another?" Is this a question from depression, a result of isolation, or evidence of inactivity?

The reports he had been receiving about the activity of Jesus did not seem consistent with his personal expectations. Here is a very human trait in even the finest of disciples. Was John trying to set the guidelines for the mission God has for the life of another? There is no indication in the text to suggest just what John's expectations were. Was he expecting Jesus to shake this world mightily in force and power? John was really seeking some affirmation of His personal mission. Had he made a mistake? And he wanted an answer. Wisely he directed it to Jesus.

Jesus affirmed the mission of John. "Go thy way," He said to John's disciples, "tell John what things you have seen and heard; how the blind see, the lame walk, the lepers are cleansed, the deaf hear, the dead are raised up, the Gospel is preached to the poor." Jesus told John that he would find his answer where he found his question. John went to his death. He probably never received satisfaction

for his question. Strangely enough, neither John or Jesus was received by men. Both of them went to their death, but the joy of life is demonstrated in the realization each of them had for his personal mission in this world. They lived and died for the mission given each of them by God.

III. *Scene Three: Across Two Thousand Years Still the Same Question, "Shall We Look for Another?"* Is it all a sad mistake? Have we wasted our years? Is Jesus done? Did we sign up in a losing cause? Is it worthwhile to make personal commitments of hands and feet, lips, heart, and life to the man, Jesus? John said that He is "the Lamb of God, which taketh away the sins of the world!" We certainly need that, but still there is the question, "Art thou he . . . or do we look for another?"

If Jesus is not the One, where shall the One be found? What do we want Him to be? What is He to be doing? Where shall we look for evidences of the "taking away the sin of the world"?

Some want to look to great government. What has great government ever produced for the souls of men. History tells this story well. The governments of Egypt, of Greece, of the Roman Empire, Germany, France and Spain were one time first-rate world powers. Government cannot produce human values. Government is usually intended to serve people, but government standing alone usually produces an arrangement where people become its servant.

Social reform can never "take away the sins of the world." Thousands of years ago Josiah discovered that social reform can help people to walk on this earth, but cannot help people to live as complete persons.

Where shall we really go, if it isn't Jesus? It is Jesus who came to bear away the sin of the world! His death on the cross is His credential. His victory over the tomb is the seal of His heavenly qualifications.

IV. *Final Scene: This Very Day and This Very Life.* John's problem was that he seemed to want to describe how God's mission would be realized in Jesus. He wanted things to happen as they had happened to him. The balance of the story and the progress of Christian history tells us another great truth: What God does in Jesus is a lot better than what we think He ought to do!

John and Jesus were certainly not exceptions to the necessity for realization of personal mission in redeemed lives. My life and yours is here for reasons known by God. We are to be "on mission." That mission is the mission of God through life. Discovery of that reason is something of what Jesus meant when He described real life as the "abundant life."

God is constantly at work in the world. He works in and through redeemed persons who will commit time, talent, and total personality to those purposes which are discovered through prayer and involvement with others.

Conclusion. The Christmas story has a deep missionary theme. John was sent from God. Jesus was sent to the world. The commission of Christ is to redeemed persons who will commit time, talent, and total personality to those redemptive purposes which are discovered through prayer and involvement with others.

WEDNESDAY EVENING, DECEMBER 11

TITLE: "The Bible Speaks to Our Condition"

SCRIPTURE READING: John 21.

Introduction. In order to receive strength and guidance from the Holy Scriptures, each one must put himself solidly and completely into the situation and let God's Word speak to his mind, his heart, to his life, to his sins, to his potential for good.

The great chapter for today discloses that our Lord revealed Himself time and time again to His disciples. There are at least ten recorded instances in the Scriptures of the appearance of the risen Lord before His Ascension. Often He was not recognized at first (21:4).

It is the teaching of the Scripture that the Christ of history becomes our contemporary through the Holy Spirit. He has promised His disciples His abiding presence as long as the ages roll. He comes to those who have faith to believe and to those who are willing to be responsive to His leadership.

I. *The Importance of Obedience* (21:5-11). All night long the apostles had labored in vain. Their nets continued to be empty. This is a parable of the life that is lived on the level of human skills and resources alone.

The risen Christ approached, and after asking a question, issued a suggestion. Without knowing who the unique person on the shore was, the fishermen followed His suggestion and caught a net so full of fish that they were unable to pull it to the shore. We are not spiritualizing this passage when we draw the conclusion that to live the life of obedience is to experience a life that is full of the resources that God makes available to the hearts and lives of men. Faith and obedience are the twin tracks that lead to fullness of life.

II. *The Restoration of An Apostle* (21:12-20). There are many significant lessons that can be drawn from this experience in a life of the Apostle Peter with the risen Lord. The major purpose of these three pointed, painful questions probably is the desire of the Good Shepherd to find, to restore, and to recommission one who had disappointed his Lord and who had lost his self-confidence and conceit by his shameful threefold denial of the Lord during His trials. After each question and answer, our Lord gave to Peter a command which was in reality an assurance of forgiveness and a recommission to service.

Each of us has disappointed our Lord and disappointed ourselves. In so many ways we have fallen short and missed the mark. There is forgiveness with the Lord and there is

a better tomorrow if we will but trust Him and obey Him.

III. *A Definition of Discipleship* (21:21, 22). In the words of our Lord to Peter, "Follow me," which was repeated twice in this passage, we have an excellent definition of what it means to be a good disciple of the Lord Jesus.

We need to follow Him in the matter of discovering and accepting His attitudes.

We need to follow Him at the point of discovering His affections and accepting these same objects of love and purposes of love as our own.

We need to discover what the compelling ambition of our Lord was and let His ambition become our ambition.

Conclusion. The risen Lord approaches each of us in the situation where life finds us today. He comes with purposes of love. He is eager to restore the drifter and the one who has failed. He is eager to lead us to the pathway that leads to a full net. The full net must not be identified with financial affluence. We can discover the fullness of life that God has planned for us by following Him all of the way throughout all of our days.

SUNDAY MORNING, DECEMBER 15

TITLE: "The Christ of Christmas"

TEXT: "But when the fulness of time was come, God sent forth his Son, made of a woman, made under the law" (Gal. 4:4).

SCRIPTURE READING: Galatians 4:4; Ephesians 1:10; 1 Timothy 2:6; Titus 1:3; Hebrews 9:26.

HYMNS: "While Shepherds Watched Their Flocks," Tate. "Gentle Mary Laid Her Child,"

Cook. "Silent Night! Holy Night," Mohr.

Dear heavenly Father, Thou art good to us all the time, but at Christmastime we take special note of Thy goodness. Now we want to thank You especially for the Christ of Christmas. We thank You and love Him for all He has done for us and for what He means to us. We thank You for His birth and we thank You for His intercession. Help us in our giving that we may give in accordance with Your will. In Jesus' name we pray. Amen.

Introduction. As a whole, people look forward to Christmas with more anticipation than any other season of the year. It is truly a time of rejoicing, bright beaming eyes, giving and receiving of gifts, much delicious food, holidays, and visiting of relatives and friends. However, Christmas would have very little real depth meaning apart from the Lord Jesus Christ. It is His birthdate that is celebrated this season of the year. It is the Christ of Christmas that is the subject for this message.

I. *The Christ of Christmas From Birth to His Present Status Is a Revelation From God.*

A. In His birth, one can see the power of God to rise above the natural and manifest Himself in a miraculous way.

The babe in Bethlehem was one of the greatest miracles of all times. This was the preexistent One now in earthly existence. This was the eternal God in the form of a fleshly child. No one but an omnipresent God could do this.

The babe in Bethlehem was born of a virgin, without an earthly father. This also reveals God at work in an unusual way. Only One, who has all power, would be able to break a natural law such as the birth of a baby and bring one into the world as God did Christ.

The babe in Bethlehem is a proof of God's fulfillment of prophecy. Hundreds of years before the birth of Jesus, God had promised such an event with many little details spelled out. This is a revelation of God's knowledge and of His ability to carry out plans.

B. In His life, one can see the nature and characteristics of God at work.

The Bible speaks of God as love and no greater revelation of love can be found and/or manifested than in Jesus Christ. He loved all. This all is all-inclusive regardless of how people might be cataloged or characterized. There are no exceptions.

The Bible speaks of God being no respecter of persons. In the life of Jesus, one can see the validity of such a statement. In Him the worth of each person is emphasized.

The Bible speaks of Jesus as a God of compassion, and the very movements of Jesus while He lived His earthly life manifests God as a God of compassion.

C. In His death one can see the sacrifice of God to redeem lost people.

This is God dying physically and spiritually to pay the price of sin. The wages of sin is death. This death is physical, but it is also separation from God, and Jesus paid the full price.

This is blood being shed for the

remission of sin. From the beginning of time, blood sacrifices played a major role in the atonement for sin. But when Jesus died, it was a sacrifice once and for all, and apart from this sacrifice, there is no remission of sin.

D. In His Resurrection, Ascension, and intercession, one can see God as might, as ruling, and as victorious.

The Resurrection reveals might—power—over enemy number one—death and the grave. When Jesus arose from the grave, He broke the power of death and the grave and so He reveals God.

The Ascension reveals God as everlasting and power over time and physical laws.

The intercession reveals God and His concern for all people of all time.

E. In His coming again, one can see the cleansing and ruling Christ.

II. *The Christ of Christmas Is Worthy of a Lofty Place in the Lives of All People.*

A. He is worthy of worship and people do worship Him.

In order to worship Him aright—in spirit and in truth—one must surrender his life to Him for salvation. Then He becomes a personal Savior and this is His purpose of coming into the world.

He is to be worshiped privately the year around. He is to be worshiped publicly in the church throughout the year.

He is to be worshiped in adoration. Everyone ought to see Him as God and as Savior and manifest reverent admiration for Him.

He is to be worshiped in praise. All Christians are to praise His name, His works, His love, and His redeeming grace.

He is to be worshiped in exhaltation because of love for Him and appreciation to Him.

B. He is worthy of one's life and possessions. In Him one's life is its very best, and apart from Him it is inferior. In Him a life is what it ought to be, and apart from Him it is less than the best. In Him one's possessions are sanctified, cleansed, and multiplied for good.

C. He is worthy of recognition and consultation of the entire world. It is nothing but natural to want to share Him. It is beneficial to consult Him in every facet of life.

Conclusion. This is the Christmas season. In your buying of gifts, do not forget Him. Think of missions. Think of the church and include Him in the expenditure of money. In your seeking of happiness and a good time, take Him into your lives and He will give supreme happiness.

SUNDAY EVENING, DECEMBER 15

TITLE: "God Is Ready When You Are!"

TEXT: "But when the fulness of the time was come, God sent forth his Son, made of a woman, made under the law, to redeem them that were under the law, that we might receive the adoption of sons" (Gal. 4:4, 5).

SCRIPTURE READING: Galatians 4:1-7.

Introduction. The subject of this message is "God Is Ready When You Are." The Apostle Paul in his writing to the people of God in the territory of Galatia reviewed the providences of God across many years to a given point in history. Then he says that when the world was ready, God was ready. It was at that moment that Jesus came.

There is a truth about the ways of our Lord which can never be matched by the ways of man. It has to do with patience—what God does in His purposes, He does in His own time and He is in no particular hurry to do it. To the contrary, what man does he wants to see accomplished in his own time. First, the seed, then the sapling, and then the sturdy oak.

Man formulates his plans and expects tomorrow to see his plan fulfilled and completed. Paul points up to the Galatian Christians that when the world was ready, but most of all when *God* was ready, it was at that time when Jesus came. Jesus came to this world as a babe in Bethlehem, lived among men for approximately thirty-three years, died on a cross, and rose from the dead appropriate to the purposes of God. And Paul summarized in the fullness of time—God was ready for the redemption of the world, and when it was just exactly the right time, Jesus came.

I. *The World Was Ready for Jesus!*

A. Politically: The dominating feature of the world to which Jesus came was "unification." This was the outstanding accomplishment of the Caesars. It was a new world; there were new horizons. There was no conglomerate of antagonistic national coalitions looking across giant barriers. The world, at the coming of Jesus, was a Roman world. The roads were Roman roads. From east to west and north to south ran the great roads of Rome. The roadbuilders were paving the way for the industries, for the movement of the merchandising processes of Rome. Little did they know that they were paving the way for the coming of the Son of God.

The language barrier was eliminated. The Greek language was spoken and understood at this time around the world. Communication between men has been, is now, and will always be a problem.

B. Economically: Underneath the magnificence and splendor of the Roman world was *unrest* and *poverty*. Two of every three men on the streets of Rome were slaves. When the poets of Rome wrote of the golden age, they were writing of the past and not of the present. There was an economic affluence but a deep moral vacuum.

C. Morally: One of the poets of yesterday said that "Jesus has taken all the gaiety and great spiritedness of Rome away" (Swineburn). Any idea that the ancient world was a happy, lighthearted one and stood at peace in the spiritual realm is neither historically or practically accurate. Paul speaks of this at length in the first three chapters of Romans. Rome had sinned its youth away. All the freshness of youth was gone and the worm and canker of grief was at work producing the spiritual vacuum.

D. Religious needs: The old

gods of Rome were dead or dying. There were two alternatives that seemed obvious. One, a new batch of gods were imported from the East. Mystical religions and oriental deities were brought in to stimulate the decayed souls of Rome. Among the philosophers that overcrowded Olympus, the place where the Gods lived was an outstanding joke! The other alternative for a supply of gods was the Caesars themselves. Caesar worship appeared. The emperor himself was accorded divine honor. His image was erected in every town square and government building.

In the backdrop of all of this was Jewish expectation of the coming Messiah. He would come to save God's people from their sins.

It is not difficult to move these truths to the present tense. The year 1974 says again to us that the world is ready for Jesus. The political needs, the economic enigma of our time, the moral vacuum and the dearth of religious commitment speaks firmly to us that the world is ready for Jesus.

II. *Our World Is Ready for the Spirit of Christ Jesus.*

A. Politically, a new world has appeared for our time. The drastic transitions that are happening in the great national and international power structures of our world speak to us of the inability of political systems to structure any kind of design that has satisfactory human consequences.

B. Economically, never has our world had so much economic goods and yet so little personal human fulfillment. Materialism has swept around our world. Commercializa-

tion is more obvious at this particular season of the year than at any other time. It is not difficult for one to point up the paradox that exists between the contents of the songs that are sung, the carols that are played, the dramas that are presented, and the decorations of the stores, the anxious looks upon people's faces, and the behavior patterns displayed these days.

C. Morals in our world have a difficult time finding an adequate foundation. The coming of Christ into this world provided once and for all a basic foundation for determination of personal and interpersonal moral relationships. By the coming of Jesus into this world one can have a basic foundation upon which he can raise the question not only, "What do I think?" but also, "Lord, what would You have me to do?"

God is ready. The world is ready too.

III. *The Human Paradox.* We usually speak of Christmas as emphasizing the joy of giving. So it is. The Bible says, "It is more blessed to give than to receive." But there is a sense in which Christmas depends upon the joy of receiving.

The purposes of God today are surely concerned with politics, economics, morals, and religion. God is concerned with the falling apart of nations, for the downward trend in human values, for lives degenerating to useless goals, and the moral and religious overtones of daily living serving as a treadmill of impractical and lifeless effort. God is ready —the world is ready—the question is, Are His people ready to receive this gift of God today?

A. Are you ready for the faith promised in Jesus? Faith is an ability of every life. When Jesus came He brought to this world the realization of faith and what it really is and does. The writer of Hebrews insists "Without faith it is impossible to please [God]" (Heb. 11:6). He describes a faith that makes the impossible possible; a faith that asks us to do what we cannot do; a faith that produces consequences for human life that cannot be produced by another.

B. Are you ready for hope? Hope expresses the circumstances of yesterday in terms of fulfillment in positive tones tomorrow. Hope takes our faith in yesterday and moves it as a reality into tomorrow. Hope lives in expectation and in expected fulfillment. Man must dream his dream. Self-pity and pessimism produce a dormant life. Jesus brought to this world, once and for all, a vital living hope. Are we ready to receive it?

C. He brings this world love! Are we ready to receive this? An eminent minister of yesterday was requested to define Christianity in a single sentence. His reply comes from an internationally beloved children's hymn: "Jesus loves me this I know, for the Bible tells me so."

Conclusion. Surely the world is ready for faith—for hope—and for love. Political science, social science, educational techniques, material affluence—all of these can produce some values for people in our time. But the vacuum is too heavy and the breach is too broad for life that has no reality in faith, hope, and love. The question for our world today: Are we ready to receive the gift of His Spirit and reflect it to our world?

God is ready when you are. He is ready to produce a fulfillment which can never be produced by another.

WEDNESDAY EVENING, DECEMBER 18

TITLE: "The Bible Speaks to Our Condition"

SCRIPTURE READING: Revelation 1.

Introduction. The great Book of Revelation is perhaps the most neglected, the most mistreated, and the most misunderstood book in the New Testament. Many have given up any attempt to try to come to understand this mysterious last book of the Bible. They have done so to their own spiritual impoverishment.

It is described as "the revelation of Jesus Christ." It is a revealing from Christ, and it is a revelation of Christ. To properly understand this book one needs to know as much as possible about the political and religious conditions that faced the early church in the last decade of the first Christian century. He also needs to understand the nature of purpose and the uses of apocalyptic literature as a means of communicating truth. Along with this knowledge of the historical situation and with an understanding of this type of literature, he would also need the leadership and the guidance of the Holy Spirit that he might understand properly.

A beatitude is pronounced upon those who read and hear and keep the teachings of this book (1:3). This particular book of the New Testament comes from John, from the Holy Spirit, and from the Lord Jesus Christ. Our Lord is described as the coming One who will one day return to the earth in triumph and victory (1:8).

"I was in the Spirit on the Lord's day." John describes his attitude of reverence and worship and openness to the truth of God while in a very difficult and dangerous situation. He had been exiled to the Isle of Patmos during a time of severe persecution, when it seemed as if Christianity would be obliterated by the policies of Domitian, the Roman emperor.

I. *The Vision of the Glorified and Exalted Lord* (1:12-16). In these words we have a description of the vision of the risen Lord which equipped the elderly Apostle John to begin a new and unique ministry as a prophet of God in a very difficult and dangerous time. God had appeared to Moses, Amos, Hosea, Isaiah, Jeremiah, Ezekiel, and had called them into a unique relationship and equipped them for significant service. In this vision, it is revealed that John experienced something similar to the great prophets of the Old Testament.

John saw the Lord—alive, triumphant, victorious, and clothed in indescribable garments. An examination of the apparel of the risen One seemingly is a combination of the robe of the high priest of the Old Testament, the robe of a prince or a king, and even the garment of a messenger of God.

As a priest he had access to God. As a king he had royal authority, and as a prophet he spoke with a message from God.

II. *The Reverent Awe of the Apostle* (1:17). Like the prophets of the past, John fell on his face as though he were dead as the eye of his soul perceived the presence of his God. The vision of God always humbles.

III. *The Triumphant Announcement* (1:17b, 18). John heard the risen Christ speak with a voice of triumphant authority concerning His victory over death and the grave and His authority over death and the abode of the dead. This vision of a triumphant and ever-present Christ was desperately needed in a time when the disciples were filled with great perplexity concerning their status and concerning their future.

IV. *The Message of the Lord* (1:19, 20). The purpose of this apocalyptic vision of the glorified Lord was to communicate an indelible impression to the mind of the apostle and to equip him with a message for the churches of that day and time. This was no mystical experience that exalted the emotions of the apostle for his own enjoyment. It was purposeful and was intended to equip him for the ministry.

Conclusion. The overall impression of this experience on the apostle was to give him a vision of the Christ who was alive, triumphant over sin, death and the grave. He was assured that Christ would be eternally victorious over all world conditions. He recognized that the Christ was spiritually present with sovereign power. He became convinced that Christ and His churches would be ultimately victorious in the present terrible crisis.

We need today a vision of our risen and exalted Lord, who is ever present with us to meet the deepest needs of our life.

May each of us pray for open eyes and hearing ears as we seek to let our Lord speak to us through this great chapter.

SUNDAY MORNING, DECEMBER 22

TITLE: "God With Us"

TEXT: "Behold, a virgin shall be with child, and shall bring forth a son, and they shall call his name Emmanuel, which being interpreted is, God with us" (Matt. 1:23).

SCRIPTURE READING: Matthew 1:18-23.

HYMNS: "Thou Didst Leave Thy Throne," Elliott. "One Day," Chapman. "I Heard the Bells on Christmas Day," Longfellow.

OFFERTORY PRAYER:

Our Father, Thou hast given us many gifts, but the greatest of all is Your Son, our Savior, Jesus Christ. We thank You that in Jesus You became identified with us. Thus, You know and understand us. As we have entered this Christmas season, help us to realize Thy presence more than ever before, and as we worship Thee in giving, accept our gifts with the purpose we give them. Use them to bring other people to a knowledge that "God is with us." In Jesus' name we pray. Amen.

Introduction. People use a number of words to describe God. One is "transcendent." This simply means God is above or beyond the earthly. He exceeds the human. Another word used to describe God is "omnipresent" and this means God is everywhere all the time. Still another word used to describe God is "imminent." This means God is present with us.

The words "imminent" and "Immanuel" mean practically the same. Immanuel means "God with us." This is the meaning found in the text.

The one prominent thing about the birth of Jesus is that God was making Himself a human being. God was becoming identified with His creation. That is the meaning of the word "incarnate." It means God in flesh.

I. *During the Earthly Life of Jesus, He Was God Identified With Man.*

A. He was tempted as a man. The Bible says in Hebrews (4:15), He "was in all points tempted like as we are, yet without sin." Man has never, nor, will he ever, suffer a temptation that was not Jesus'. This identifies Jesus as a person in reach by sinful, struggling human beings. He knows all the struggles, weaknesses, and problems of those with whom He came to be identified.

By such coming, Jesus became Savior. He suffered temptation, but never yielded; therefore, He was able to offer Himself as a perfect sacrifice for the sinner's sin.

B. He was called "The Man of Sorrows." Several hundred years before His birth, it was prophesied that He would be a "man of sorrows" (Isa. 53:3). In Luke (19:41), one sees Him fulfilling this prophecy. Here He is pictured weeping over the city of Jerusalem. He was identified with the sin and it caused much sorrow.

All during Jesus' earthly life He grappled with the problems with which human beings are confronted.

C. He was involved in human situations. When there was physical pain and handicap, He was right there dealing with it.

The gospel of Matthew tells of His healing a woman diseased with an issue of blood for twelve years. The same chapter also tells of His opening the eyes of two blind men and enabling them to see. The gospel of Luke tells of His healing a man with palsy and enabling him to take up his bed and walk. The gospel of Mark tells of Jesus putting His hand upon an untouchable leper and cleansing him of the dreaded disease.

When there was mental disorder and emotional disturbances, Jesus was also found ministering to them. Matthew (8:28) tells of two men, possessed with devils, being healed. The same gospel (9:32) gives a similar instance and there Jesus gave the man ability to speak.

When there was social differences, Jesus dealt with the issues in a redemptive fashion. He made no distinction in people. He went through Samaria the same as He went through Judea. In doing so, He dealt with an outcast from the Jewish standpoint. He ate with a hated tax collector and showed His interest in the unlovely.

When there was economic problems, Jesus was equally concerned.

He kept Himself busy helping the poor. He gave parables to teach human relations in the economic world.

When there were religious problems, Jesus was in the middle of them seeking to find a solution.

When there were domestic problems, Jesus gave sound advice and helpful suggestions, as well as resourceful strength to deal with them.

When there was sin and guilt, Jesus forgave the sin and removed the guilt.

When there was joy in the hearts of the people, Jesus rejoiced with them and added to the joy.

Thus, one can see that when Jesus was born in Bethlehem of Judea, He was "God with us" in every need of man.

II. *God Is Equally Identified With Man Today.*

A. Just as He was identified with man in the person of Jesus Christ, He is now identified with man in the person of the Holy Spirit.

There is not one thing that can happen to any man today, but what God is right there. No problem is ever faced, but what God is present and ready to help deal with it. No heartache has ever been overlooked or ignored by the ever-present God in the person of the Holy Spirit. He is truly everywhere now as He was at the time when Jesus was born.

B. There is a difference in God's presence in the Holy Spirit and in the Son. In the Son, God took on self-limitations, whereas, in the Holy Spirit, there are no limitations. This is true geographically, timewise, and in regard to circumstances.

Conclusion. This is the time of year when special attention is given to God's identity with us. If you know Him as your personal Savior, recommit your life to Him for joys and victories. Lean on Him for the strength you need. If you have not received Him as your Savior, let this be the greatest Christmas you have ever experienced by trusting Him now and letting Him have complete control of your life.

SUNDAY EVENING, DECEMBER 22

TITLE: "And Jesus Begat . . ."

TEXT: "He came unto his own, and his own received him not. But as many as received him, to them gave he power to become the sons of God, even to them that believe on his name" (John 1:11, 12).

SCRIPTURE READING: Matthew 1:1-14.

Introduction. In a Christmas occasion of yesteryear there is a story about a group of English school children constructing a manger scene in one corner of their classroom. They built a barn and covered the floor with hay. The figures of Mary, Joseph, the shepherds, the wisemen, and the animals faced the cradle. A tiny doll represented the baby Jesus. The children were all excited, but one little fellow seemed troubled. He kept returning again and again to the corner of the room to study the manger scene. Finally, the teacher asked if something was wrong. Revealing wisdom typical of a child's ability to confound the wise he said, "What I would like to know is—where does God fit in?" This is an important question.

There are four books which begin our New Testament. Three of these set forth to introduce Jesus in the backdrop of a genealogy. The genealogy in Matthew's gospel is usually read through quickly and taken quite lightly. There is a repetitiousness involved. Matthew keeps reminding his readers of the fact that certain people came and did certain things and "begat" other people and other things. John's gospel went right to the core of the spirit of the Incarnation and identified Jesus as the One who was from the beginning, who was with God, and was God, who became flesh and dwelled among us, who influences life eternally. The genealogy in Matthew's gospel points up the historical continuity of people relating to other people. These people, whose names for some of us are almost unpronounceable, are bound together by the word "begat," but the continuity moves forward toward the coming of Jesus. When Matthew gets to the place where he points out the continuity that begat Jesus, there is no further use of the word. However, as we look back across history and into the details of personal lives today, it is not difficult for us to recognize the fact that continuity continues. For there are some things that Jesus has begotten also. Jesus was never married, He had no sons, He had no daughters, but Jesus did begat—the word itself means "bring to life."

I. *Jesus Begat His Church.* It would take a great amount of time to go in depth to the details of this genealogy. Wiping away all the clutter of names, Matthew is tracing the story of a covenant God had with Abraham, continued through David, and now fulfilled in Jesus who Matthew says is the Messiah of God. This covenant essentially says, "If you will be My people, I will be Your God," and Jesus begat a covenant people—the people of God.

The Gospel is specific about what Jesus begat. He touched people of every walk and level of life from the person on the top rungs of the ladders of life to those on the lowest. Jesus paid attention to them. He saw them, He called them, He touched them, He helped them and He blessed them. Out of these ranks came His disciples, the chosen ones, the holy people of the Lord. When we get to the last pages of this gospel we get to see again what Jesus has begotten. He is in His resurrected body, and a great crowd is with Him from the mountain. He is surrounded by people. He speaks, "All power is given unto me in heaven and in earth. Go ye therefore, and teach all nations ... Teaching them to observe all things whatsoever I have commanded you: and, lo, I am with you alway, even unto the end of the world."

Jesus begat a people of a covenant, a people of redemption, a people with God in their hearts and the message for their world. This is His Church. He expressed the divine intention for the Church to be the cutting edge to bring to pass the kingdom of God.

He gave His Church something brand new and has never taken it away from her. He gave to His Church a divine presence—the Holy Spirit. He gave to His Church a new day—the Lord's day, the celebration of His Resurrection. He gave to His Church two new ordinances—baptism and the Lord's Supper—covenant relationships internally with an external expression for the people of God. And he gave to His Church a glorious hope—"I shall be with you alway, even until the end of the [age]."

Our loyalty to God and His Church have lofty motives and designs far superior to the customary viewpoint. We identify with loyalties far too small. By this time in our century, this loyalty is whittled down to one determined by attendance in services, giving in the offering plate, and a few kindly benevolent deeds. But Jesus begat a people who claimed Him the Lord of their life! These people count loyalties in terms of a commitment to a Christ who lives in their hearts, provides a guidance and a presence which cannot be produced by loyalties other than divine lordship in Jesus.

Sometimes we are inclined to think of goodness among the Lord's people in terms of specific loyalties that are congregational. It is not unusual to hear it said of certain persons of the fellowship, "This person has served the church for thirty years!" The response of the Gospel to such an understanding is one of shame and wasted life. Basic to the claims of a total life is a first loyalty to Jesus Christ who came that we might have life, and who came to be served.

Christ begat a brotherly fellowship. The people of God are redeemed persons who bear compassion and fellowship for each other. This is the common life. The vertical dimension of relationships of an individual with God corresponds always in an outward expression of horizontal relationships of that total life and personal mission to others. The mere erection of buildings, construction of programs, design of techniques can never replace the commitment of a total personality bound together in mutual relationships of Christian love. The first one hundred years of the Church were vital, vigorous, and victorious. The spirit of Christ permeated their presence. The dark years of the medieval ages were dark indeed in the loss and lack of a vital relationship which God intends in a redemptive fellowship.

II. *And Jesus Begat a Divine Discontent With Things As They Are.* When Jesus came to this earth, He ran head-on into the religious world of His day. He was divinely discontented at two specific places.

A. The way religious people handled their precedent. They made the law, the prophets, and the spiritual values an end in themselves instead of a means to an end. They forgot the covenant and worshiped the system.

B. The way the religious people treated other people. They could not accept this One from Galilee. They said He kept paying attention to the ragtag and bobtail of humanity. In answer to this accusation, Jesus gave them a parable about a fellow who was away from his father and in the hog lot with pigs, and when he came home he was welcomed to the open arms of a father who loved him. Jesus was no avowed rebel. He loved people and wept over a whole city, but He would not bend to the kind of religious living that would pass by on the other side.

III. *Jesus Begat a New Hope.* When the life of every man great and small is written, it usually closes— "and he died!" But this is not true in the life of Jesus. Renan, a wise French philosopher, wrote one of the lovely stories of the life of Jesus. When he told the story of the cross he wrote on that last page, "Finis." Renan could not see the hope that had been begotten eternally for the world by Jesus. The grave is not the end. He came forth from the tomb. The words spread like wildfire around the province: "He is not here—he is risen!" And because He rose from the dead He assures us of a glorious hope of tomorrow.

Conclusion. The Christmas story is prelude. Jesus was born but there were some things that God did by His death in the Resurrection. Jesus begat a new people. He gave birth to an astounding movement. He gave His Church to the world. He set the pattern for divine discontent with things as they are and He gives to redeemed people a glorious new hope.

When we come to the conclusion of our annual celebration of the coming of Christ into this world, we must recognize dramatically and conclusively that we have not really come to a conclusion of the meaning of Christ for life. The purposes of God are eternal involving all persons of every kind in every generation. There are things beyond today which our minds cannot understand. There are things beyond today which our being cannot comprehend. There are things beyond today which will not be the same tomorrow as we have found them today. Beyond today is the vital necessity of the glorious reality of a Christian hope through Christ Jesus.

TITLE: "The Bible Speaks to Our Condition"

SCRIPTURE READING: Revelation 22.

Introduction. On this Christmas Day, when the thoughts of those who make up the Christian world are focused on the birth and first coming of our Lord, it could be most helpful to us if we would also let Him speak to us concerning His final victorious return to the earth.

I. *Behold, I Come Quickly* (22:7, 12, 20). In the last chapter of the last book of the New Testament, we find three clear, definite plain promises from the lips of our Lord that He will return to the earth. Our Lord spoke these words with greater determination and with greater authority than did General MacArthur when he left the Philippines during the second World War with the promise, "I shall return." It is the clear teaching of the New Testament from the lips of our Lord, from angelic messengers, from all of the apostles, that one day the Lord Jesus Christ will return triumphant and victorious for His own.

II. *Eden Restored* (22:1-5). It is interesting to note that man began his earthly existence in a garden which God had prepared for him. In this final chapter we find a picture of the redeemed in the garden of God enjoying that which God had prepared from the beginning and which man had forfeited because of sin. Everything that sin wrecked, grace has restored. The activity of the redeemed is described in terms of, "His servant shall serve him." Heaven will not be a place where we sit and rust, but it will be a place where we serve and worship and praise.

III. *The Great Final Invitation* (22:17). The last chapter of the book of the Bible contains one of the greatest invitations from the heart of God to the hearts of men. It is like our gracious God that, after extending so many invitations to the hearts of sinful men, He would not let the Holy Book come to a close without extending this most extensive, intensive invitation that could possibly be extended to the hearts and lives of men.

As individual Christians and as congregations, it is our present task to publish and to make known this gracious invitation from God to the hearts and lives of those about us. Let us not neglect our opportunity and responsibility.

IV. *The Rewards of the Lord* (22: 12). Forgiveness is full and free by the grace of God. Eternal life is the gift of God through faith in Jesus Christ. We do not merit a position of favor in the sight of God either by observing religious ceremony or by keeping a legalistic law. We become the children of God by God's pure grace through faith.

It is in the plan and purpose of God to bestow rewards upon His servants who labor faithfully and unselfishly. Let each of us pray that we might respond to God's grace and to God's commandments in such a way that He will be pleased with our stewardship and have words of commendation to bestow upon us at the end of the way.

V. *Our Abiding Hope* (22:20b). Some dread to even think of the

Second Coming of Jesus Christ. In this last chapter of the Bible, the beloved Apostle John reveals His attitude toward the return of Jesus in the words, "Even so, come, Lord Jesus." When the Lord's victorious return is properly understood, this would be the joyous and abiding hope of every living believer. There could be only one reason why we would not want Him to come immediately: that reason would be that some are not ready.

Conclusion. Let us thank God for the fact that Christ came the first time. Let us rejoice in the promise of His return. Let us respond to that promise by giving of ourselves in service to Him that others might let Him be born within their own heart and life today.

SUNDAY MORNING, DECEMBER 29

TITLE: "Retrospective and Perspective"

TEXT: ". . . lo, I am with you alway" (Matt. 28:20).

SCRIPTURE READING: Matthew 28:18-20.

HYMNS: "O God, Our Help in Ages Past," Watts. "The Nail-Scarred Hand," McKinney. "Lead On, O King Eternal," Shurtleff.

OFFERTORY PRAYER:

Holy Father, Thou hast blessed us in a bountiful way in the year that is about to come to a close. We thank You for each blessing. As we make our offering today, help us to particularly express our love and appreciation for the multiple blessings that have been ours. Then take the offering and use it to bring similar blessings to people all over the world. In Jesus' name we pray. Amen.

Introduction. This is the last Sunday in 1974. One cannot come to the end of a year without reflecting on the past. Neither can one project his thoughts into the incoming year without thinking what it holds for him.

Whether one reflects on the past or projects into the future, he can be assured of God's presence with him. He is with each person always, even unto the end of the age.

I. *The Word "Retrospective" Is Used to Look Backward on the Year That Is Coming to a Close.*

A. There is a group of words that deal with the physical and psychological, but also the spiritual is affected.

Paul uses the word "forget" (Phil. 3:13). He says "forgetting those things which are behind." To make one's reflections on the past fruitful, forgetting must be thought of in two ways. It may be good and it may be bad. The thought here is to forget the things that are bad.

Every person needs to forget the unpleasant and unhappy. Such experiences as defeat, disappointments, and guilt are events in the life of many that should be forgotten.

This can be done by an unconditional surrender to Jesus for forgiveness and cleansing (1 John 1:9).

Each person needs to forget the attitudes that make for pride and egotism. The Bible says that "pride goeth before destruction" (Prov. 16:18). The Bible also says "every good gift and every perfect gift is from above, and cometh down from the Father of lights" (James 1:17).

The word "remember" is used many times in the Bible and is also helpful as one seeks to be retrospective. In order to make the past productive, it is necessary to remember that one is dependent upon God for all he has and is. He also needs to remember the blessings of the past year, as well as the opportunities it afforded.

Another word that ought to be prevalent in the mind of each person as he reflects on the past is "learn." Most honest and/or intelligent persons will learn from their mistakes. They will also learn from their achievements and take these lessons to build the future.

"Look" is still another word that will aid the retrospective mind. One needs to look at what happened and use it. A good hard look at what happened and an intelligent analysis of it should be profitable to each person. The same thing is true of what could have happened.

B. There is another group of words that are applicable to the spiritual.

To reflect on the past and God's dealings with a person is to cause him to stand in "awe." One is amazed when he comes to realize how sinful he really is and how merciful and long-suffering the Lord is toward him.

Then the awe leads to repentance. Any conscientious person will turn from his wicked ways after reflecting on the past. To behold one's sinfulness and God's goodness in that past is to provoke repentance.

One of the greatest words in the Christian's vocabulary is "forgiveness." The Bible assures each sinner of forgiveness when his sins are confessed. It is indeed a spiritually healthy experience to be retrospective and realize one is forgiven of all his sins.

II. *The Word "Perspective" Is Used to Project One's Thought Into the Future.*

A. There are some words that apply to the physical which are helpful.

The word "vision" looms high in one's mind as he thinks of the future. Proverbs 29:18 says, "Where there is no vision, the people perish." This applies to an individual or a church. It applies to the vocation and/or physical, as well as the spiritual.

One word that is prevalent in the minds of many on the eve of a new year is "resolution." This word implies purpose. For adequate plans to be had and motivation to expedite them, there must be purpose.

Closely related to resolution is the word "determination." This puts firmness into the resolutions. Before much can be accomplished in the incoming year, a determination is necessary. This will involve work, sacrifice, planning, and dedication.

In order for one to be truly successful in his endeavors for the incoming year, one must feed into his subconscious the thought of victory. The Christian religion is a triumphant, victorious religion. Jesus came to triumph over evil. He is victorious and His followers have the same assurance.

B. There are some words that

apply to the spiritual realm which are applicable to the perspective attitude.

Paul says, "be filled with the Spirit" (Eph. 5:18). This means to be controlled by the Holy Spirit and is a must for great accomplishments in kingdom work and personal aggrandizement.

Paul also says, "pray without ceasing" (1 Thess. 5:17). "Prayer is like a vast continent, the shores of which one can touch from many directions, but a lifetime of exploration will not reveal its secrets" (Bruce E. Mills, *Help in Troubled Times*, Valley Forge, Pennsylvania: The Judson Press, 1962, p.139). Prayer takes on the aspects of eternity and is also a must to make the incoming year a fruitful one.

Obedience to the will of God is the one greatest desire for next year. Whatever He says, do. Wherever He leads, follow. Complete obedience is one's assurance of a full and meaningful life.

III. *There Is a Word That Stands Between Retrospective and Perspective and That Word Is "Now."* Now is between the past and future. In order to use the past and anticipate the future, each person needs to act now. The past is gone and the future is yet to come. Each person must learn his lessons from the past and start trying now to be ready for the future. God has spoken in the past. He has worked in the past, but He also has plans for the future. Now is the time to respond to the touch of His Spirit.

Conclusion. As you reflect on the past year and God's goodness to you, give Him your thanks. As you look forward to the year just ahead, surrender your life to Him. Place your hand in His nail-scarred hand and say, "Lead on, O King eternal."

SUNDAY EVENING, DECEMBER 29

TITLE: "You Can Take It From Here"

TEXT: "Go ye therefore, and teach all nations, baptizing them in the name of the Father, and of the Son, and of the Holy Ghost: Teaching them to observe all things whatsoever I have commanded you: and, lo, I am with you alway, even unto the end of the world" (Matt. 28:19, 20).

SCRIPTURE READING: Matthew 28:16-20.

Introduction. Very appropriate to the concluding Sunday service of a year is the scene in the last verses of Matthew's gospel. Jesus has gathered His disciples closely about Him and reviews for them their base of authority and gives to them their marching orders into the world. At no other place in the history of the world is it more obvious that our Lord has committed the Gospel to the people of His Church. There is a fourfold account of the Great Commission of our Lord. Matthew declares that the content of the Gospel is "Good News," and instructs His disciples to cross the barriers of geography, socio-economic disparities, cultural and racial differences, and interpersonal relationships by the good news of God in Christ Jesus.

It is further appropriate that in the concluding Sunday evening service of this year we be reminded of the three great missionary motives. There is the command of Christ to go; there is the inner compulsion of the spirit that says, "I must go"; and then there is the voice from God that keeps saying "Go!" The needs of the world are obvious. The mission task of the people of God is not a matter of emotion or feeling. It is not a work to be carried on at our convenience. We are under orders of our Lord. He said, "You take it from here!"

There are at least three characteristics of this command of our Lord:

I. *The Authority for the Command.* A religion which has no authority is a worthless one. Some have emphasized the autonomy of the individual to ridiculous extremes. In the backdrop of this principle we might conclude that things pertaining to the Christian life are arbitrary or optional. We can do them or not do them as our souls command. But the flip-side of that record is the authority of Christ, and Jesus leaves no question. "All power is given unto me in heaven and in earth." These are the orders of our King. If the church had asked you to do it there might be a wavering; if the preacher had asked you to do it there might be a decision; if the only reason we had for our missionary enterprise was that other churches are doing it there would be a question. But our Lord, whose authority is beyond question, has given this command. Forever the principle is established!

This is the authority of the King. The task of the Church and the task of the minister is to show people who God is in Christ Jesus. The One who left the glory of heaven and came among men; who lived as a man in the form of sinful flesh; who gave His life sacrificially on Calvary's cross; who demonstrated the power of God over death and the grave by the glorious significance of the Resurrection; it is He who says, "The authority belongs to Me." This is the One who so majestically and regally certifies His work. He is the One who so royally stands by His disciples and gives the marching orders. The cross was behind Him, the Resurrection was the sealing bond. He lived, He loved, He taught, He served and He died for people of all time. He has a right to say to His Church, "Go make disciples."

II. *It Is a Steady Task.* Our Lord has not merely given us something to believe but something to do. Here in a few sentences is the scope of our task. The command leaves no question mark. What is the business of the Church, the business of the Christian? It is to bring men to God through Jesus Christ. It is to baptize those who are won; it is to teach the way and the work and the purposes of our Lord. It is written indelibly in the history of the Church that a Christian thrives spiritually when he is passing on his faith to others.

Significant and appropriate for the needs of our world and our day is an individual review of personal mission. The mission God gives to us is expressed in personal terms. It is not meant to be done by professionals; it is meant to be an expression of the faith and hope and the love of an individual found in personal relationships with Christ Jesus. It is the task of each life and every Christian.

A church may have some admirable characteristics. She may be financially successful, physically attractive, organizationally complete; but if she does not reflect a flame of missionary zeal, surely, "The glory of the Lord" has departed from her.

The symptoms of the need for this study task by the people of God is clear for our time. There are 220 giant metropolitan areas of our nation in which individual people are groping, seeking, longing, dreaming and looking for the filling of a spiritual vacuum. Personal face to face relationships of the people of God can provide the good news of God through Christ Jesus. There are the domestic problems, the youth dilemma, the economic anxieties, the social and cultural enigmas of our time. Great barriers exist in the minds and behavior patterns of thousands and thousands of persons. Jesus Himself said, "I am the way, the truth, and the life; no man cometh unto the Father, but by me" (John 14:6). In these concluding days of a year when review is being given of our yesterdays, let's take a new look at tomorrow and understand that God is saying in Christ Jesus, "As you go, make disciples."

III. *A Divine Presence.* Jesus expressed His authority for this mission, defined the continued and steady task of personal relationships with others, and concluded His commission with a promise, "Lo, I am with you alway, even until the end of the world." One of the traumatic experiences of personal relationship is the moment in which you must say good-by to a dear friend. It is difficult to express feelings in a moment like this. Sometimes we say, "I will be thinking of you." By this, you probably mean that you would be sharing his experience, helping, sustaining and encouraging him in his new venture though separated physically from him. Certainly it does help to know that you are not forgotten, and continuing relationships can be maintained by correspondence and modern technology which assists in filling the communications gap.

But our Lord goes farther than that. He says, "I will go with you." The promise of the living Christ is not just a dream. It is the promise of a very real presence. John expresses this truth in the fourteenth, fifteenth and sixteenth chapters of his gospel.

"Always!" is the word that he uses. This means all the days of summer, winter, spring and fall, the sunshine days and the cloudy ones, the days of storm and the days of joy, the days of faith and those of doubt, the days of victory and those of defeat, the days of strength and those of weakness, the days of peace and the days of war, those days of youth where significant decisions are made and the days of mid-life where decisions are being carried through, the days of life, and yes, even the days of death and those years of eternity. God meant it when He said, "I will be with you *always!*"

Conclusion. Here then is the final word of our Lord to His people, "You take it from here."

At the highest moment in the ministry of Christ He expresses the royal authority of the King. It is by the authority of heaven and the authority of the earth entrusted to Him that He says to every Christian, "You take it from here."

MESSAGES ON THE LORD'S SUPPER

TITLE: "The Lord's Supper: on Being Involved"

TEXT: "And he said to them all, If any man will come after me, let him deny himself, and take up his cross daily, and follow me" (Luke 9:23).

SCRIPTURE READING: Luke 9: 23-26; 1 Corinthians 11:26.

Introduction. In Luke 9:23-26 we find only one of many places in which Jesus told what it meant to be involved as one of His disciples. He often warned men to count the cost of such involvement but He also warned against overlooking the cost of not becoming involved.

In Matthew 10:32 Jesus warns against the high cost of non-involvement. On another occasion Jesus remarked that "They that are not with me are against me." The Lord's Supper speaks to us about involvement.

I. *The Cross of Christ Is God's Involvement* (Luke 9:23). The cross reminds us that God was not content merely to create a world and to create men but was concerned about the welfare of His creation. God became involved in the affairs of men on many occasions in the course of history in order to redirect men to the only way of life. The supreme involvement came as the Word became flesh and dwelt among us, full of grace and truth. The involvement of our Lord in the problems of men found its zenith at the cross of Calvary. The cross reminds us that a Savior who is willing to become involved at the point of death can never be content with disciples who are uncommitted.

II. *Discipleship Is Our Involvement* (Luke 9:23, 24). Somehow the tragic heresy has entered the minds of some people that says a man's soul can be saved without his life becoming involved in daily discipleship. No such alternative is offered. Conversion is equivalent to involvement with Christ as Savior. This is why Christ says to His disciples, "I am the way, the truth, and the life."

I remember three years ago in New York City when I was wanting to know the way back to my hotel, I asked a man for directions and he obligingly chose rather to show me the way himself. He led me to the proper bus stop and missed his own bus in order to stay there and help me get on the right bus. Rather than give me directions which would have been hard to follow, he became my way. So it is with Jesus. He becomes our Way into life.

III. *Communion Is Joint Involvement.* We have often shied away from the word "Communion" when speaking of the Lord's Supper but it is a perfectly valid Biblical word which is used to speak of genuine Christian fellowship (*koinonia*). A part of our gathering at the Lord's table is involvement.

A. Involvement by identification. One of the darkest moments in the life of Simon Peter was when he denied his involvement with Christ. Gathering at the Lord's table identifies each of us as one who is involved with Christ and what He stands for. This is why the Lord's Supper is for Christians and has no meaning for anyone else.

The Lord's Supper is an identification with the message of the Gospel. First Corinthians 11:26 literally says that as often as we do this we "proclaim the Lord's death." This is why we believe that the Lord's Supper is for those of like faith who proclaim the same Gospel and mean the same things by it.

B. Involvement by way of reminder. After the war some people found a French soldier obviously suffering from amnesia. When they picked him up at a railway station, he looked at his questioners blankly and kept saying, "I don't know who I am. I don't know who I am." Because he had been disfigured by facial wounds, there were three different families who claimed him as belonging to them. He was taken to one village after another where these different families lived and

was allowed to walk around by himself. When he entered the third village, a sudden light of recognition came into his eyes. He walked unerringly down a side street, through a small gate, and up the steps of his father's home. Like a prodigal son he had "come to himself." The old familiar surroundings had restored his mind. Once again he knew who he was and where he belonged.

Conclusion. So we come to the upper room like amnesia victims in a shell-shocked world. We have often forgotten who we are and where we belong. Let us, with minds of faith, make our way down a side street and up a flight of stairs to a room in an old Jerusalem and thus find our way home. Here it is that we shall find our way back to God, restored in mind and heart. Here is the promised land of our souls. (Leonard Griffith, *The Eternal Legacy from an Upper Room*, New York: Harper and Row, 1963, p. 77).

TITLE: "The Atmosphere of the Lord's Supper"

TEXT: "And they began to inquire among themselves, which of them it was that should do this thing. And there was also a strife among them, which of them should be accounted the greatest" (Luke 22:23, 24).

SCRIPTURE READING: Luke 22: 22-38.

Introduction. We are familiar with the meaning of the wine and the bread in the Lord's Supper.

They symbolize the body and the blood of Christ which made forgiveness of sin a reality. Jesus is not present in the wine and the bread as some believe but the wine and the bread are here to remind us that Jesus is present with us. It is a time when we realize in a special way the heritage which is ours and the faithful ones who have preceded us. As the writer of Hebrews said, "We also are compassed about with so great a cloud of witnesses." I would like for us to think together about the atmosphere which surrounds the Lord's Supper and to let that atmosphere speak to us.

I. *The Atmosphere Says a Word About Betrayal* (Luke 22:22). The disciples are struck with awe at the words of their Lord that someone is to betray Him. Betrayal is always present in our world and few are the Christians who have not felt betrayed at some time. We too need to be awestruck by the possibility that we might in some way betray our Lord even as did Simon Peter in his denial, or even as Judas in his disillusionment. This word about betrayal reminds us of the power and the pull of the world upon us. It reminds us of the possibility of letting that which can be seen overcome in our own lives that which cannot be seen.

II. *The Atmosphere Has a Word About Greatness* (Luke 22:24, 25). It is a rather shocking thing to find that in the midst of the Lord's Supper activities the disciples have an argument about who is the greatest: "And there was also a strife among them, which of them should be accounted the greatest." Jesus reminds them that His kingdom is not like the earthly kingdoms: "The kings of the Gentiles exercise lordship over them; and they that exercise authority upon them are called benefactors. But ye shall not be so: but he that is greatest among you, let him be as the younger; and he that is chief, as he that doth serve."

In the first World War one of the most savage sections of the Western Front was the Ypres Salient. For weeks and months it was the center of an unending, monotonous, rugged trench warfare. In this British sector of the Allied fortifications there was erected a wooden hut a few miles back from the front line. It was named Talbot House. It was the meeting place of men going up to the trenches and men coming down. Over its entrance door was carved the inscription: "Abandon rank all ye who enter here." Every night the Lord's Supper was observed in the loft overhead, literally a last supper in an upper room for so many men. Thousands had knelt in that room. The survivors never forgot it. When a soldier trudged upstairs to the loft, the abandoning of rank was a necessity for that kind of fellowship. Talbot House was only a tarrying place, a way station on the road from the rear billets to the front line. There men had a chance to take time out before they entered the muddy trenches and the battle. (James Cleland, *Wherefore Art Thou Come?*, pp. 116-118.)

The Lord's Supper is very similar. It is a place where we tarry from time to time to remember some things and to gain a new strength as we go on to face the conflict into which Christ has called us. The first supper was just a stopping place on the way to the cross and ours must always have about it this aspect. There must be a setting aside of all classes and ranks and human categories as we gather together here at the Lord's table and realize that greatness is found only in humble service, and that in the kingdom of God there is no lording it over others.

III. *The Atmosphere Has a Word About Purpose* (Luke 22:29). Jesus mentions that each of those present is indeed appointed to a kingdom. He mentions the necessity of serving in this world. The atmosphere of the Lord's Supper has a great deal to say to us about the real purpose of life which is so often lost amidst our confused activity. There are times when it seems that what we do has no purpose. The story is told of a group of laborers who were given the meaningless task of digging holes three feet deep and filling them in again. During lunch hour they delegated one of their number to approach the foreman. "We quit!" he announced. "We're tired of just digging holes." The boss replied, "Well, that's the only way to find a broken pipe." The man walked over to the others, conferred with them for a moment, then came back to the foreman and said, "All right, where do you want us to dig?" Once the men knew there was purpose in their work they were willing to go on with it. The Lord's Supper reminds us that though at times it may seem like we are digging holes and filling them in there is purpose behind trying to witness to people on behalf of Christ.

The Lord's Supper reminds us that into our hands have been committed certain problems of life. Men everywhere about us are bound down by sin and God has chosen to set us in this world as a witness and a help to these men. This is not something which we can hand over to someone else. The task is ours. In one of his novels, Dickens presents a despicable character named Mr. Skimpole, a human parasite who specializes in passing his problems to other people. We all have something of this in us but at the Lord's Supper we are reminded that they are our problems under God. (Leonard Griffith, *The Eternal Legacy From An Upper Room*, New York: Harper and Row, 1963, pp. 165-167.)

IV. *The Atmosphere Has a Word About the World* (Luke 22:35-38). Note the strange words of Jesus: "And he said unto them, When I sent you without purse, and scrip, and shoes, lacked ye any thing? And they said, Nothing. Then said he unto them, But now, he that hath a purse, let him take it, and likewise his scrip; and he that hath no sword, let him sell his garment, and buy one." The key to this passage is in Jesus' admonition to buy a sword. The hallmark of an outcast was that he carried a sword. "Buying a sword" was a symbolic phrase in that day for equipping oneself for an outcast's life. If a man criticized the government, his friend would humorously say, "You had better go and buy a sword." For any civilian to carry a sword in Jerusalem at Passover time was a criminal offense. Jesus knew He was now an outcast and His disciples would no longer be looked upon as conventional peace-loving citizens. Thus He said, "Buy a sword for you are now outcasts from prevalent society." When the disciples tell Jesus that they already have two swords He says in verse 38, "It is enough." This was Jesus' way of saying that He did not mean a literal sword, and that His disciples have again completely misunderstood Him.

What Jesus is saying to His disciples is that now they must make their own way in the world. They must take their purse and their scrip and no longer depend upon the world for provisions. The world will no longer support Christ's movement nor should it. God's people must support their own campaign for the Lord for if the world pays the check, the Church will lose power.

Conclusion. The Lord's Supper reminds us that we live in an alien world and must therefore depend upon our Lord. We must plan to make sacrifices. We must plan to pay the cost of our campaign. We go forth from this moment today to go the separate ways that each of us has, but each way must somehow go by way of the cross. We must walk from this place tonight with the realization that with the morning sun will come the conflict of the week with the world about us.

MEDITATIONS FOR FUNERAL SERVICES

TITLE: "Mixed Emotions"

TEXT: "For thou hast delivered my soul from death, mine eyes from tears, and my feet from falling" (Ps. 116:8).

SCRIPTURE READING: Psalm 116.

Introduction. Any time a group of people are gathered around the corpse of a Christian loved one, there are mixed emotions. This is the subject for this message.

I. *There Are Emotions of Sorrow Because a Friend or Loved One Has Departed in Death.*

A. Any human finds it difficult to give up a loved one. Often the survivors have seen the deceased loved one suffer long and much in life, and just prior to death. They have observed a gradual failing for an extended time. They have known the anxiety that death was inevitable. Now that death has occurred, there is assurance that the loved one is in an eternal place of rest and freedom from things described above. Yet, even with this assurance, there is still sorrow in seeing one go.

B. Any friend has grief in the departure of a friend. This friendship may be a business associate, a fellow church member, or a neighbor. Once friendship has been established, it is a traumatic experience to part.

II. *There Are Emotions of Joy Because of the Eternal Welfare of the Deceased Who Are Christians.*

A. Death for a Christian is a glorious thing. It is a transformation from a sickly, frail, suffering body to a glorified body.
The Bible gives assurance of the wonderful state now (Rev. 21:1-4).

B. Death for the Christian is a blessed or happy experience. "And I heard a voice from heaven saying unto me, Write, Blessed are the dead which die in the Lord from henceforth: Yea, saith the Spirit, that they may rest from their labours; and their works do follow them" (Rev. 14:13).
This passage gives assurance of another life after this one. "If a

man die, shall he live again?" (Job 14:14a). "Jesus said unto her, I am the resurrection, and the life: he that believeth in me, though he were dead, yet shall he live" (John 11:25).

"And have hope toward God, which they themselves also allow, that there shall be a resurrection of the dead, both of the just and unjust" (Acts 24:15).

C. There are emotions of joy because of the promises of God. "But God will redeem my soul from the power of the grave: for he shall receive me" (Ps. 49:15). "Verily, ver-ily, I say unto you, The hour is coming, and now is, when the dead shall hear the voice of the Son of God: and they that hear shall live" (John 5:25). "Knowing that he which raised up the Lord Jesus shall raise up us also by Jesus, and shall present us with you" (2 Cor. 4:14).

Conclusion. If you are in grief because of your loved one's death, then do not be ashamed of it. Thank God that you have human feelings, but then also thank God that He has provided for your loved one in death and that now He is realizing this provision.

TITLE: "Blessed Are the Dead Which Die in the Lord"

TEXT: "And I heard a voice from heaven saying unto me, Write, Blessed are the dead which die in the Lord from henceforth: Yea, saith the Spirit, that they may rest from their labours; and their works do follow them" (Rev. 14:13).

SCRIPTURE READING: Psalm 23.

Introduction. Funeral services are designed to be of help to the loved ones of the deceased, as well as memorializing the one who has died. That is the purpose of the content of this message.

I. *What Does It Mean to Die in Christ?*

A. To die in Christ simply means the death of a Christian. This passage says they are blessed. The word "blessed" means happiness. So the Bible is confirming the fact that death for a Christian is a happy experience. There are two reasons for this joy.

One is, "they . . . rest from their labours." For a person who labors and toils all of his or her life, it is a great joy to look forward to rest from such. The idea of rest implies refreshment. Thus, when a Christian dies, he is refreshed from the toils of life.

The other reason for the happiness in the death of a Christian is, "their works . . . follow them." Those who have devoted a life to good things, such as helping the helpless, ministering to the poor, serving in the name of Christ, and simply being a friend, have works that follow them long after they are dead.

B. The Bible uses some terms for death that are of help in time of sorrow. It is referred to as sleep. For a tired, worn-out person, nothing is more meaningful and helpful than sleep. One goes to sleep with the anticipation of arising rested and refreshed for a new day. This is what death is for a Christian—going to sleep in the earthly world, exhausted from days of toil, to awake in the heavenly world refreshed for the new day.

A term is used as the unyoking of an animal. This term is almost obsolete for many people today, but it, too, is a word description of laying down burdens. It is the removal of the things that gall and make uncomfortable. It is the cessation of burden bearing. Another term found in the Bible in reference to death is a release from bonds. In this life, a person is shackled with the weakness of the flesh. He is imprisoned by fleshly limitations. Death breaks the shackles, destroys the prison walls, and frees the Christian from all limitations forever.

Still another Biblical concept of death is loosening the tent rope and striking camp. The idea here is that of changing residence. The Christian changes his place of abode in death. He moves from one dwelling place to a better one. Closely associated with tent ropes are mooring ropes of a ship. One loosens the mooring ropes and sails the deep waters into the presence of God.

Other concepts that help one understand the blessedness of death are coronation and moving from one room to another. The only way God can crown His own in the way He desires to do so, is by taking His own from this life into the greater one—moving them from one room to another by means of death.

II. *The Heart of the Whole Matter Is That All This Applies to a Christian.* A non-Christian cannot expect such blessings. Death serves as an inclination to cause all to want to become Christians.

Conclusion. A word to you who are in sorrow because of the homegoing of your loved one: Recognize you are hurt and make no pretense of it. Then turn your face toward the heavenly Father and thank Him for the wonderful provisions He has made for His own in death.

A word to anyone present who is not a Christian: Take comfort in God's love for you. Then surrender to Him for eternal life.

TITLE: "Areas of Comfort"

TEXT: "I will not leave you comfortless: I will come to you" (John 14:18).

SCRIPTURE READING: John 14: 1-27.

Introduction. There is never a time when someone needs comfort more than when death claims a loved one. This is one of the deepest hurts the human being suffers. This is the experience of the day. This is the purpose of such a gathering. This is the reason for such a service. A loved one has died and there is bereavement. Where can one go for comfort? Comfort comes from three directions.

I. *Comfort Is From Above or Godward.*

A. The greatest source of comfort anyone can have is the Holy Spirit. This is the Comforter mentioned in the text.

John 14:16 tells the bereaved of

the abiding presence of the Holy Spirit. John 14:17 tells of the believer being indwelt by the Holy Spirit, and John 14:26 tells of the Holy Spirit's teaching ministry. Also, the same verse tells of calling to remembrance.

Each of these verses is an identity of the all-loving, ever-present God, ministering to the loved ones of a deceased one.

B. God has also provided comfort for the bereaved in Christ, His Son. The real comfort here is the redemption from sin. A child of God has been redeemed from sin. Then he has eternal blessedness with God in heaven. To know a loved one is forever with the Lord because of the work of Christ, is a comfort only God can provide.

II. *Comfort Is From Without or Outward.* It comes from friends. Often it has been said that one does not know how many friends he has until a crisis arrives in his life. This is especially true when death invades a family and removes a loved one. Tokens of friends' comfort are seen in flowers, presence in the home, at the funeral, and in places of need. Friends use soft-spoken words that are used for comfort. Friends also lend a helping hand. The many acts of kindness that friends bestow upon the bereaved are true sources of comfort.

III. *Comfort Is From Within—the Self.*

A. Each Christian is indwelt by the Holy Spirit as was mentioned earlier. For this divine Holy Spirit to adequately fulfill His role as a comforter, one must depend upon Him. One must pray to Him and seek His leadership.

B. Each Christian can use his mind to recall memories. The reason death hurts is because it separates the survivors from the deceased, but there are many wonderful memories of a loved one that can bring comfort. As each person relies upon his memory, he can find comfort that is needed.

C. Prayer is a wonderful source of comfort. Regardless of the thought, each person can tell God about it. His ear is always bent to hear. It is always uplifting to talk to Him and listen to Him. Prayer is one of the bereaved's main sources of comfort.

Conclusion. You who suffer sorrow now because of a lost loved one, look for sources of comfort. You will find them from above, from without, and from within.

MESSAGES FOR CHILDREN AND YOUNG PEOPLE

TITLE: "The Temptations of a Young Man"

TEXT: "And she caught him by his garment, saying, Lie with me: and he left his garment in her hand, and fled, and got him out" (Gen. 39:12).

SCRIPTURE READING: Genesis 39:1-20.

Introduction. William James said, "No man has matriculated in the university of life till he has been well tempted." Every one is tempted. If a person is alive, he is tempted. Every one who has a body to live in will be tempted through it. Every one who has a mind will be tempted at the point of his thoughts.

I. *Whom Do Temptations Attack?* (Gen. 39:2, 3). Temptations always attack those who are trying to do right. We learn that "the LORD was with Joseph. . . . and his master saw that the LORD was with him" (Gen. 39:2, 3). Temptations attack the young person who is trying to live the Christian life, trying to do what is good and honorable and respectable. Those who are not seeking to do right have already succumbed to temptation and their struggle is over. We learn early that Satan travels God's roads and appeals to us in an attempt to twist and pervert all those good appetites that God has given us. Therefore every person needs to treat his temptations with respect.

II. *When Do They Attack?* (Gen. 39:6). Temptations come with every new liberty that is given. It was when the total welfare of the household was left in Joseph's hand that his greatest temptation struck. This is what makes liberty so dangerous. Joseph is entrusted with everything in Potiphar's household. A man is never tempted to take money from someone's cash register until he first has been given access to it. This is the liberty of grace that the Scripture warns us about. We are never to use our liberty as an occasion, or a beachhead through which the flesh can destroy us.

III. *What Are the Earmarks of Temptation?*

A. They appeal to one's pride. This means that temptations often come to us in the form of flattery. They make us feel wanted, important, masterful. Joseph was merely a slave. Slaves were never looked upon by women of position and wealth, and yet here is a beautiful woman who throws herself at him.

B. Temptations make refusal embarrassing and often dangerous. Joseph no doubt knew the danger of scorning such a woman who was in effect his employer. A weaker person would have justified his sin by saying that it was the command of his master, and that disobedience on the part of a slave could be met by the death penalty. It could be embarrassing for a girl to have to slap a boy's face and get out of a car and walk home. It can equally be embarrassing for a boy to have to tell a girl that he is not interested in premarital relationships.

C. Temptations appeal to a natural desire. The attraction of a man for a woman is part of the handiwork of God. The day will come when Joseph will take a woman for his wife and enter into all the relationships of marriage made holy by God. But here the temptation is to become soiled by using outside of marriage that which God has ordained for the sanctity of the man and woman who become one flesh in holy matrimony. The Apostle Paul warns against temptation by urging that we always stand against them "lest Satan should get an advantage of us: for we are not ignorant of his devices" (2 Cor. 2:11).

IV. *How Serious Are Temptations?* (Gen. 39:9).

A. They lead us to sin against God. Joseph is a young man for whom God has great plans. One moment of weakness can ruin those plans. As a youngster growing up on a farm, I remember several occasions in which I stood and watched a gathering storm cloud, filled with rumbling thunder and criss-crossed with lightning, its green ominous color revealing the presence of destructive hail, and knew that it threatened all the labor of the past year as it swept down upon the fields of ripening wheat. Sin can ruin an entire life.

B. Temptations lead us to let others down. Potiphar, Joseph's employer, had placed supreme trust in his hand. Joseph was not aware of it at the moment, but his own father and brothers, which were to become the nation of Israel, would in the years to come depend on his faithfulness in the plan of God. There will come a time when Joseph will be used to bring his people together in deliverance, and the temptation which he faces can ruin all of that.

V. *How Are Temptations Overcome?* (Gen. 39:12). We overcome temptations by fleeing from them. We must never suppose that we can toy with them and enjoy them without yielding to them. This is not to say that temptations are easily overcome. Because Joseph stood true to his faith, he finds himself falsely accused and cast into prison. It will only be after much suffering that he is vindicated. Yet the time will come when his faithfulness, and the wisdom of his choice, will be manifest. Spurgeon once said: "No man can keep the birds of passion from flying about his head; the trouble is when he allows them to begin building nests in his hair." To fight temptation we must learn the secret of watching and praying. Watching refers to the human side and praying refers to the divine side. As we cooperate with God, we overcome our temptations.

Conclusion. Temptation has no power of itself. This is its Achilles' heel. Temptation can win only with your help. There is only one knob to the door of man's life, and that is on the inside. The door never opens except when you open it. God is more powerful than Satan, and if we are willing to look to Him, He will give us the strength to overcome every temptation (1 Cor. 10:13).

TITLE: "An Unlikely Disciple"

TEXT: "And after these things he went forth, and saw a publican, named Levi, sitting at the reccipt of custom: and he said unto him, Follow me" (Luke 5:27).

SCRIPTURE READING: Luke 5:27-32.

Introduction. Because of His nature, God is always doing the impossible and dealing in unlikely places with unlikely people. From the human standpoint, calling Matthew as an apostle was very unwise. It might be likened in our day and time to the election of a community fund chairman of a man just released from prison for embezzling funds from a bank. From the human standpoint one feels that he needed to pull Jesus aside and tell

Him a few things about the kind of world we live in and what people think about certain things. The calling of a man like this for a helper did not bespeak a bright future. Matthew truly was an unlikely disciple.

I. *Notice the Difficulties Involved* (Luke 5:27). Matthew was a publican. This is another term for tax collector. If one wanted to become financially independent there were few ways which offered this any quicker than did that of becoming a tax collector. By pulling strings and with much effort Matthew had at last secured a portion of the fat plum possessed by the tax collectors. His bid had been accepted for the portion of the taxes he was to render to Caesar and of course all over that amount which he could collect became his.

When Matthew gained his position as a tax collector he at the same time closed the doors to the homes of his Jewish friends. No respectable person would have him as a guest. His money was not even acceptable in the synagogue. By Jewish law a tax collector was barred completely from the synagogue and was included with things and beasts unclean. He could not be a witness in any court case. Robbers, murderers, and tax collectors were all classed together by the Jewish people.

II. *Notice the Demands of the Bargain* (Luke 5:28). As this Jesus of Nazareth came by the customs place where Matthew worked He challenged Matthew's heart to give up all his opportunity and to become a Christian. To the amazement of all Matthew arose from his table of customs, gave up his world

of opportunity, and became a Christian.

Matthew lost everything he had labored for years to achieve. He lost a comfortable job, a good income, and the security which worldly wealth can bring with the approaching of old age. He lost his ability to provide anything his family wanted in the way of worldly goods. He gave up everything our world calls success in order to have honor, to become an heir to the riches of Christ, to be a man on a thrilling adventure pursuing the will of God, and most important of all, to be a man who now had a destiny.

III. *Notice the Talk* (Luke 5:30). Broadly speaking, in Palestine people were divided into two groups. There were the orthodox who rigidly kept the law in every petty detail and regulation; and there were the people who did not keep the petty regulations of the law. The second group were classed as "people of the land"; and it was forbidden to the orthodox to go on a journey with them, to do any business with them, to give anything to them or to receive anything from them, to entertain them as guests or to be guests in their homes. By companying with people like this Jesus was doing something which the pious people of His day could never have done. The self-righteous said it was a disgrace for such people to meet together and propose to discuss religious matters.

Jesus answers by saying that people who claim that they are whole and have no sin are in no frame of mind to accept a physician. Jesus said, "I am coming to call those who will admit their sin and admit their sickness and out of this be willing to repent."

IV. *Notice the Outcome.* Matthew may have been an unlikely prospect, but when the power of God is considered there are no unlikely prospects. Matthew immediately calls his fellow tax collectors together that they too may meet Jesus. This is the fundamental principle of Christian growth. A man begins to grow when he begins to become concerned about helping other people find Christ. This is the fundamental principle which later Alcoholics Anonymous has come to use. They find that an alcoholic is on his way to recovery when he can become responsible for helping another alcoholic.

Levi the tax collector became Matthew the disciple. I think it is significant that the name Matthew itself means "Gift of God."

How did this unlikely prospect turn out? Weeks later, when after a night in prayer Jesus chose twelve to be apostles, the list included the name of Matthew.

The first book of the New Testament bears Matthew's name. Alexander Whyte has said, "When Matthew rose up and followed Jesus the only thing he took with him was his ink and pen and it is well for us that he did since he made such good use of them."

The last words in Matthew's gospel are, "Lo, I am with you always, even unto the end of the age." The tax collector once shut out from the congregation of Israel was never shut out from the fellowship of the Lord Jesus Christ. Christ remained with him always.

Conclusion. It is significant that in the building of the Church, our Lord used moral rubbish—a tax collector, a traitorous Simon Peter, and a fanatical Zealot. The reason God can use such material is found in 2 Corinthians 5:17 where we read, "If any man be in Christ, he is a new creature: old things are passed away; behold, all things are become new."

TITLE: "A Man Who Forgot God"

TEXT: "In the same hour came forth fingers of a man's hand, and wrote over against the candlestick upon the plaster of the wall of the king's palace: and the king saw the part of the hand that wrote" (Dan. 5:5).

SCRIPTURE READING: Daniel 5: 1-31.

Introduction. Picture if you will a successful business man who has learned to take what he wants, say what he pleases, live as he chooses.

Suddenly a tragedy envelops him. There is no reason to be too specific—whether a heart attack, a blinding crash on the highway, or some other tragedy—the result is the same. He suddenly is confronted by his mortality. There is the overwhelming sense that the God who has been ignored has drawn near in judgment.

Such is the setting for our Scripture. Though Belshazzar lived centuries ago, he was as modern in his outlook as tomorrow. We look into his life at a very crucial moment and discover a man who has completely forgotten God and who has chosen to live as if there were no

God. This not only happened in far-off, forgotten Babylon. But it happens today! Tonight! Tomorrow!

I. *His Secularized Life* (Dan. 5:1-4). We find in Belshazzar a totally secular outlook. The word "secular" has come to the place where it denotes a kind of "this age-ism." It is not that Belshazzar did not believe in the possibility of another life beyond this one; it is merely that he has chosen to consume himself with the present moment.

Strange indeed that men have feasts in the presence of great peril. Just outside the city's walls was encamped the army of Cyrus. Belshazzar felt secure within his walled city because he supposed it to be impregnable. It is said that the walls of Babylon were wide enough at the top for six chariots to race abreast. What he did not realize was that under the cover of darkness the enemy was quietly diverting the Euphrates River into an overflow canal that had been built years before and was in disuse. Once the waters had been so diverted, the enemy would be able to slip in under the walls of the city through the dry river bed. One hundred and fifty years before, Isaiah had prophesied that Babylon would fall to Cyrus (Isa. 13:17-22; 45:1, 2).

II. *His Interruption* (Dan. 5:5, 6). The banquet is at its peak. The king, together with his leading nobles, is seated at one end of the great banquet hall on an elevated stage. The great candelabra illuminate the hall and cast shadows on the white glistening plaster of the walls. It is at the precise moment that we see God's interruption: "In the same hour came forth fingers of a man's hand, and wrote over

against the candlestick upon the plaster of the wall of the king's palace: and the king saw the part of the hand that wrote" (Dan. 5:5).

At last we see the arrival of what Belshazzar had sought to ignore. Guards can shut out human intruders, but God cannot be shut out. No matter how hard we try to shut out all crises from our life, they at last descend upon us with the suddenness of a summer storm.

III. *His Blindness* (Dan. 5:20-24). If any one would have told Belshazzar that he would invite the preacher to his great feast he would have laughed in his face. But now the situation has changed. It is Daniel who then reminds him of some of the handwriting that he should have heeded long ago. One episode written on the walls of time before the very eyes of Belshazzar had to do with Nebuchadnezzar, a relative of Belshazzar. Daniel reminds the king that Nebuchadnezzar had once been the most powerful monarch in the world. He had held in his hand the power of life and death over many people. Yet there came a time in his life "when his heart was lifted up, and his mind hardened in pride" (Dan. 5:20). It was the living God who deposed him from his throne and took his mental powers from him, causing him to live like the beasts of the field.

IV.. *His Judgment* (Dan. 5:25-30). In this vivid account we find the fate of every man who shuts out the supernatural and chooses to know only a half existence—a half life. Belshazzar's judgment awaits every man who leaves God out of his life. Daniel announces to the great potentate that the word "Mene" indicates that God has numbered the kingdom. In other words, God has announced: "Time's up!" Each life has its limit. God has allowed· Belshazzar to run his course, and now the course has ended. There will be no further opportunity. There will not be another time. There is no other chance. Time is up!

The next word in the mysterious writing is "Tekel." It means: "Thou art weighed in the balances, and art found wanting." Thus Belshazzar's whole life has been weighed by a divine standard. "The LORD is a God of knowledge, and by him actions are weighed" (1 Sam. 2:3). The customs of ancient warfare were that when a monarch had been defeated, all his prized possessions were weighed and divided among the conquerors. Therefore to be weighed was to be defeated. It was to lose all one's possessions. It was to lose all one's power. It was to be deposed from the throne forever. (Albert Barnes, *Daniel*, Volume I and *Notes on the Old Testament*, Grand Rapids: Baker Book House, 1957, pp. 229, 300.)

The third word of the writing was "Peres." It meant the kingdom of Belshazzar was to be divided and given to the Medes and the Persians. Opportunity had indeed vanished. The kingdom would be no more.

Ancient history tells us that the army of Cyrus did indeed divert the channel of the river and slip under the great iron gates by means of the dry river bed. While the town slept, while the king reveled amidst his banquet, the enemy was slipping quietly into the midst of the city to take it.

Conclusion. So we look into the life of a man who did not deny God, but who lived as though God were not important.

It is almost an afterthought, almost an anticlimax, for Daniel to tell us in the following few verses: "And that night was Belshazzar the king of the Chaldeans slain" (Dan. 5:30). His death that night was not the real tragedy. It was his failure at life that was the tragedy.

THEMES FOR WEDDING CEREMONIES

‖ TITLE: "The Permanence of Love"

"In this life we have three great lasting qualities—faith, hope and love. But the greatest of them is love" (1 Cor. 13:13, Phillips). It is suggested that the minister performing the ceremony read 1 Corinthians 13 from a modern version of the scriptures, such as Phillips translation or from the New English Bible. Preliminary remarks could include a review of the importance of Christian love, the nature of Chris-

tian love and close with the permanence of Christian love. It could be pointed out that while romantic love is important for the achieving of happiness in marriage that Christian love, that is, a persistent unbreakable spirit of goodwill, will undergird and help guarantee the highest possible human happiness.

The kind of love described in 1 Corinthians 13 is not limited to the emotions. It primarily is a matter of the intellect and the will of a Christian who has experienced the love of God through faith in Jesus

Christ. The kind of love described here is the supreme gift of the Holy Spirit. If Christians would achieve the highest possible happiness in marriage, they should recognize the indwelling presence of the Holy Spirit and respond to His leadership day by day that they might develop a relationship as husband and wife that will be mutually creative and stimulating and helpful. To make marriage abundantly happy, Christian love should be practiced by each member of the new partnership that comes together to establish a home.

The minister may now inquire, "Who gives this woman to this man in marriage?" The father may reply, "I do," or he may reply, "Her mother and I."

If you, then, ... and ...., have freely and deliberately chosen each other as partners in this holy estate, and know of no just cause why you should not be so united, in token thereof you will please join your right hands.

Groom's Vow

........, in taking the woman you hold by the right hand to be your lawful and wedded wife, before God and the witnesses present you must promise to love her, to honor and cherish her in that relation, and leaving all others cleave only unto her, and be to her in all things a true and faithful husband so long as you both shall live. Do you so promise?

Groom's Answer

"I do."

Bride's Vow

........, in taking the man you hold by the right hand to be your lawful and wedded husband, before God and the witnesses present you must promise to love him, to honor and cherish him in that relation, and leaving all others, cleave only unto him, and to be to him in all things a true and faithful wife so long as you both shall live. Do you so promise?

Bride's Answer

"I do."

Pastor's Response

Then are you each given to the other in advances or reverses, in poverty or in riches, in sickness and in health, to love and to cherish, until death shall part you.

The Ring(s)

For unnumbered centuries the ring has been used on important occasions. It has reached its loftiest prestige in the symbolic significance which it vouches at the marriage altar. It is a perfect circle having no end. It symbolizes your desire, and our desire, and God's desire, that there be no end to the happiness and success for which your heart hungers. It is thus a symbol of the unending plan and purpose of God for your happiness and well being.

Pastor's Question

Do you give these rings to each other as a token of your love for each other?

Couple's Answer

"We do."

Pastor's Question

Will each of you receive this ring as a token of your companion's wedded love for you, and will you wear it as a token of your love for your companion?

Couple's Reply

"We will."

Closing Proclamation

Here in the presence of your parents, your relatives, and your friends; here in the presence of your pastor and in the presence of the living God you have made vows. These vows are binding upon you by the laws of this state. They are binding upon you by the law of God. And they are binding upon you by the law of your own love for each other. You have sealed these vows by the giving and by the receiving of rings. Acting in the authority vested in me as a minister of the Gospel by this state, and looking to heaven for divine sanction, I now pronounce you husband and wife. What therefore God hath joined together do not let anything put asunder.

The pastor may now request the relatives and friends to join with him in a prayer for the Lord's blessing upon the couple.

Following the prayer, the minister may speak to the groom and say, "You may now claim your bride with a kiss."

Following the kiss, the minister may instruct the couple to face their friends or the congregation and then say, "May I introduce to you Mr. and Mrs. _____."

‖ TITLE: "A Marriage Ceremony"

At the very dawn of human history, the Holy Scriptures tell us that God saw that it was not good for the man to be alone. Marriage is God's first institution for the welfare and the happiness of the human race. The divine Creator made for man a helpmate suitable for him and established the rite of marriage while heavenly hosts witnessed this wonderful scene in reverence.

Our Lord sanctioned the contract of marriage and honored it with His presence and power at a marriage in Cana of Galilee. It was on this occasion that He demonstrated His glory and rendered a ministry to the family that prevented them from being embarrassed.

The relationship of a man and a woman in marriage is declared by the Apostle Paul to be honorable among all men. It is ordained by God that a man shall leave his father and mother and cleave to his wife and they twain shall be one flesh, united in hopes and aims and sentiments until death alone shall part them.

(The minister may now ask, "Who gives this woman to this man in marriage?") The father may reply, "I do." Or he may reply, "Her mother and I."

The minister may then address the couple and present to them the vows as follows:

If ye, then, _____ (Groom), and _____ (Bride), after careful consideration, and in the fear of God, have deliberately chosen each other as partners in this holy estate, and know of no just cause why you should not be so united, in token thereof you will please join your right hands.

Groom's Vow

_____, wilt thou have this woman to be thy wedded wife, to live together after God's ordinance in the holy estate of matrimony? Wilt thou love her, comfort her, honor and keep her in sickness and in health, and forsaking all others keep thee only unto her so long as you both shall live?

Answer: "I will."

Bride's Vow

_____, wilt thou have this man to be thy wedded husband, to live together after God's ordinance in the holy estate of matrimony? Wilt thou love him, honor him and keep him in sickness and in health, and forsaking all others keep thee only unto him so long as you both shall live?

Answer: "I will."

Vows to Each Other

I, _____ (Groom), take thee, _____ (Bride), to be my wedded wife, to have and to hold from this day forward, in prosperity or adversity, in sickness or in health, in advances or reverses, to love and to cherish till death do us part, according to God's holy ordinance, and thereto I plight thee my troth.

I, _____ (Bride), take thee, _____ (Groom), to be my wedded husband, to have and to hold from this day forward, in prosperity or adversity, in sickness or in health, in advances or reverses, to love and to cherish till death do us part, according to God's holy ordinance, and thereto I plight thee my troth.

Then are you each given to the other for richer or poorer, for better or worse, in sickness and in health, till death alone shall part you.

From time immemorial the ring has been used to seal important covenants. The golden circlet, most prized of jewels, has come to its loftiest prestige in the symbolic sig-nificance which it vouches at the marriage altar. Its untarnishable material is of the purest gold. Even so may your love for each other be pure and may it grow brighter and brighter as time goes by. The ring is a circle, thus having no end. Even so may there be no end to the happiness and success that come to you as you unite your lives together.

Do you, _____ (Groom), give this ring to your wedded wife as a token of your love for her?

Will you, _____ (Bride), receive this ring as a token of your wedded husband's love for you, and will you wear it as a token of your love for him?

Do you, _____ (Bride), give this ring to your wedded husband as a token of your love for him?

Will you, _____ (Groom), receive this ring as a token of your wedded wife's love for you, and will you wear it as a token of your love for her?

Having pledged your faith in and love to each other in the sight of God and these assembled witnesses, and having sealed your solemn marital vows by giving and receiving the rings, acting in the authority vested in me as a minister of the Gospel by this State, and looking to heaven for divine sanction, I pronounce you husband and wife.

Therefore, what God hath joined together, let not man put asunder.

The minister should then pray for the couple that God might unite them in an indissoluble manner and that their lives might ever be a blessing to each other and to those about them.

The minister may then say to the groom, "You may now claim your bride with a kiss."

If the wedding ceremony was re-hearsed, the minister may have instructed the couple at this point to turn and face the congregation and pause before the recessional. At this point the minister could introduce the new couple as Mr. and Mrs. ---------- .

BULLETIN SERMONETTES

1. "If you live a Christless life, you will die a Christless death."

2. "Prayer is the key to the day and the lock to the night."

3. "Time will not tarry."

4. "The life of a Christian is like breathing in and out: in for strength and training, and out for ministry and service."

5. "Conditions are changed only as men are changed."

6. "Walk your talk."

7. "To step out of God's will is to step down, never up, in quality of life."

8. "The love of God never dims or dies."

9. "The most expensive thing God ever did was to love you and me."

10. "The cross reveals God at His best."

11. "Man was made for God, like notes were made for music."

12. "All spiritual life begins with a birth."

13. "The love of God never fades or fails."

14. "The Bible is not the book of the month, rather it is the Book of the Ages."

15. "God feeds the sparrow but He never throws the food into the nest."

16. "Prayer is the greatest power that we have on earth."

17. "Prejudice melts in the face of compassion."

18. "We are a product of our thoughts."

19. "When it comes to giving, some folks stop at nothing."

20. "The smallest deed is better than the grandest intention."

21. "Life does not give you a dress rehearsal. There is one try, either you succeed or fail."

22. "Behind every Calvary there is an Easter Sunday."

23. "God operates on eternal standard time."

24. "God always raises a solution in the midst of the pollution."

25. "Hell is eternal separation from God."

26. "Eternity is in the tiny little minute that is yours right now."

27. "Do you have an eternal relationship with Jesus Christ?"

28. "The Bible is from everlasting to everlasting."

29. "There is no ignorance like an educated ignorance."

30. "The heart of God is filled with love for all men."

31. "Self-made men stop when the job is half done."

32. "Is your heart on its knees?"

33. "Love is the only effective way to deal with a problem."

34. "Blue Monday has no place on the Christian's calendar."

35. "If a church does not evangelize its environment, its environment will paganize it."

36. "Every problem is in reality an opportunity."

37. "A life without Christ is an empty existence."

38. "Our fates are sealed at death."

39. "Christ came not to preach the gospel, but that there might be a gospel to preach."

40. "You are young only once, but you can stay immature indefinitely."

41. "The darkness of the night cannot extinguish the smallest candle."

42. "No joy is complete unless it is shared."

43. "Jesus Christ is no security against storms, but He is perfect security in storms."

44. "A man is as big as the things which made him angry."

45. "Tact is the ability to close your mouth before someone else wants to."

46. "An optimist laughs to forget; a pessimist forgets to laugh."

47. "Your calendar shows the passing of time. Your face and character shows what you are doing with it."

48. "Fortune or misfortune does not change men. It only unmasks them."

49. "Coasting through life means a downhill plunge."

50. "Worry never robs tomorrow of its sorrow; it only robs today of its strength."

INDEX OF TOPICS

INDEX OF SCRIPTURE TEXTS